STOP!

This is the back of the book.
You wouldn't want to spoil a great ending!

This book is printed "manga-style," in the authentic Japanese right-to-left format. Since none of the artwork has been flipped or altered, readers get to experience the story just as the creator intended. You've been asking for it, so TOKYOPOP® delivered: authentic, hot-off-the-press, and far more fun!

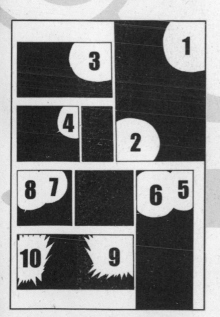

DIRECTIONS

If this is your first time reading manga-style, here's a quick guide to help you understand how it works.

It's easy... just start in the top right panel and follow the numbers. Have fun, and look for more 100% authentic manga from TOKYOPOP®!

LEADING • THE MANGA REVOLUTION • LEADING • THE MANGA REVOLUTION

漫画革命

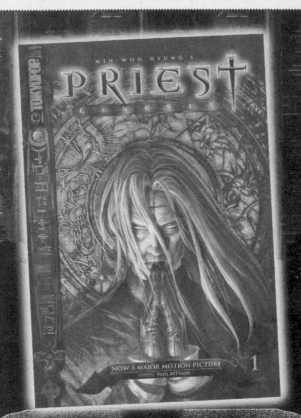

♥3 Alice IN THE COUNTRY OF Hearts
·········WONDERFUL WONDER WORLD·········

WHAT HOLE WILL SHE FALL INTO NEXT?
THE ADVENTURE CONTINUES...

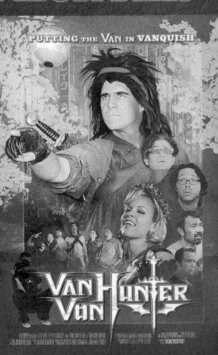

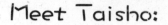

WHEN YOU CAN OWN ANY SERIES
FOR UNDER 30 BUCKS,
ONLY ONE QUESTION REMAINS UNANSWERED...

WHICH ONE DO I CHOOSE?!

THIS ONE?

OR... BOTH

WALTER
Addictus Animemus

Animal ACADEMY

HAKOBUNE HAKUSHO

はこぶね白書

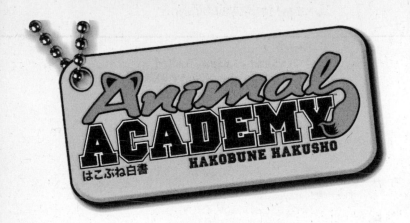

Volume 5

by

MOYAMU FUJINO

TOKYOPOP®

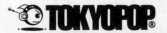

HAMBURG // LONDON // LOS ANGELES // TOKYO

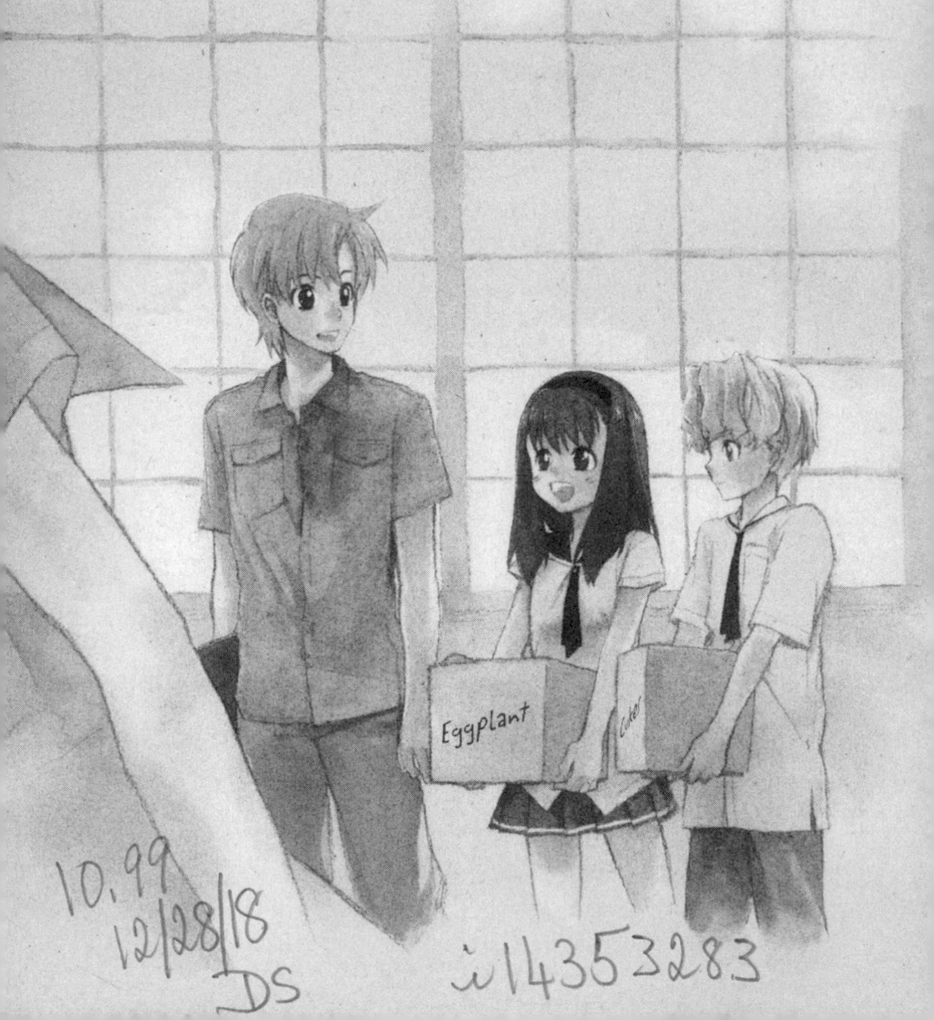
Eggplant

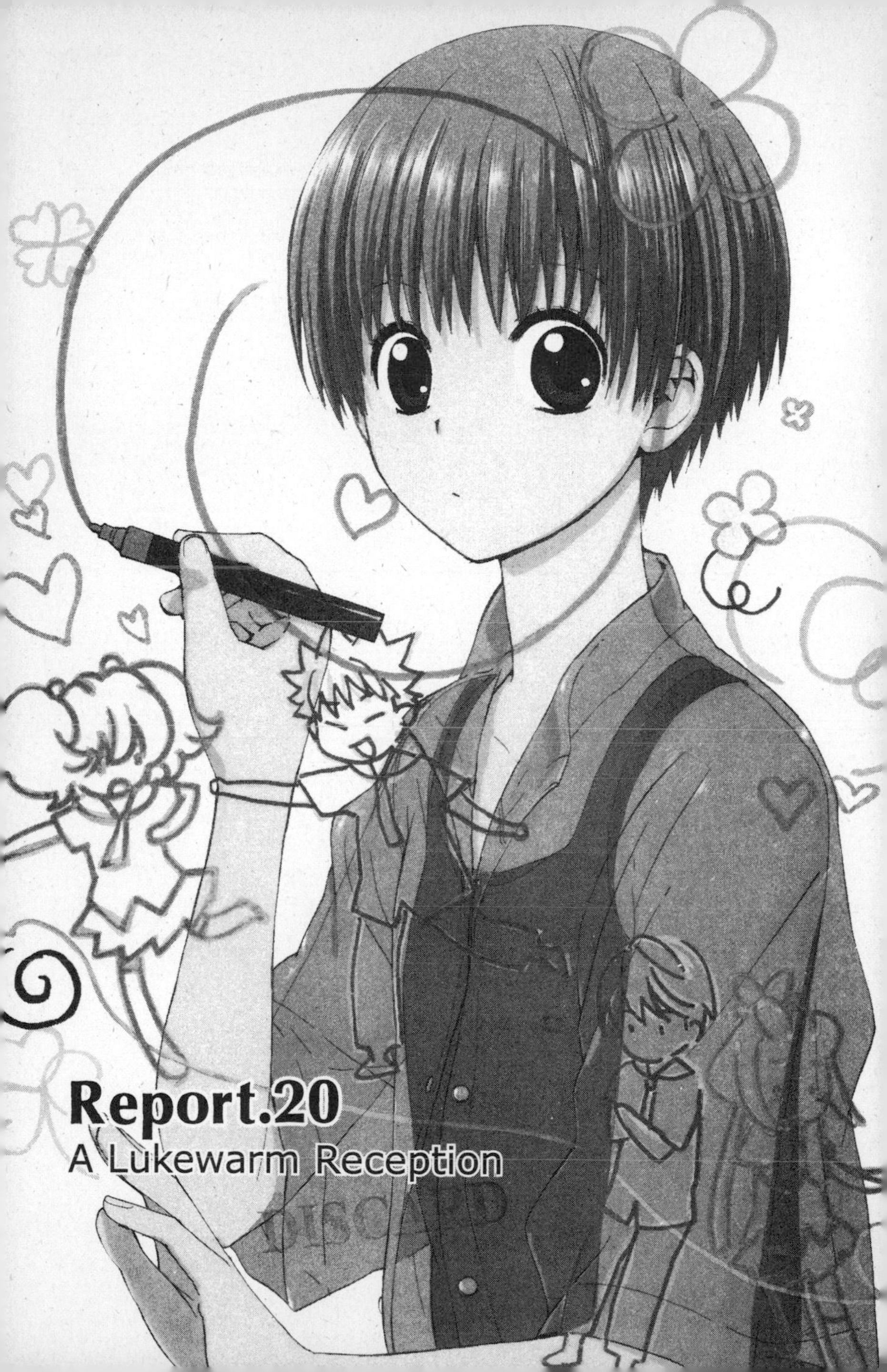

Report.20
A Lukewarm Reception

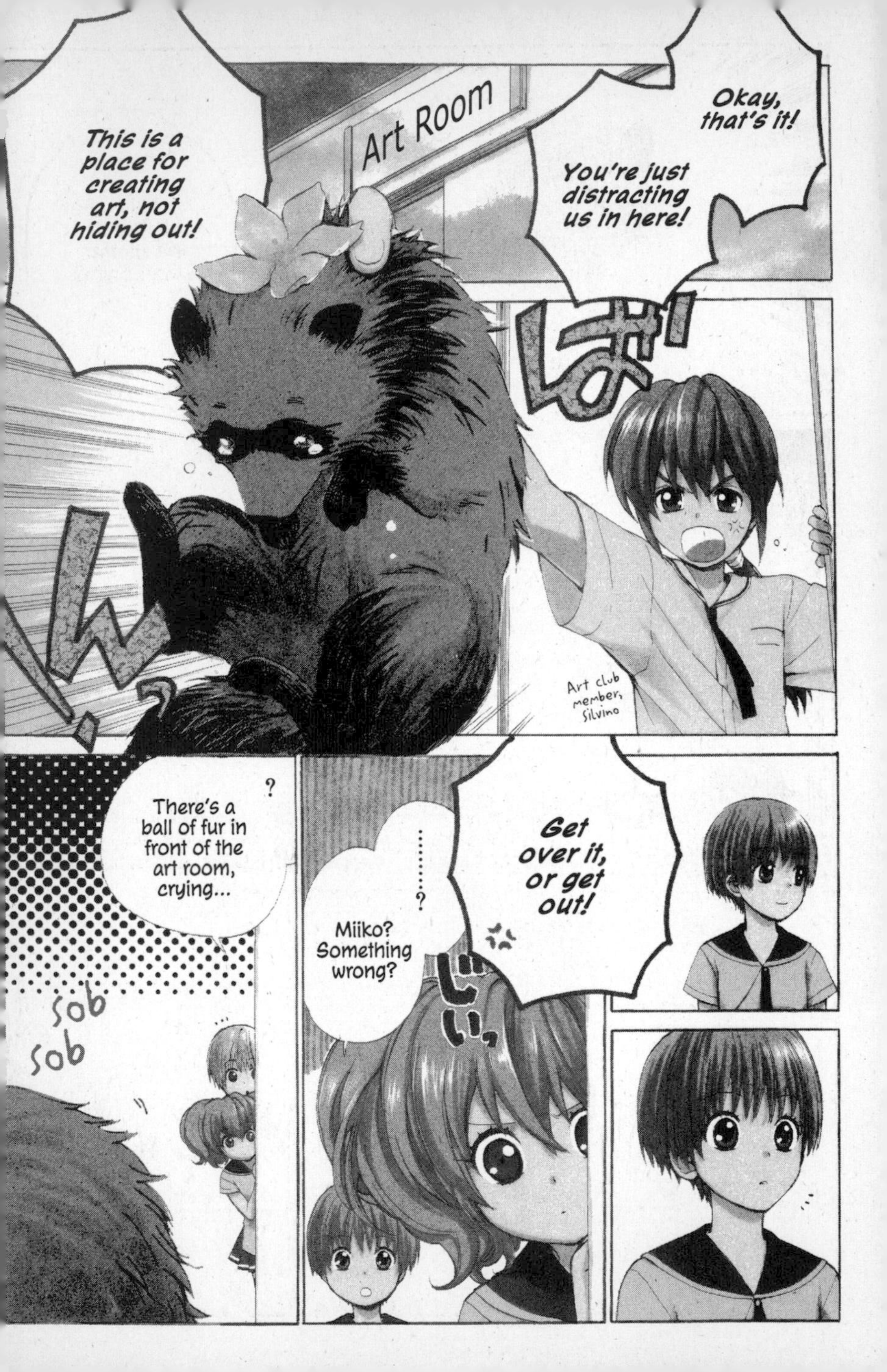
Okay, that's it!
You're just distracting us in here!
Art Room
This is a place for creating art, not hiding out!
Art club member, Silvino
Get over it, or get out!
......?
Miiko? Something wrong?
?
There's a ball of fur in front of the art room, crying...
sob sob

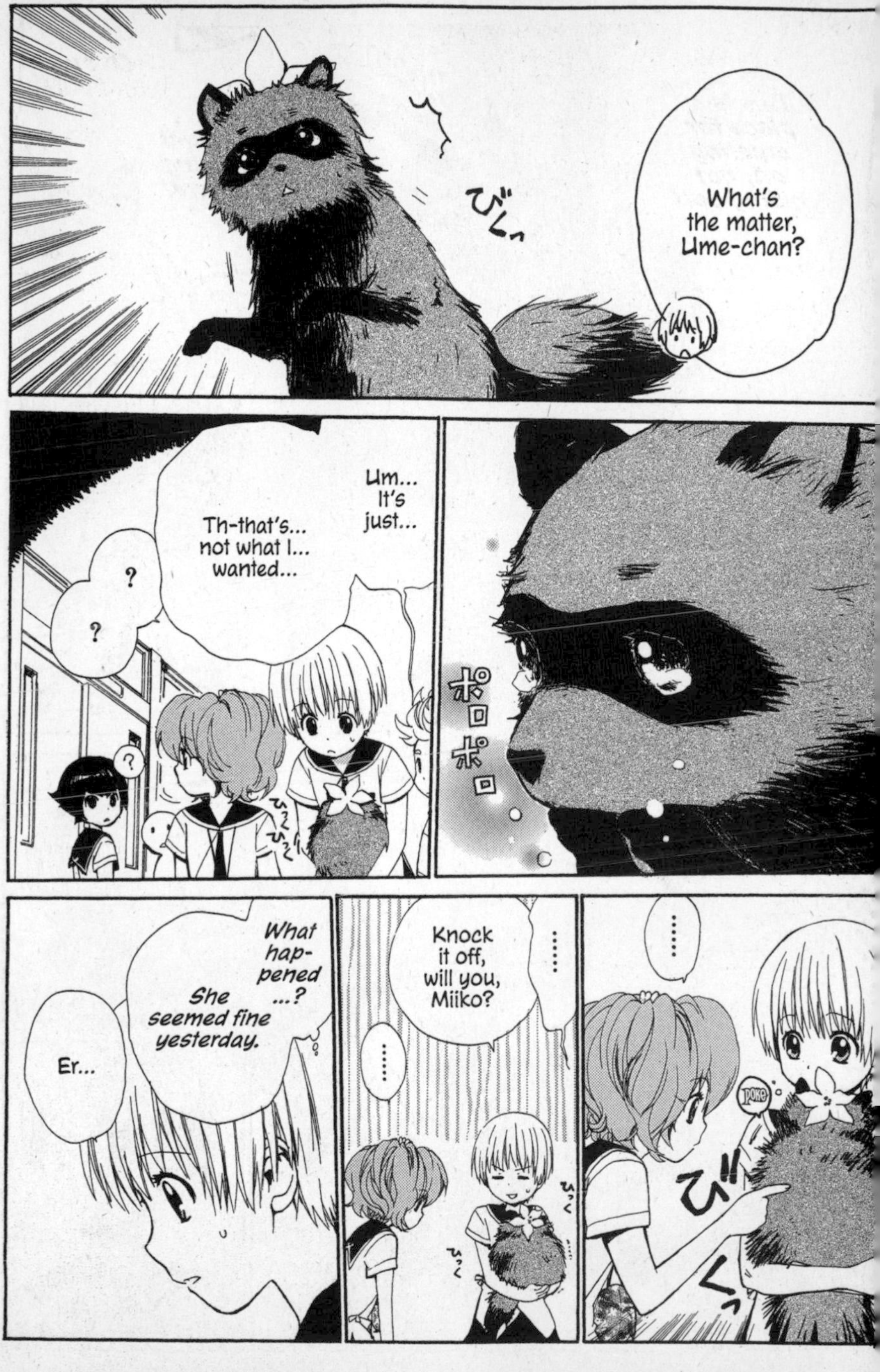
What's the matter, Ume-chan?
ポロポロ
Um... It's just...
Th-that's... not what I... wanted...
?
?
?
......
POKE
Knock it off, will you, Miiko?
......
......
What hap-pened ...?
She seemed fine yesterday.
Er...

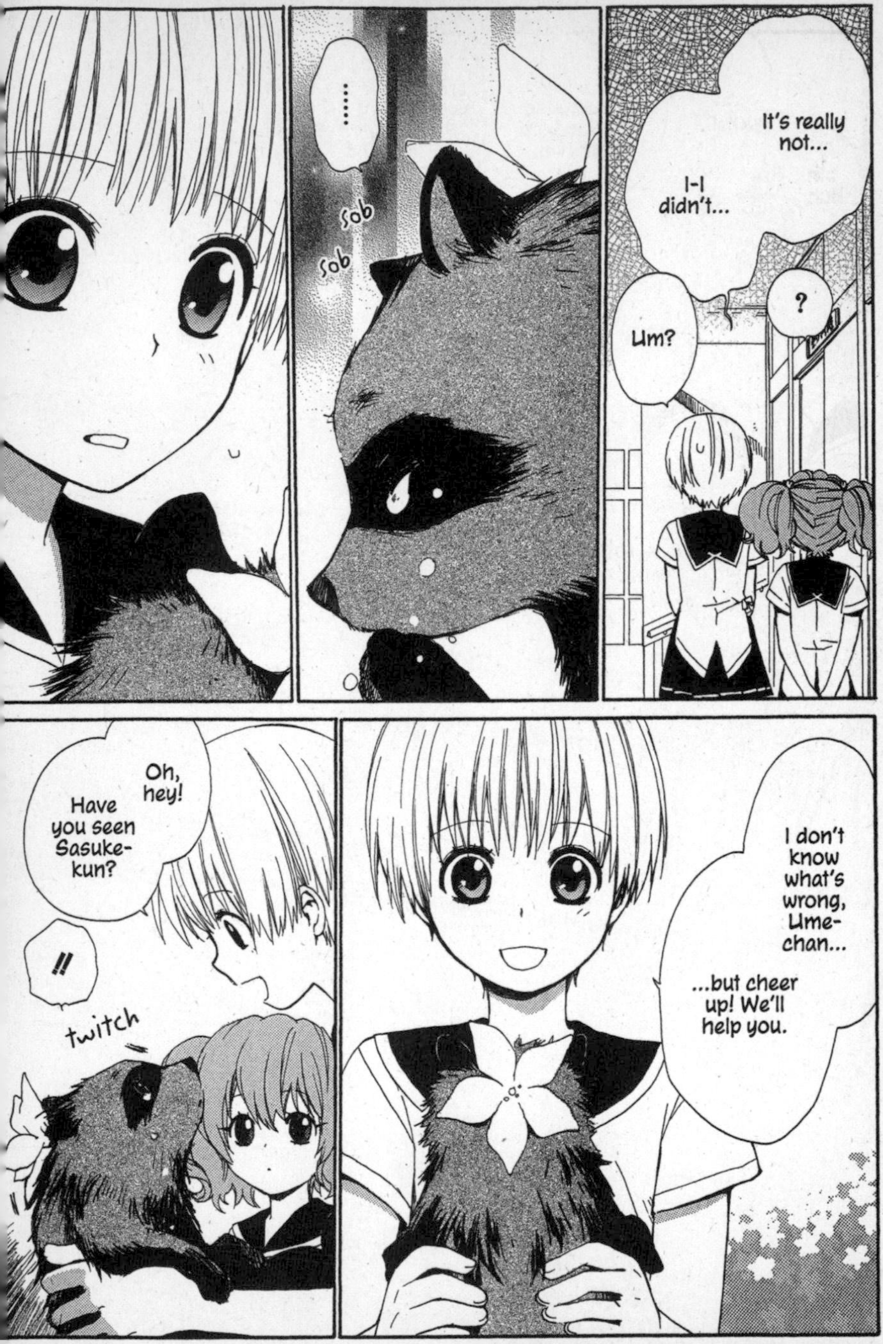
It's really not...
I-I didn't...
?
Um?
......
sob
sob
I don't know what's wrong, Ume-chan...
...but cheer up! We'll help you.
Oh, hey! Have you seen Sasuke-kun?
!!
twitch

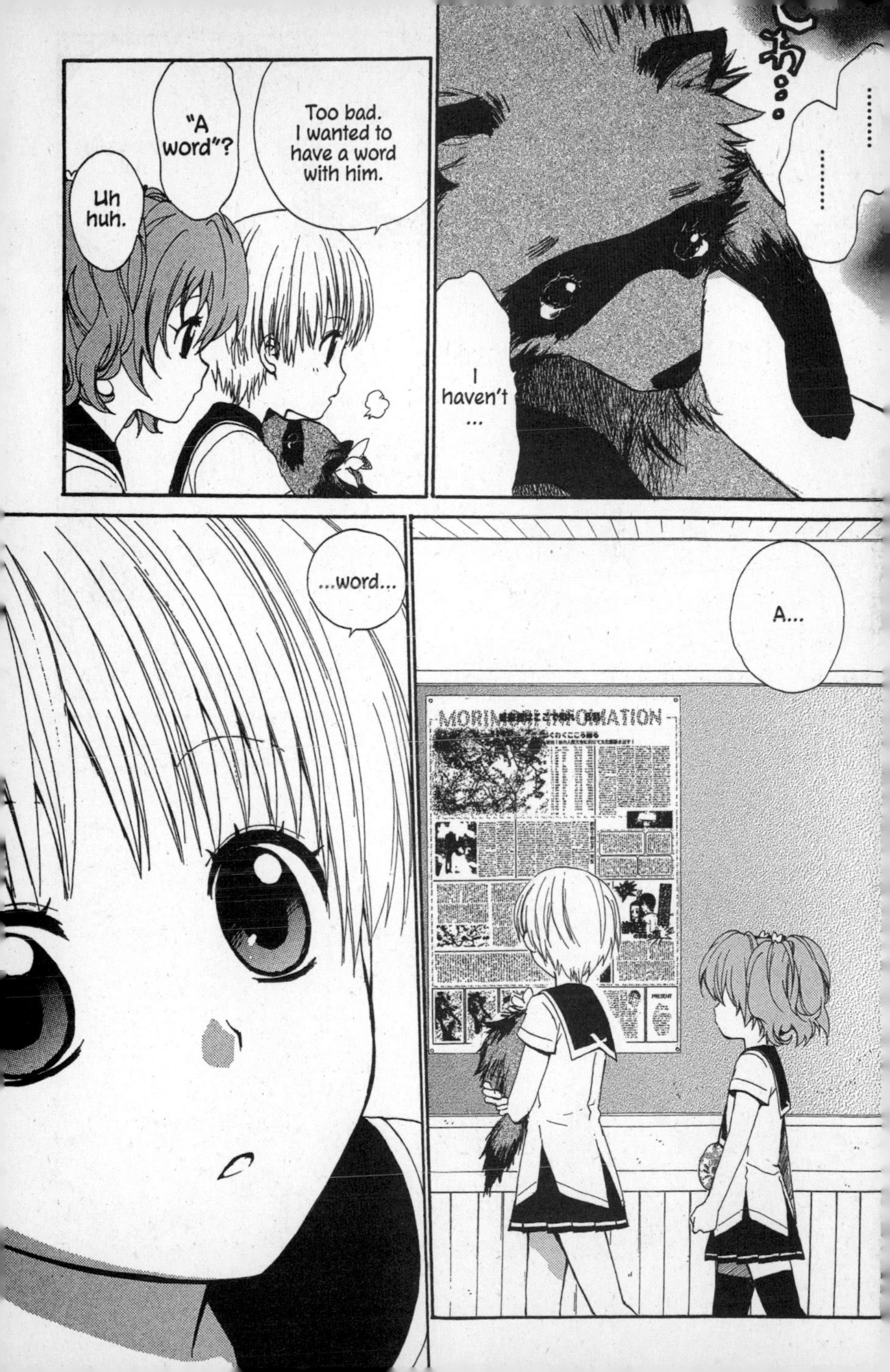
......
......
I haven't ...
Too bad. I wanted to have a word with him.
"A word"?
Uh huh.
A...
...word...

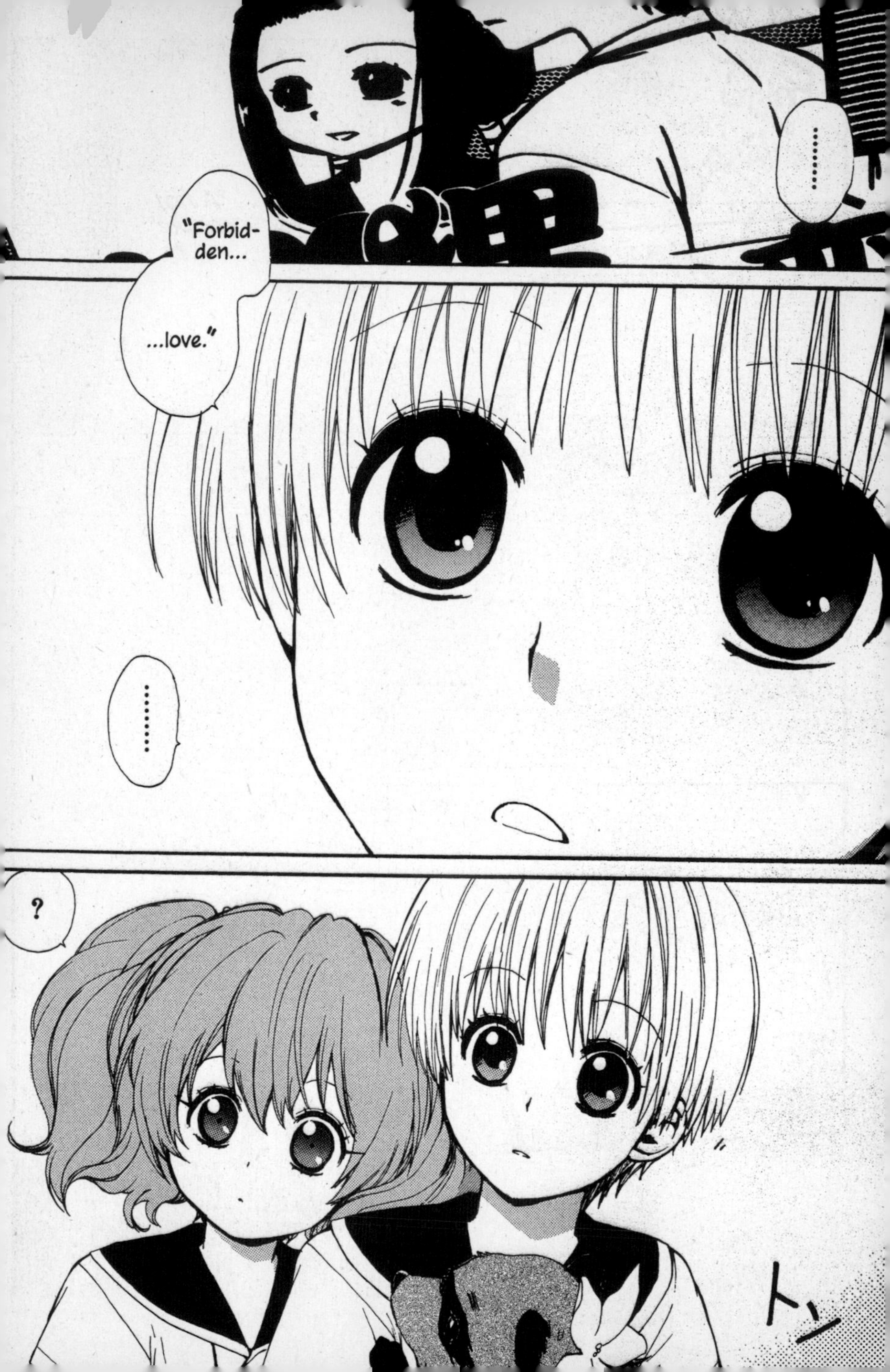
......
"Forbid-
den...
...love."
......
?
トン

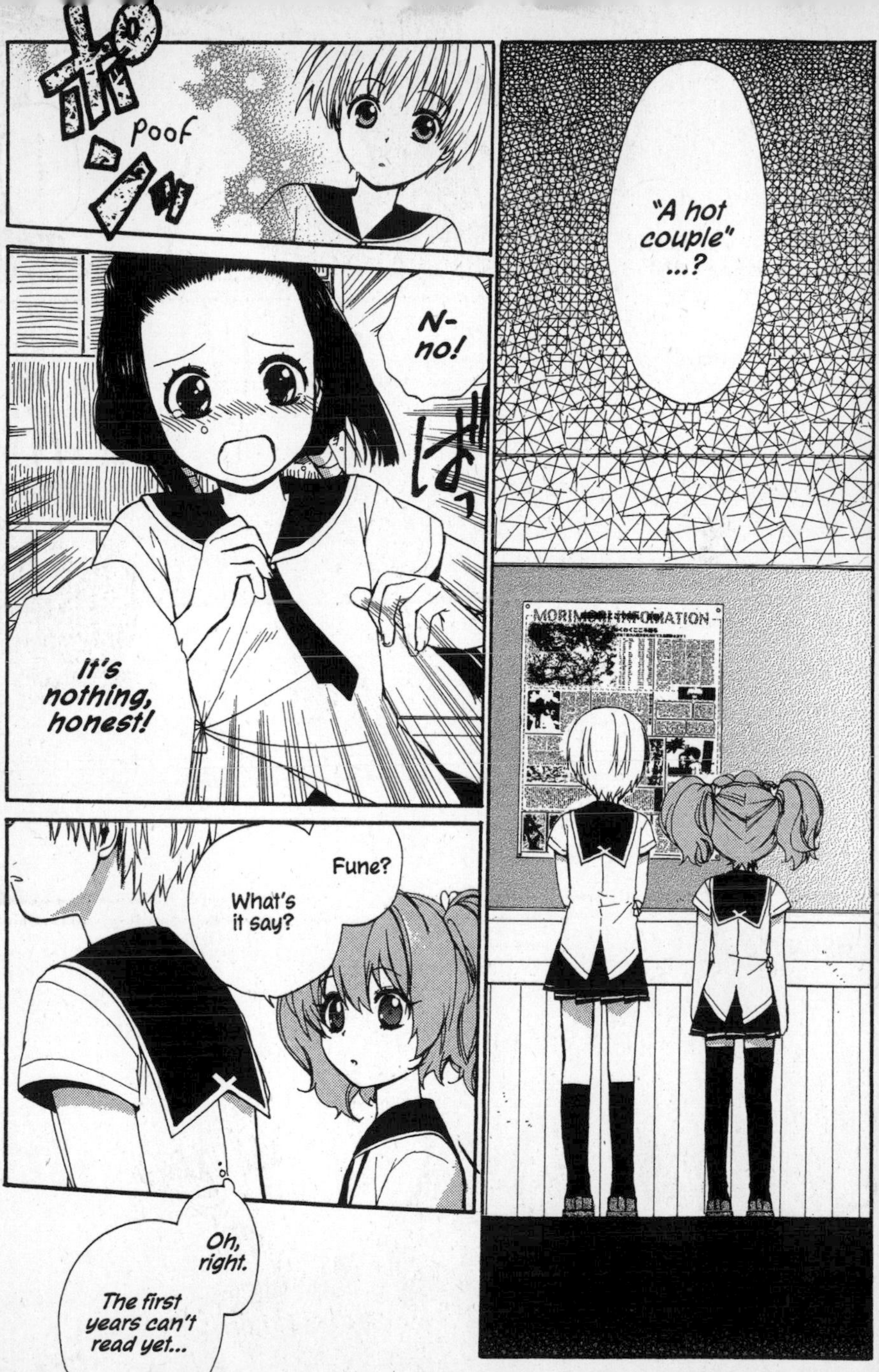
"A hot couple" ...?
poof
N-no!
It's nothing, honest!
Fune?
What's it say?
Oh, right.
The first years can't read yet...

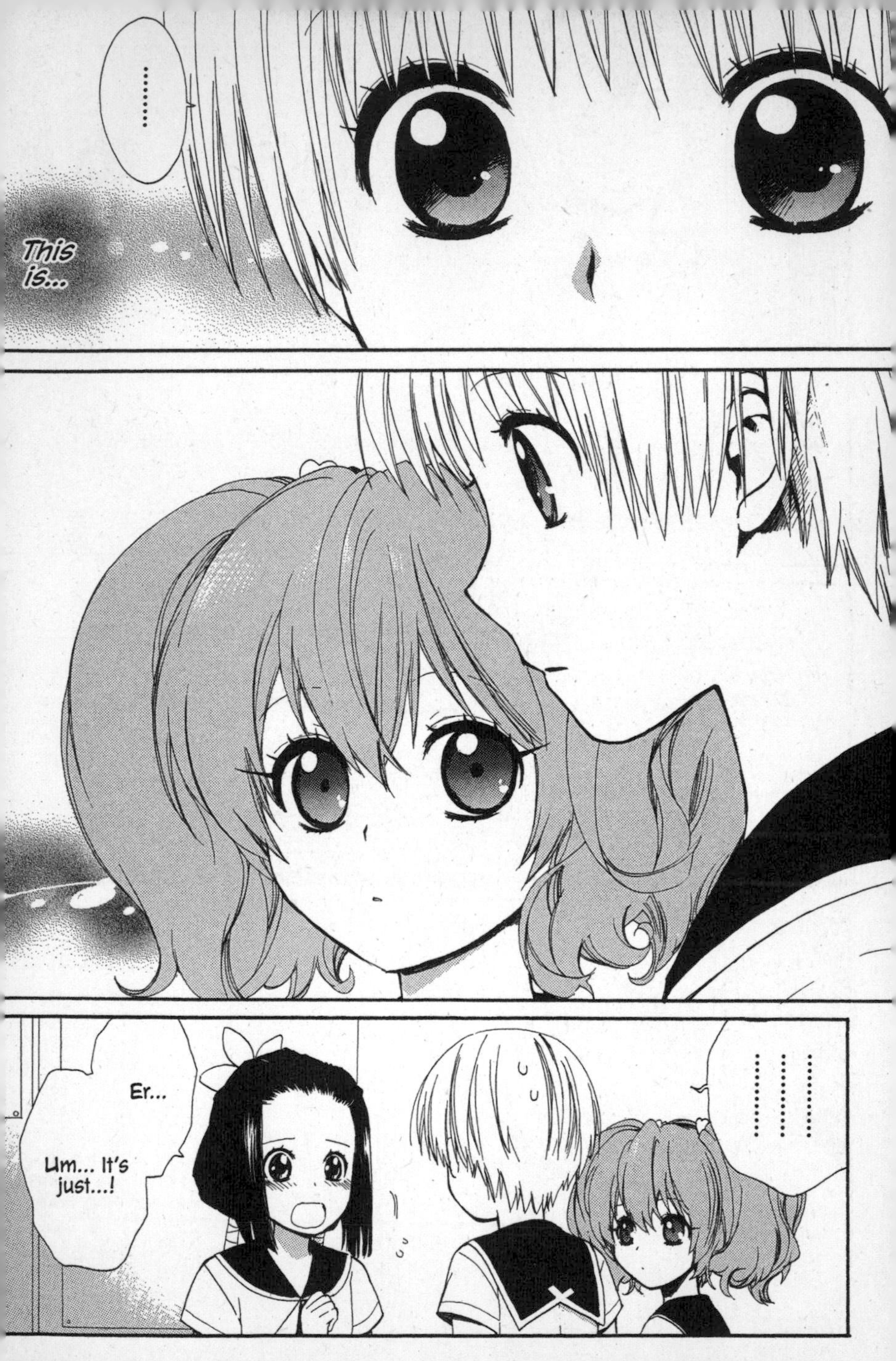
……
This is...
……
Er...
Um... It's just...!

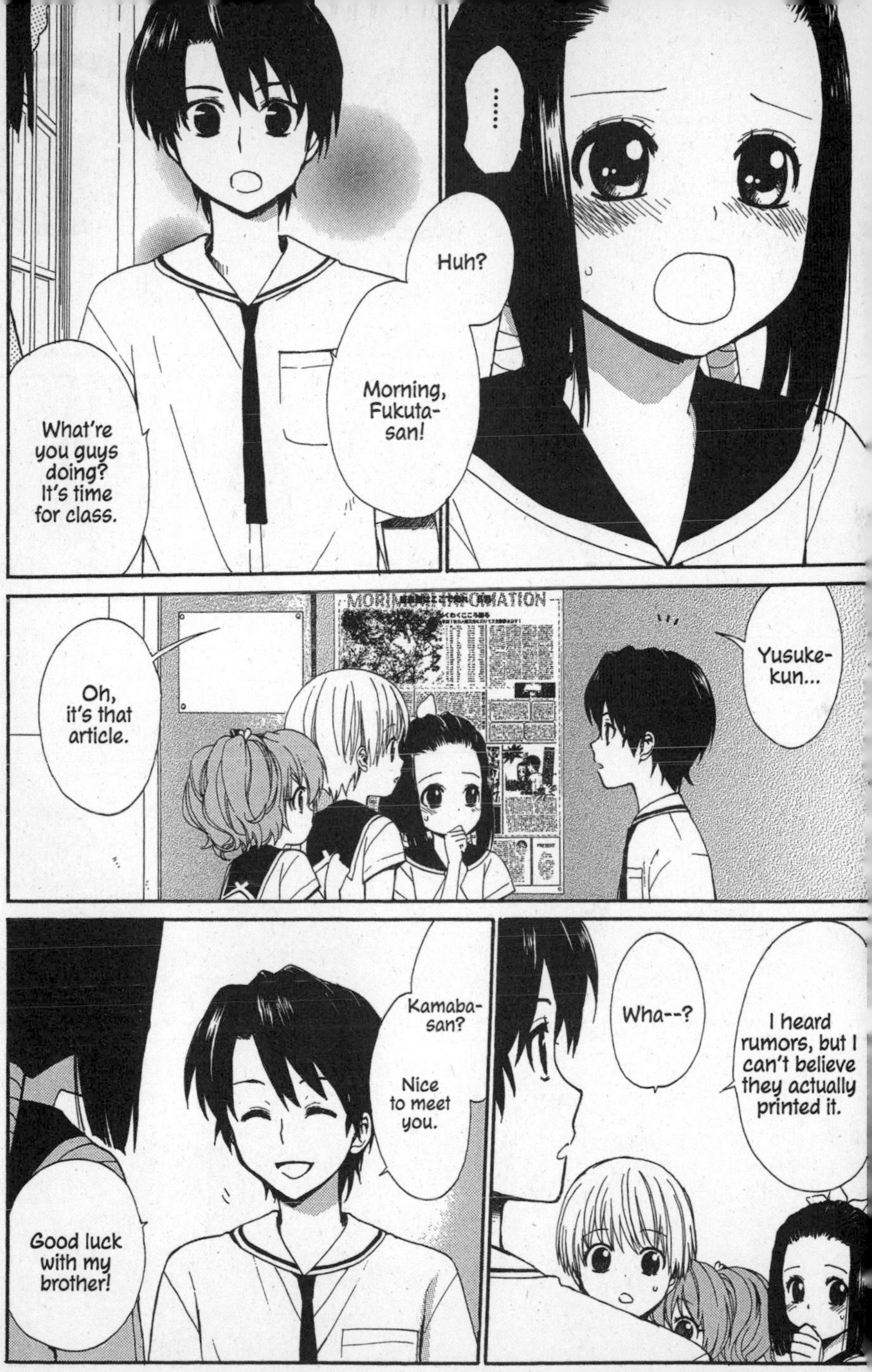
......
Huh?
Morning, Fukuta-san!
What're you guys doing? It's time for class.
Yusuke-kun...
Oh, it's that article.
I heard rumors, but I can't believe they actually printed it.
Wha--?
Kamaba-san?
Nice to meet you.
Good luck with my brother!

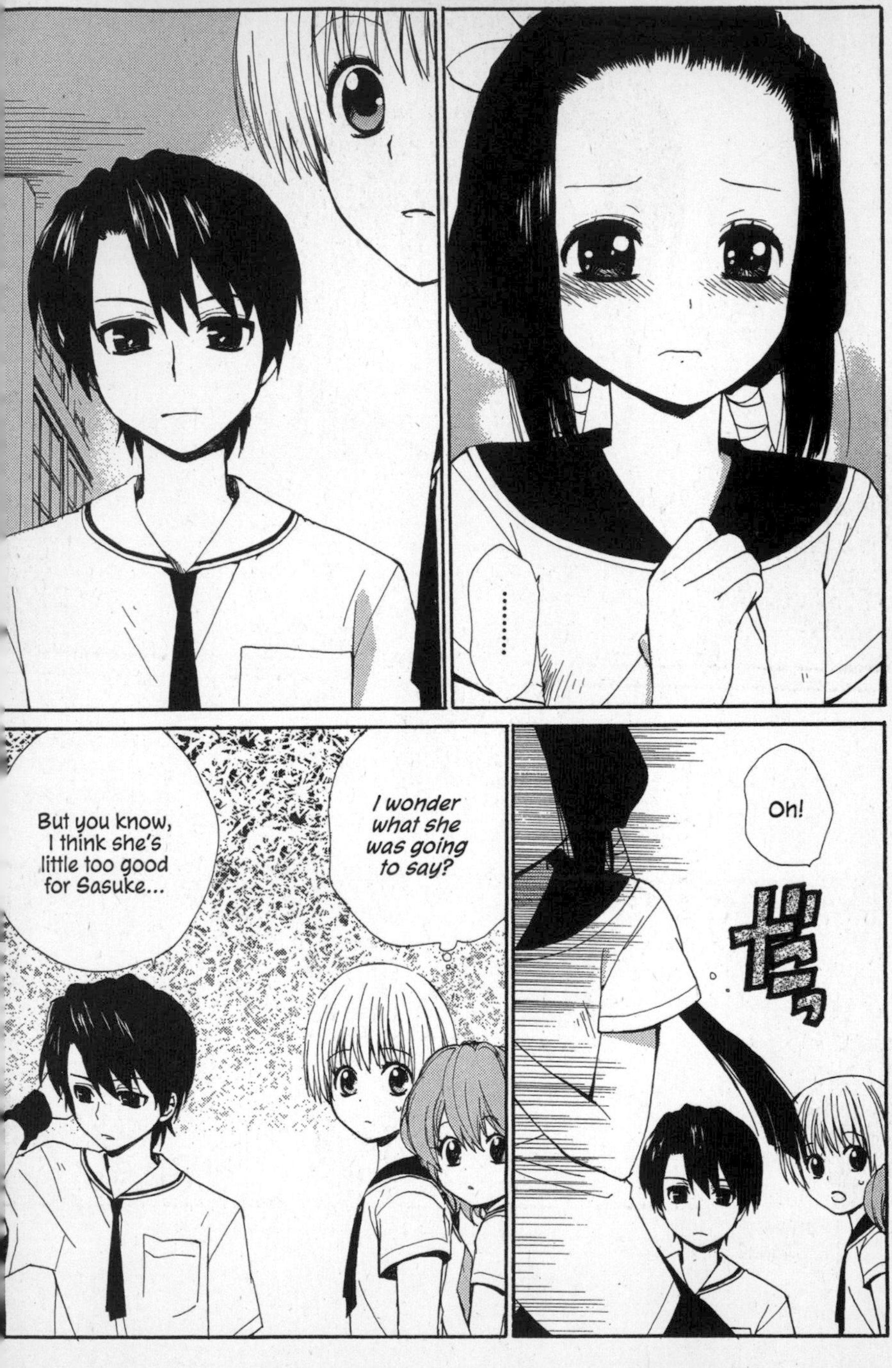
......
Oh!
I wonder what she was going to say?
But you know, I think she's little too good for Sasuke...

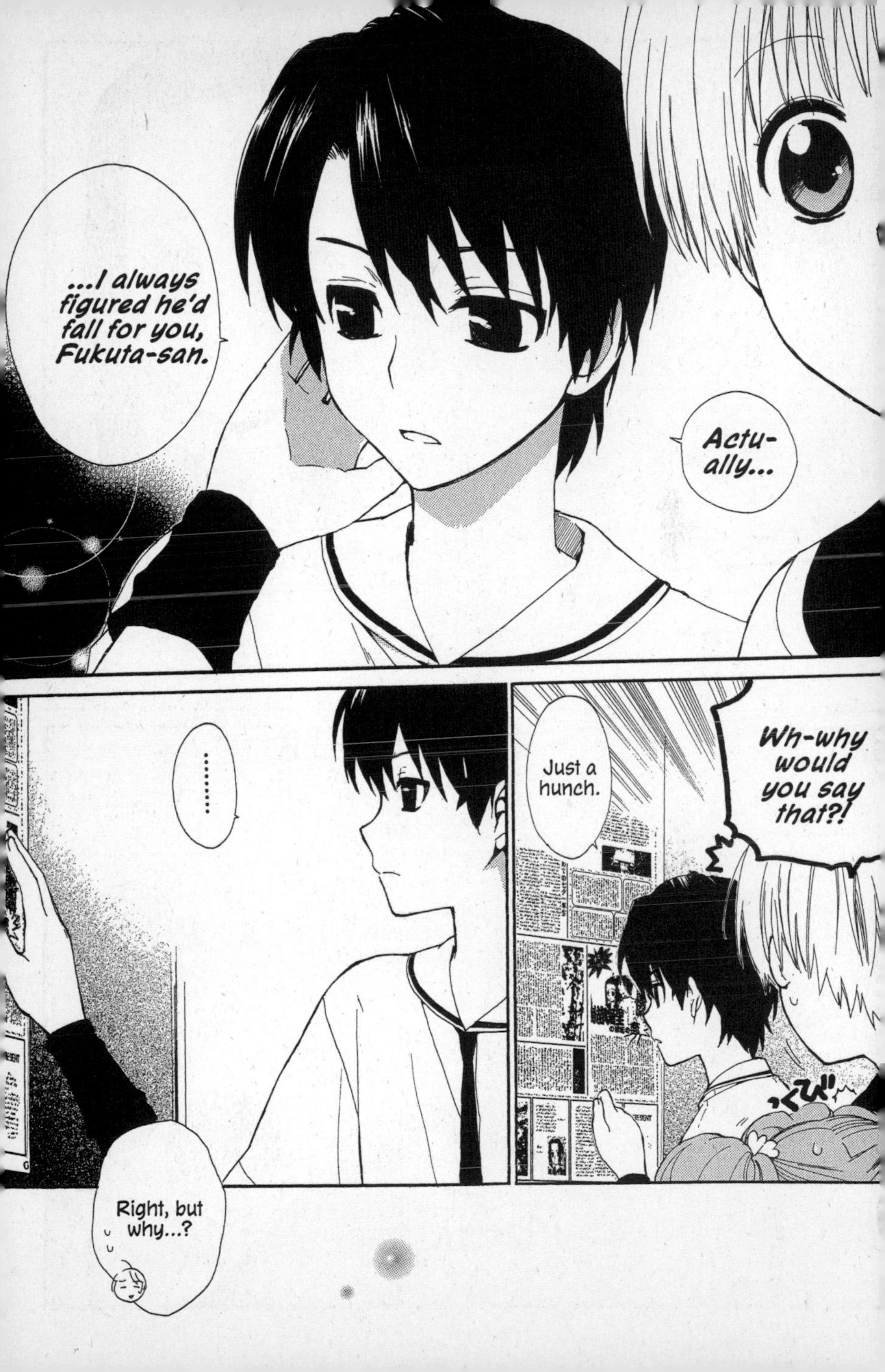
Actu-ally...
...I always figured he'd fall for you, Fukuta-san.
Wh-why would you say that?!
Just a hunch.
......
Right, but why...?

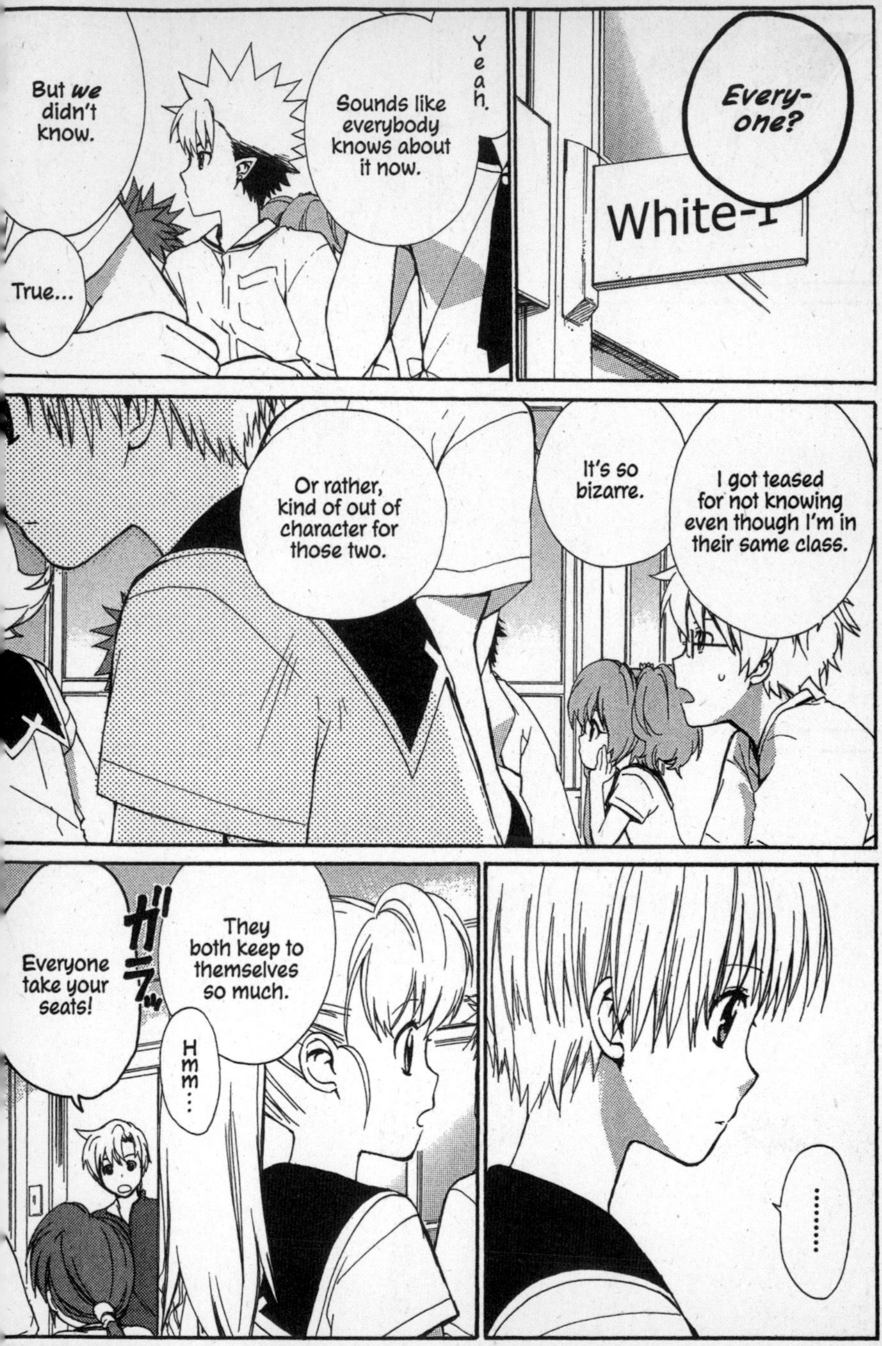
Every-one?
White-1
Yeah.
Sounds like everybody knows about it now.
But *we* didn't know.
True...
I got teased for not knowing even though I'm in their same class.
It's so bizarre.
Or rather, kind of out of character for those two.
......
They both keep to themselves so much.
Hmm...
ガラッ
Everyone take your seats!

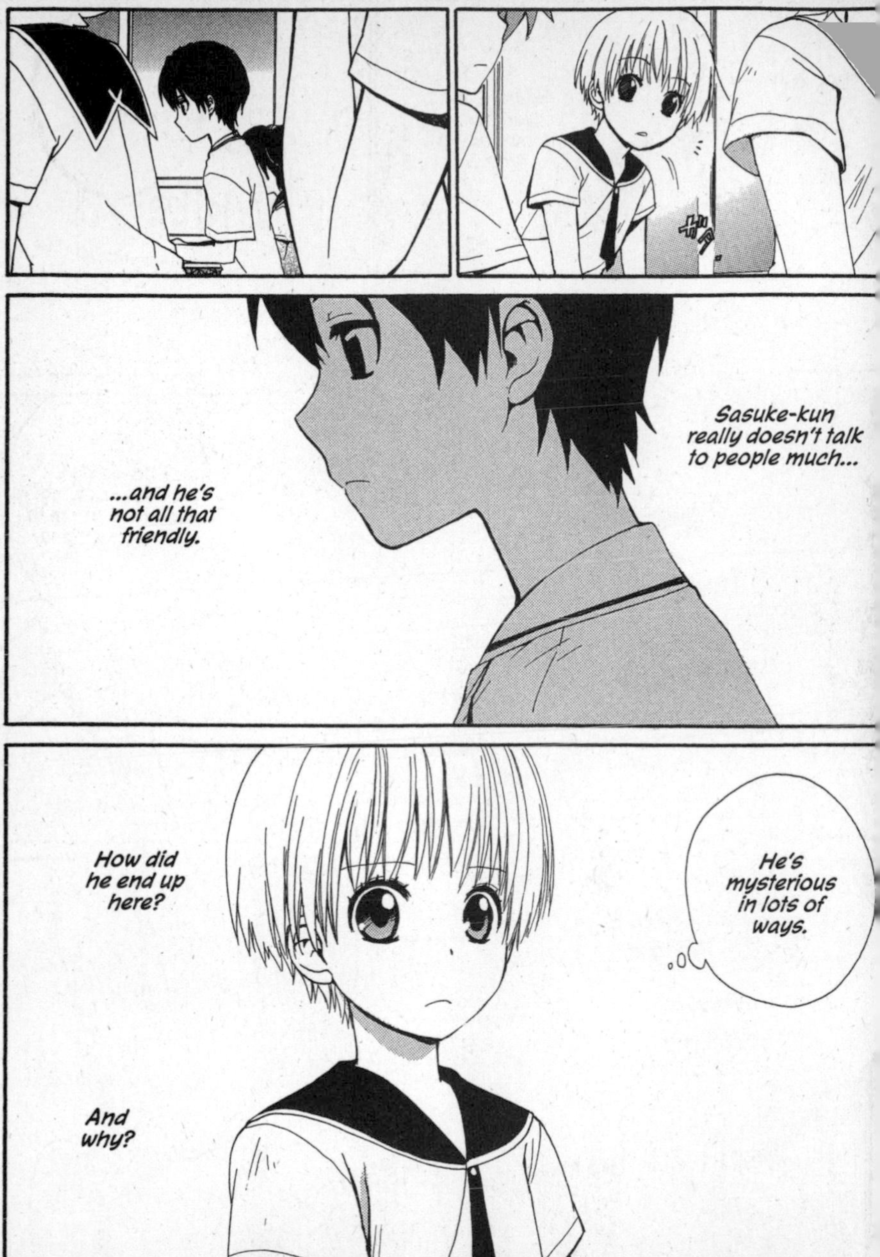
Sasuke-kun really doesn't talk to people much...
...and he's not all that friendly.
He's mysterious in lots of ways.
How did he end up here?
And why?

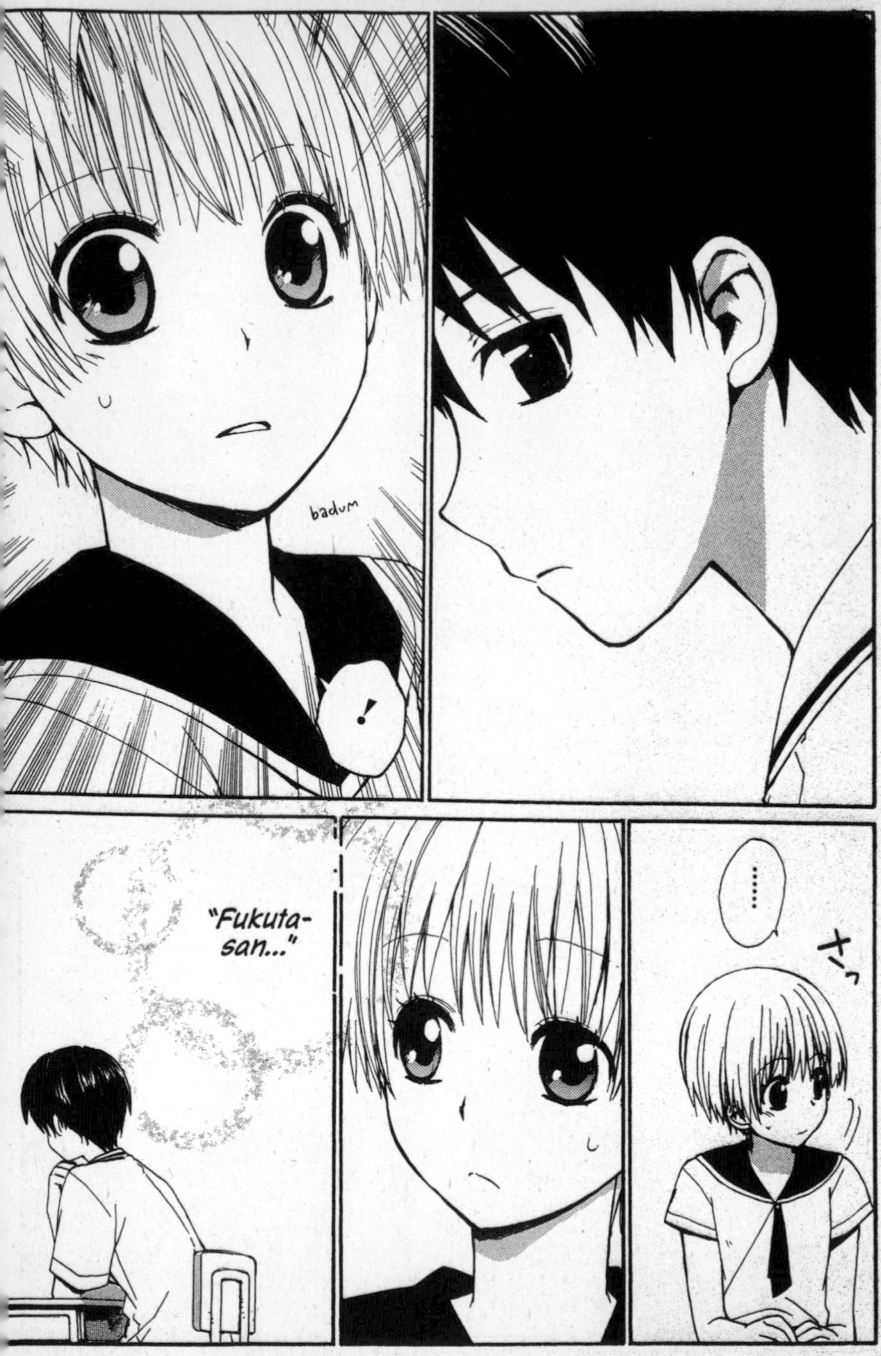
badum
!
......
さっ
"Fukuta-san..."

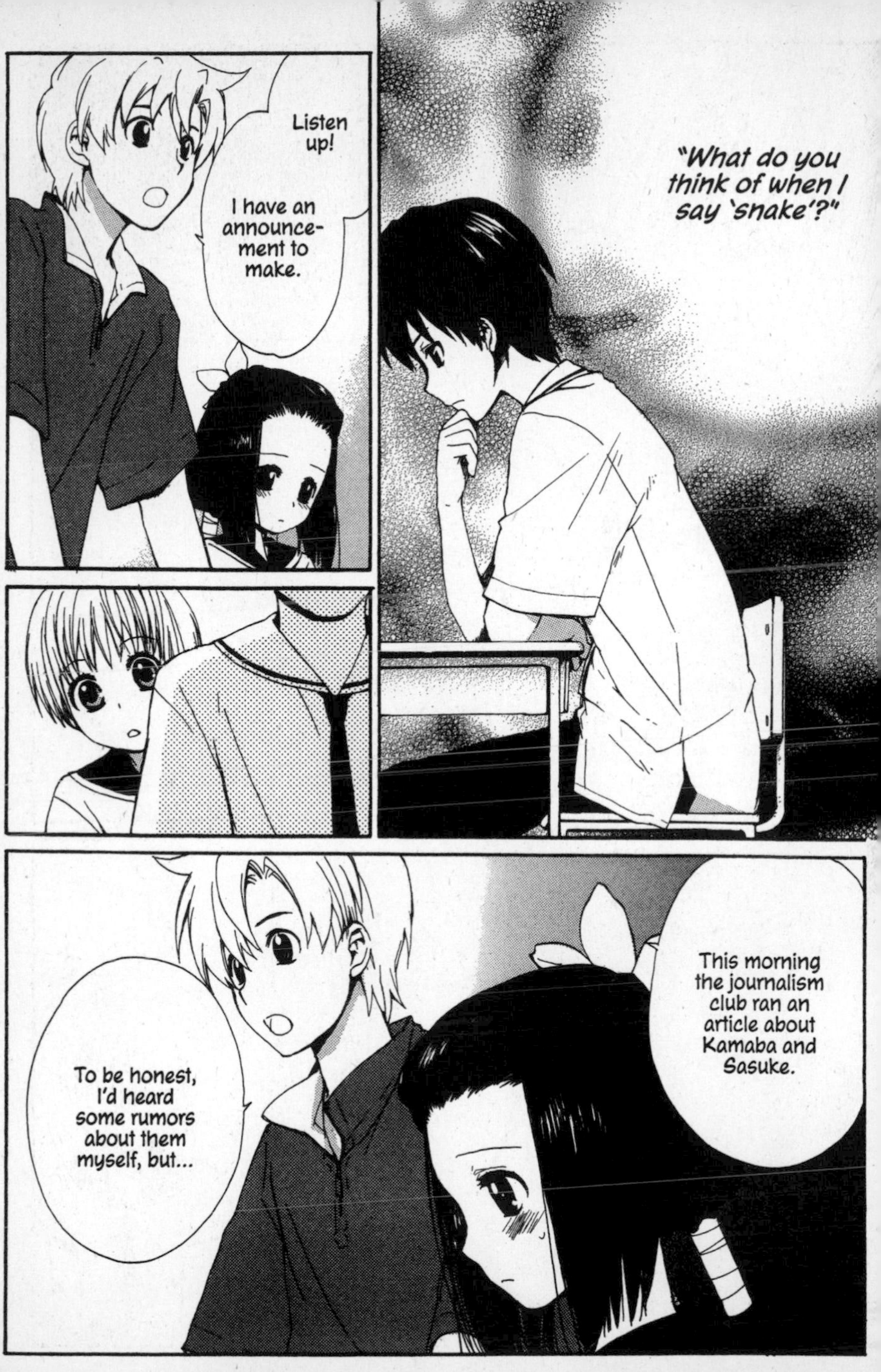
"What do you think of when I say 'snake'?"
Listen up!
I have an announcement to make.
This morning the journalism club ran an article about Kamaba and Sasuke.
To be honest, I'd heard some rumors about them myself, but...

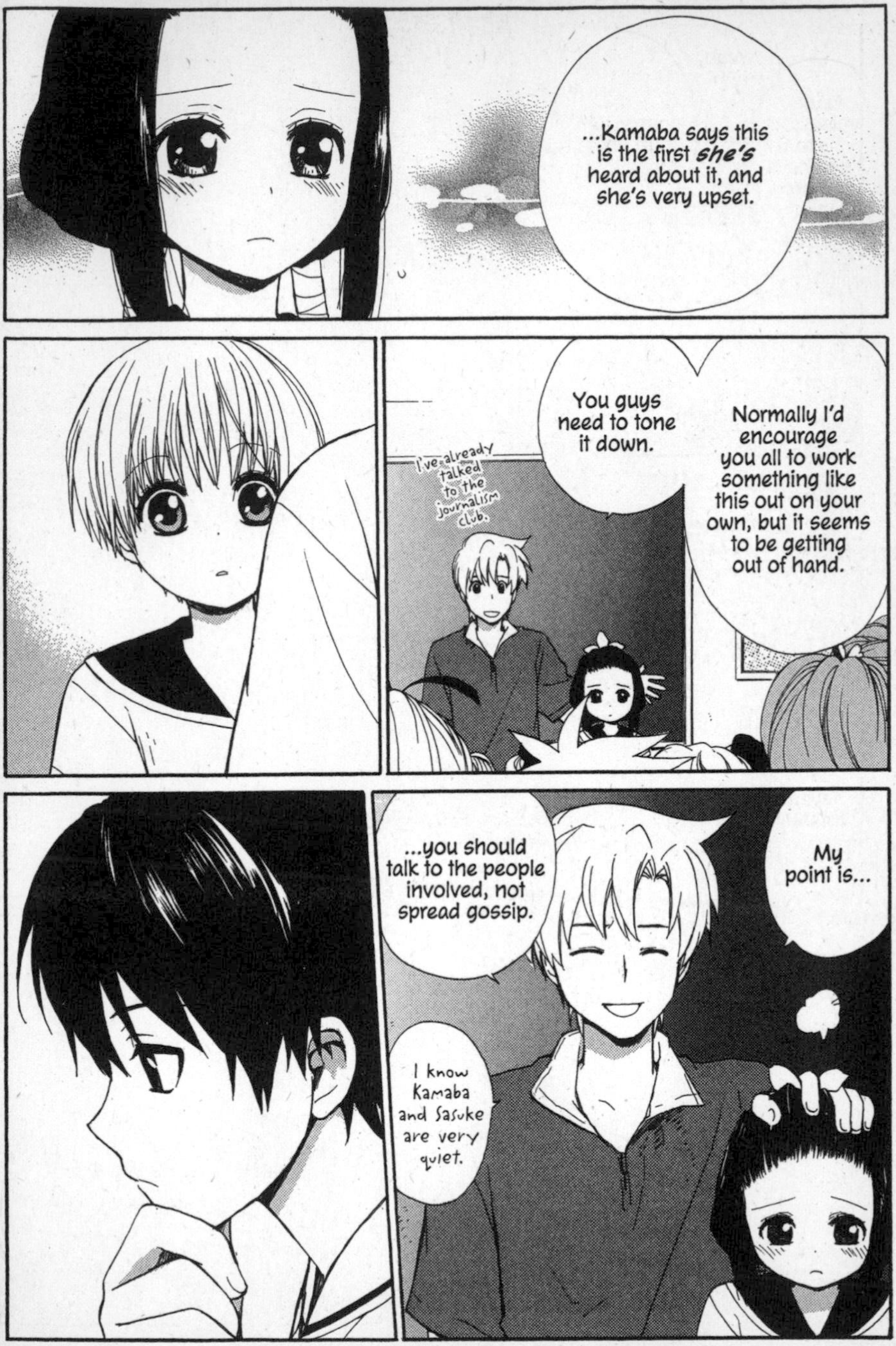
...Kamaba says this is the first *she's* heard about it, and she's very upset.
Normally I'd encourage you all to work something like this out on your own, but it seems to be getting out of hand.
You guys need to tone it down.
I've already talked to the journalism club.
My point is...
...you should talk to the people involved, not spread gossip.
I know Kamaba and Sasuke are very quiet.

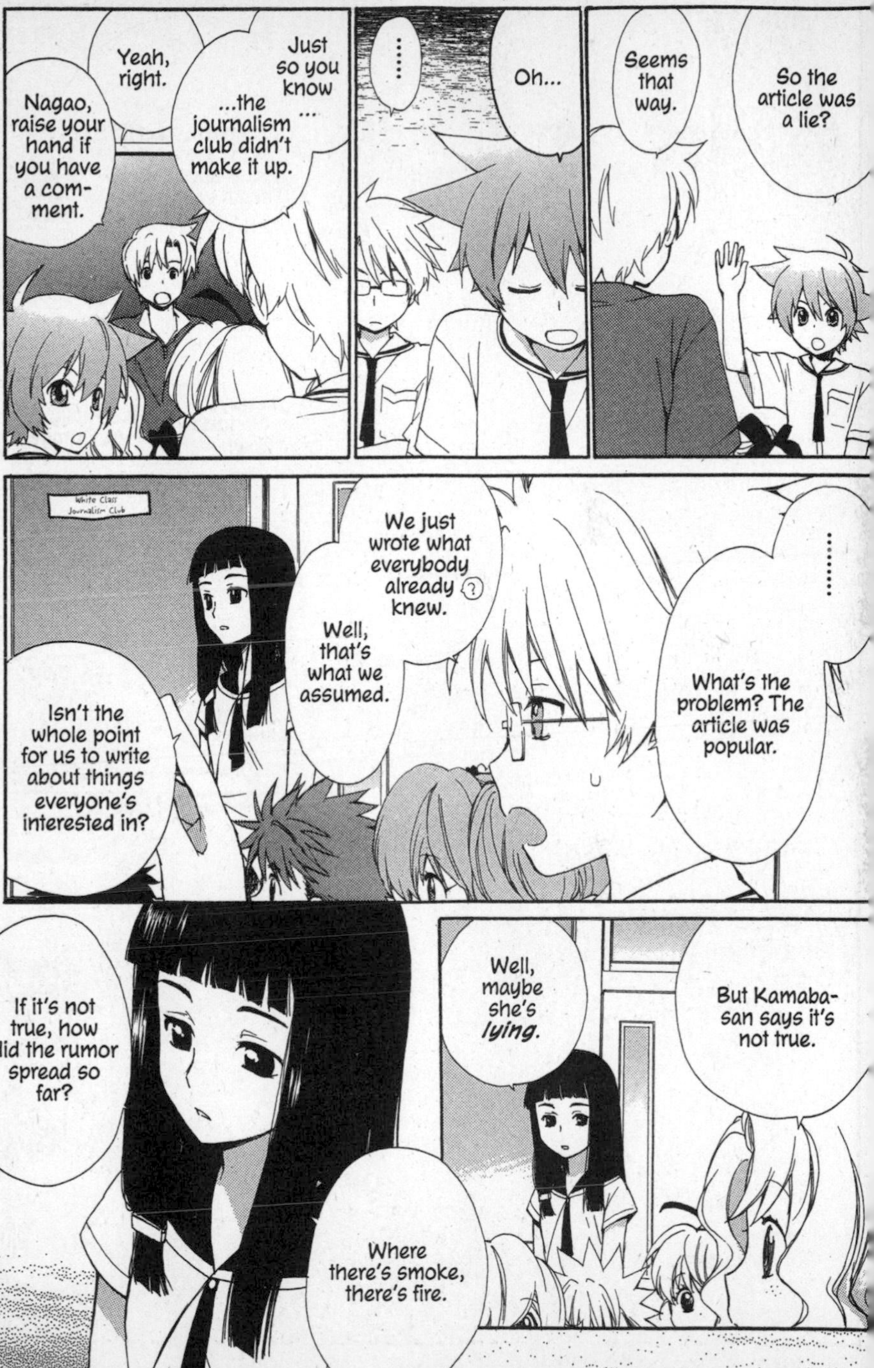
So the article was a lie?
Seems that way.
Oh...
......
Just so you know ...
...the journalism club didn't make it up.
Yeah, right.
Nagao, raise your hand if you have a comment.
......
What's the problem? The article was popular.
We just wrote what everybody already knew.
?
Well, that's what we assumed.
White Class Journalism Club
Isn't the whole point for us to write about things everyone's interested in?
But Kamaba-san says it's not true.
Well, maybe she's *lying*.
If it's not true, how did the rumor spread so far?
Where there's smoke, there's fire.

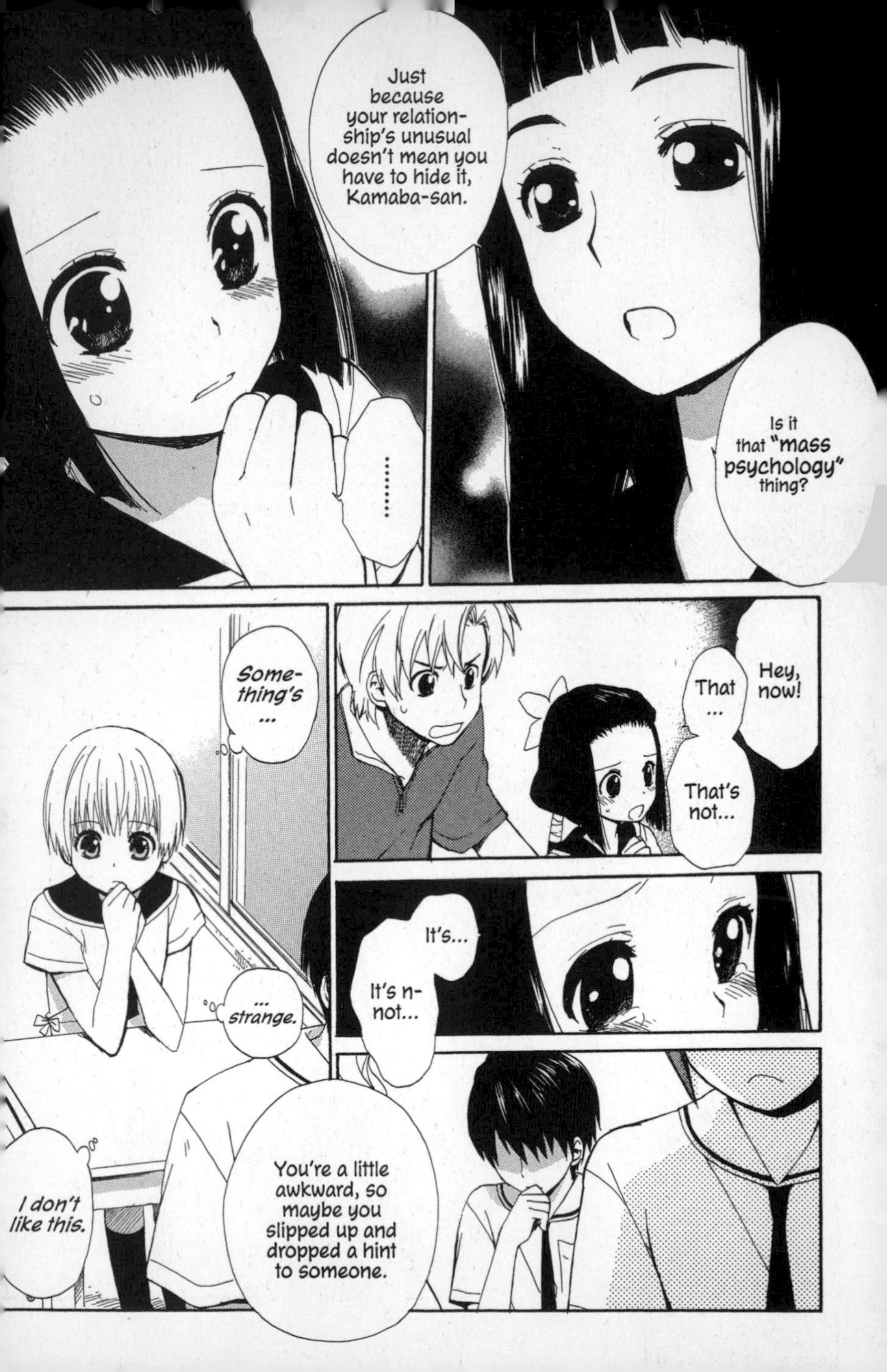
Just because your relationship's unusual doesn't mean you have to hide it, Kamaba-san.
Is it that "mass psychology" thing?
....
Hey, now!
That...
That's not...
It's...
It's n-not...
You're a little awkward, so maybe you slipped up and dropped a hint to someone.
Some-thing's ...
... strange.
I don't like this.

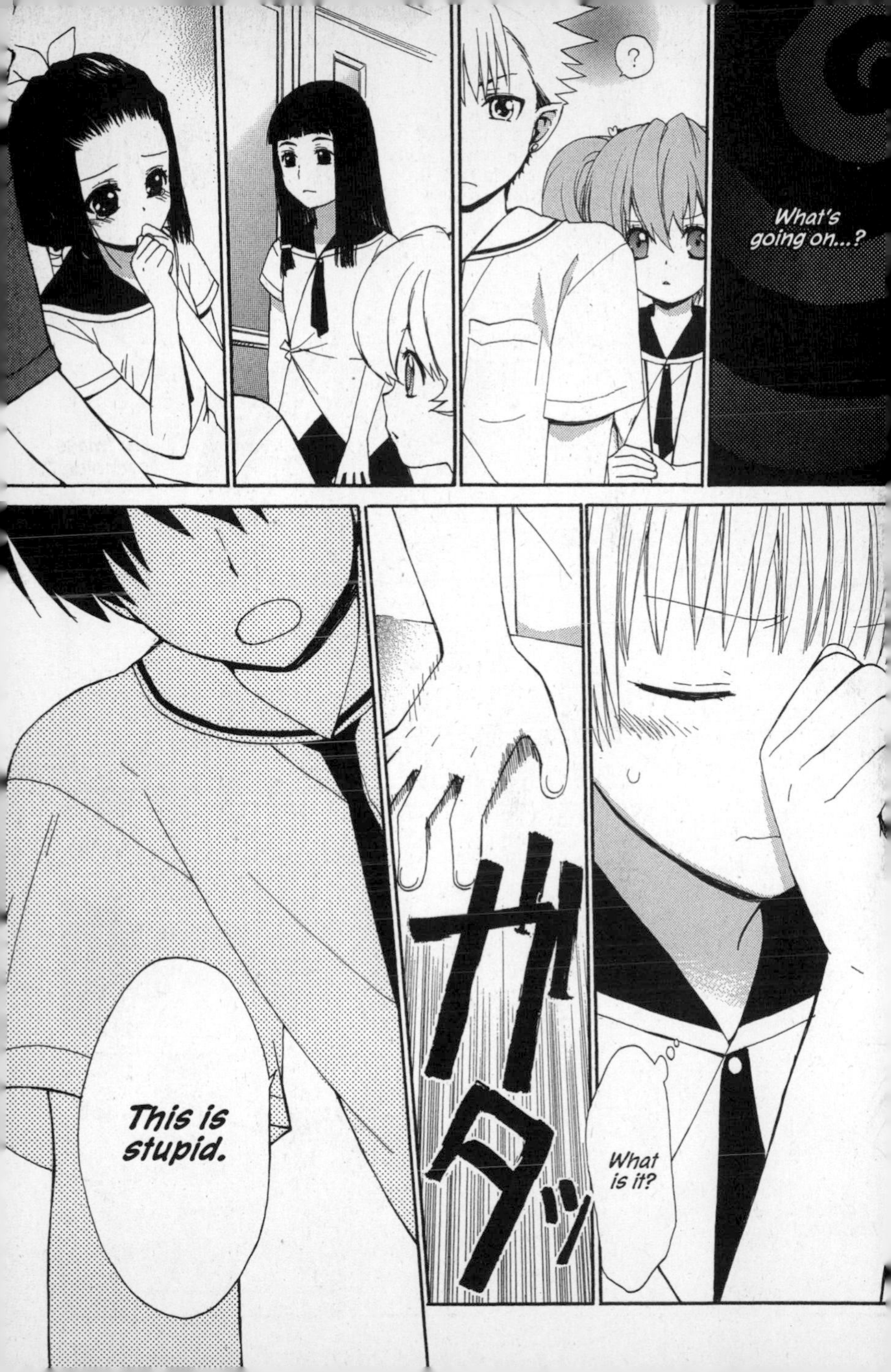
What's going on...?
?
What is it?
ガタッ
This is stupid.

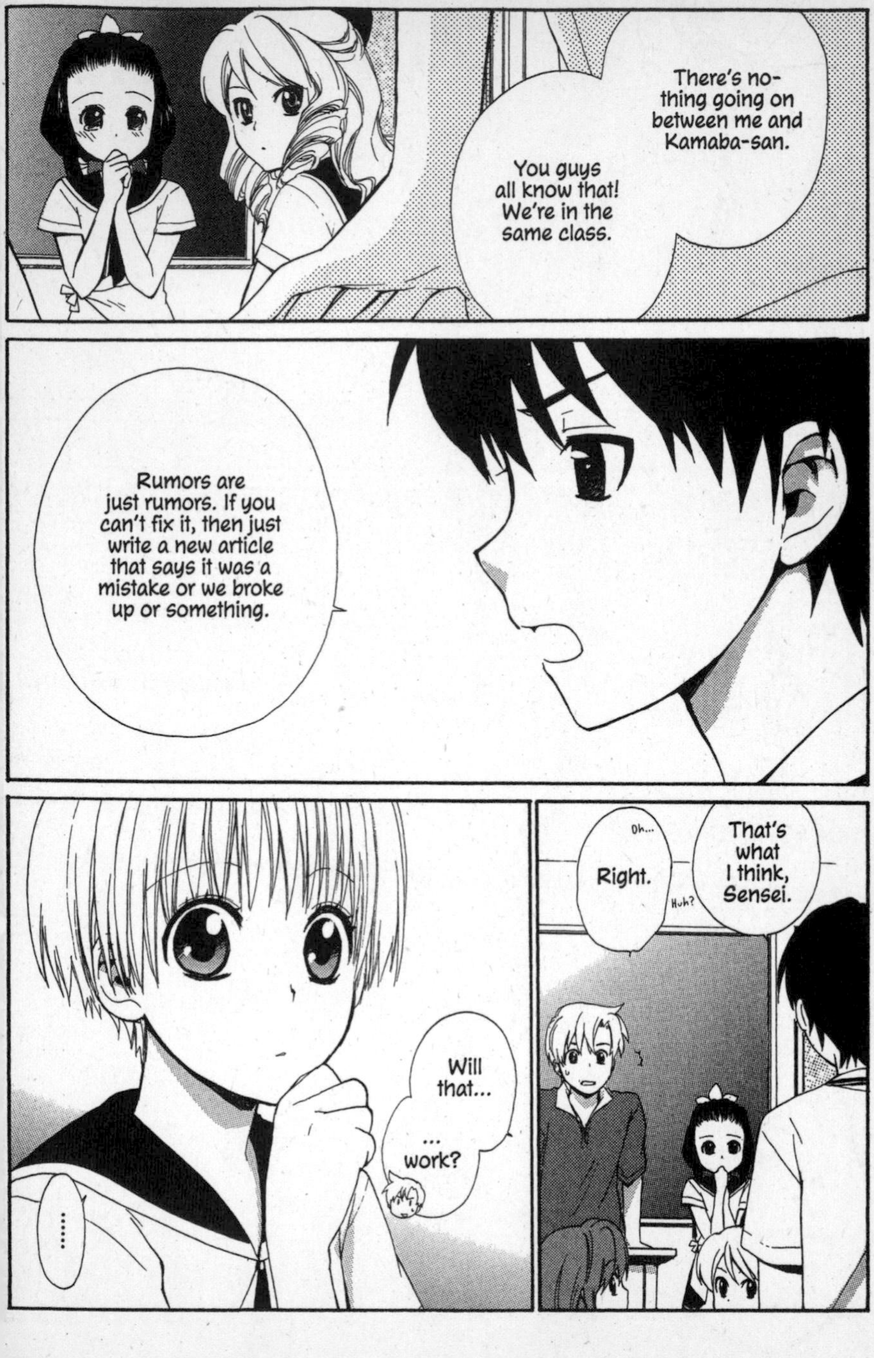
There's no-thing going on between me and Kamaba-san.
You guys all know that! We're in the same class.
Rumors are just rumors. If you can't fix it, then just write a new article that says it was a mistake or we broke up or something.
That's what I think, Sensei.
Huh?
Oh...
Right.
Will that...
... work?
......

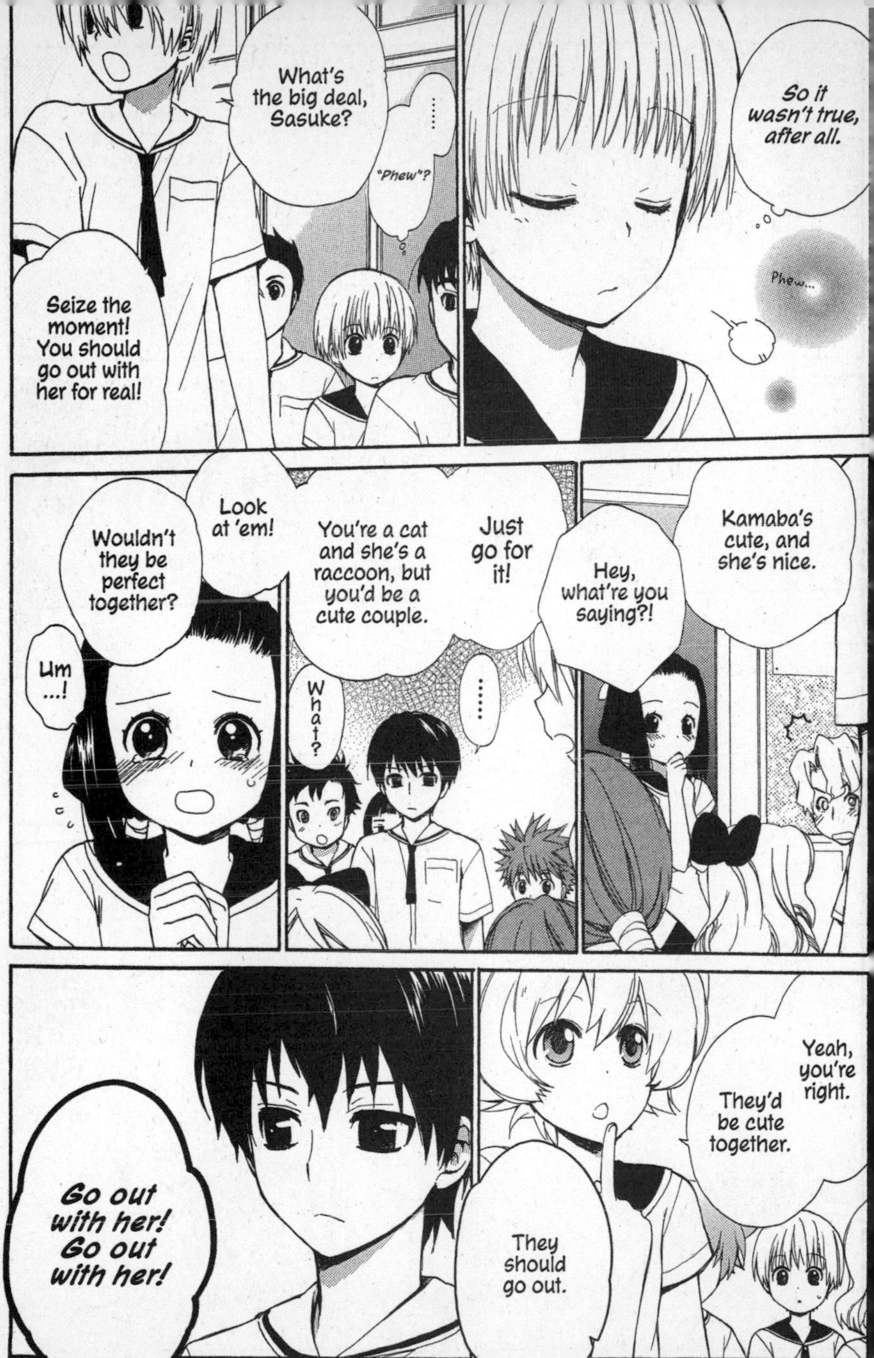
So it wasn't true, after all.
Phew...
What's the big deal, Sasuke?
......
"Phew"?
Seize the moment! You should go out with her for real!
Kamaba's cute, and she's nice.
Hey, what're you saying?!
Just go for it!
You're a cat and she's a raccoon, but you'd be a cute couple.
Look at 'em!
......
What?
Wouldn't they be perfect together?
Um ...!
Yeah, you're right.
They'd be cute together.
They should go out.
Go out with her! Go out with her!

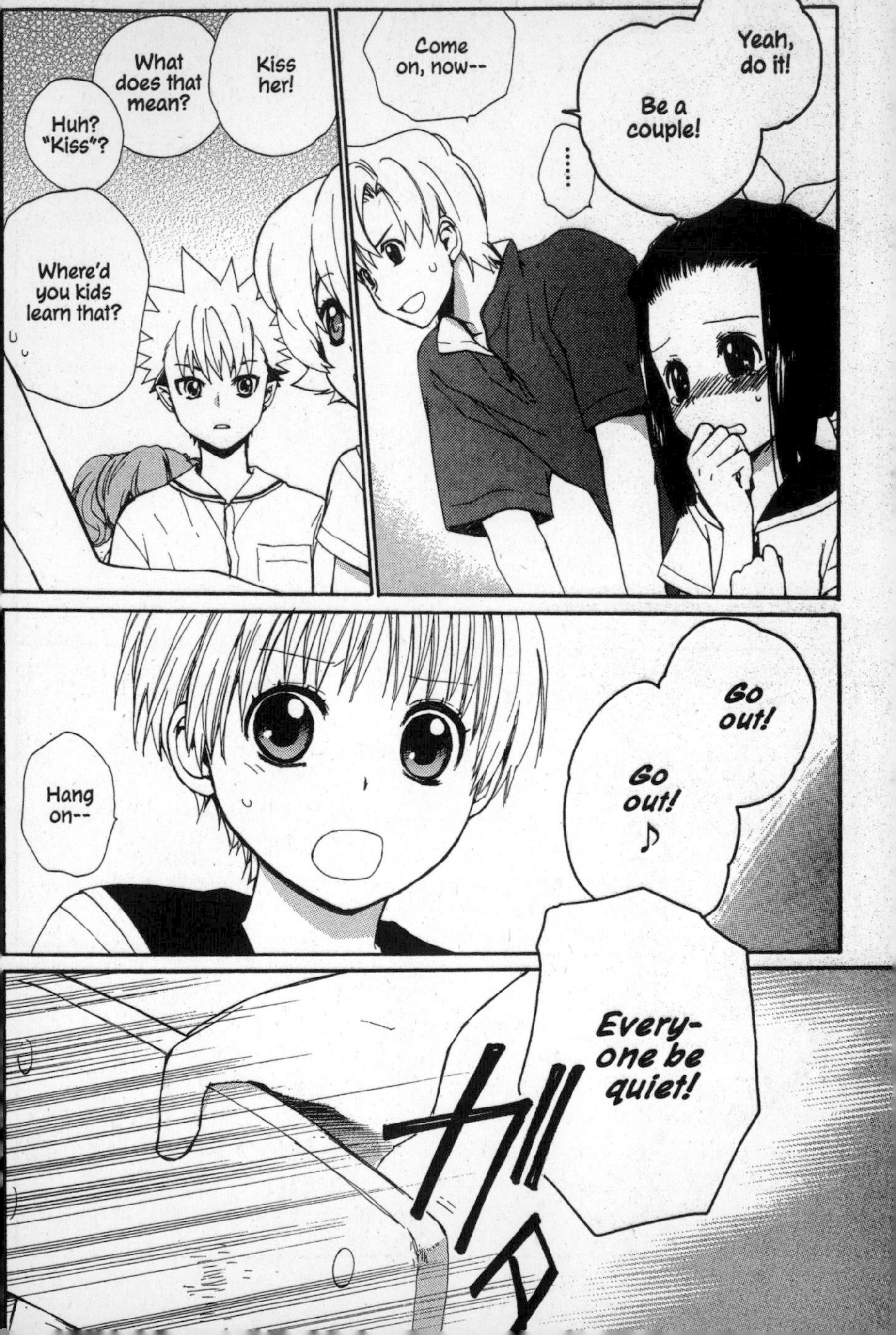
Yeah, do it!
Be a couple!
......
Come on, now--
Kiss her!
What does that mean?
Huh? "Kiss"?
Where'd you kids learn that?
Go out!
Go out! ♪
Hang on--
Every-one be quiet!
ガタ

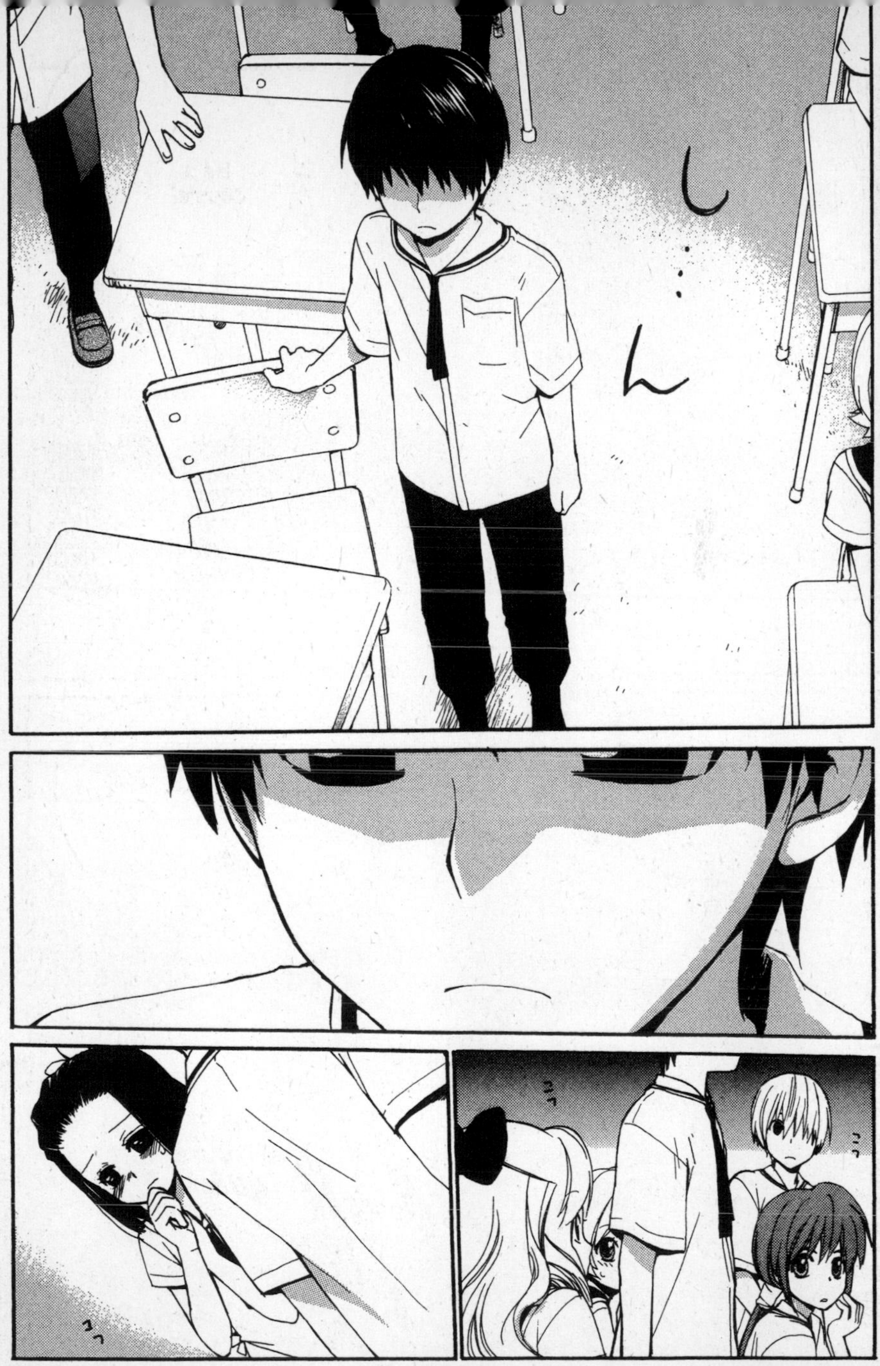
し…ん
コソ
コソ
コソ

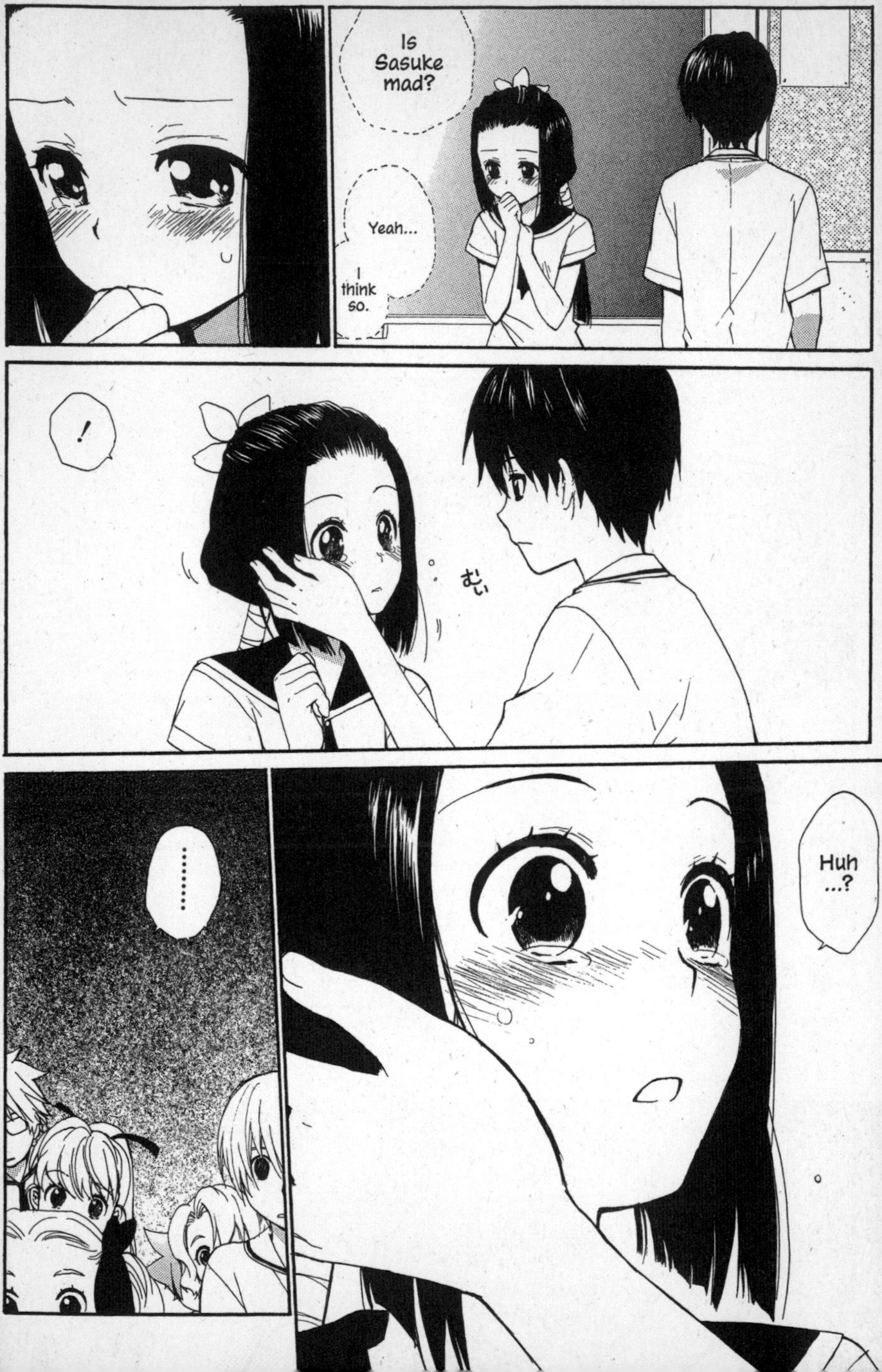
Is Sasuke mad?
Yeah...
I think so.
!
むい
Huh ...?
....

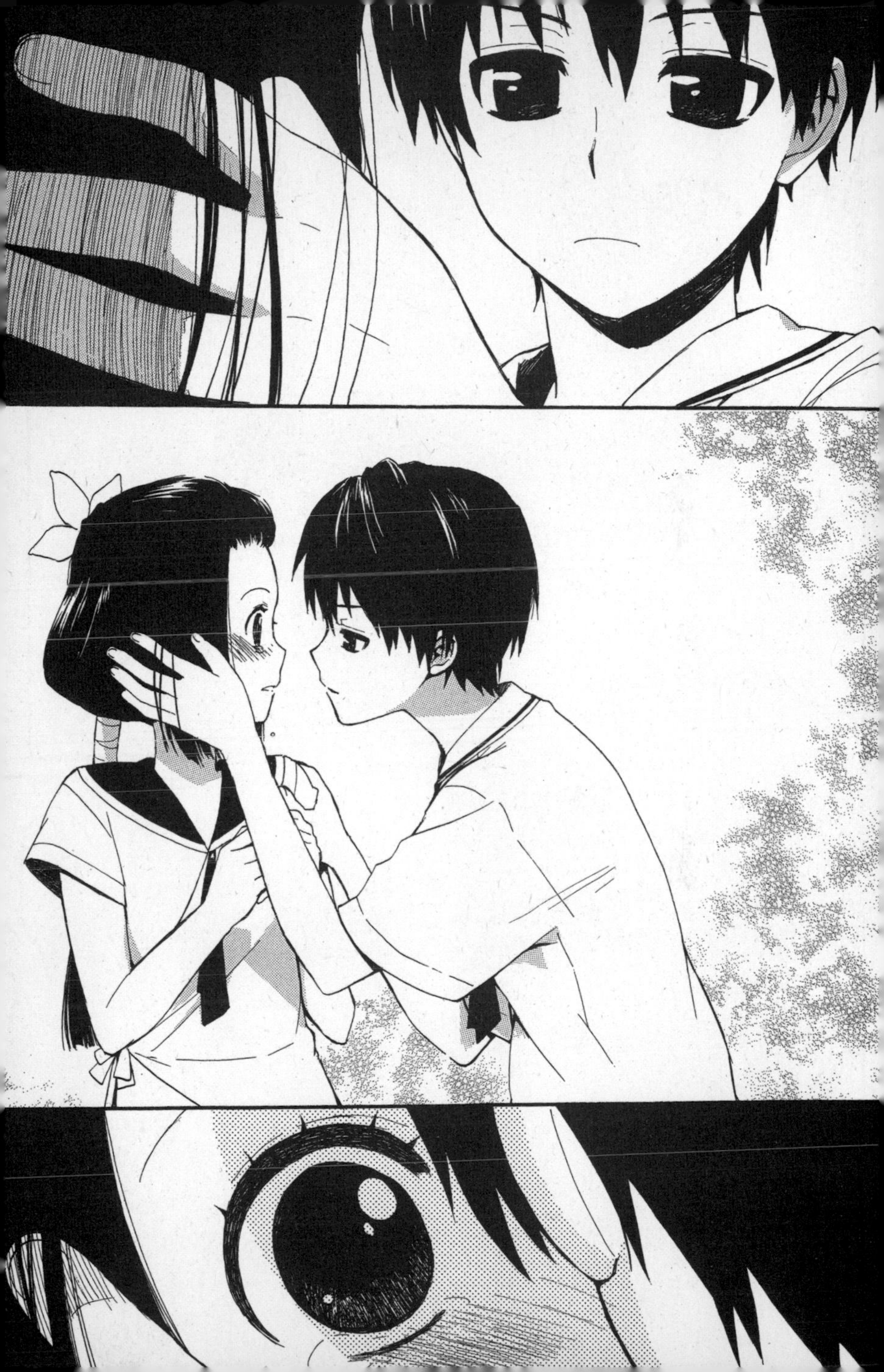

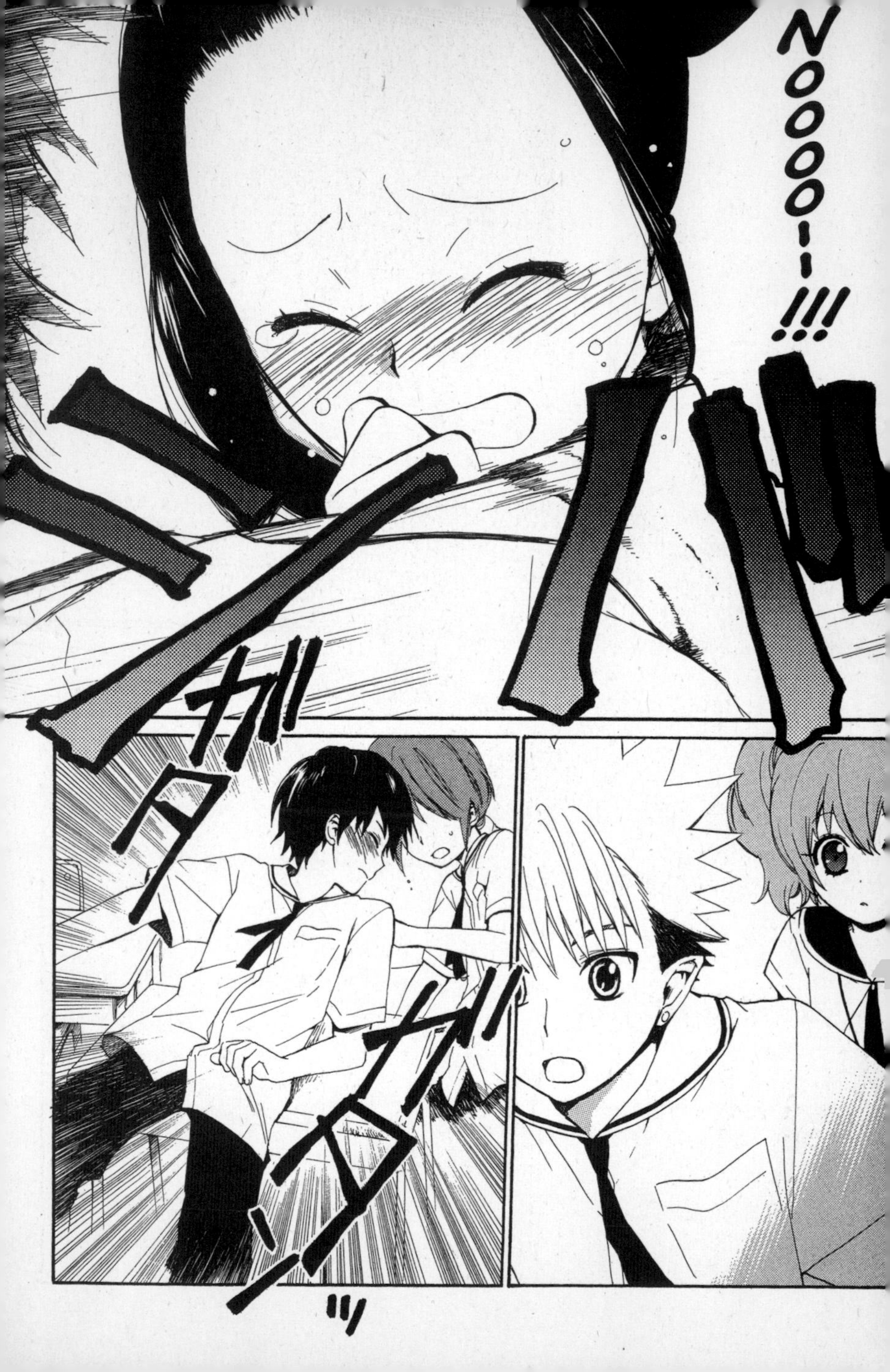
NOOOOO!!!!!

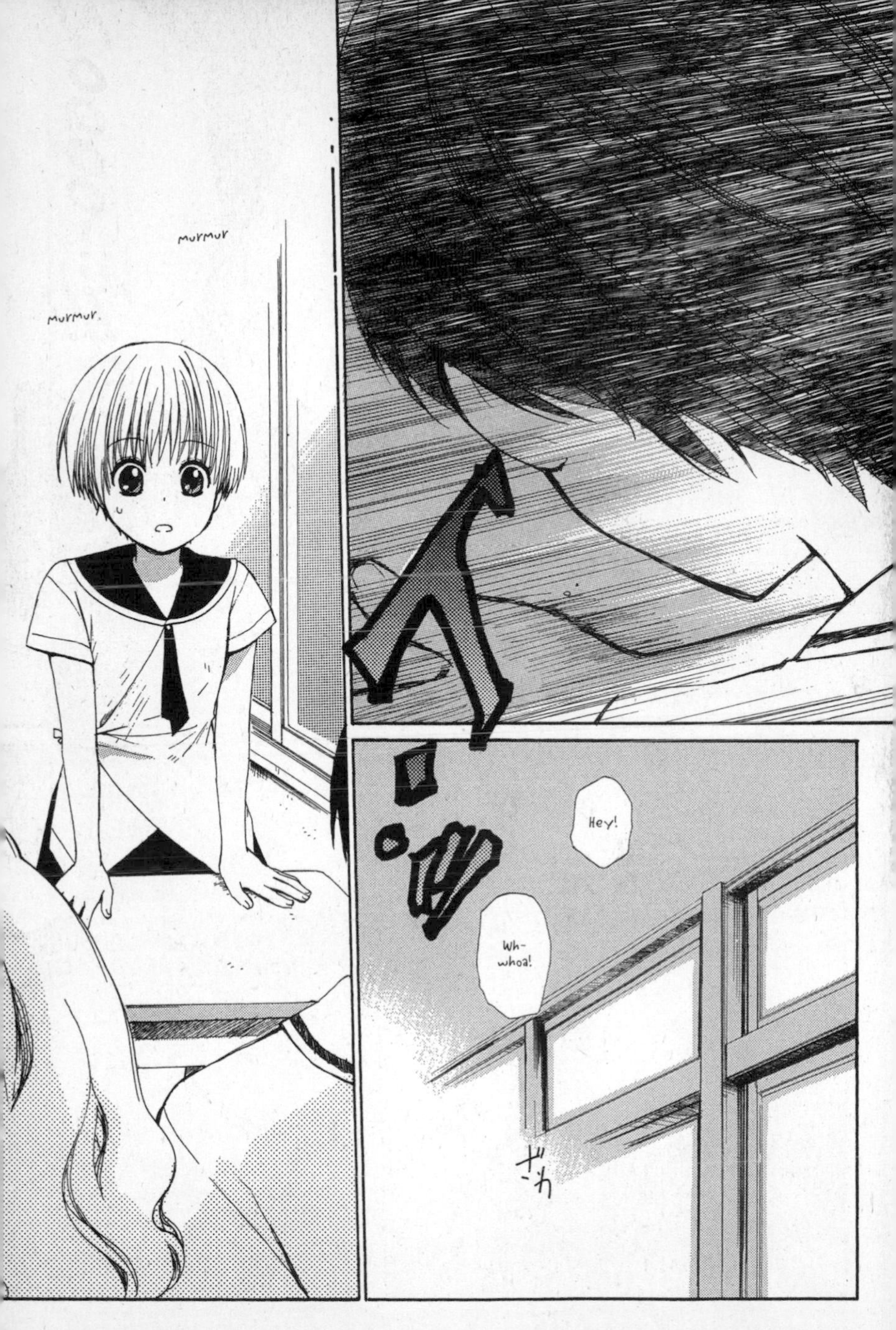
Hey!
Wh-
whoa!
ざわ
murmur
murmur.

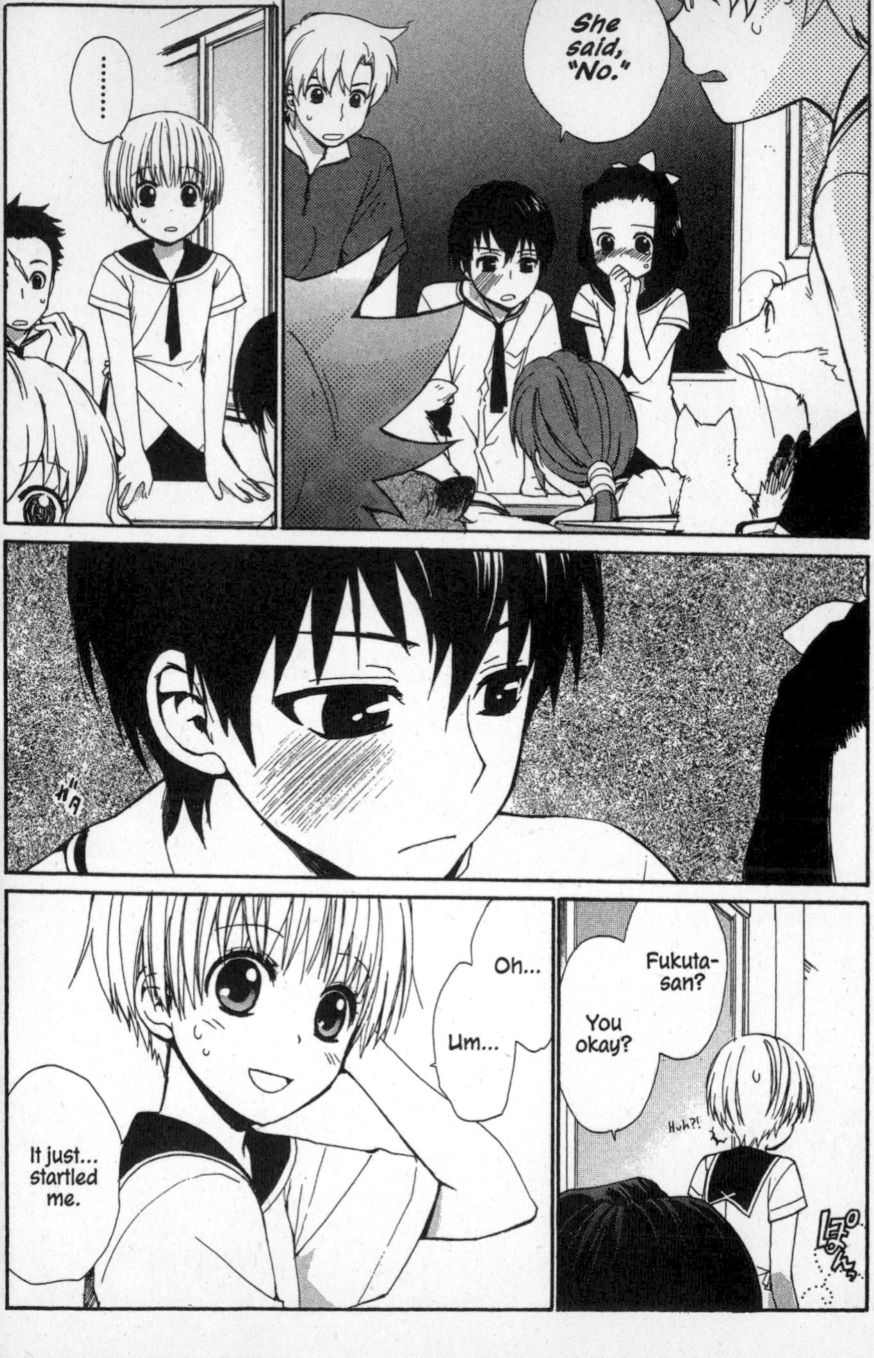
She said, "No."
......
HA
Fukuta-san?
You okay?
Huh?!
Oh...
Um...
It just... startled me.

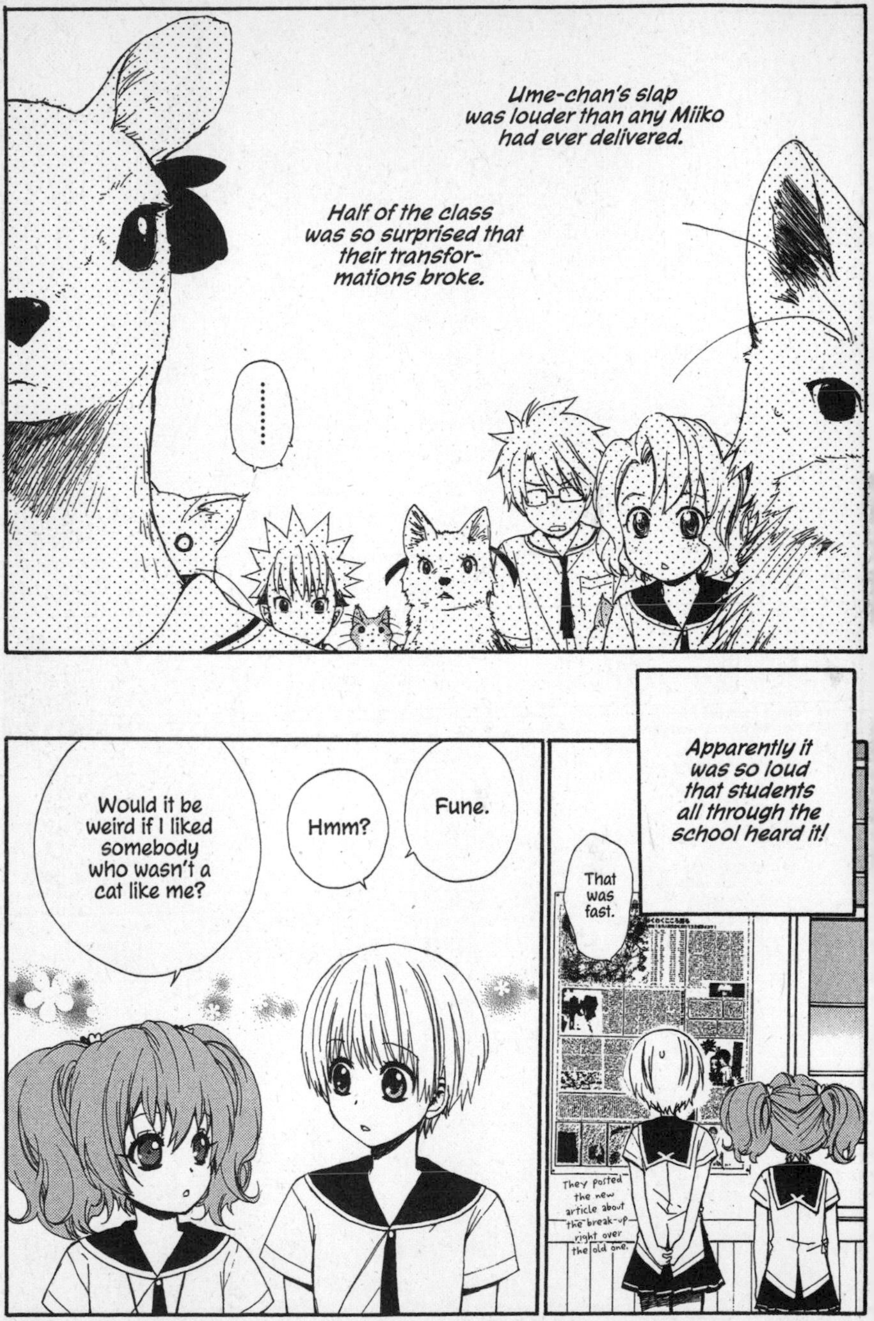
Ume-chan's slap was louder than any Miiko had ever delivered.
Half of the class was so surprised that their transfor-mations broke.
……
Apparently it was so loud that students all through the school heard it!
That was fast.
They posted the new article about the break-up right over the old one.
Fune.
Hmm?
Would it be weird if I liked somebody who wasn't a cat like me?

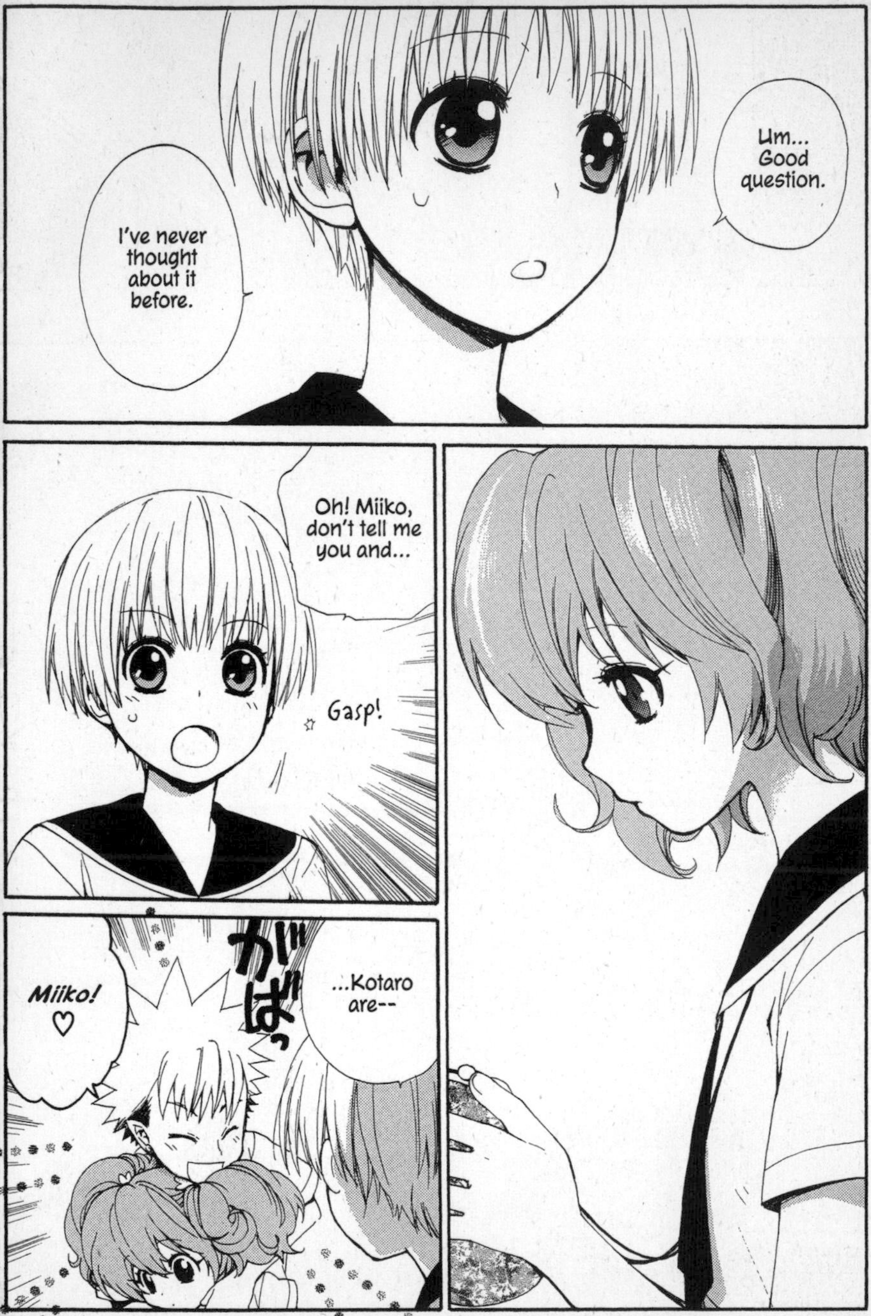
Um... Good question.
I've never thought about it before.
Oh! Miiko, don't tell me you and...
Gasp!
...Kotaro are--
がばっ
Miiko! ♡

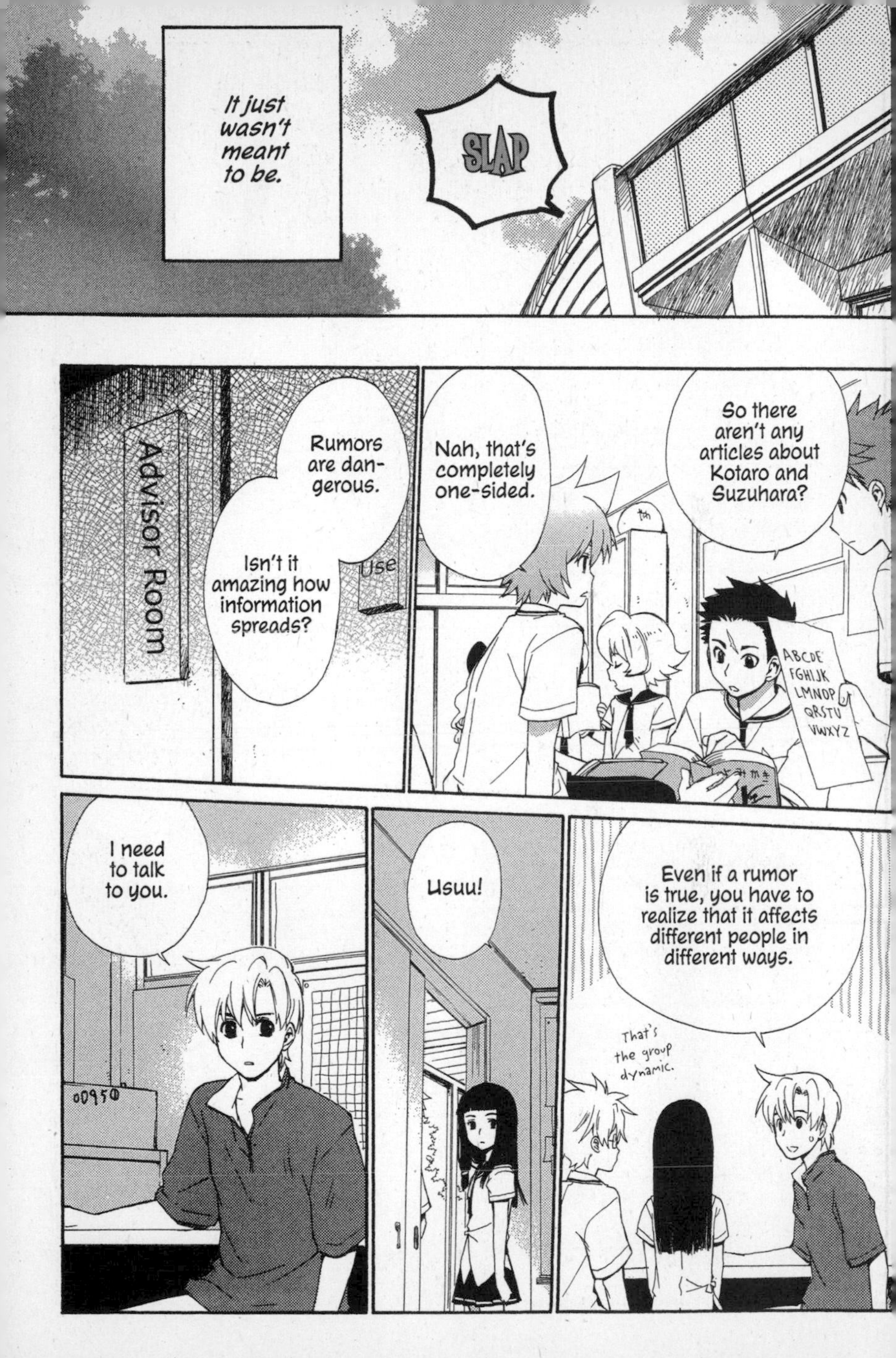
SLAP
It just wasn't meant to be.
So there aren't any articles about Kotaro and Suzuhara?
ABCDE FGHIJK LMNOP QRSTU VWXYZ
Nah, that's completely one-sided.
Rumors are dangerous.
Use
Isn't it amazing how information spreads?
Advisor Room
Even if a rumor is true, you have to realize that it affects different people in different ways.
That's the group dynamic.
Usuu!
I need to talk to you.

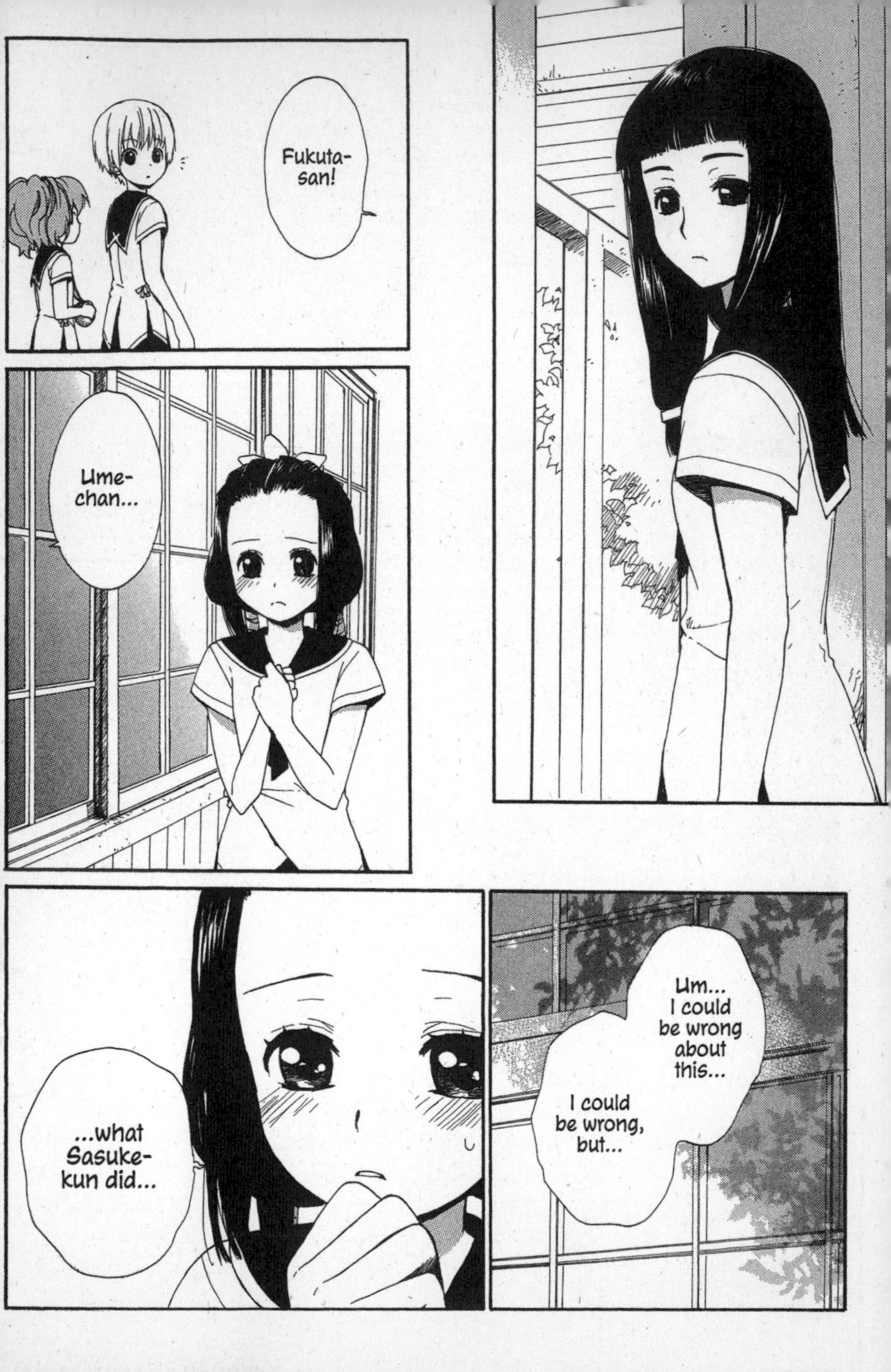
Fukuta-san!
Ume-chan...
Um... I could be wrong about this...
I could be wrong, but...
...what Sasuke-kun did...

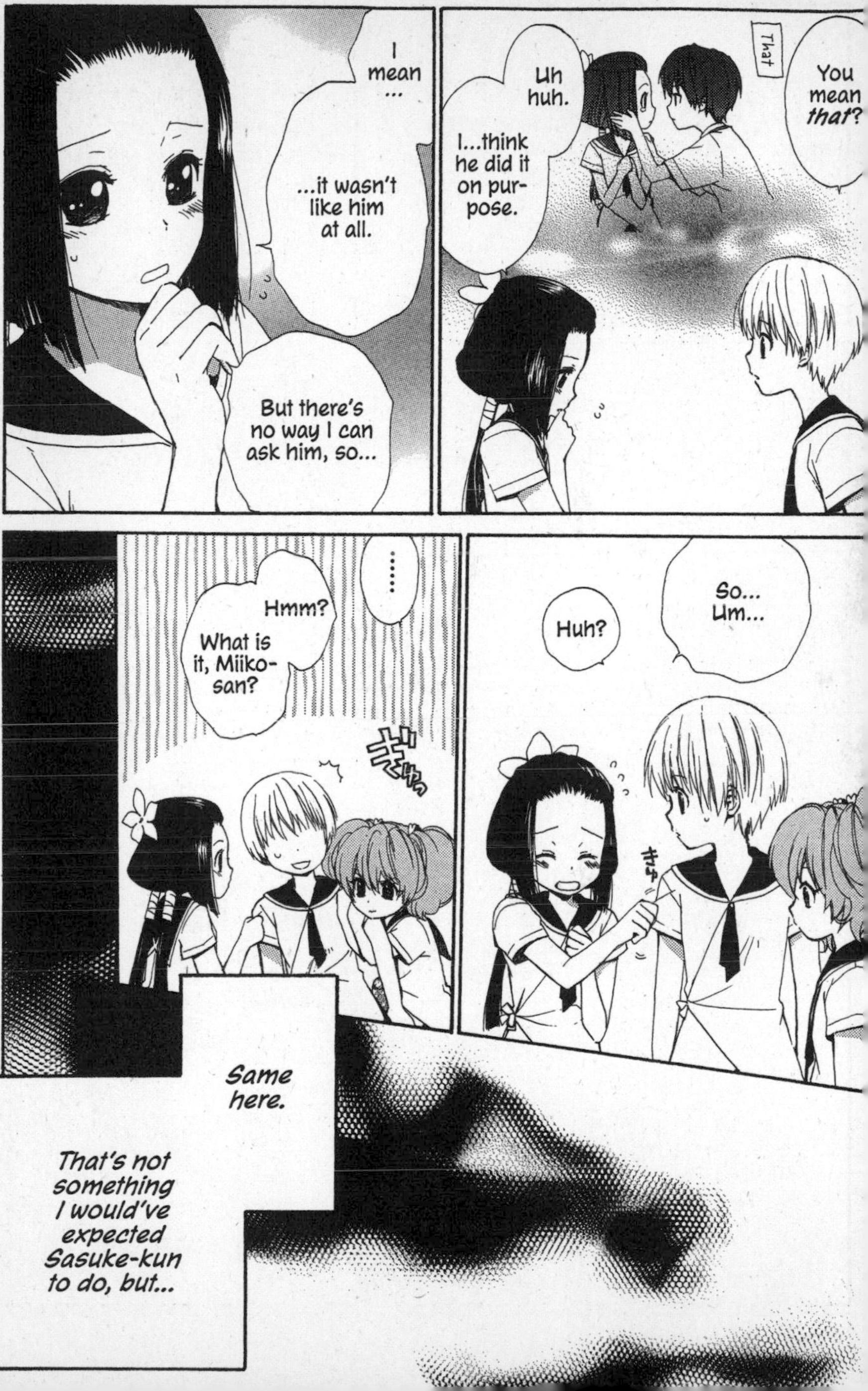
That
You mean *that*?
Uh huh.
I...think he did it on purpose.
I mean...
...it wasn't like him at all.
But there's no way I can ask him, so...
So... Um...
Huh?
......
Hmm? What is it, Miiko-san?
Same here.
That's not something I would've expected Sasuke-kun to do, but...

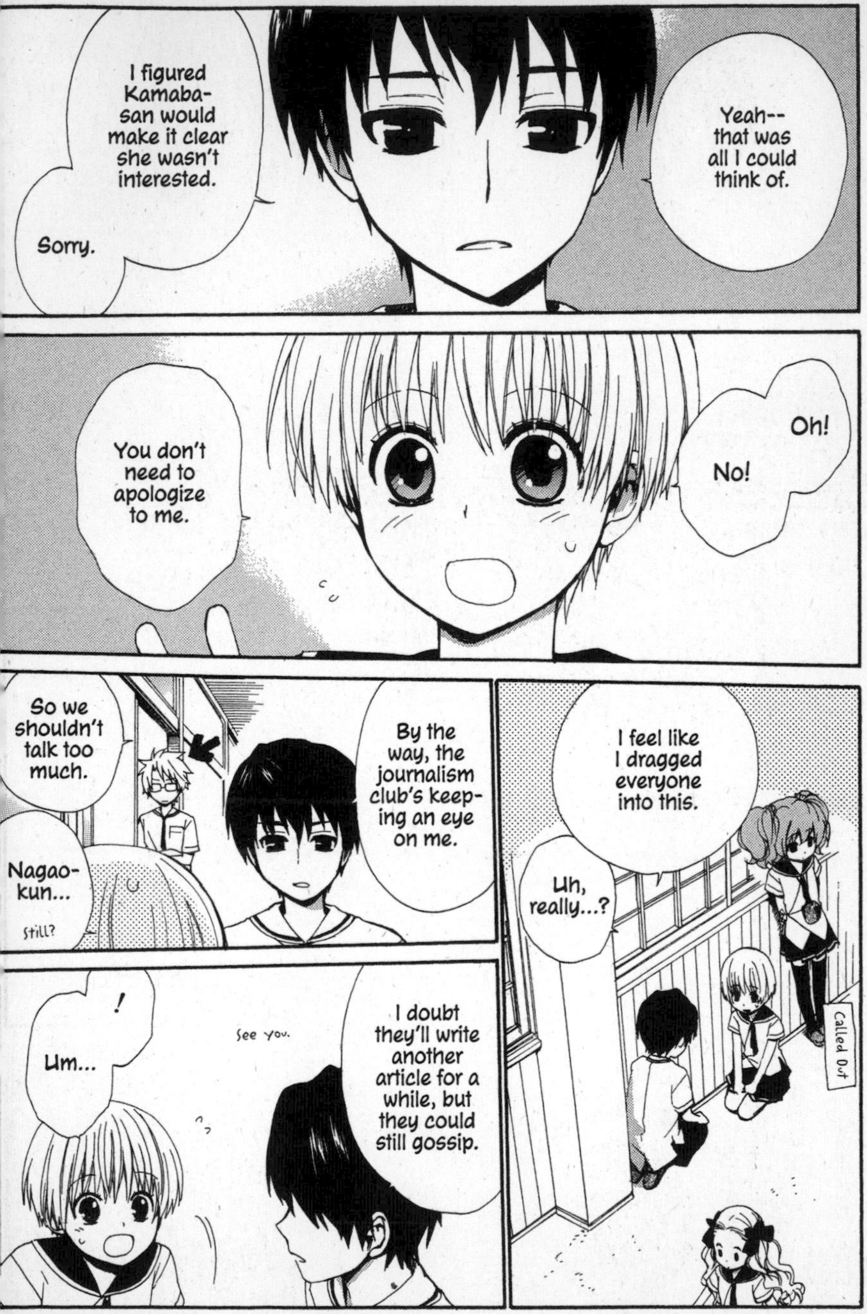

Yeah-- that was all I could think of.
I figured Kamaba-san would make it clear she wasn't interested.
Sorry.
Oh!
No!
You don't need to apologize to me.
I feel like I dragged everyone into this.
Uh, really...?
Called Out
By the way, the journalism club's keeping an eye on me.
So we shouldn't talk too much.
Nagao-kun...
Still?
I doubt they'll write another article for a while, but they could still gossip.
See you.
!
Um...

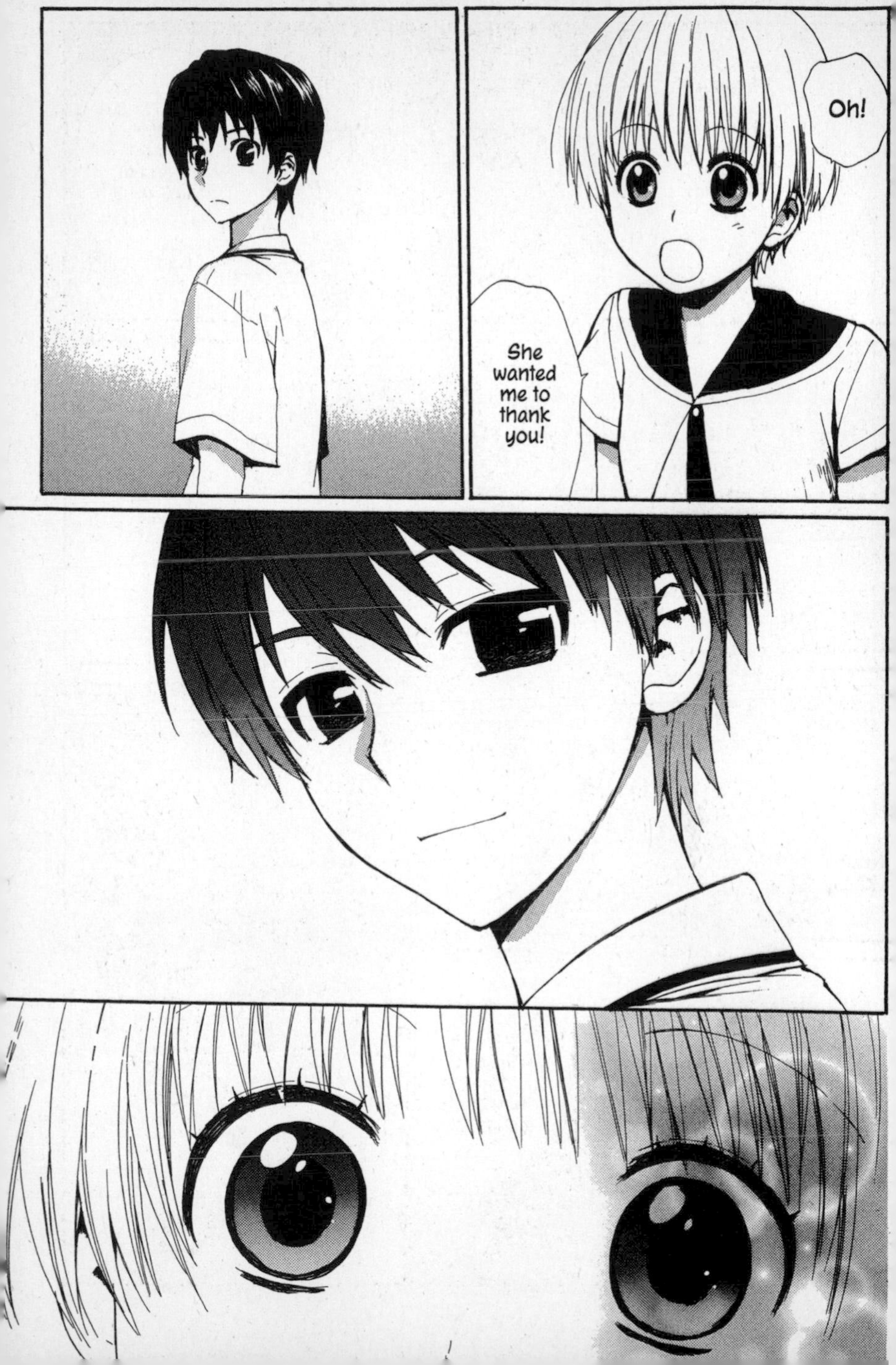
Oh!
She wanted me to thank you!

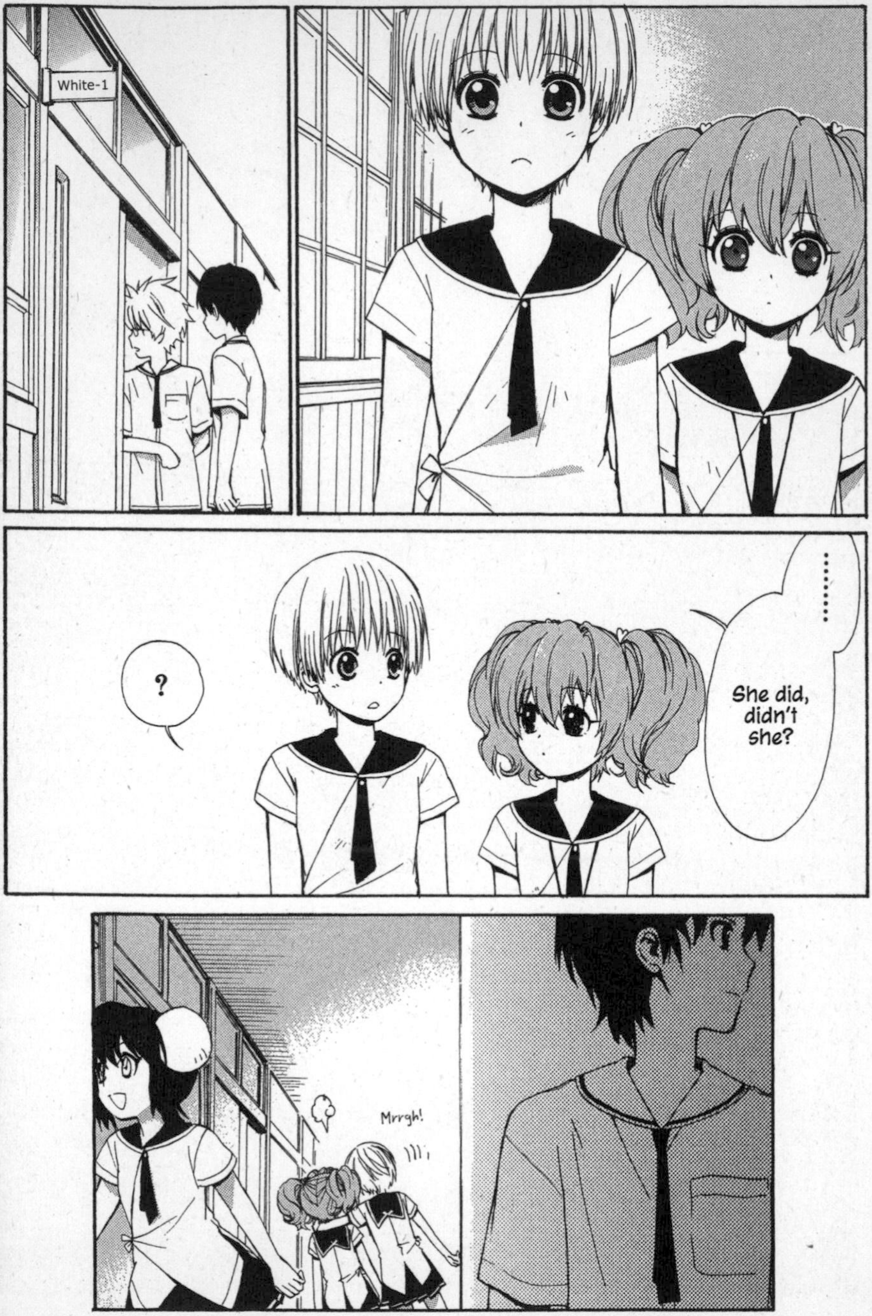
White-1
......
She did, didn't she?
?
Mrrgh!

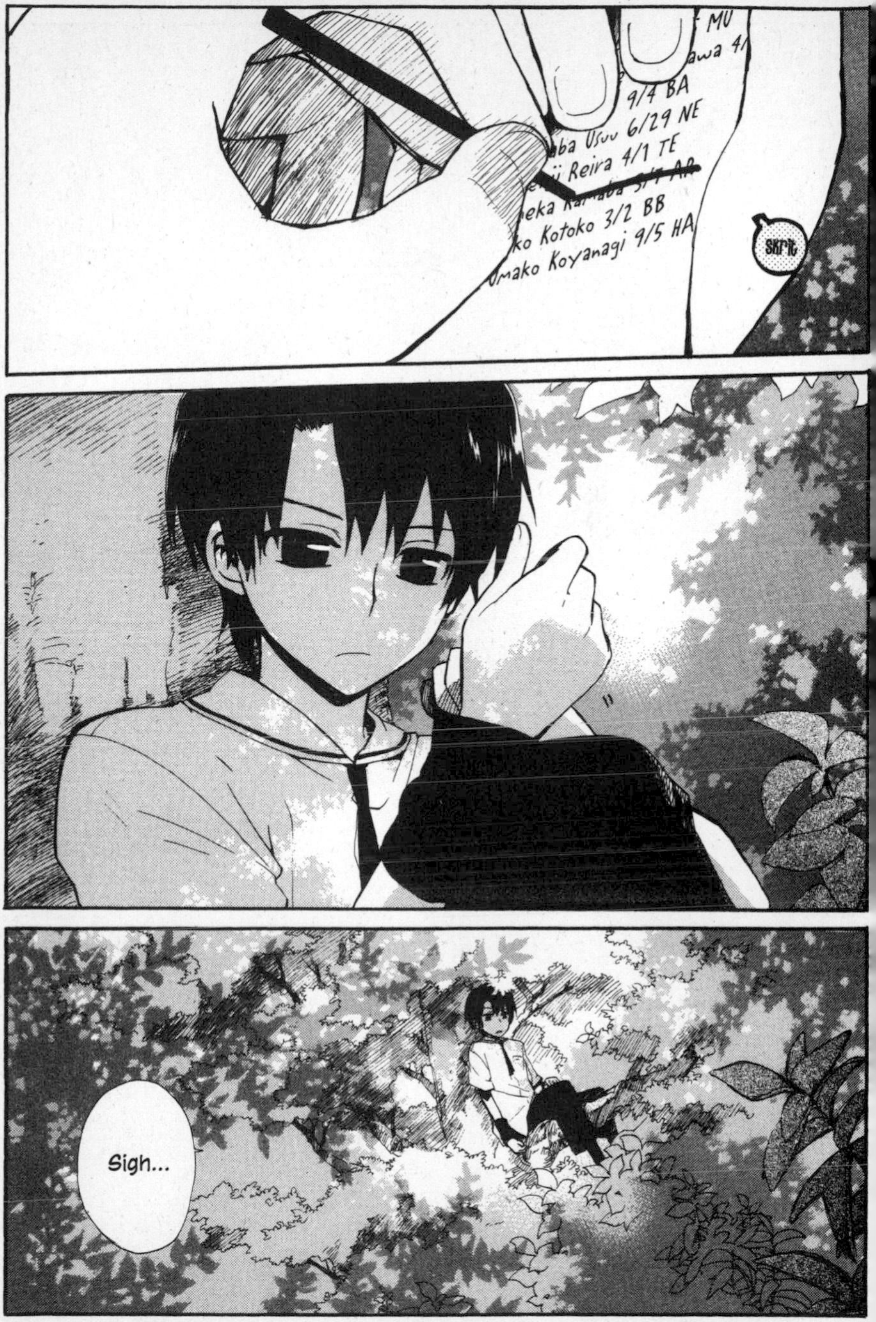
MU
9/4 BA
aba Usuu 6/29 NE
ü Reira 4/1 TE
ko Kotoko 3/2 BB
Umako Koyanagi 9/5 HA
SKRIT
Sigh...

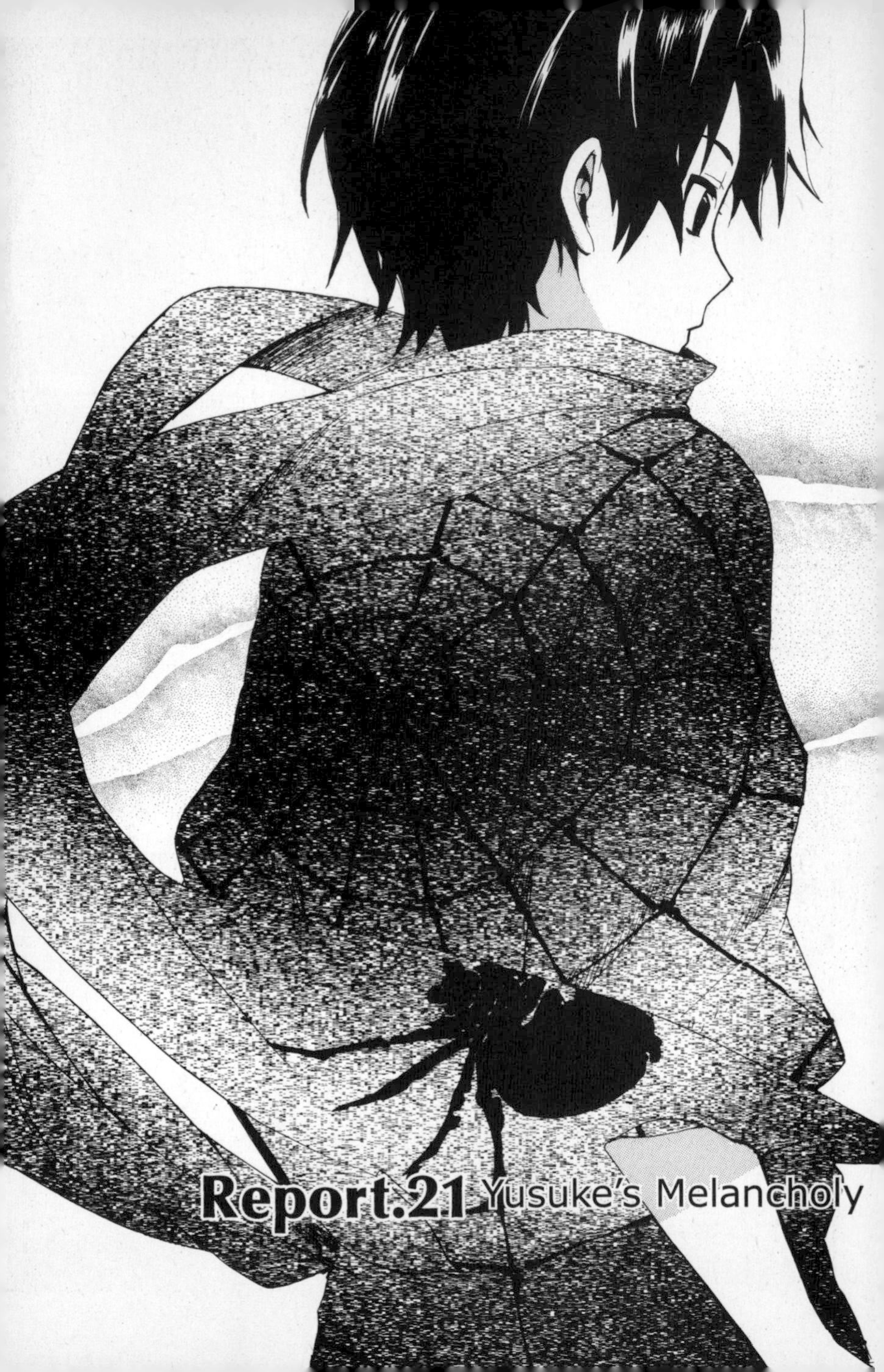
Report.21 Yusuke's Melancholy

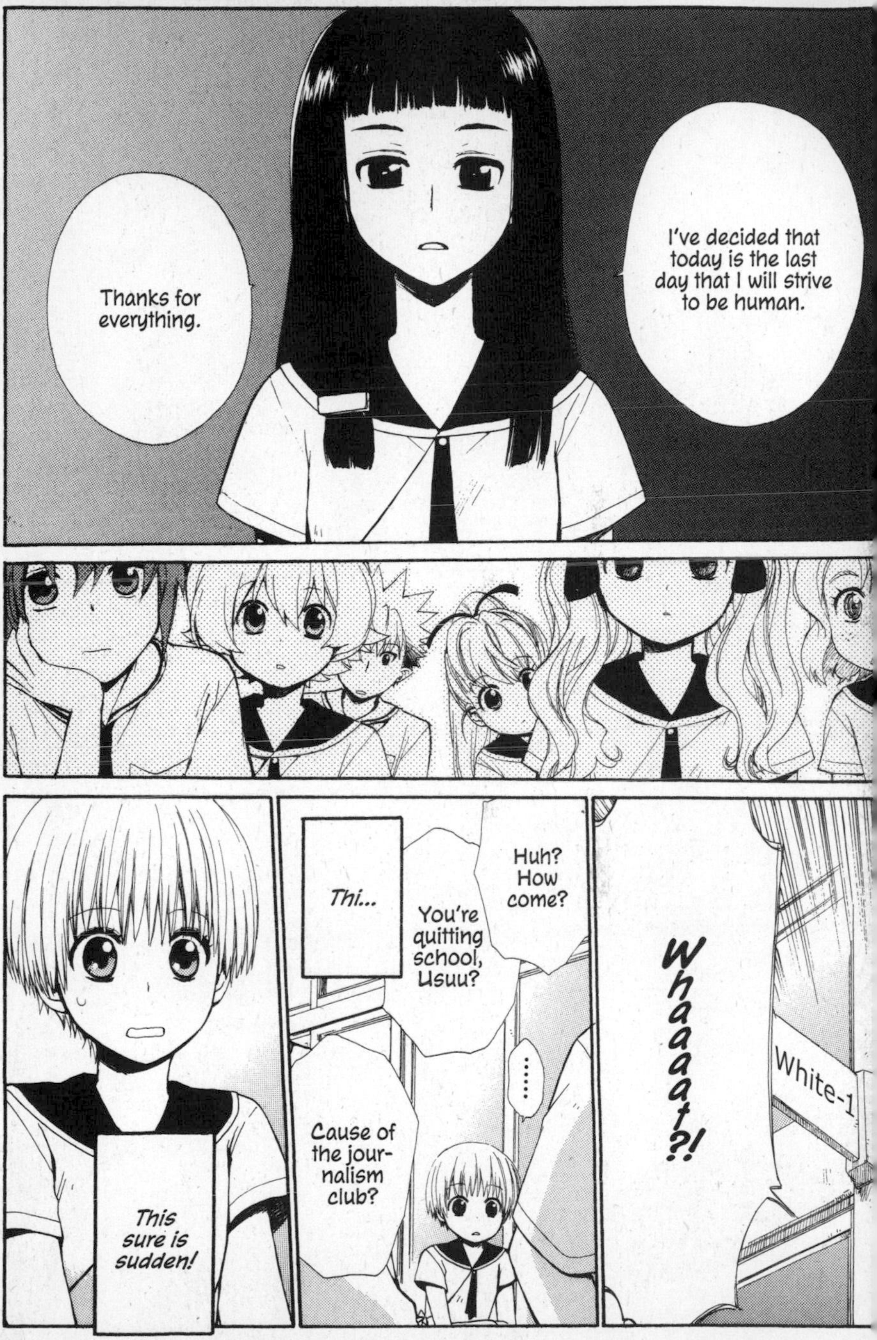
I've decided that today is the last day that I will strive to be human.
Thanks for everything.
Whaaaat?!
White-1
Huh? How come?
You're quitting school, Usuu?
Thi...
......
Cause of the jour-nalism club?
This sure is sudden!

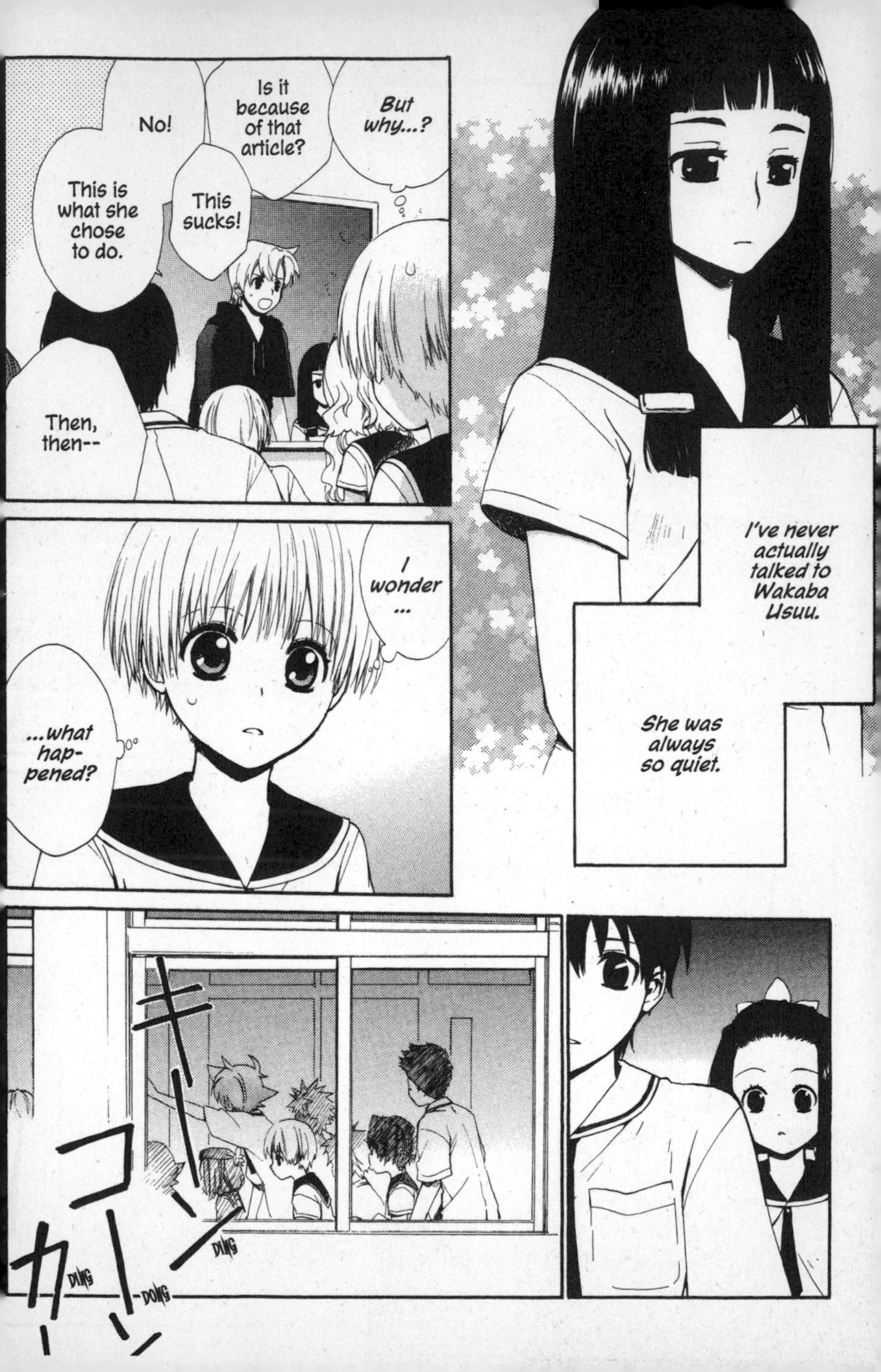
I've never actually talked to Wakaba Usuu.
She was always so quiet.
But why...?
Is it because of that article?
No!
This sucks!
This is what she chose to do.
Then, then--
I wonder ...
...what hap-pened?
DING
DING
-DONG

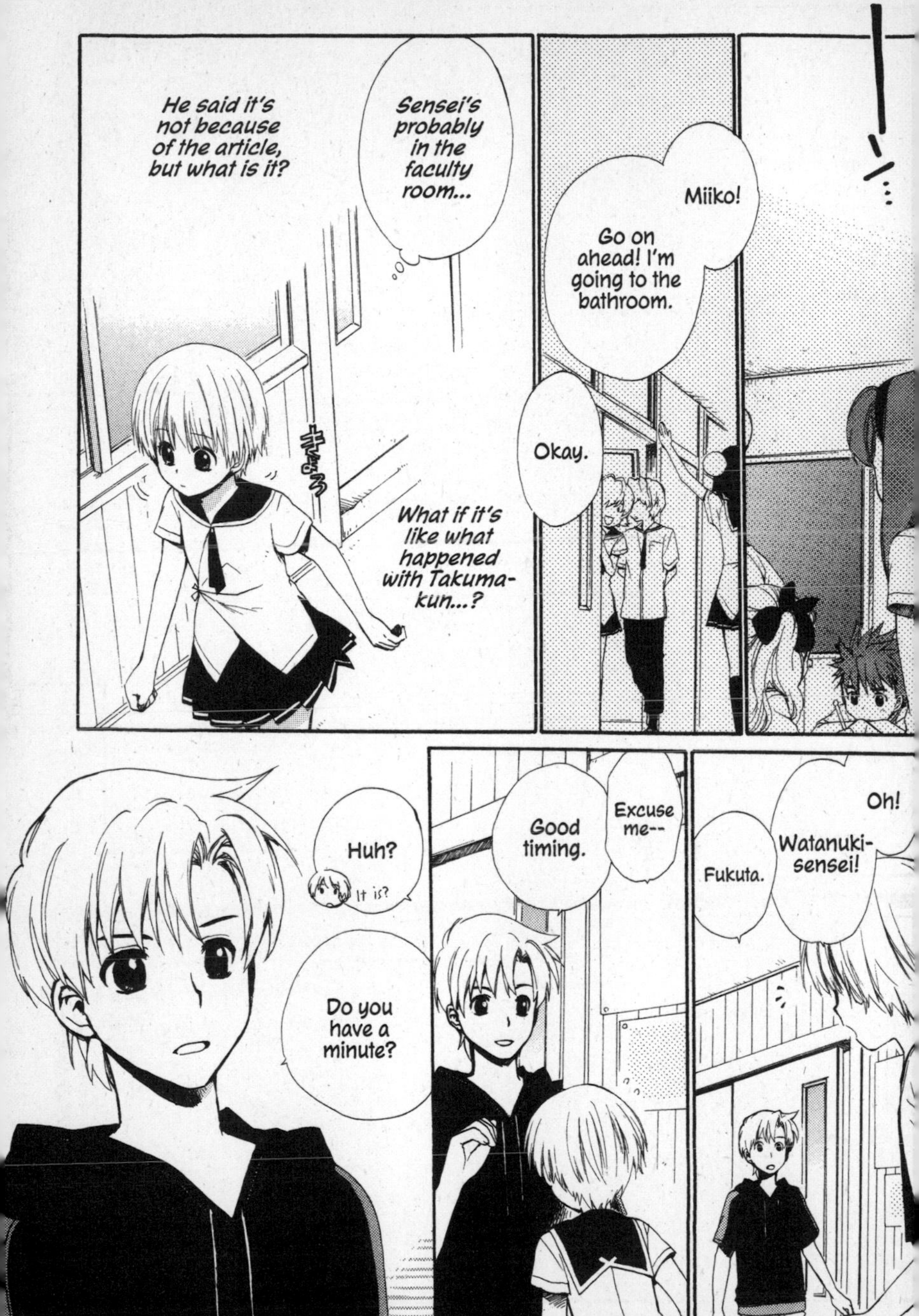
Miiko!
Go on ahead! I'm going to the bathroom.
Okay.
Sensei's probably in the faculty room...
He said it's not because of the article, but what is it?
What if it's like what happened with Takuma-kun...?
Oh!
Watanuki-sensei!
Fukuta.
Excuse me--
Good timing.
Huh?
It is?
Do you have a minute?

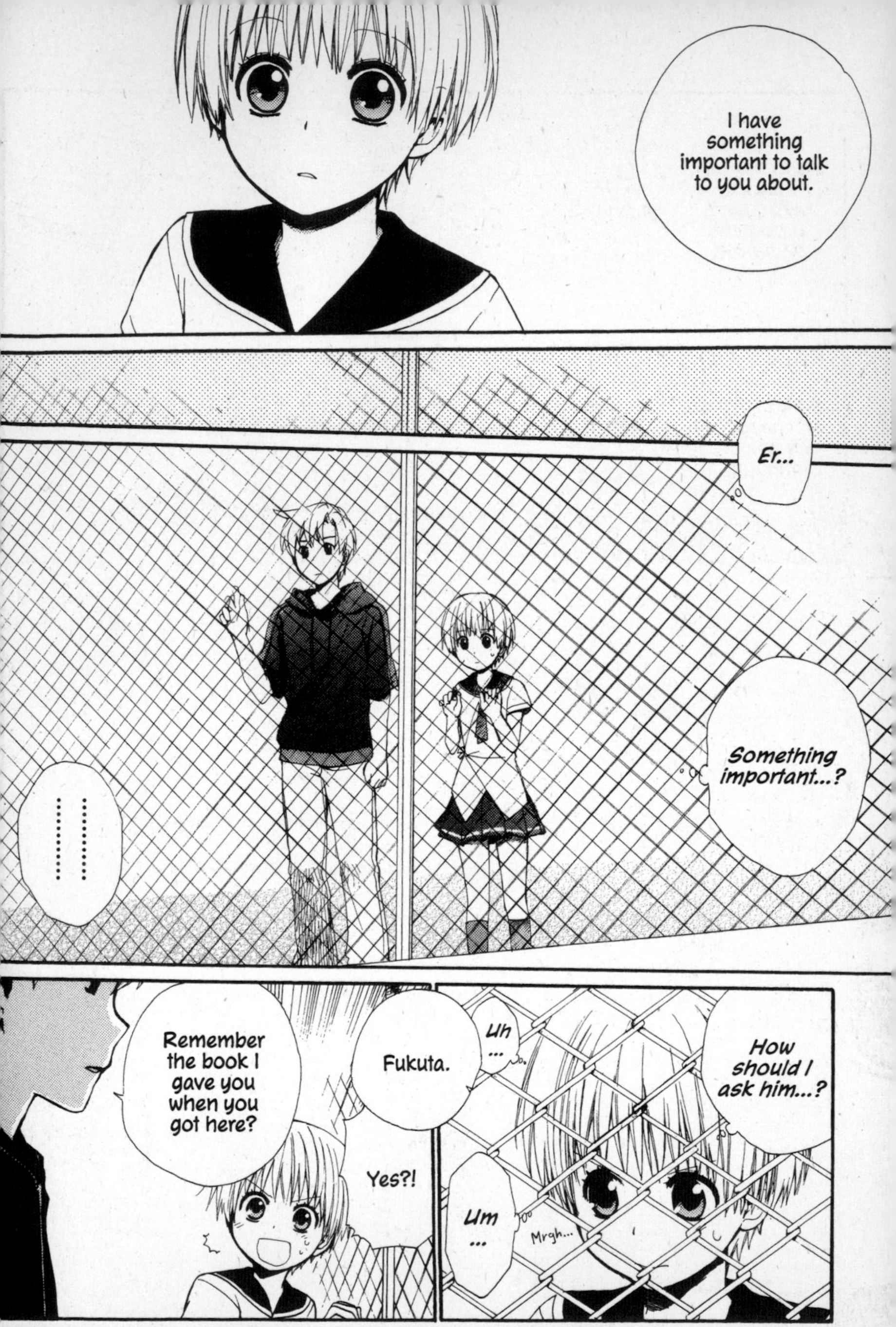
I have something important to talk to you about.
Er...
Something important...?
......
How should I ask him...?
Uh ...
Um ...
Mrgh...
Fukuta.
Remember the book I gave you when you got here?
Yes?!

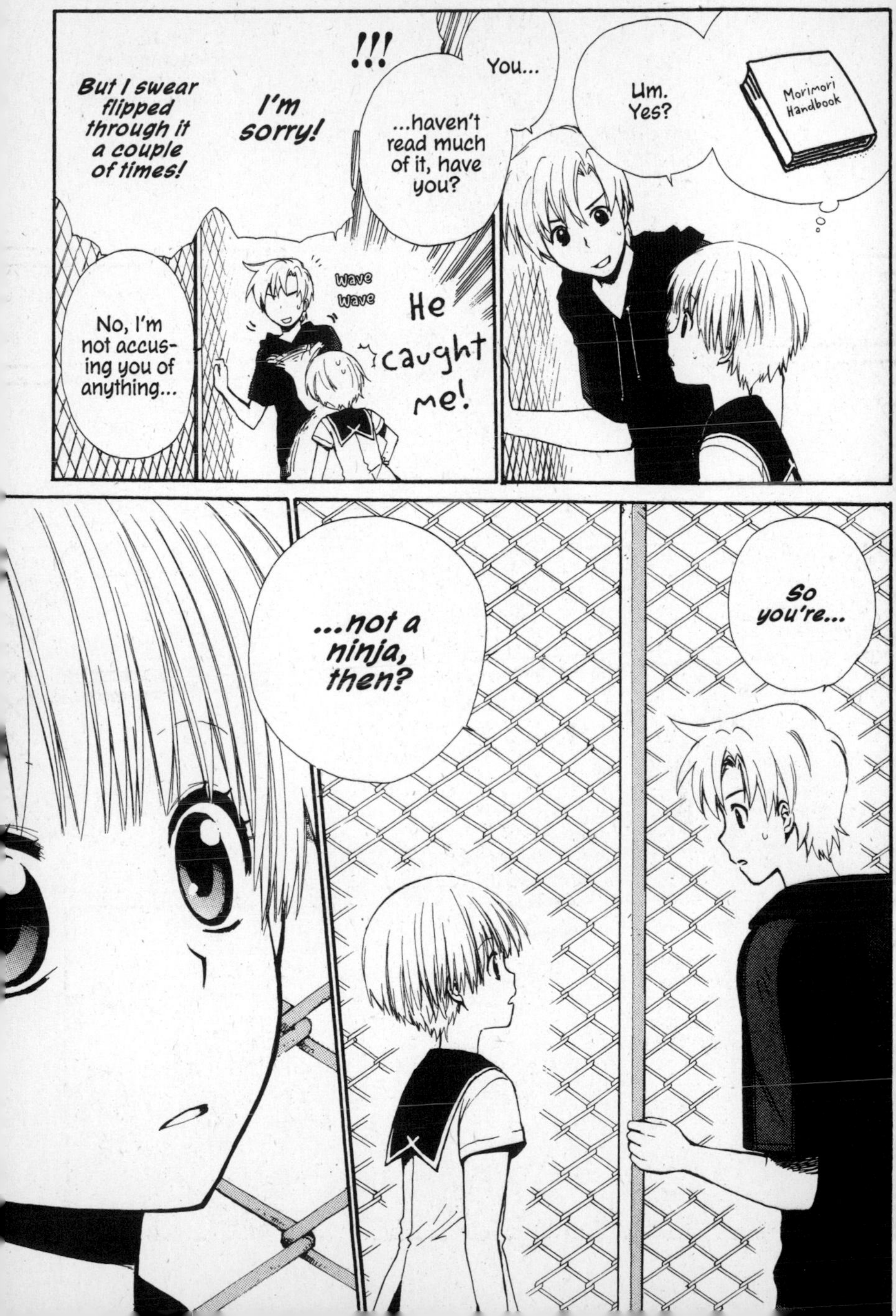
Morimori Handbook
Um. Yes?
You...
...haven't read much of it, have you?
!!!
I'm sorry!
But I swear flipped through it a couple of times!
He caught me!
Wave wave
No, I'm not accusing you of anything...
So you're...
...not a ninja, then?

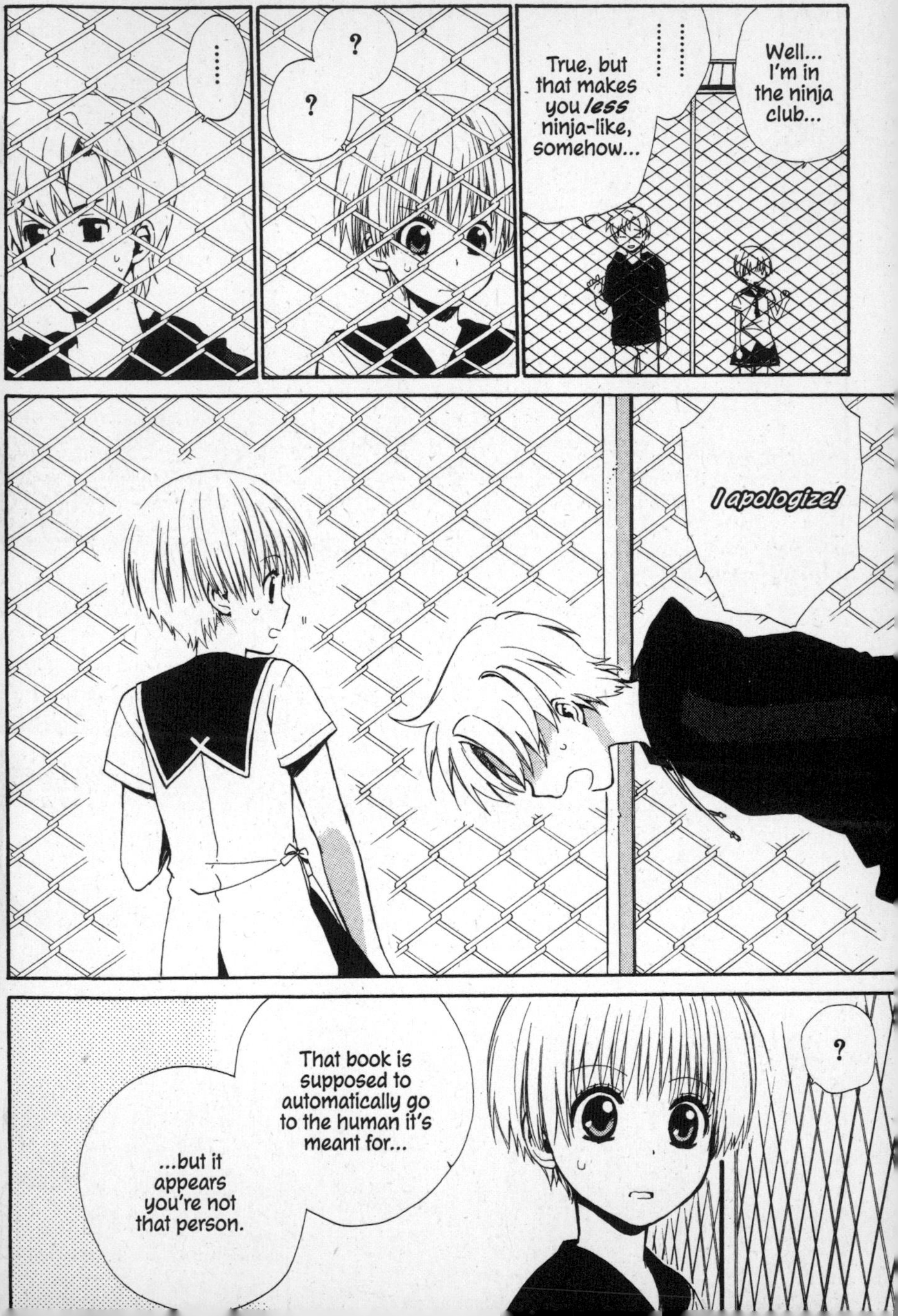

Well... I'm in the ninja club...
......
True, but that makes you *less* ninja-like, somehow...
?
?
......
I apologize!
?
That book is supposed to automatically go to the human it's meant for...
...but it appears you're not that person.

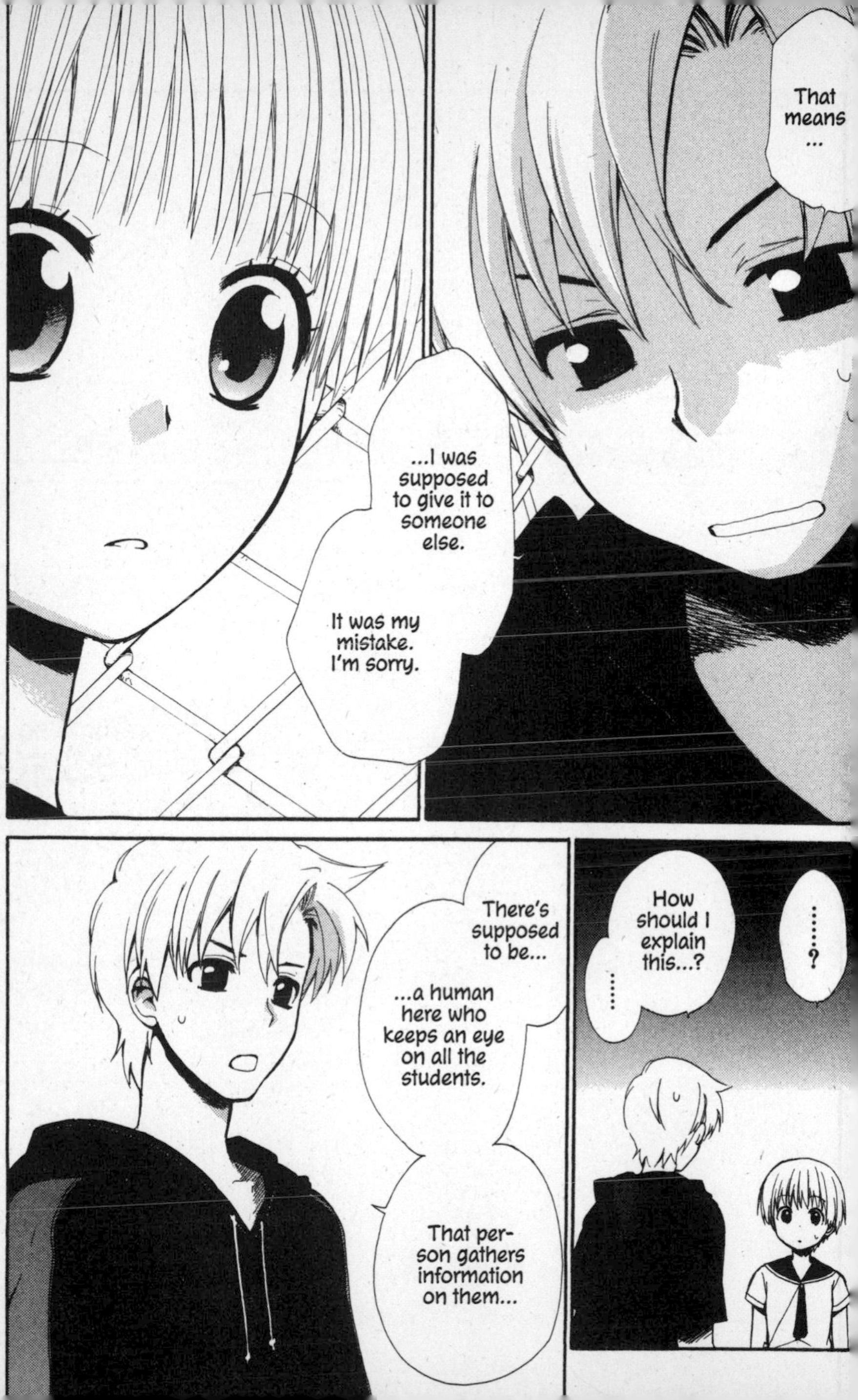
That means ...
...I was supposed to give it to someone else.
It was my mistake. I'm sorry.
......?
How should I explain this...?
......
There's supposed to be...
...a human here who keeps an eye on all the students.
That person gathers information on them...

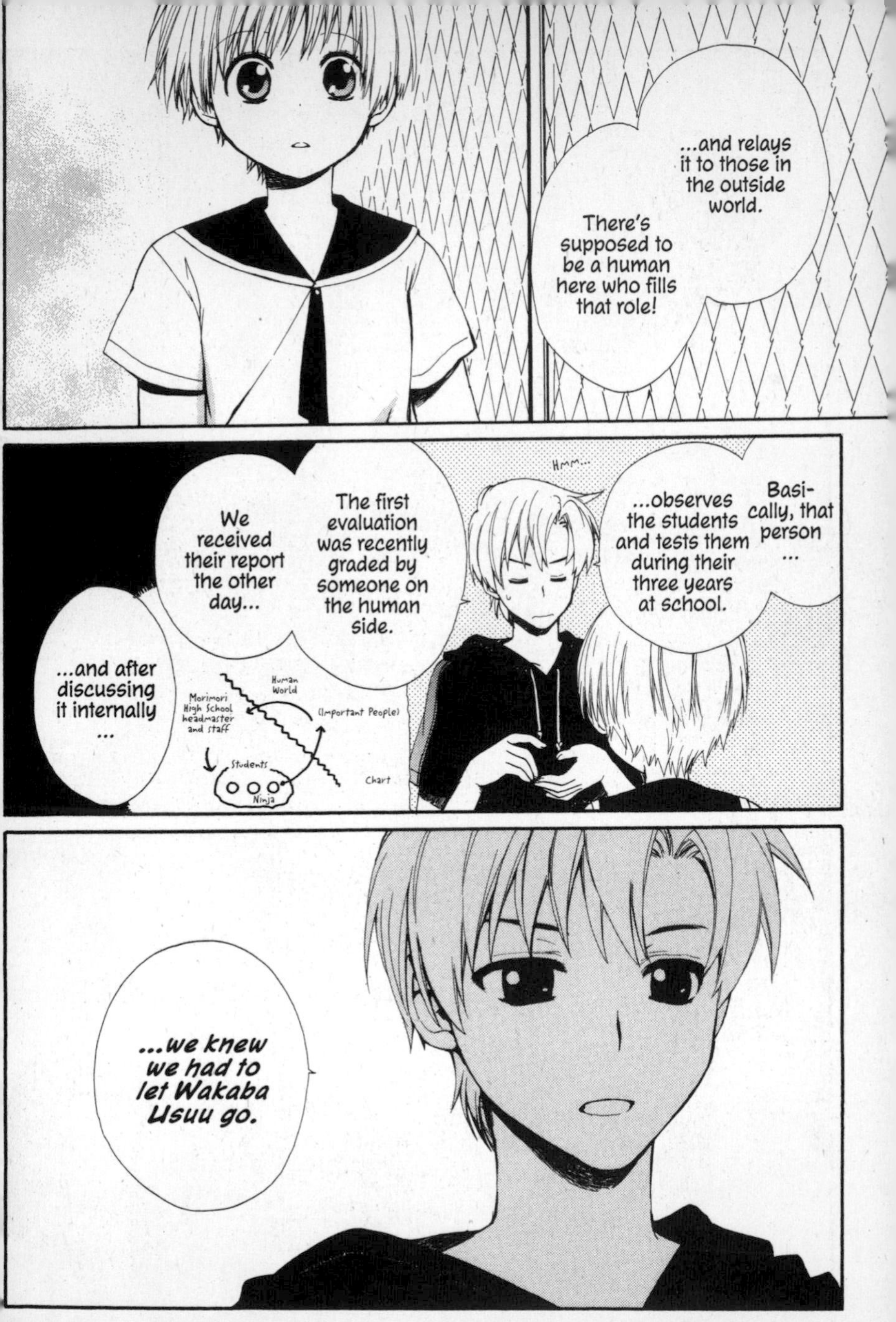
...and relays it to those in the outside world.
There's supposed to be a human here who fills that role!
Basically, that person...
...observes the students and tests them during their three years at school.
Hmm...
The first evaluation was recently graded by someone on the human side.
We received their report the other day...
...and after discussing it internally...
Human World
(Important People)
Morimori High School headmaster and staff
Students
Ninja
Chart
...we knew we had to let Wakaba Usuu go.

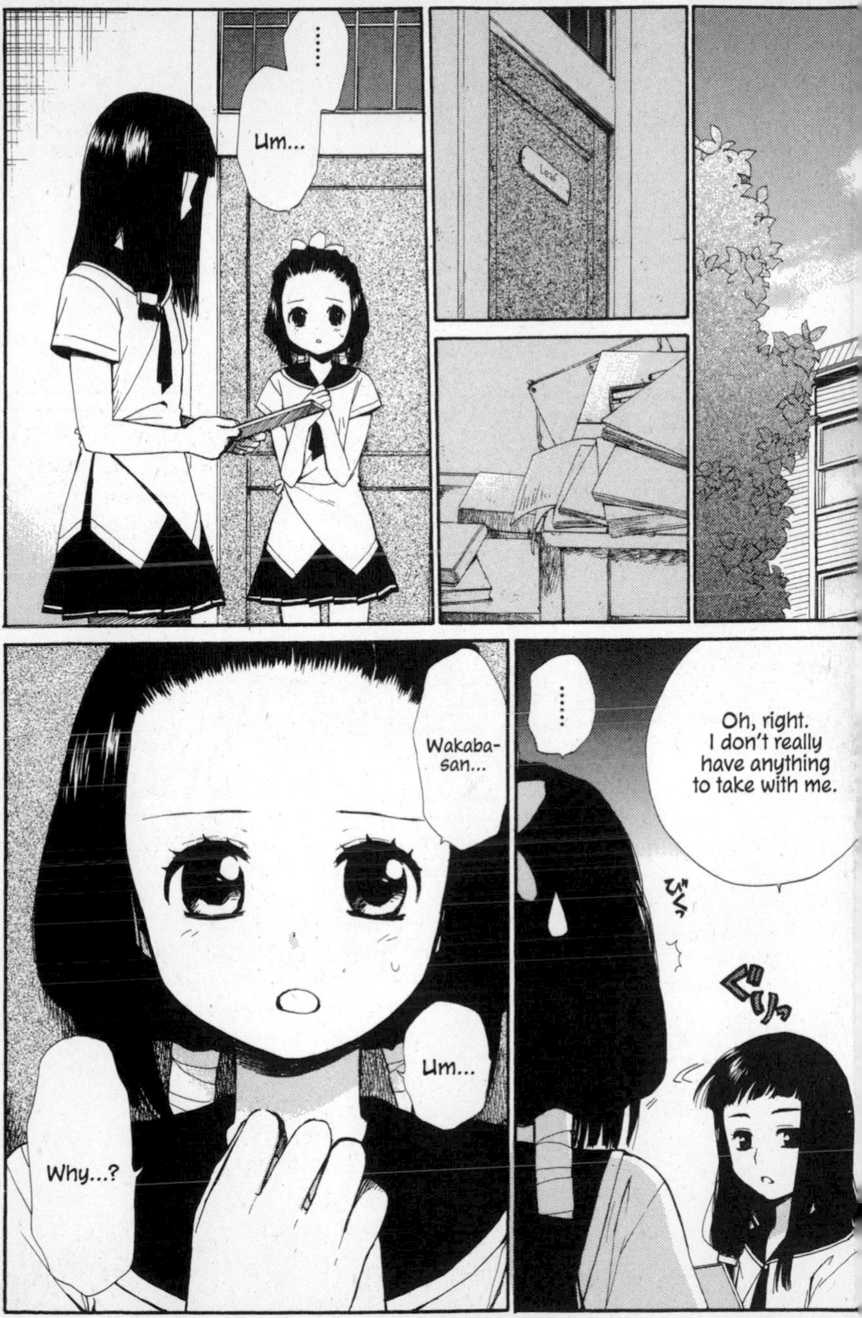
......
Um...
Oh, right. I don't really have anything to take with me.
......
Wakaba-san...
Um...
Why...?

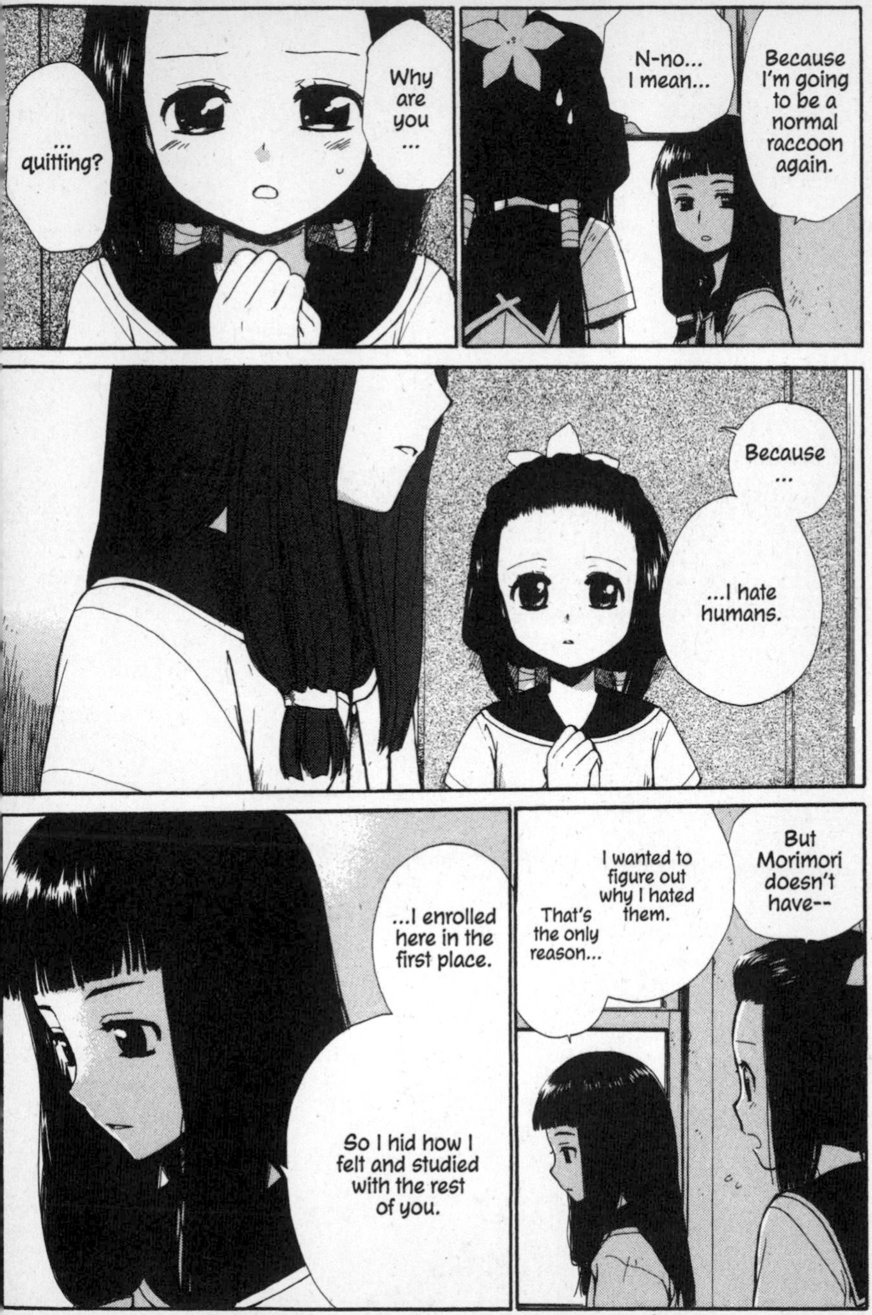
Because I'm going to be a normal raccoon again.
N-no... I mean...
Why are you ...
... quitting?
Because ...
...I hate humans.
But Morimori doesn't have--
I wanted to figure out why I hated them.
That's the only reason...
...I enrolled here in the first place.
So I hid how I felt and studied with the rest of you.

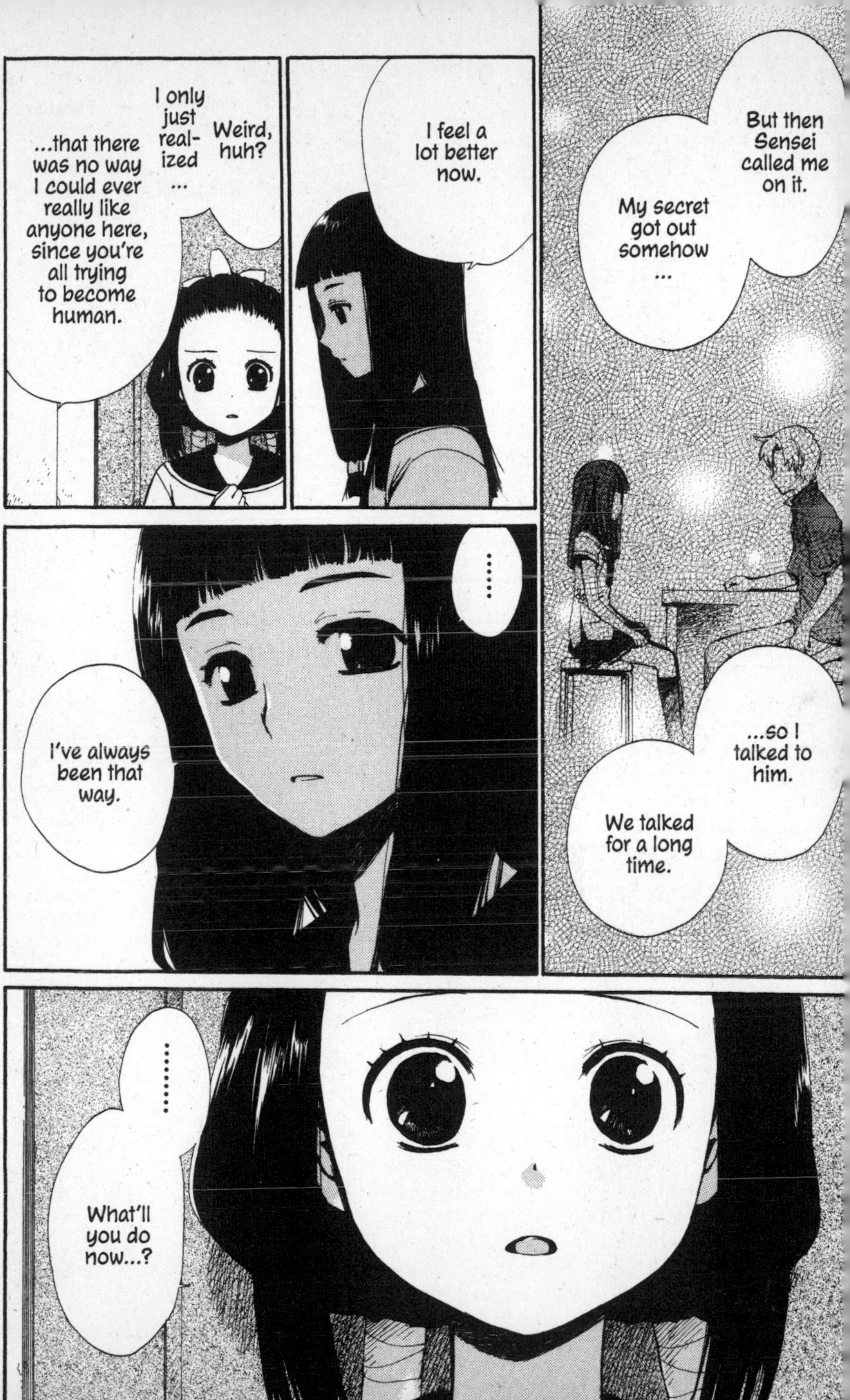

But then Sensei called me on it.
My secret got out somehow ...
...so I talked to him.
We talked for a long time.
I feel a lot better now.
Weird, huh?
I only just realized ...
...that there was no way I could ever really like anyone here, since you're all trying to become human.
......
I've always been that way.
....
What'll you do now...?

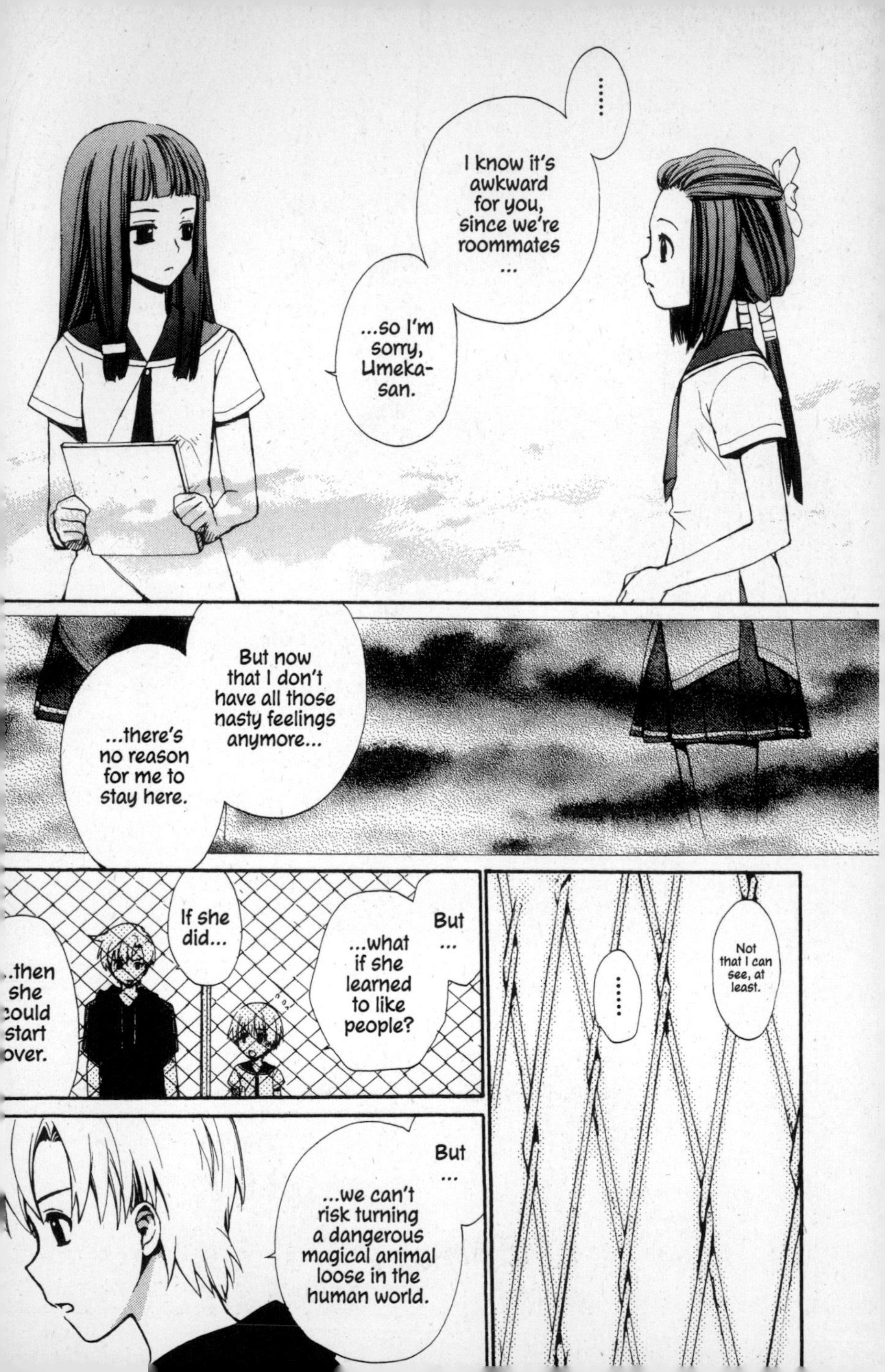
......
I know it's awkward for you, since we're roommates ...
...so I'm sorry, Umeka-san.
But now that I don't have all those nasty feelings anymore...
...there's no reason for me to stay here.
Not that I can see, at least.
......
But ...
...what if she learned to like people?
If she did...
..then she could start over.
But ...
...we can't risk turning a dangerous magical animal loose in the human world.

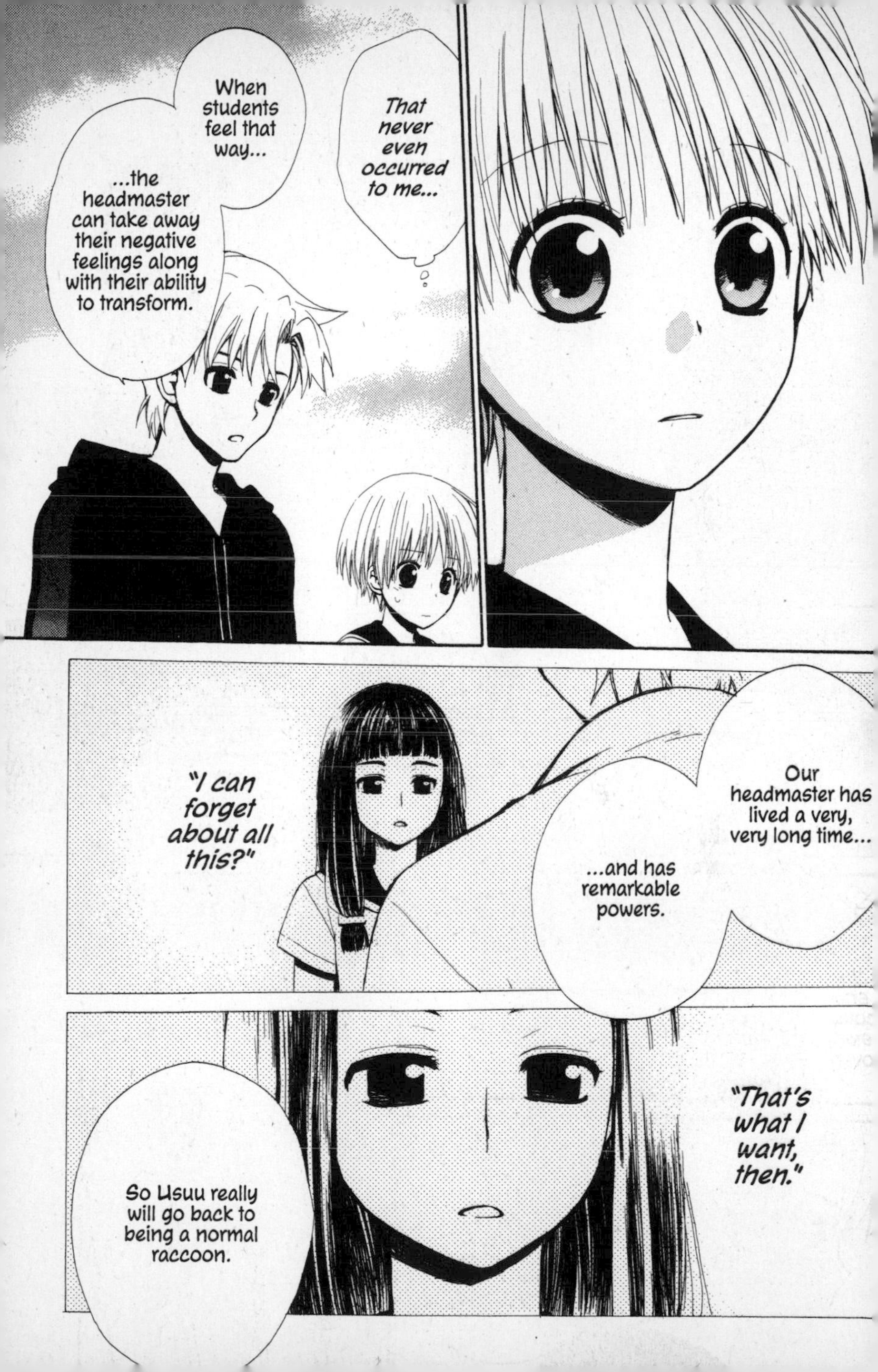
When students feel that way...
...the headmaster can take away their negative feelings along with their ability to transform.
That never even occurred to me...
Our headmaster has lived a very, very long time...
...and has remarkable powers.
"I can forget about all this?"
"That's what I want, then."
So Usuu really will go back to being a normal raccoon.

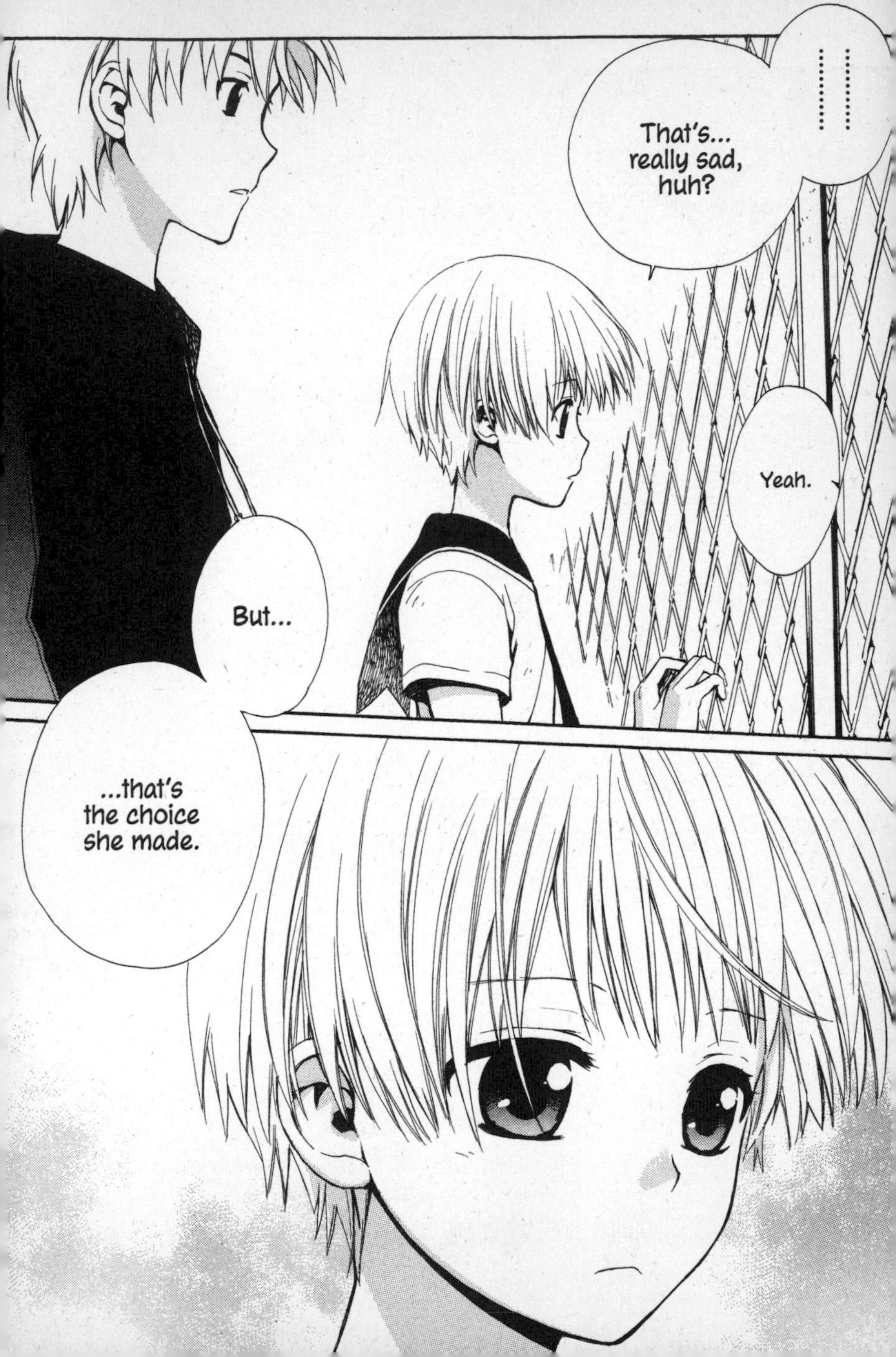
……
That's... really sad, huh?
Yeah.
But...
...that's the choice she made.

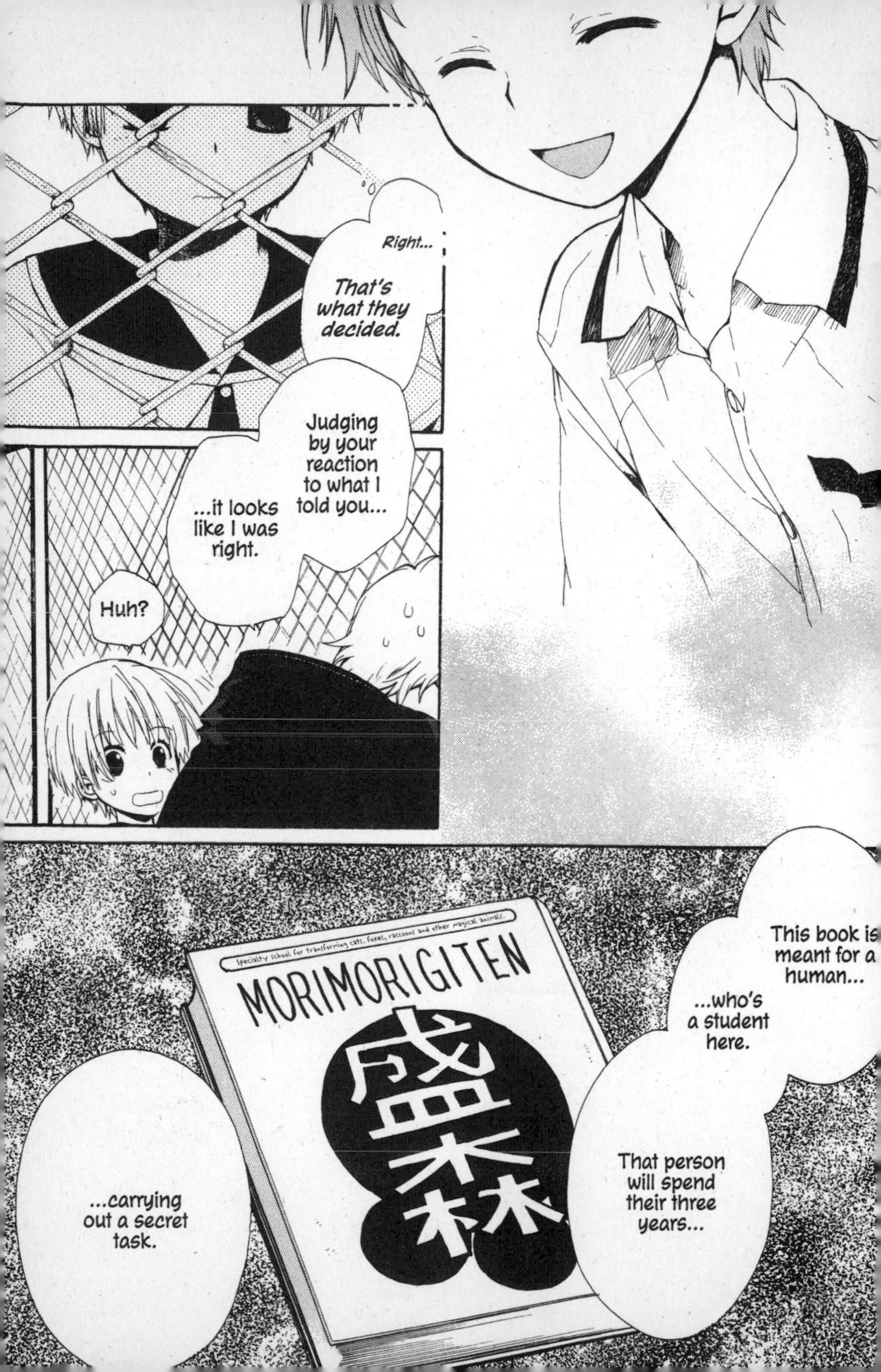
Right...
That's what they decided.
Judging by your reaction to what I told you...
...it looks like I was right.
Huh?
This book is meant for a human...
...who's a student here.
Specialty school for transforming cats, foxes, raccoons and other magical animals.
MORIMORIGITEN
盛林
That person will spend their three years...
...carrying out a secret task.

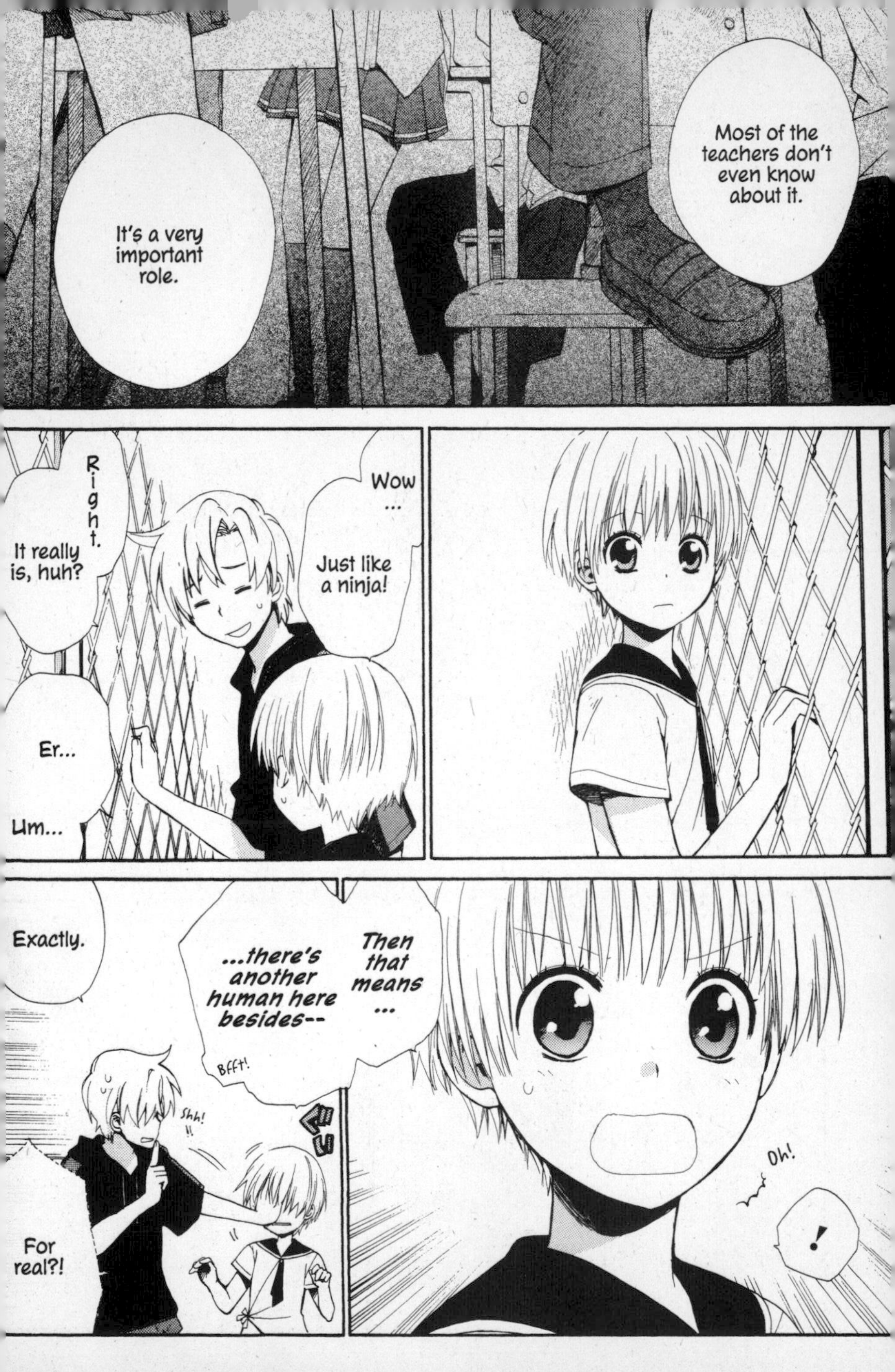
Most of the teachers don't even know about it.
It's a very important role.
Wow... Just like a ninja!
Right.
It really is, huh?
Er...
Um...
Oh!
!
Then that means...
...there's another human here besides--
Bfft!
Shh!!
Exactly.
For real?!

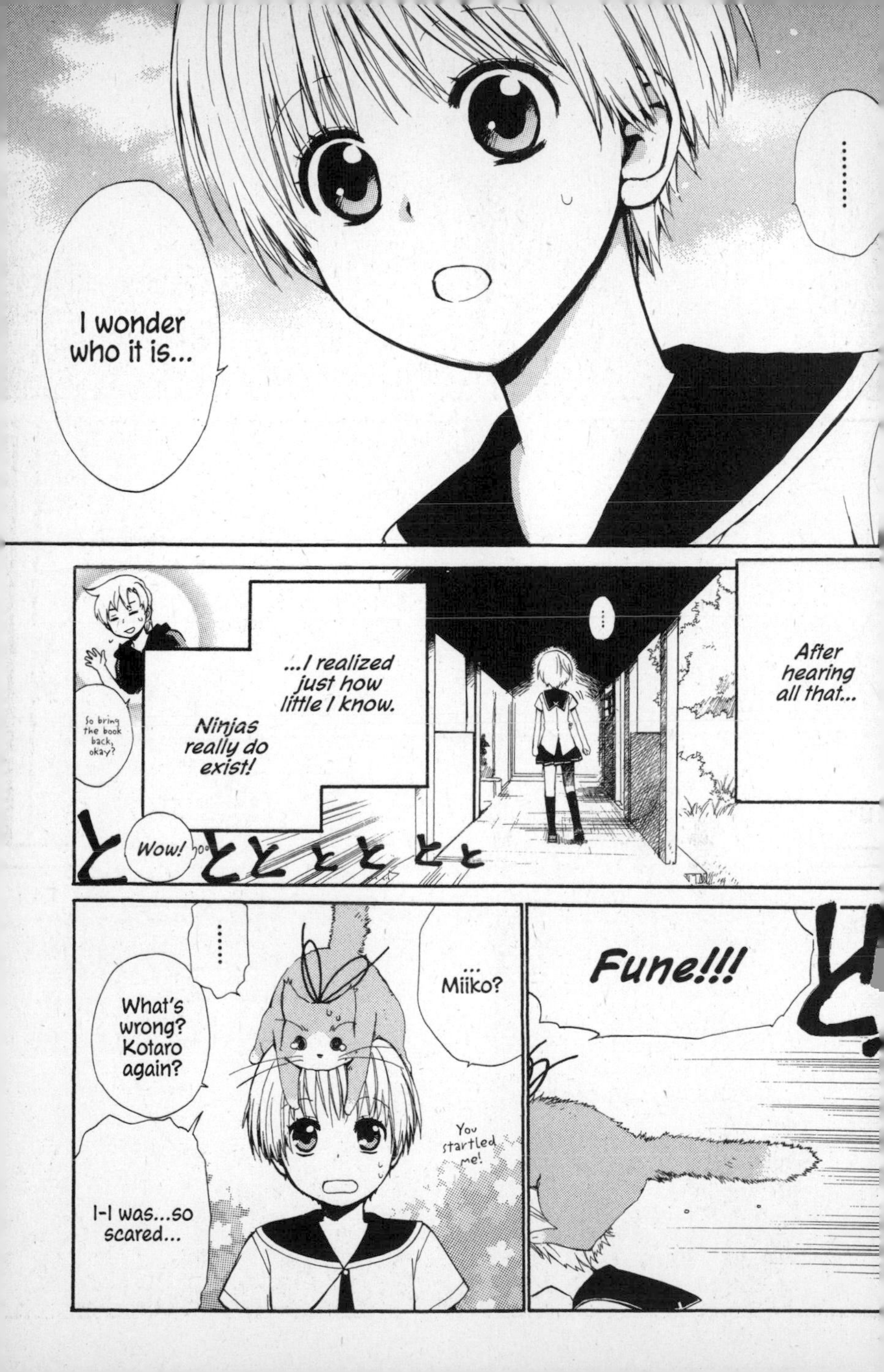

......
I wonder who it is...
After hearing all that...
...
...I realized just how little I know.
Ninjas really do exist!
So bring the book back, okay?
Wow!
とととととととと
と!
Fune!!!
... Miiko?
......
What's wrong? Kotaro again?
You startled me!
I-I was...so scared...

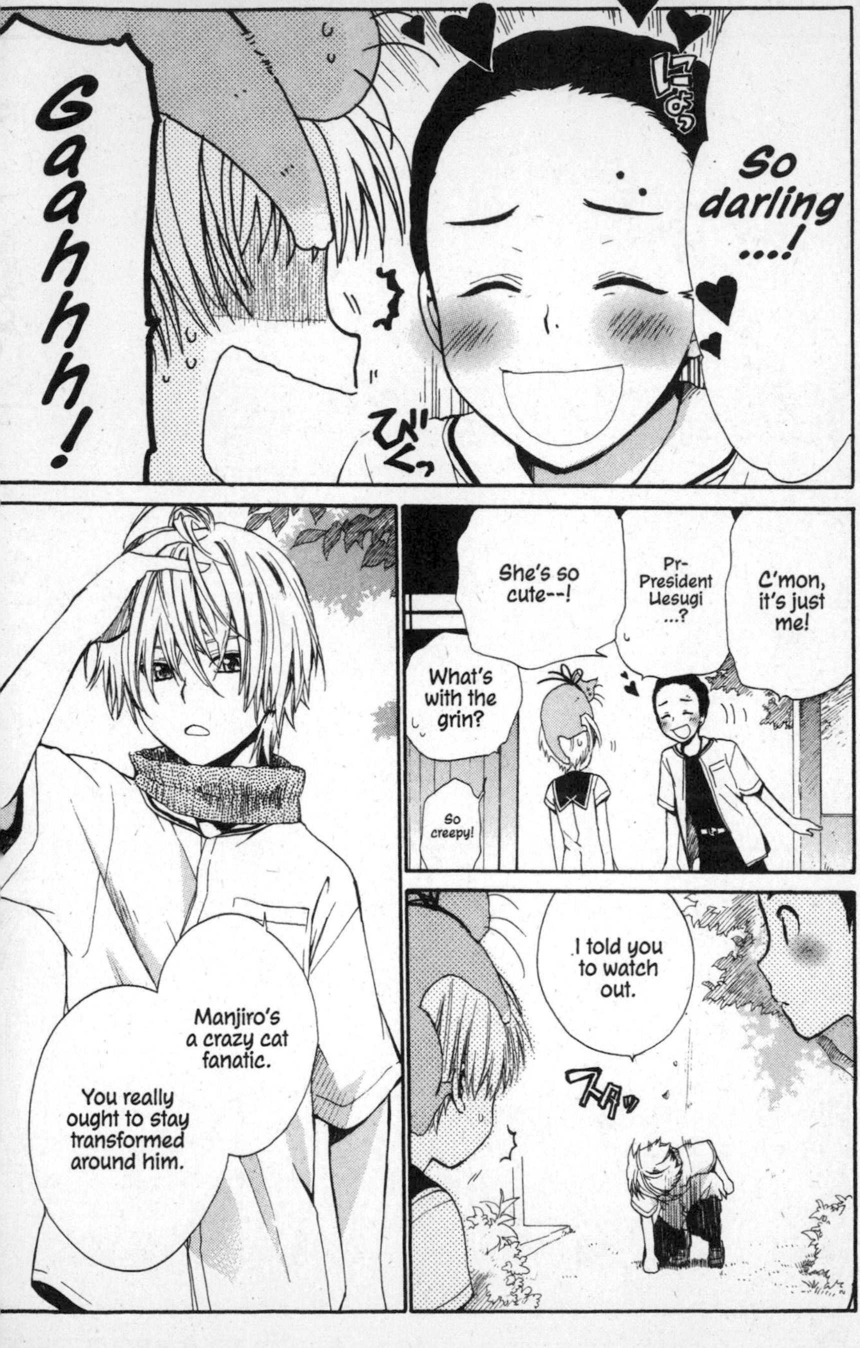
So darling ...!
Gaahhh!
びくっ
C'mon, it's just me!
Pr-President Uesugi ...?
She's so cute--!
What's with the grin?
So creepy!
I told you to watch out.
スタッ
Manjiro's a crazy cat fanatic.
You really ought to stay transformed around him.

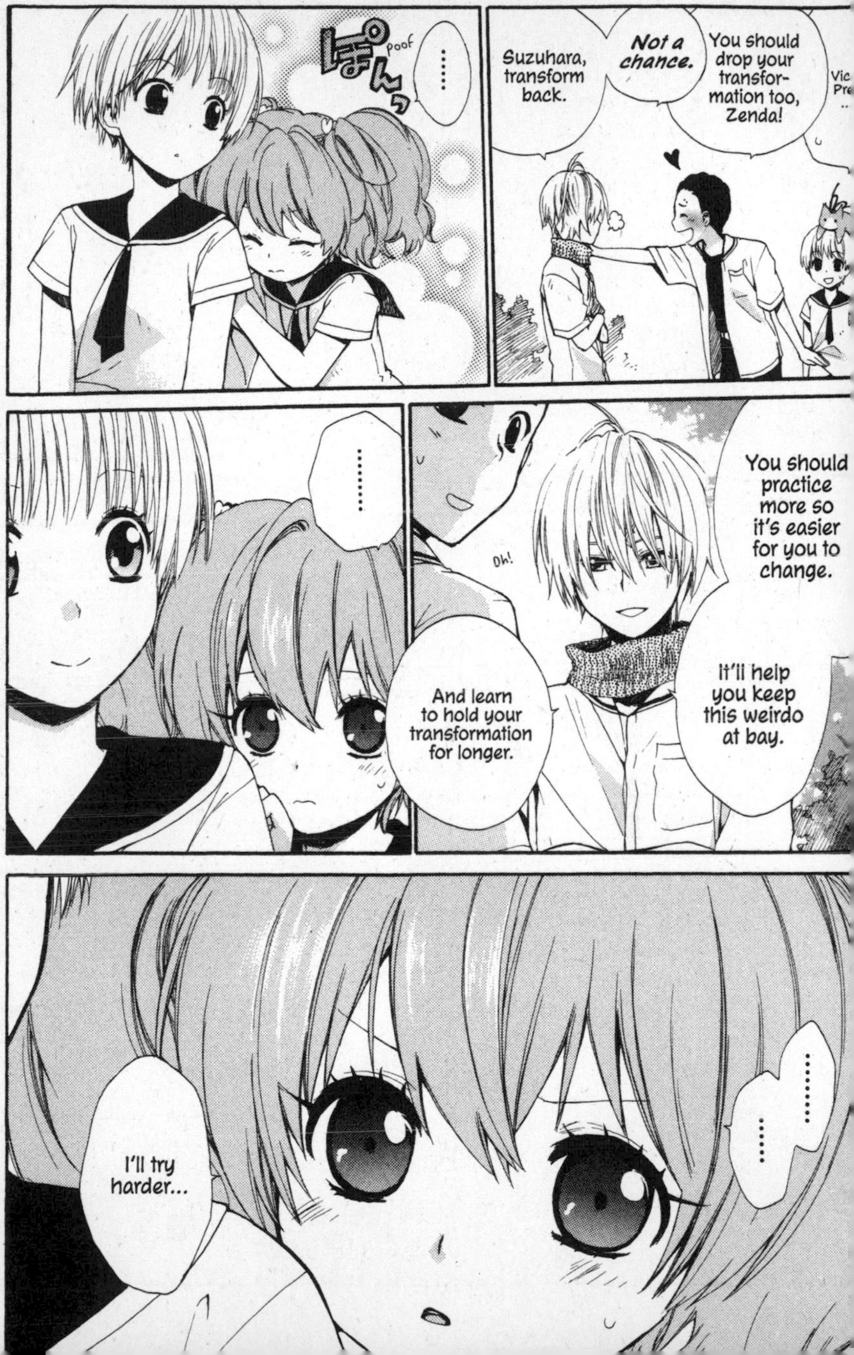

You should drop your transformation too, Zenda!
Not a chance.
Suzuhara, transform back.
......
poof
You should practice more so it's easier for you to change.
It'll help you keep this weirdo at bay.
Oh!
And learn to hold your transformation for longer.
......
......
......
I'll try harder...

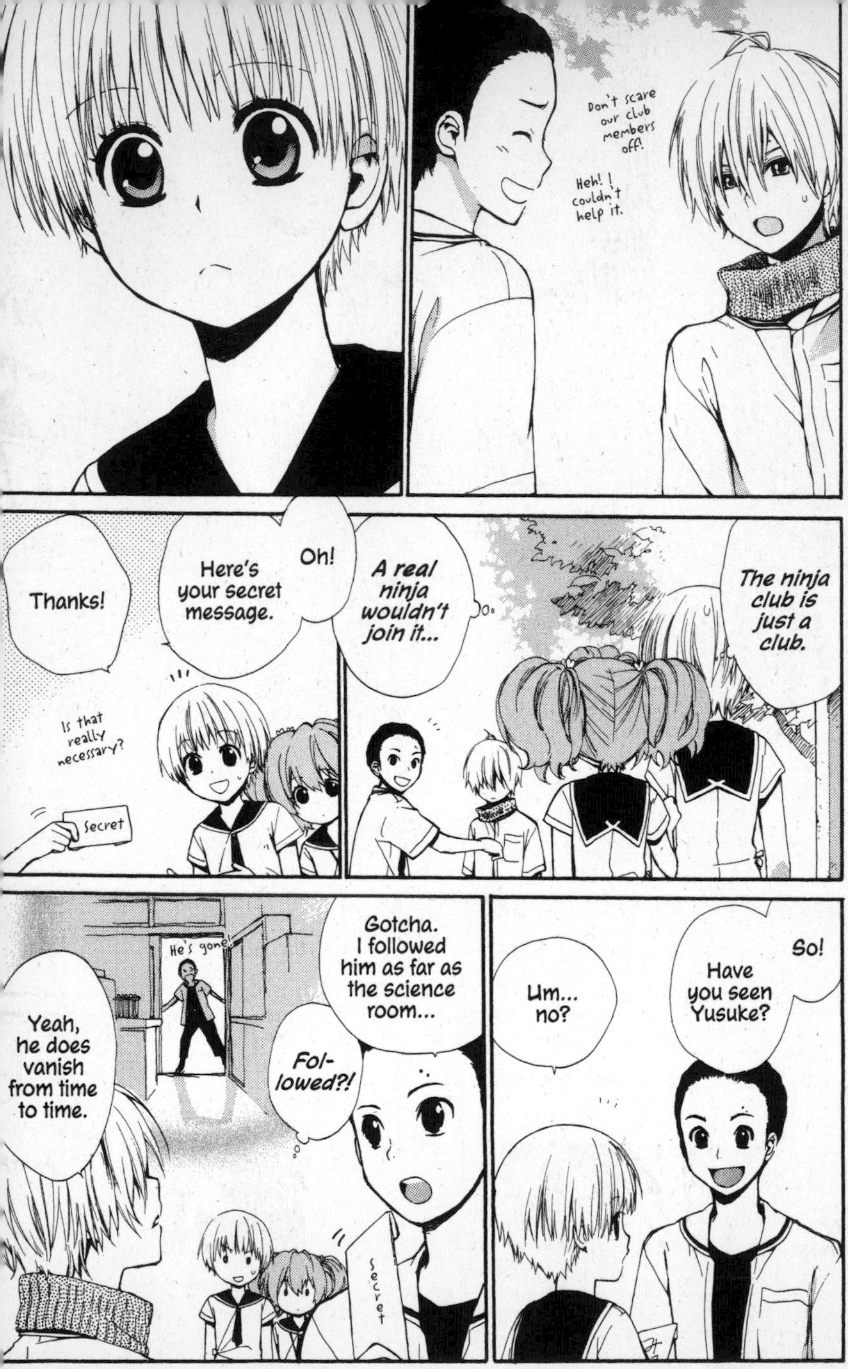
Don't scare our club members off.
Heh! I couldn't help it.
The ninja club is just a club.
A real ninja wouldn't join it...
Oh!
Here's your secret message.
Thanks!
Is that really necessary?
Secret
So!
Have you seen Yusuke?
Um... no?
Gotcha. I followed him as far as the science room...
Fol-lowed?!
Secret
He's gone!
Yeah, he does vanish from time to time.

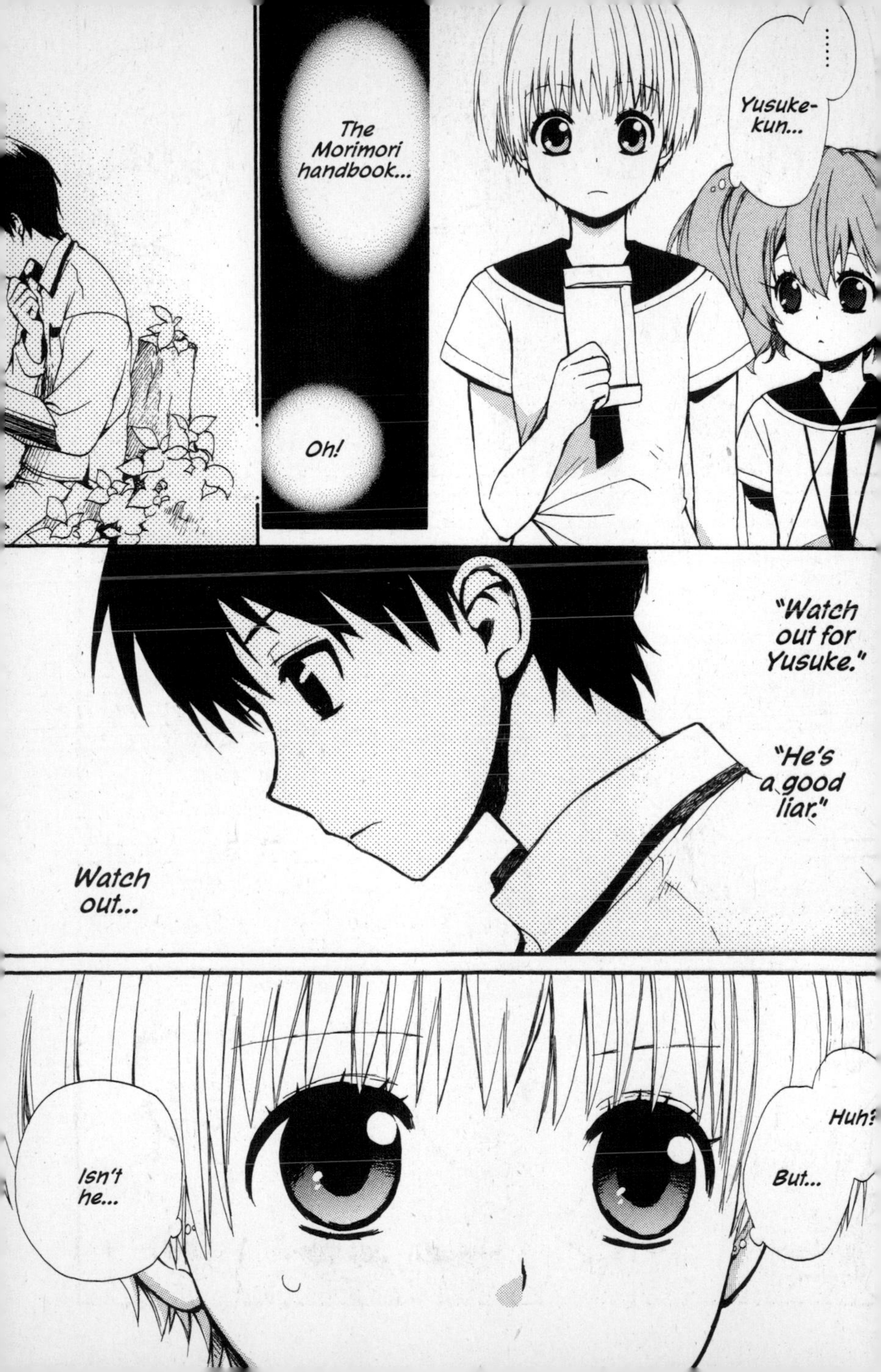
……
Yusuke-kun...
The Morimori handbook...
Oh!
"Watch out for Yusuke."
"He's a good liar."
Watch out...
Huh?
But...
Isn't he...

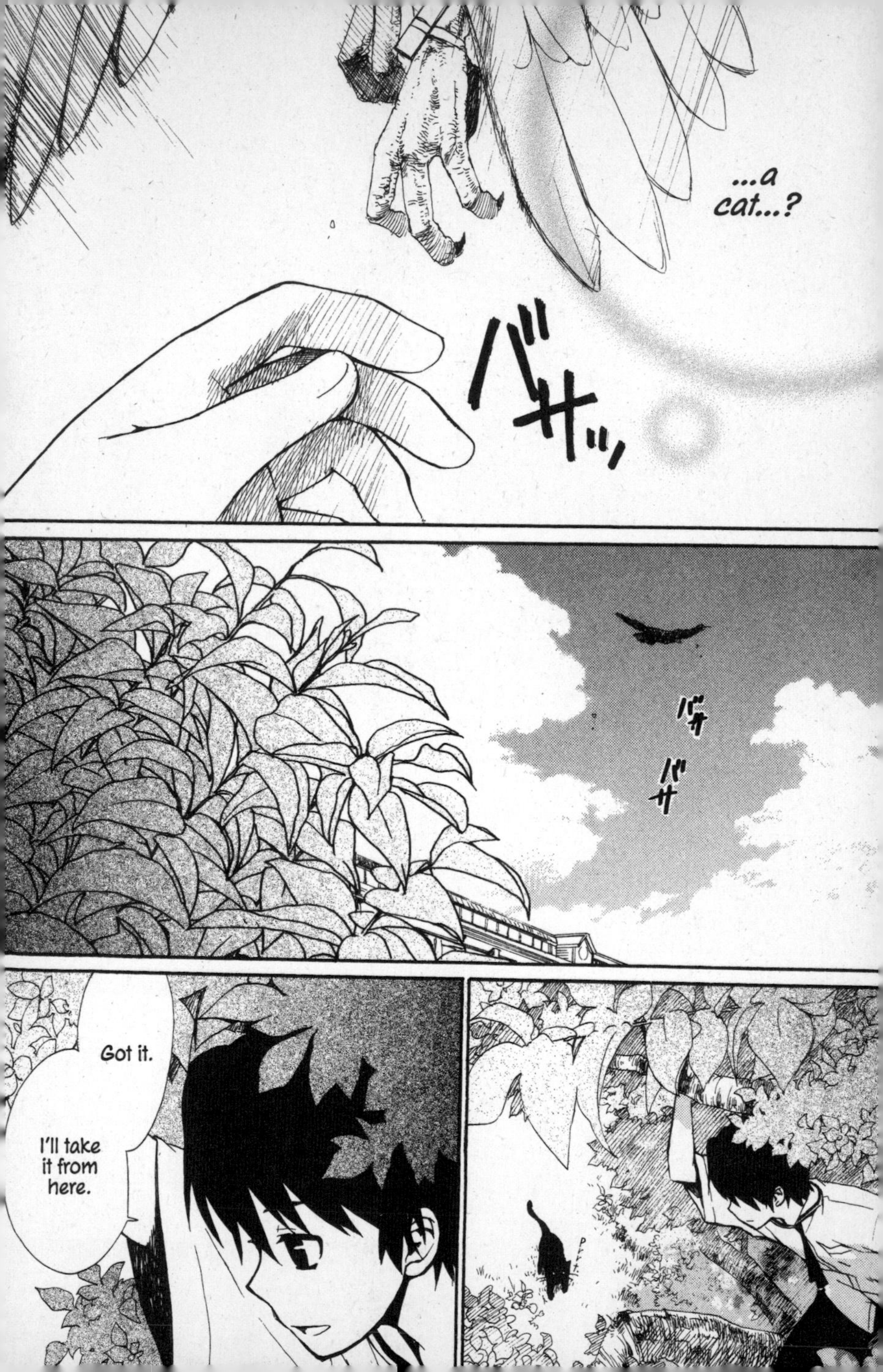
...a cat...?
バサッ
バサ
バサ
Prrrt.
Got it.
I'll take it from here.

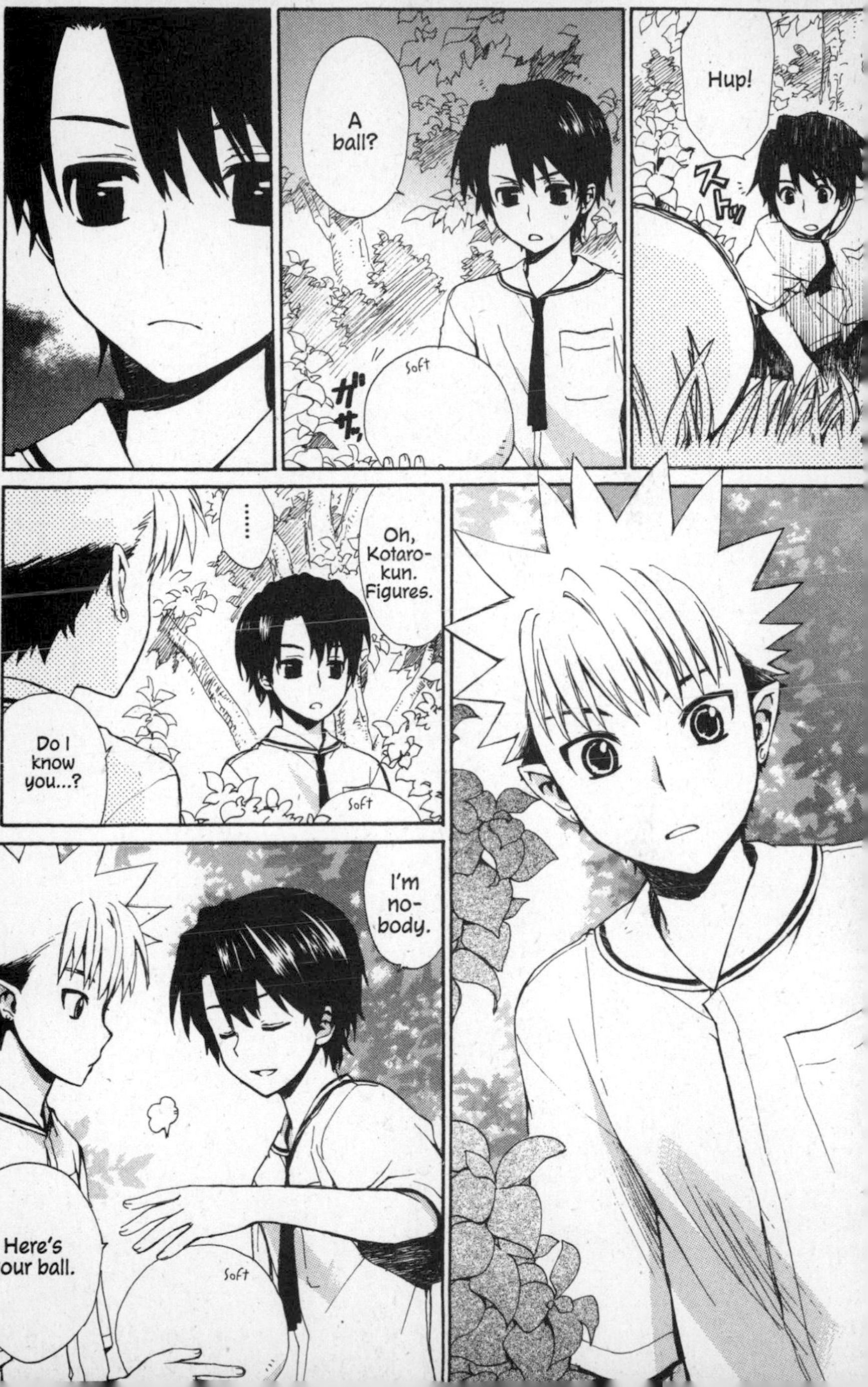
Hup!
ストッ
A ball?
Soft
ガサッ
Oh, Kotaro-kun. Figures.
……
Do I know you...?
Soft
I'm no-body.
Here's your ball.
Soft

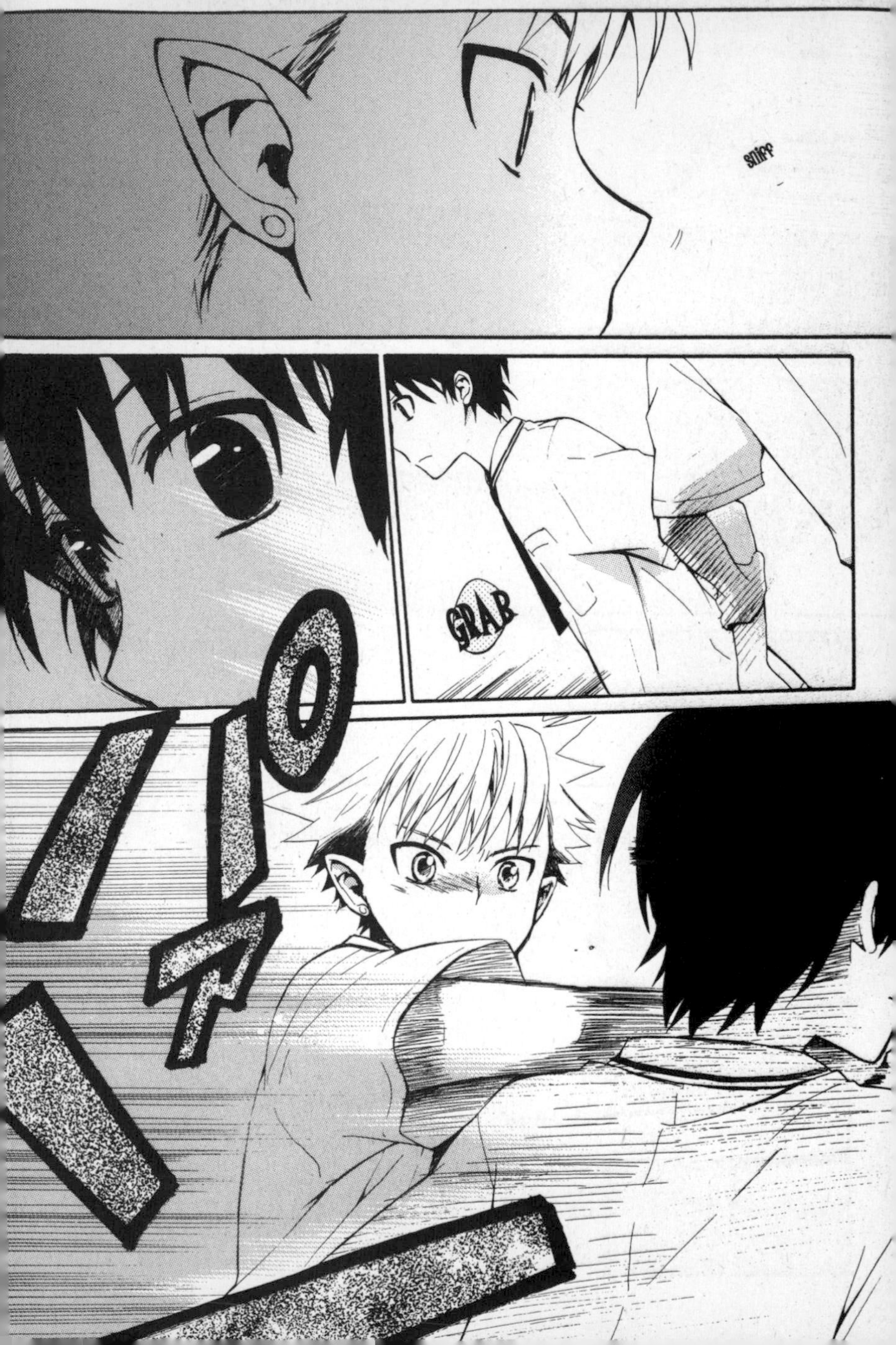
SNIFF
GRAB

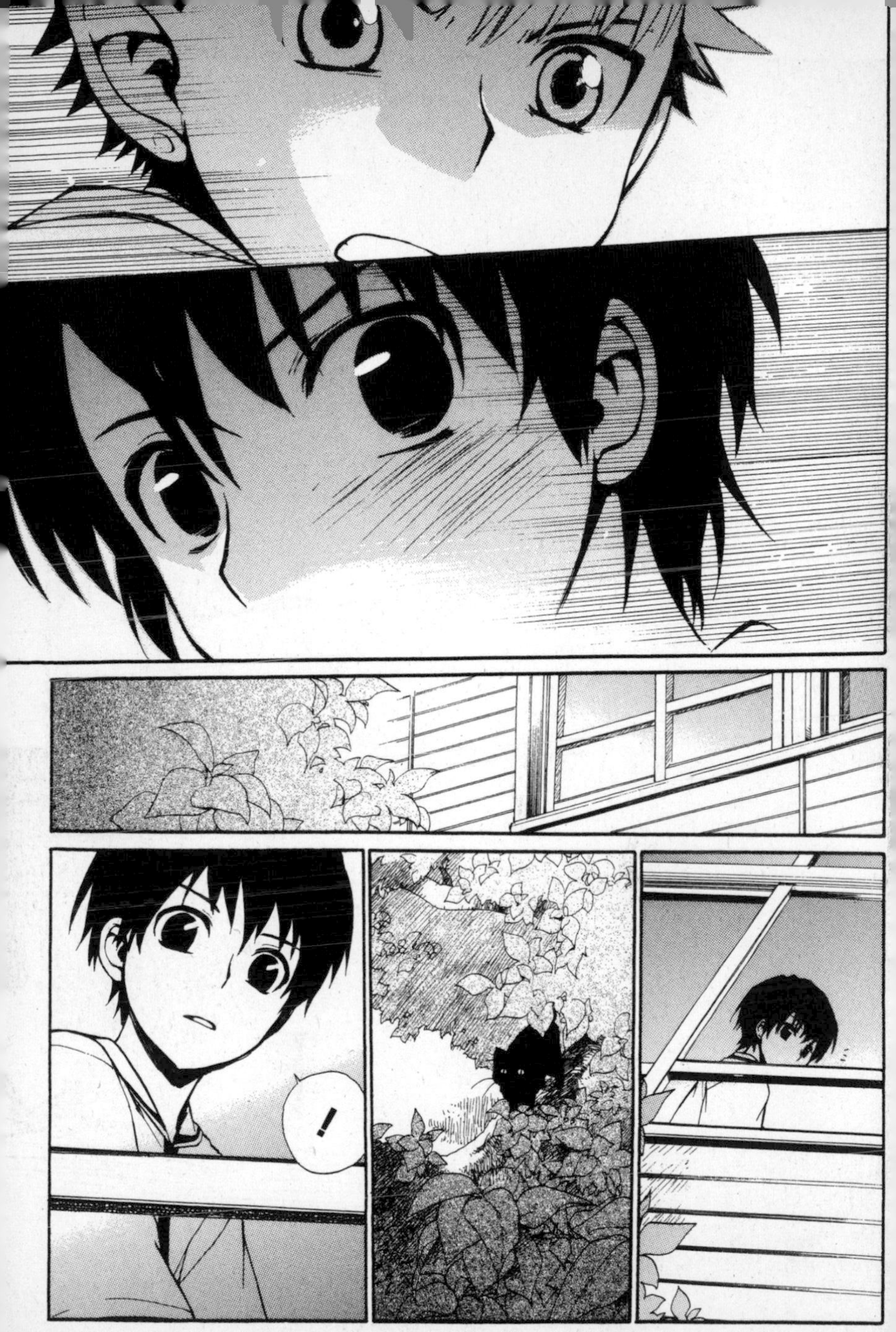
!

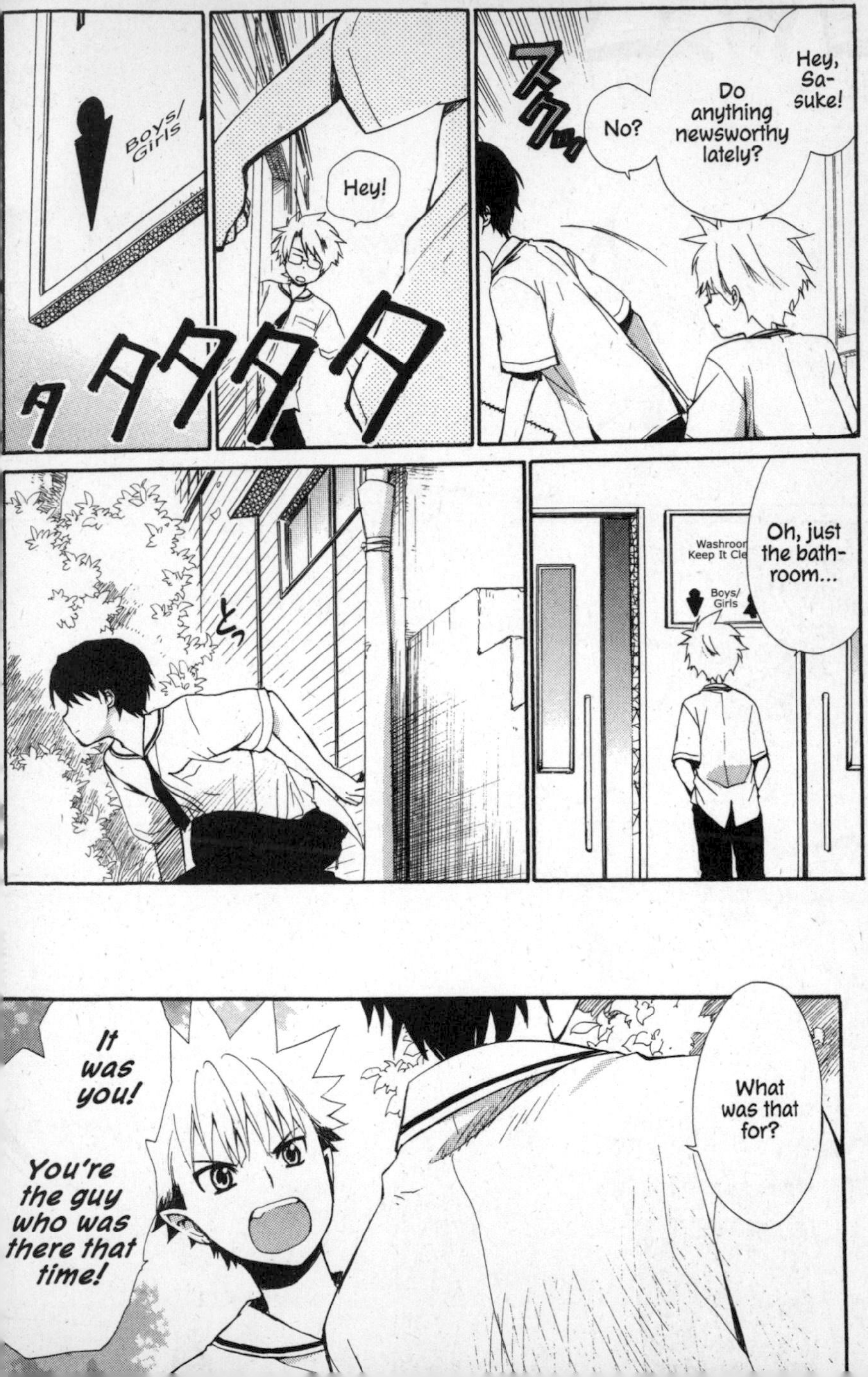
Hey, Sa-suke!
Do anything newsworthy lately?
No?
Hey!
Boys/ Girls
タタタタタ
Oh, just the bath-room...
Boys/ Girls
とっ
What was that for?
It was you!
You're the guy who was there that time!

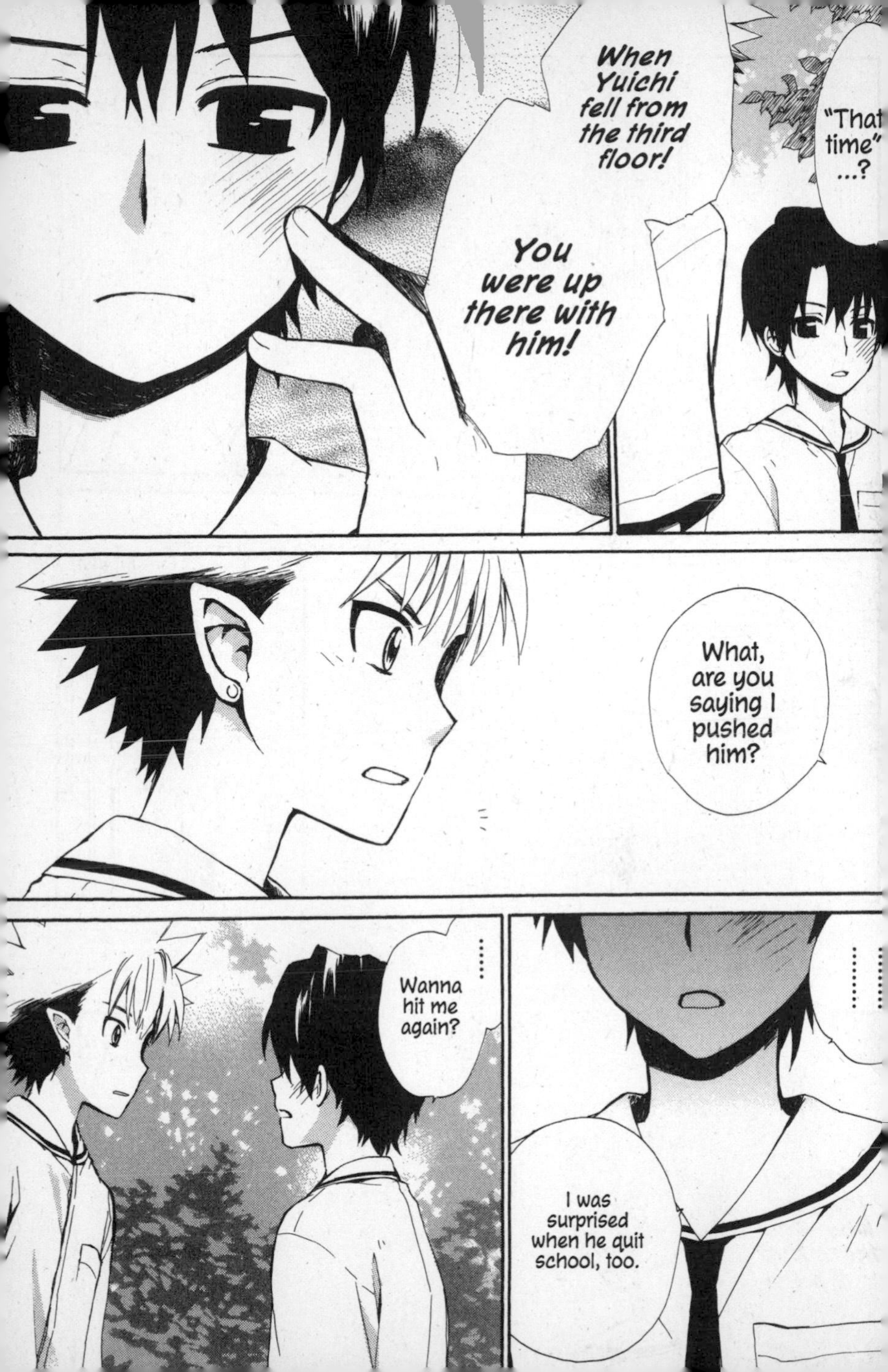
"That time" ...?
When Yuichi fell from the third floor!
You were up there with him!
What, are you saying I pushed him?
......
I was surprised when he quit school, too.
......
Wanna hit me again?

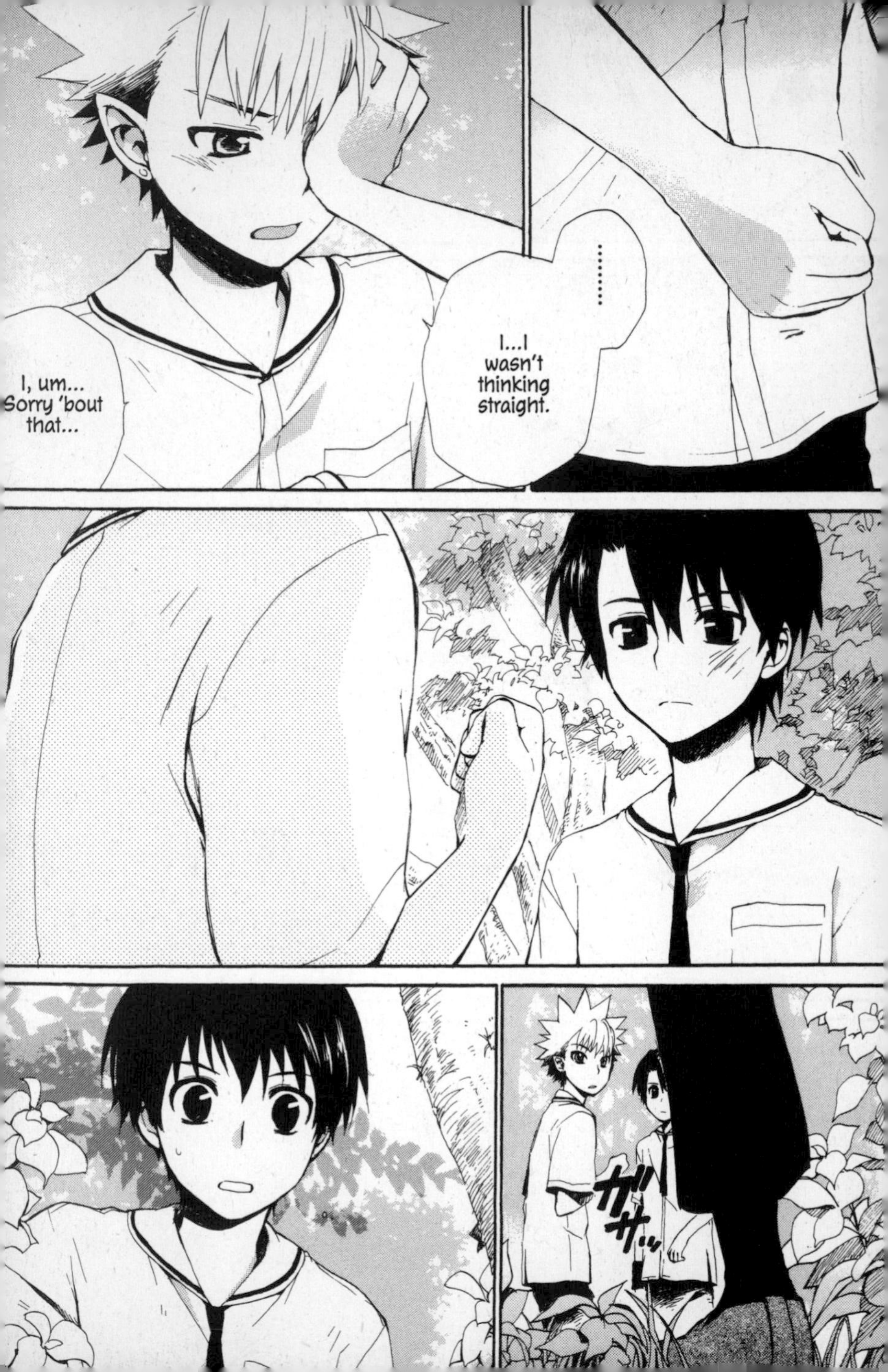
......
I...I wasn't thinking straight.
I, um... Sorry 'bout that...
ガサッ

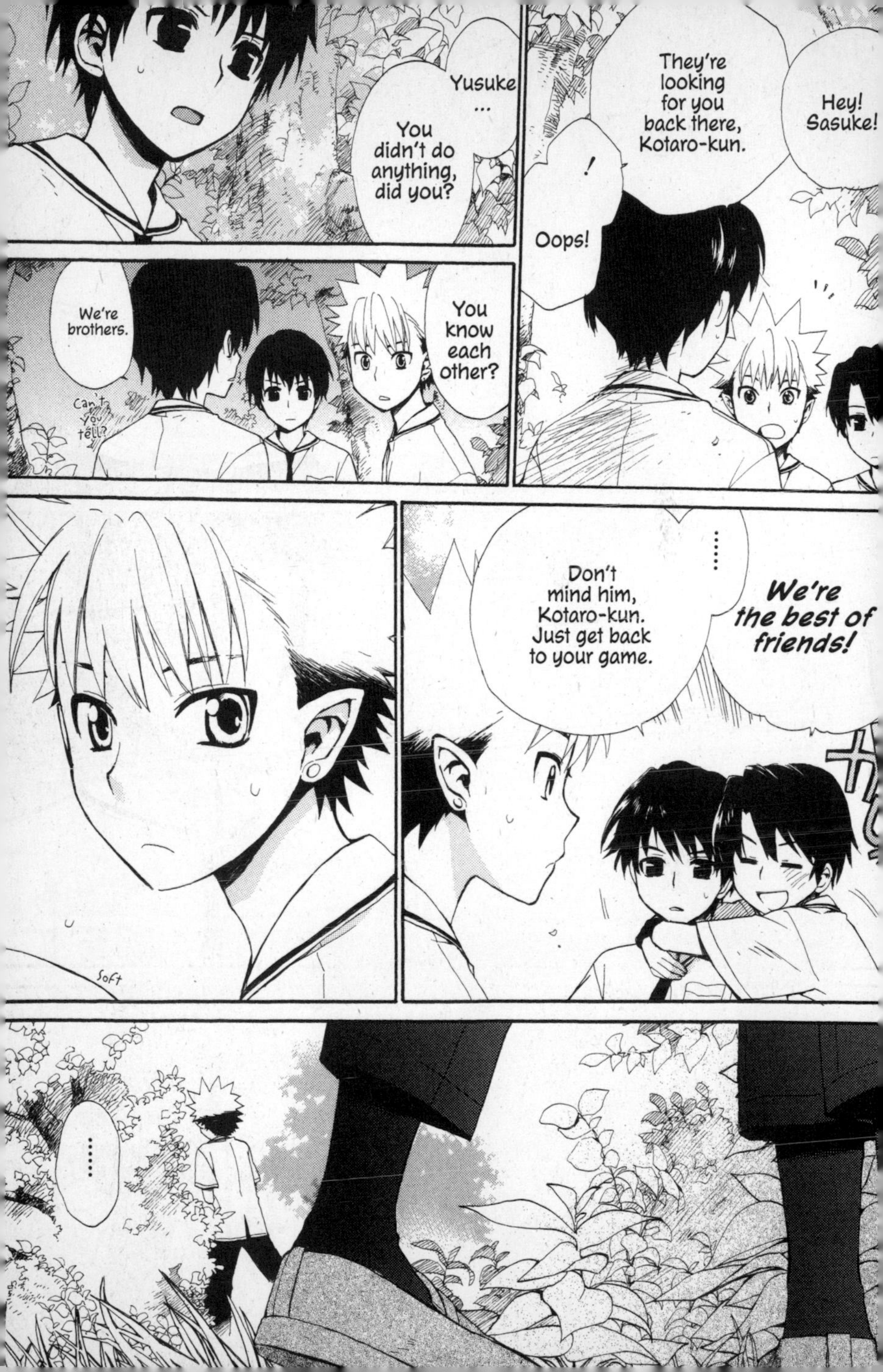
Hey! Sasuke!
They're looking for you back there, Kotaro-kun.
!
Oops!
Yusuke ...
You didn't do anything, did you?
You know each other?
We're brothers.
Can't you tell?
We're the best of friends!
......
Don't mind him, Kotaro-kun. Just get back to your game.
Soft
......

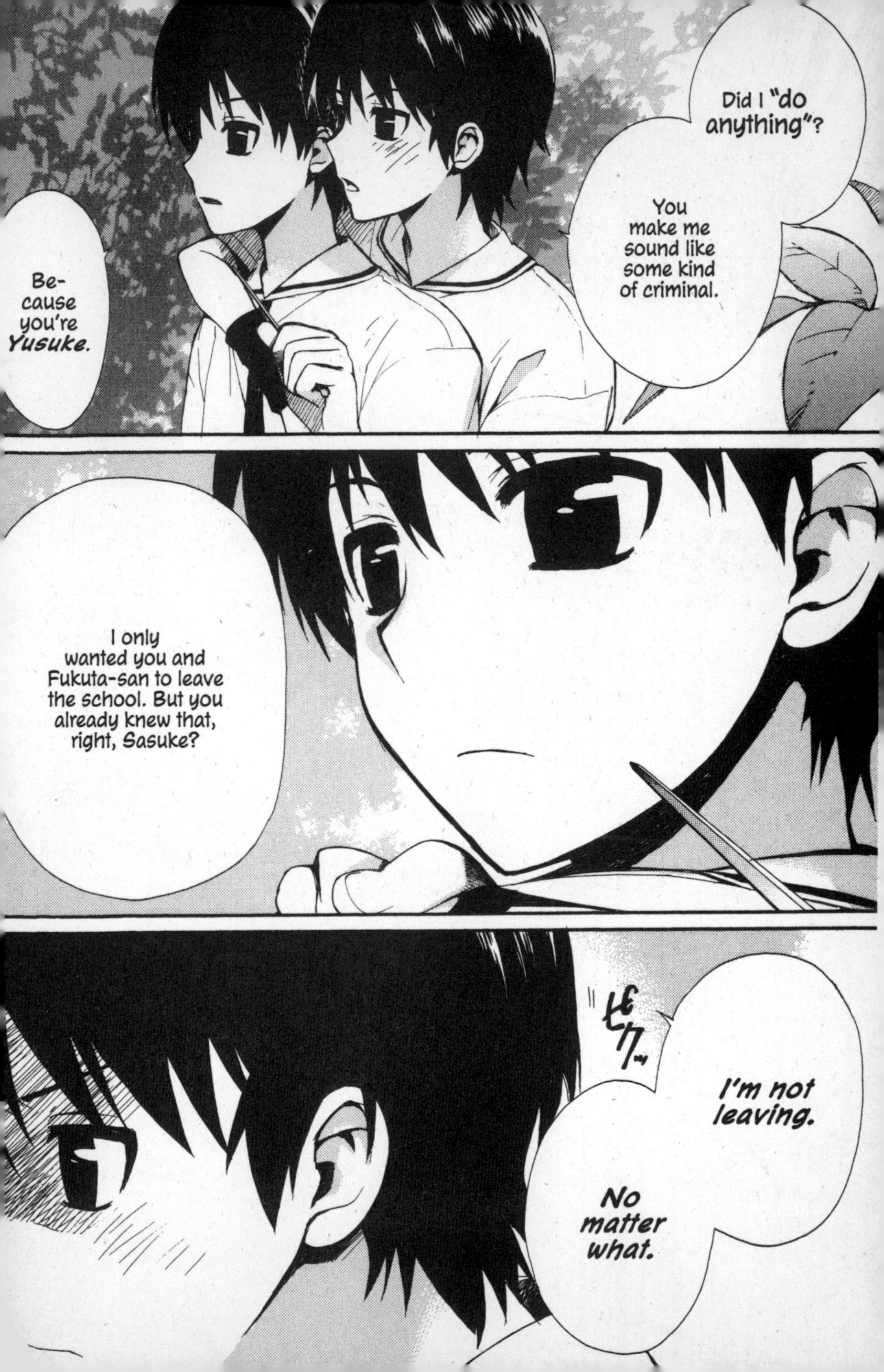
Did I "do anything"?
You make me sound like some kind of criminal.
Be-cause you're *Yusuke*.
I only wanted you and Fukuta-san to leave the school. But you already knew that, right, Sasuke?
I'm not leaving.
No matter what.

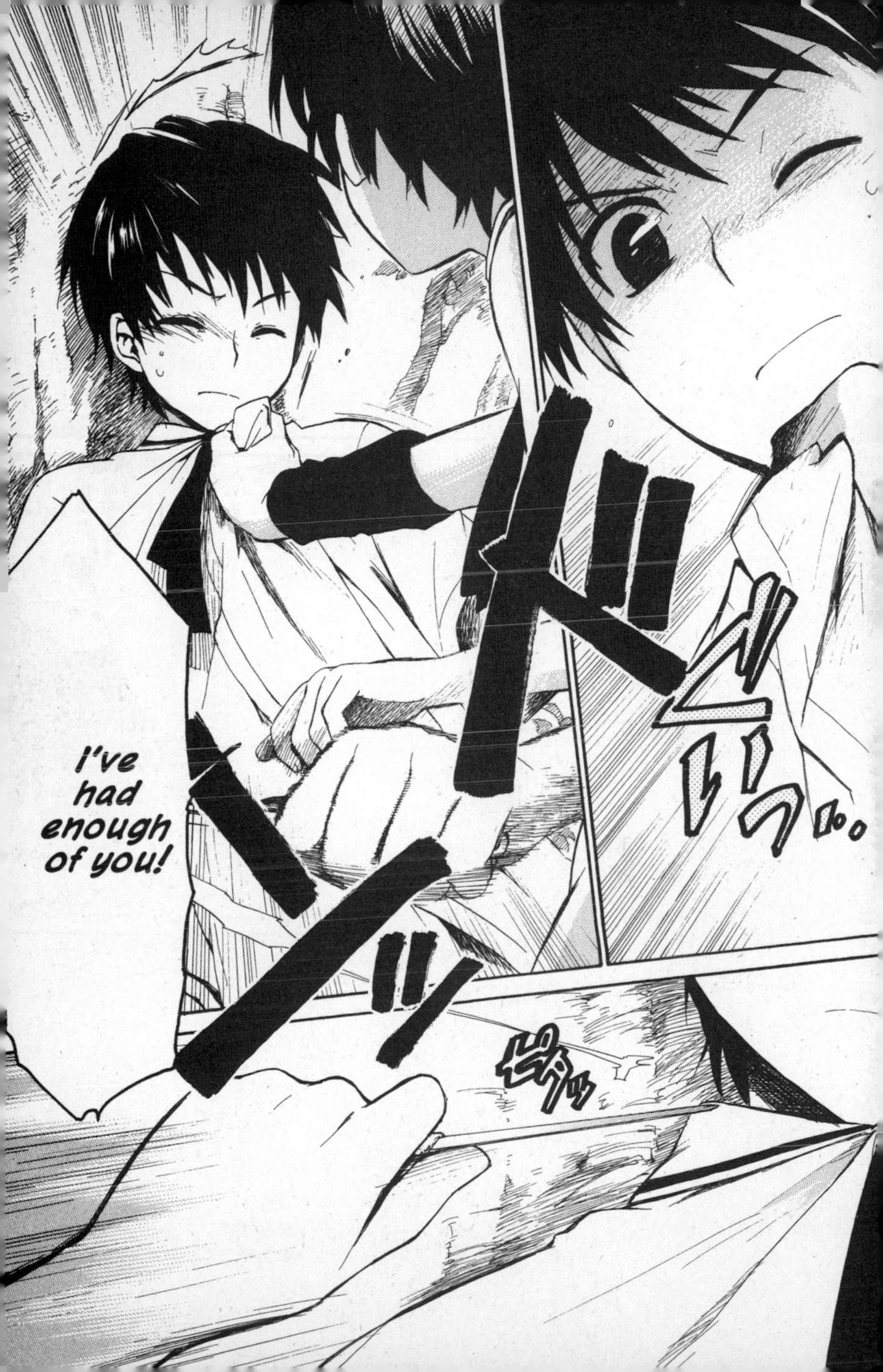
I've had enough of you!

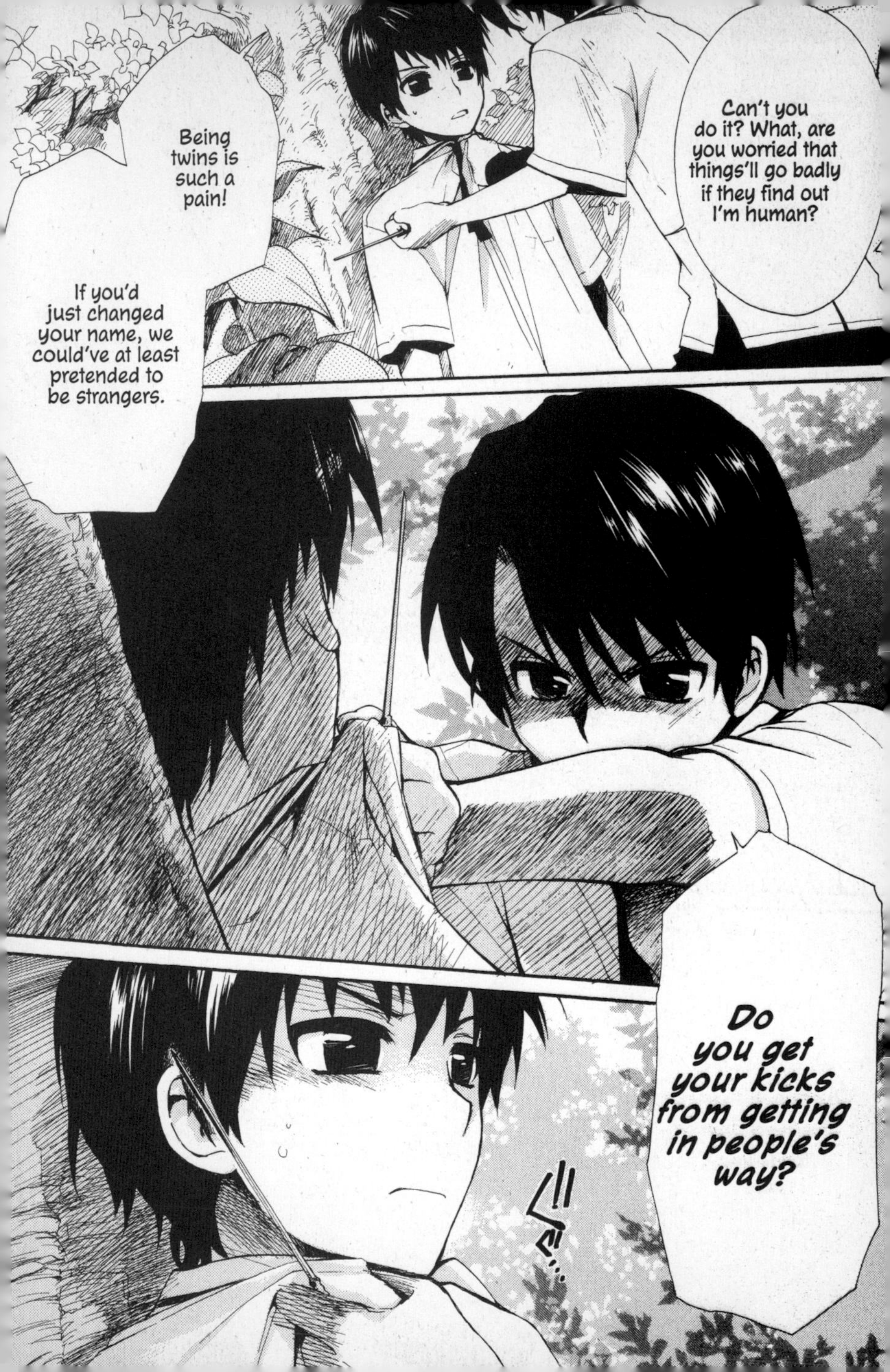

Can't you do it? What, are you worried that things'll go badly if they find out I'm human?
Being twins is such a pain!
If you'd just changed your name, we could've at least pretended to be strangers.
Do you get your kicks from getting in people's way?

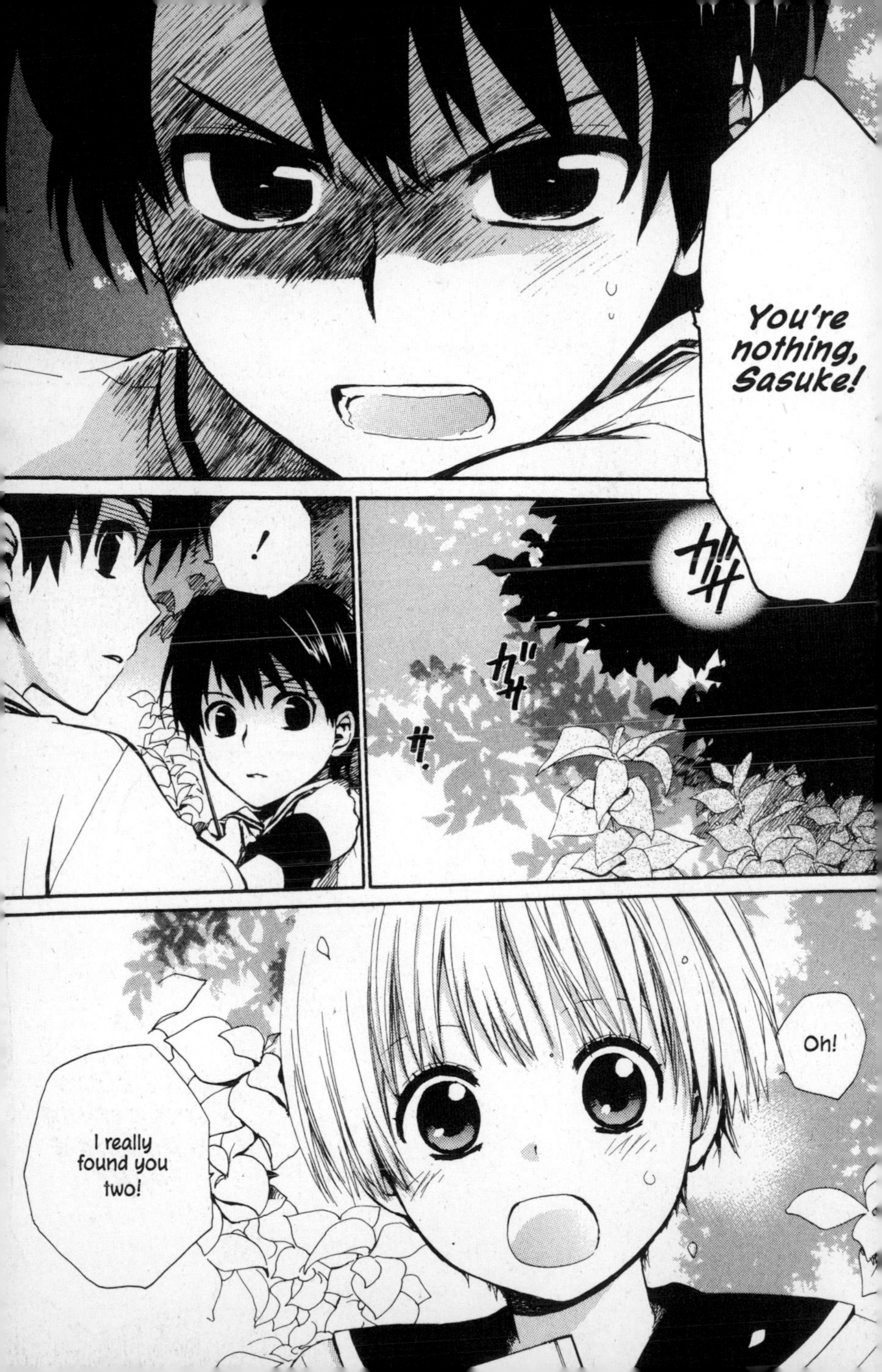
You're nothing, Sasuke!
!
Oh!
I really found you two!

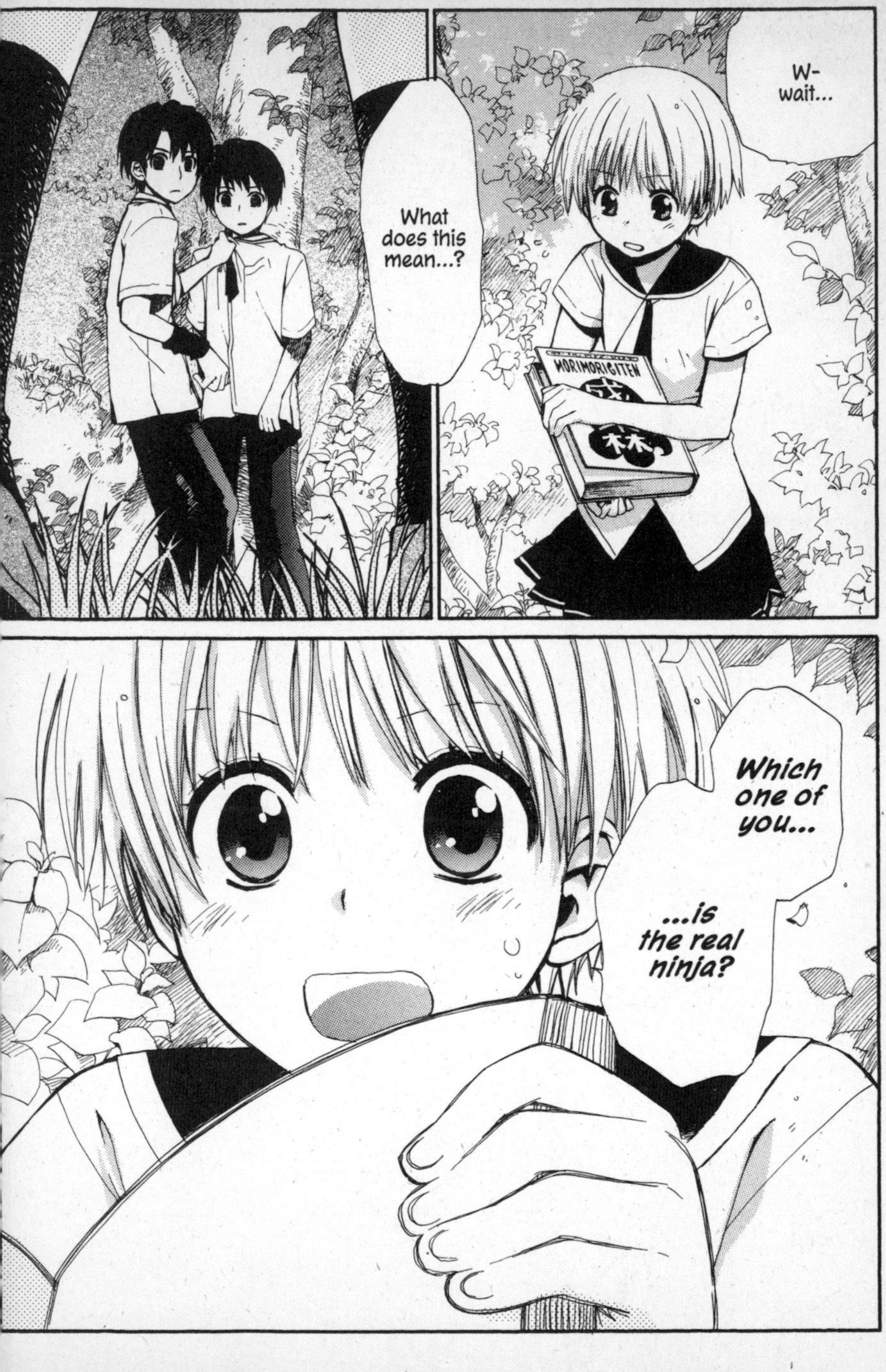
W- wait...
MORIMORIGITEN
What does this mean...?
Which one of you...
...is the real ninja?

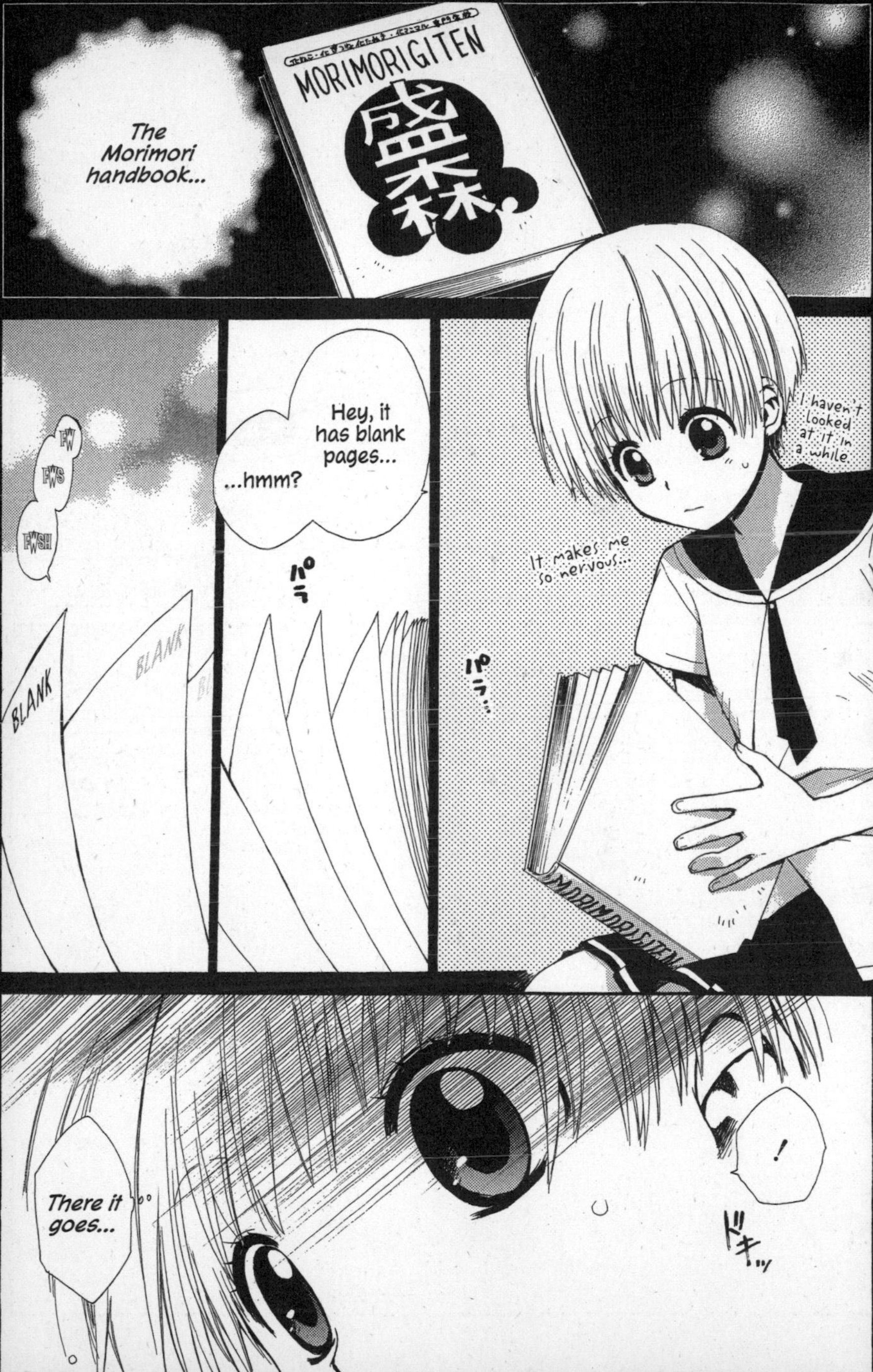

MORIMORIGITEN
The Morimori handbook...
I haven't looked at it in a while.
It makes me so nervous...
パラ...
Hey, it has blank pages...
...hmm?
パラ
FW
FWS
FWSH
BLANK
BLANK
!
ドキッ
There it goes...

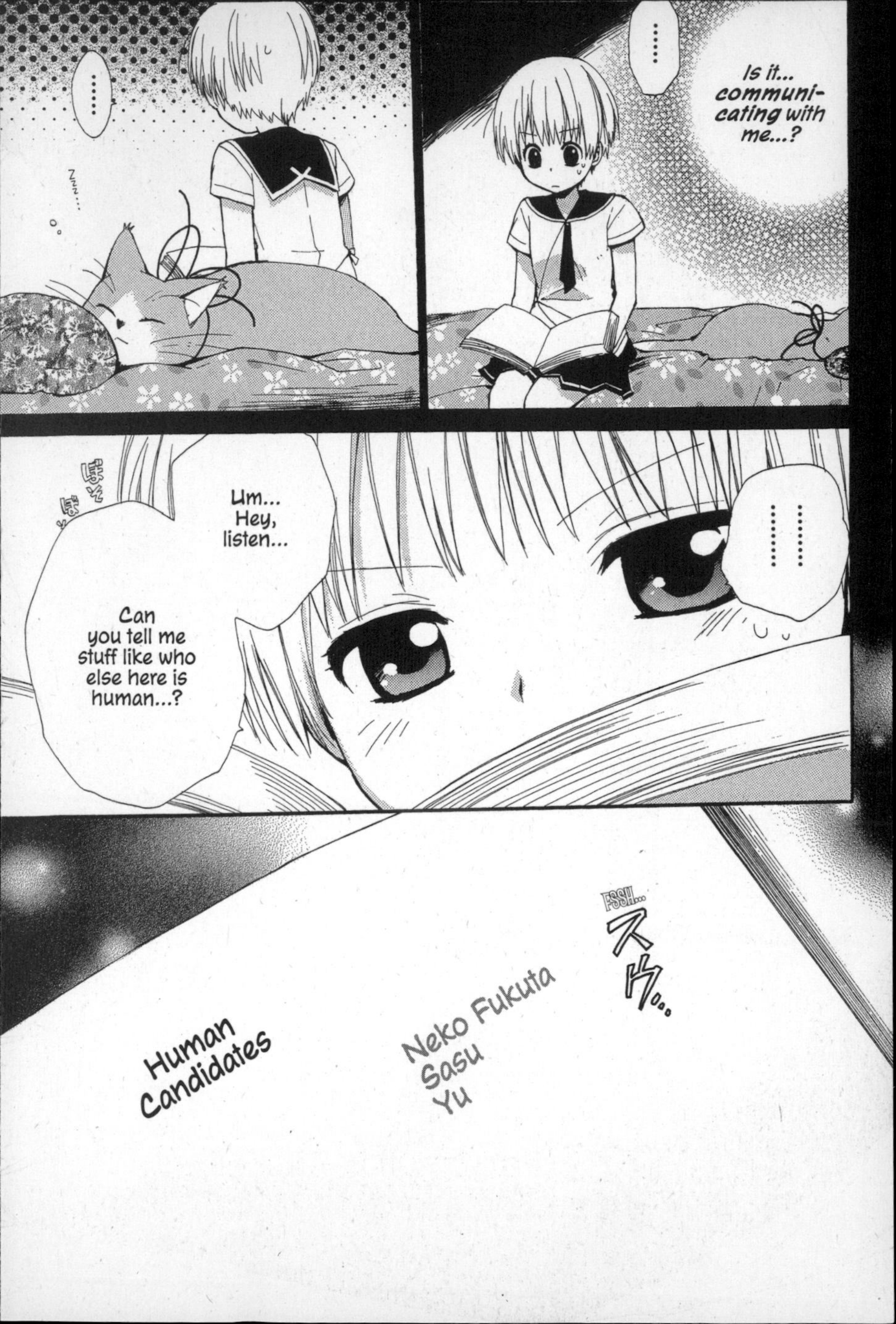
……
Is it... communicating with me...?
……
Zzz...
……
Um... Hey, listen...
Can you tell me stuff like who else here is human...?
FSSH...
スゥ...
Neko Fukuta
Sasu
Yu
Human Candidates

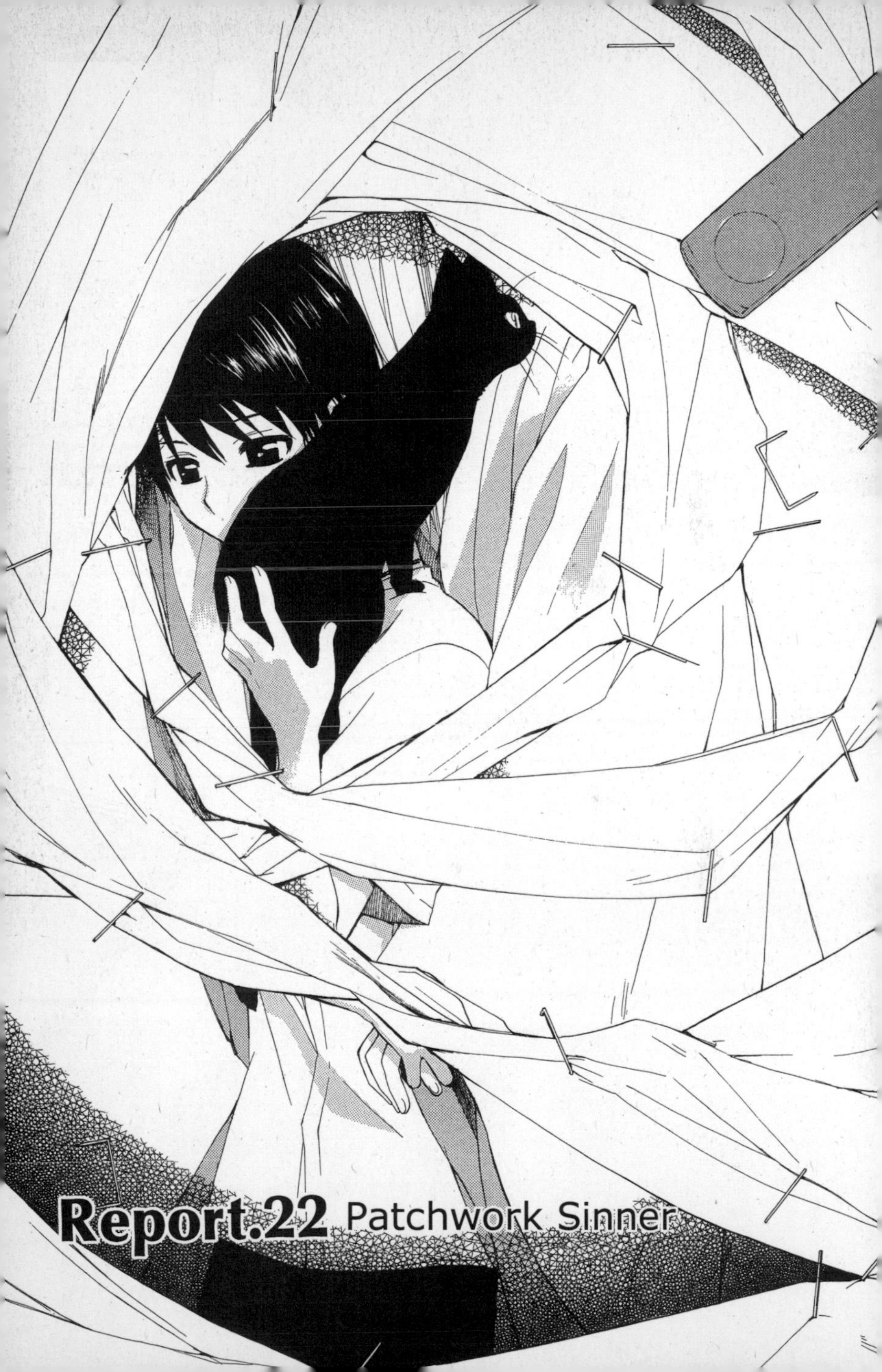
Report.22 Patchwork Sinner

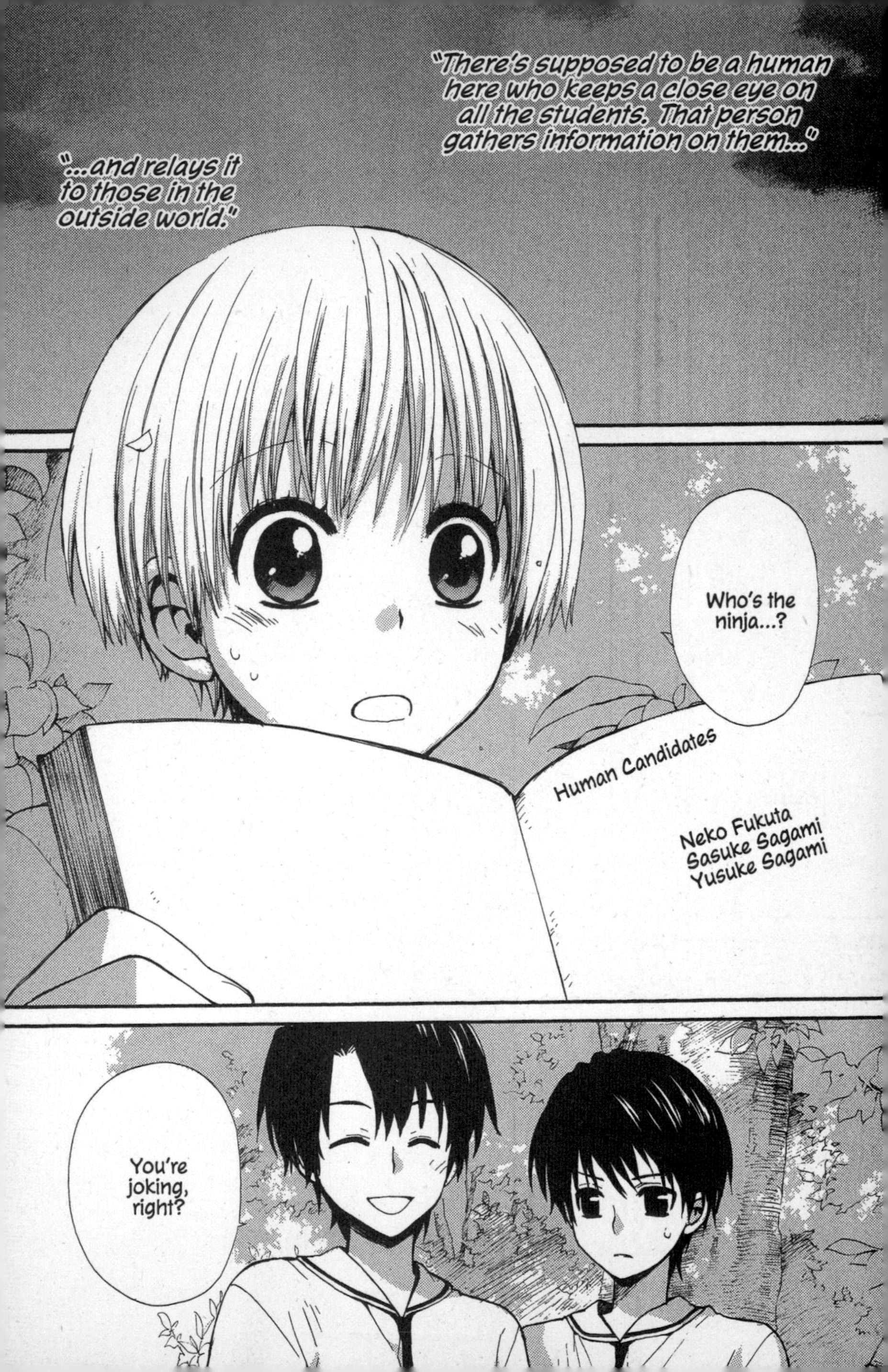
"There's supposed to be a human here who keeps a close eye on all the students. That person gathers information on them..."
"...and relays it to those in the outside world."
Who's the ninja...?
Human Candidates
Neko Fukuta
Sasuke Sagami
Yusuke Sagami
You're joking, right?

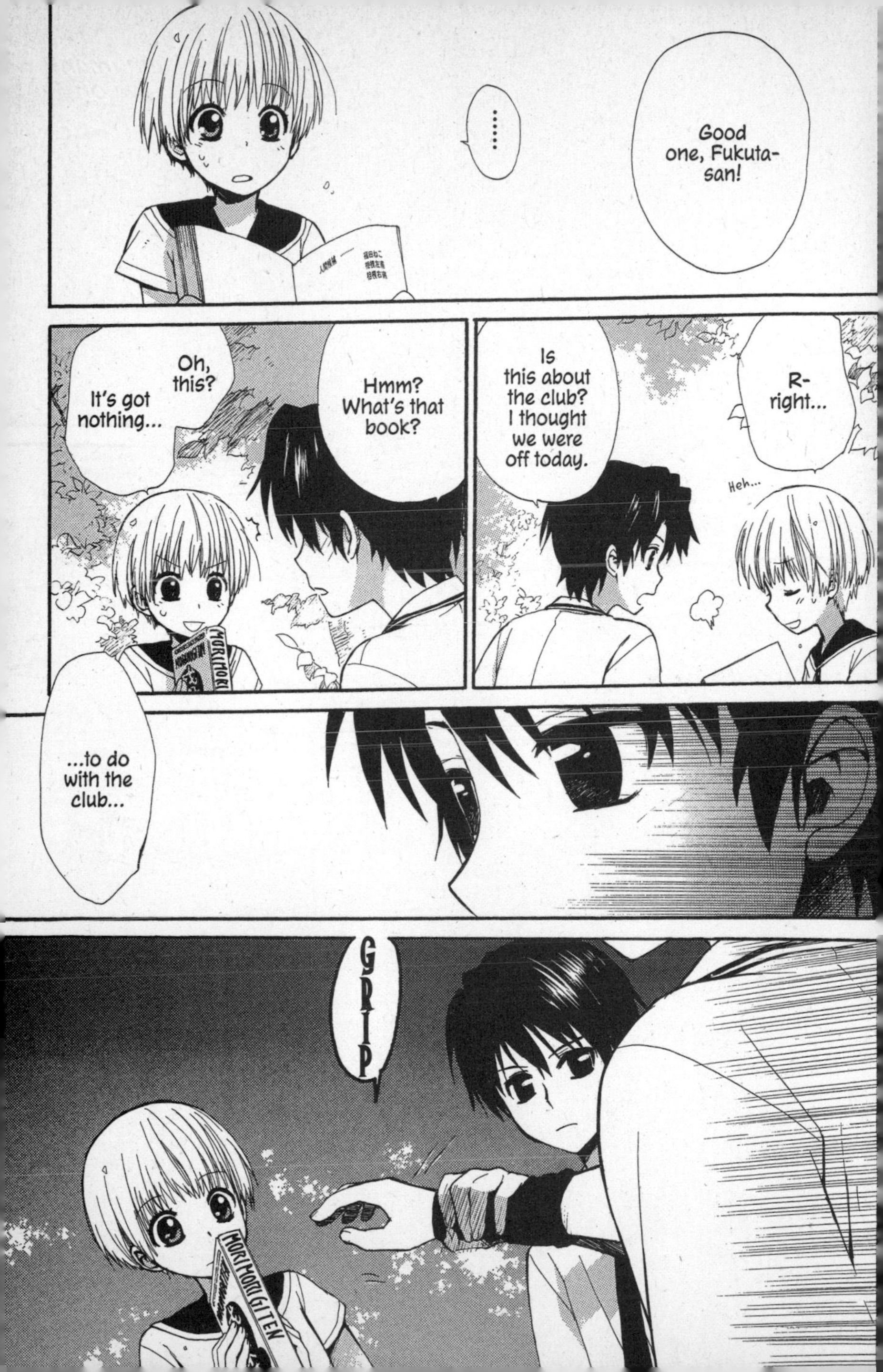
Good one, Fukuta-san!
......
R-right...
Is this about the club? I thought we were off today.
Heh...
Hmm? What's that book?
Oh, this?
It's got nothing...
...to do with the club...
GRIP

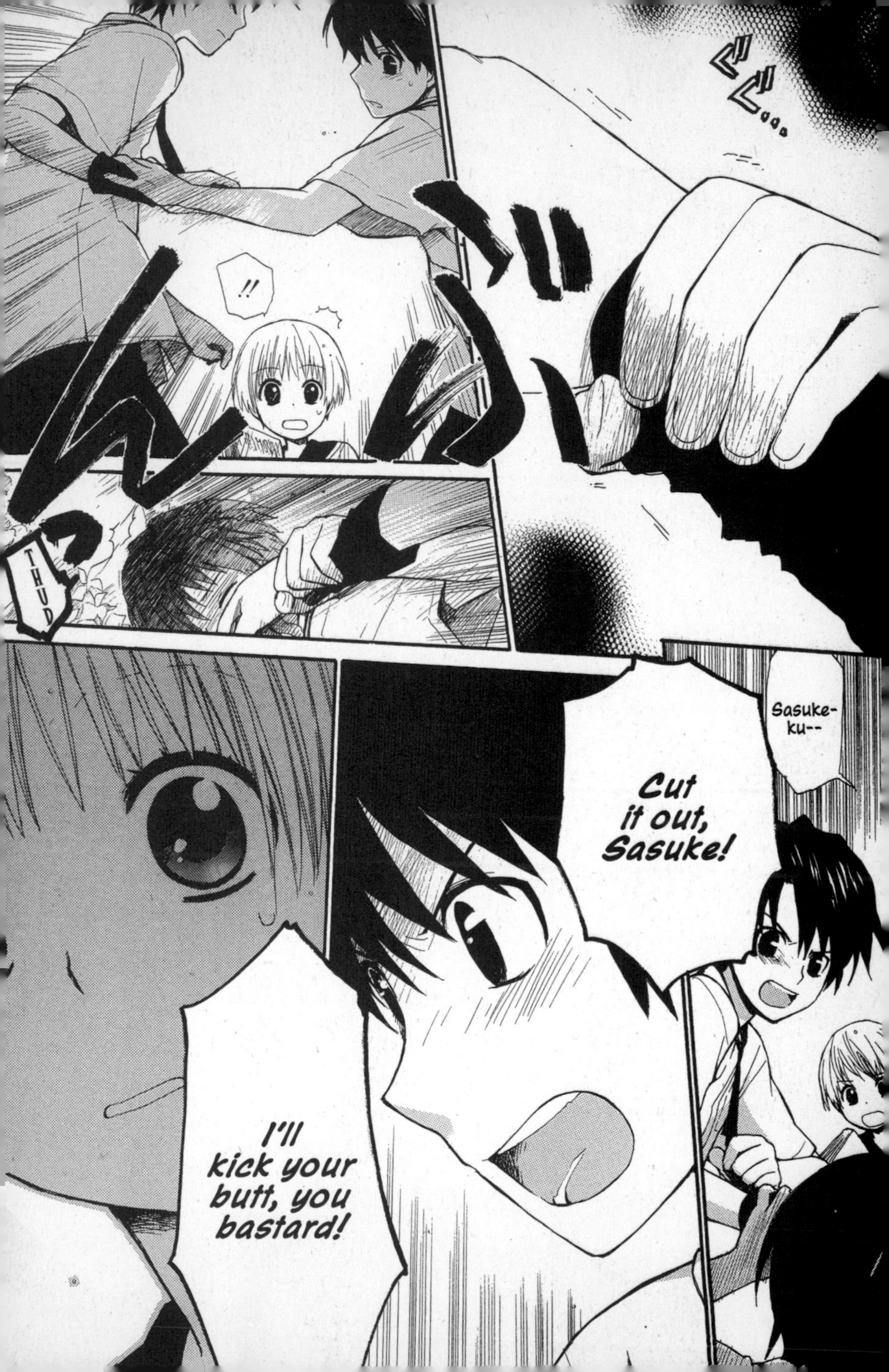
!!
THUD
Sasuke-ku--
Cut it out, Sasuke!
I'll kick your butt, you bastard!

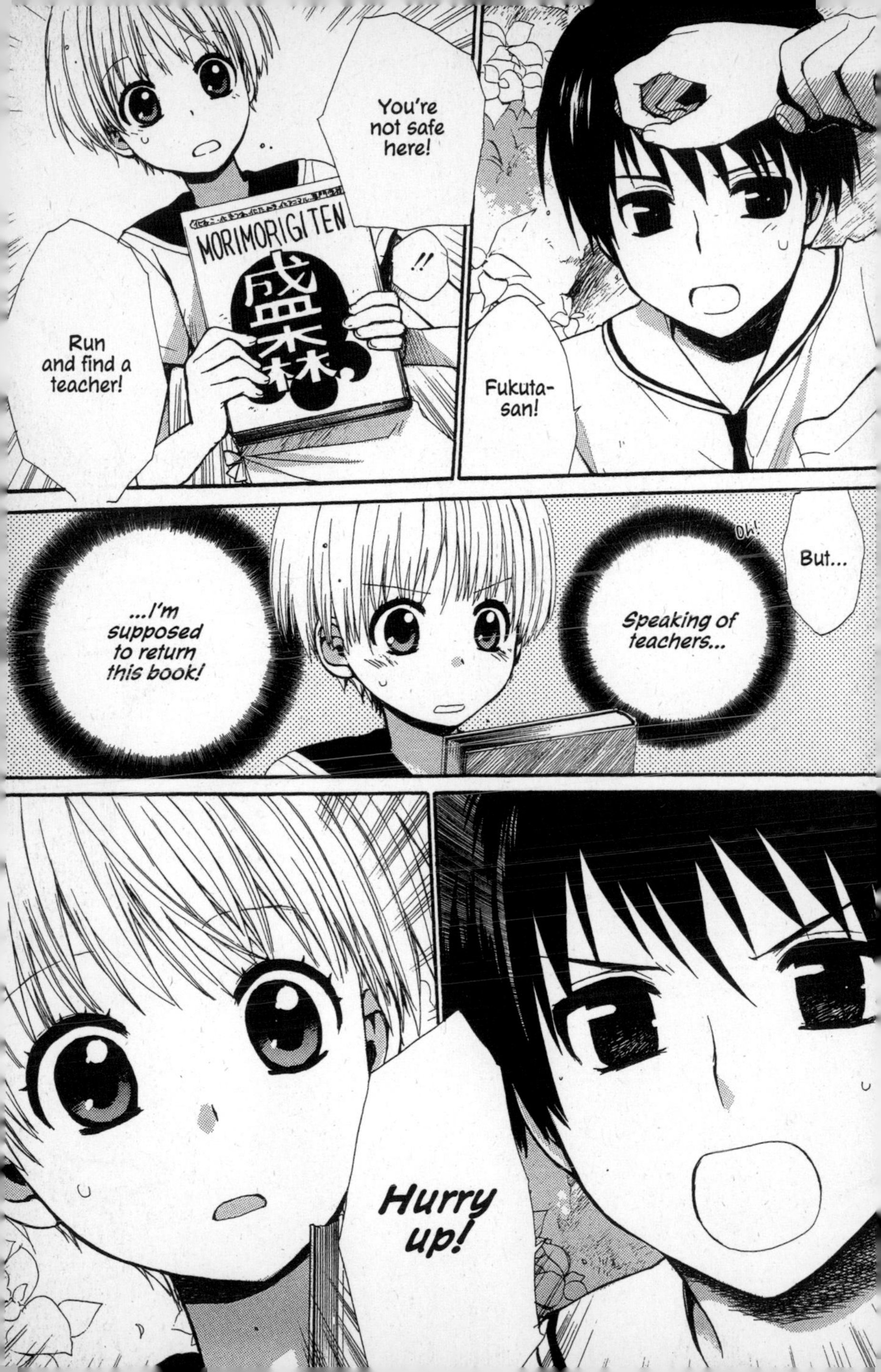

Fukuta-san!
You're not safe here!
!!
Run and find a teacher!
MORIMORIGITEN
But...
Oh!
Speaking of teachers...
...I'm supposed to return this book!
Hurry up!

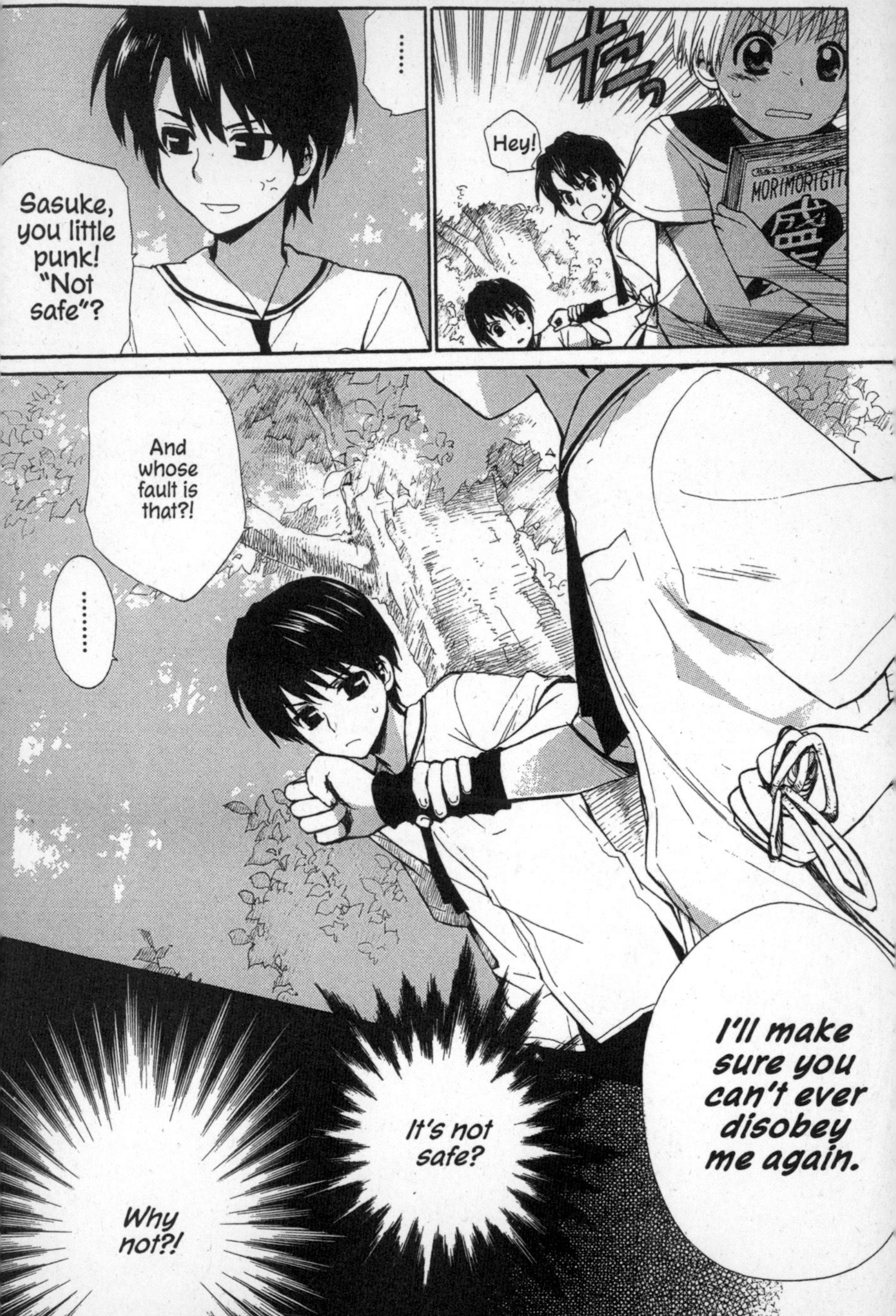
Hey!
......
Sasuke, you little punk! "Not safe"?
And whose fault is that?!
......
I'll make sure you can't ever disobey me again.
It's not safe?
Why not?!

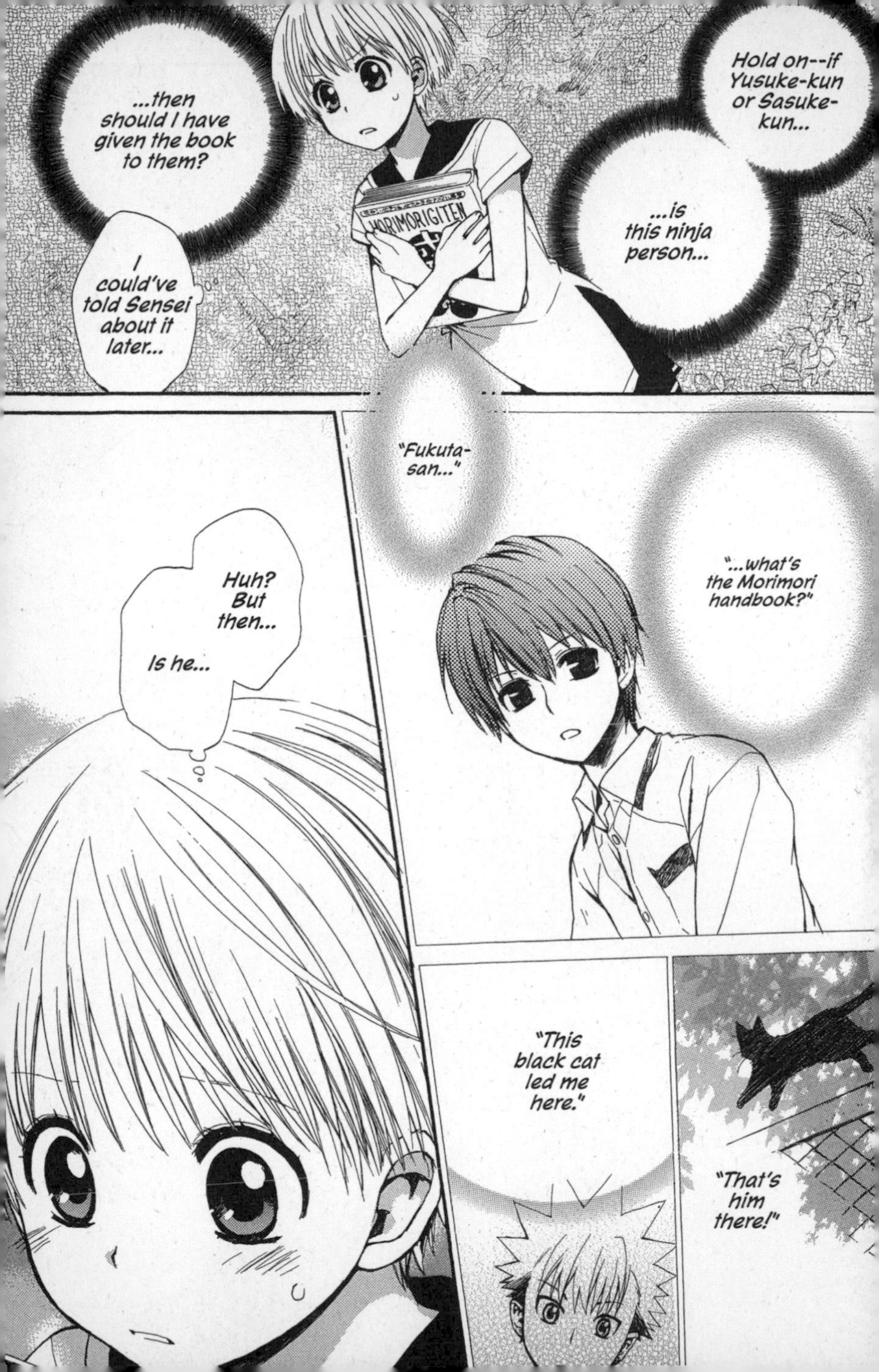
Hold on--if Yusuke-kun or Sasuke-kun...
...is this ninja person...
MORIMORIGITEN
...then should I have given the book to them?
I could've told Sensei about it later...
"Fukuta-san..."
"...what's the Morimori handbook?"
"This black cat led me here."
"That's him there!"
Huh? But then...
Is he...

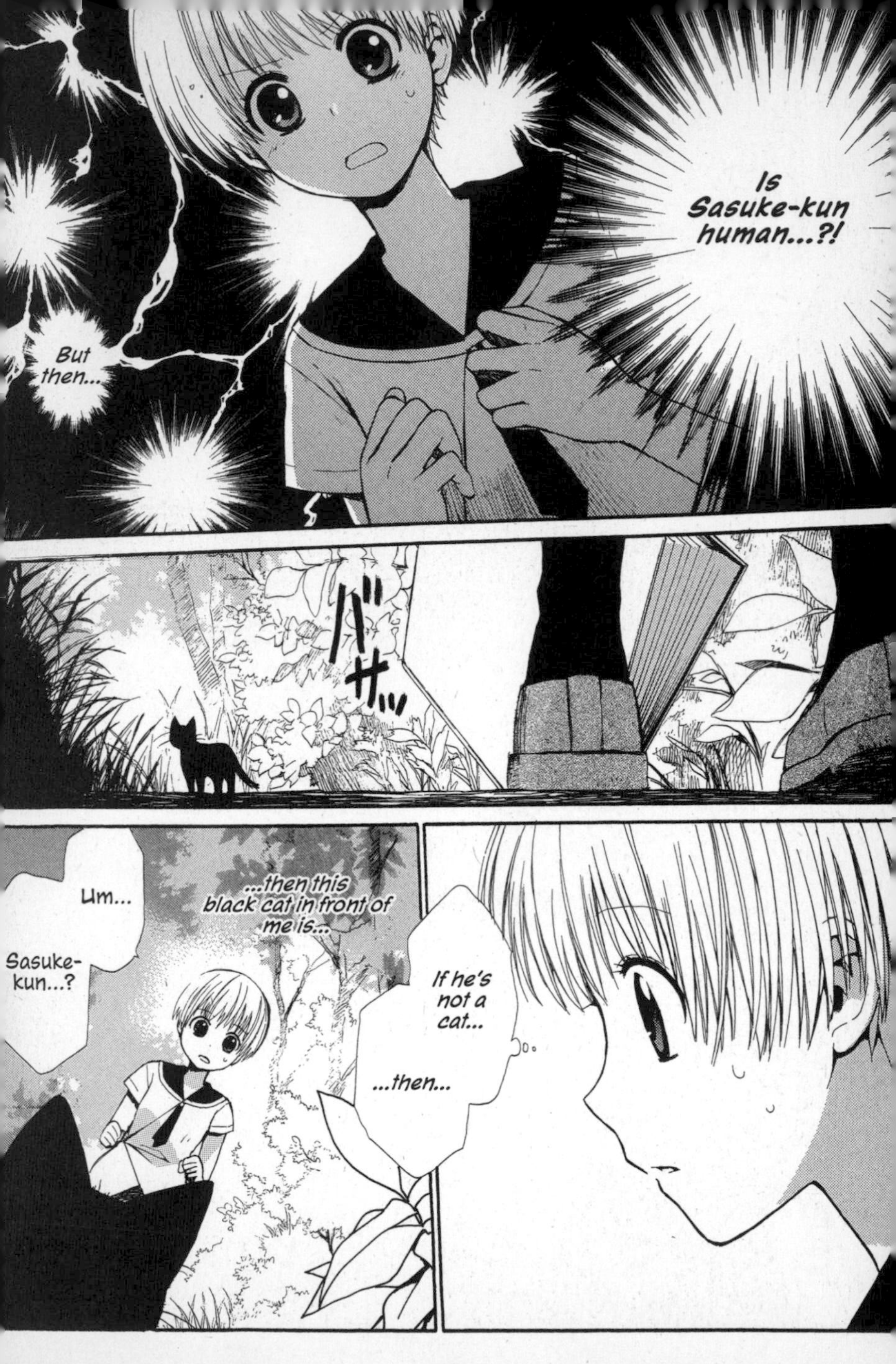
Is Sasuke-kun human...?!
But then...
バサッ
If he's not a cat...
...then...
...then this black cat in front of me is...
Um...
Sasuke-kun...?

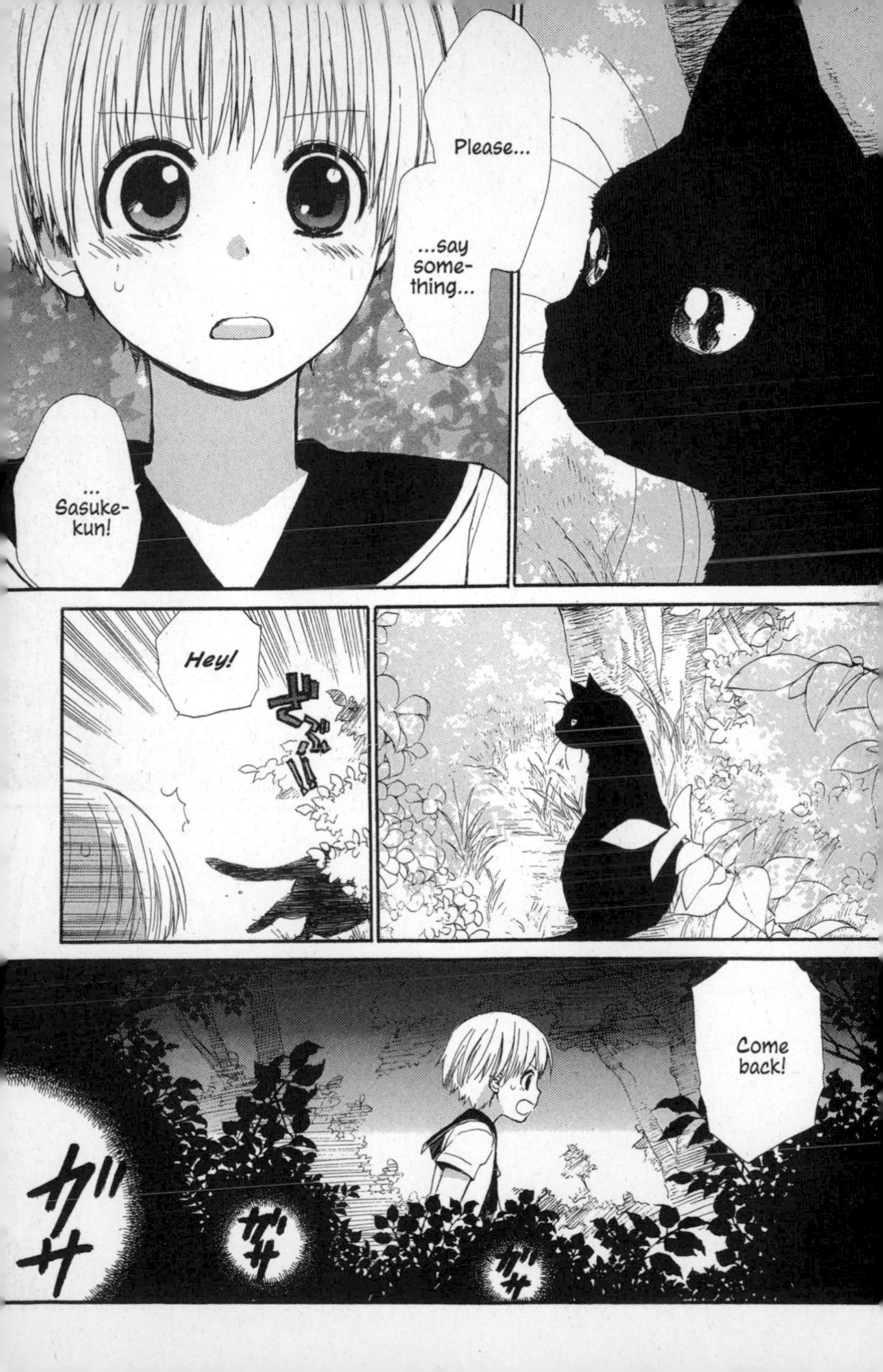
Please...
...say something...
...Sasuke-kun!
Hey!
Come back!
ガサ
ガサ
ガサ

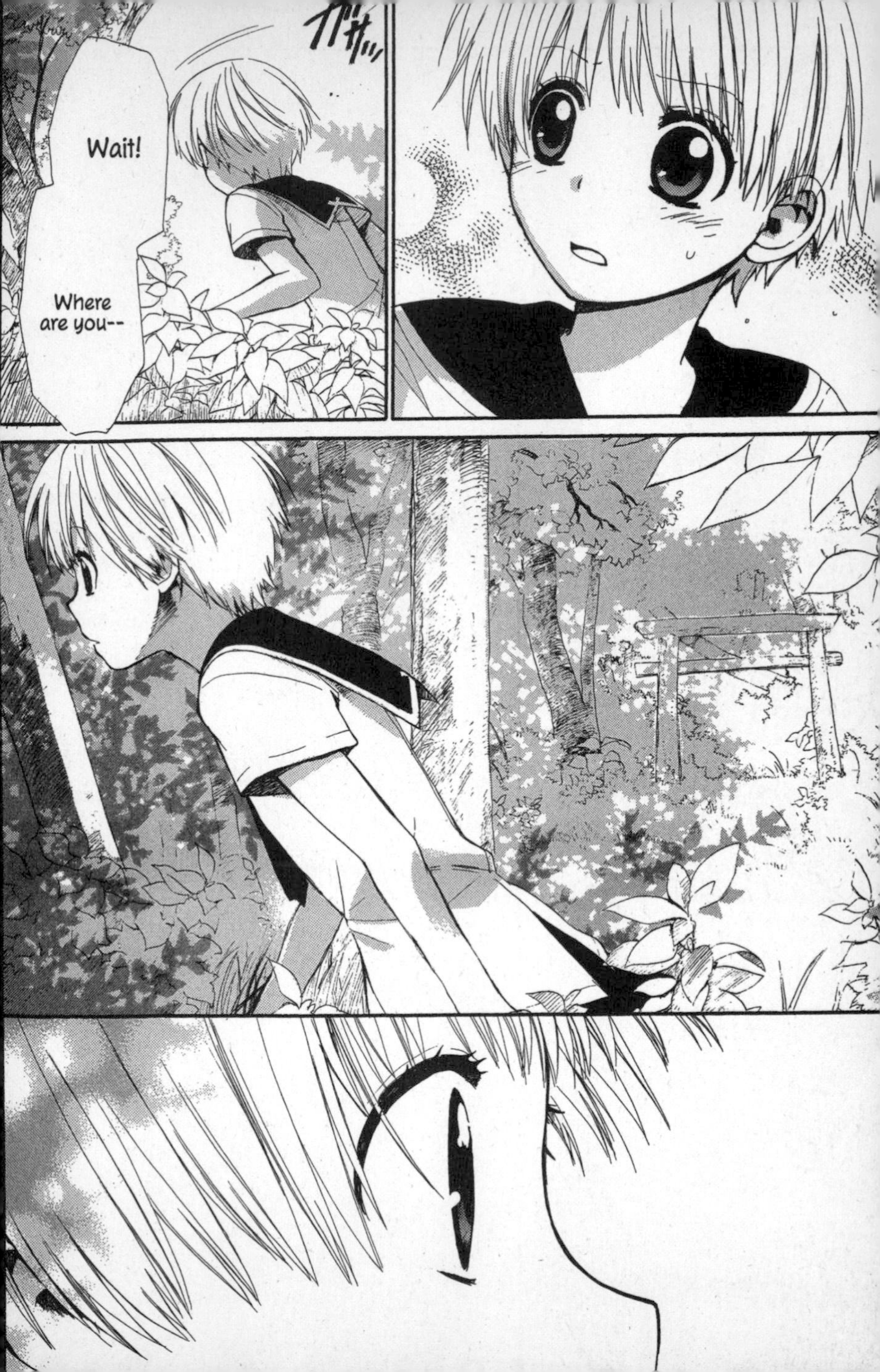
Wait!
Where are you--

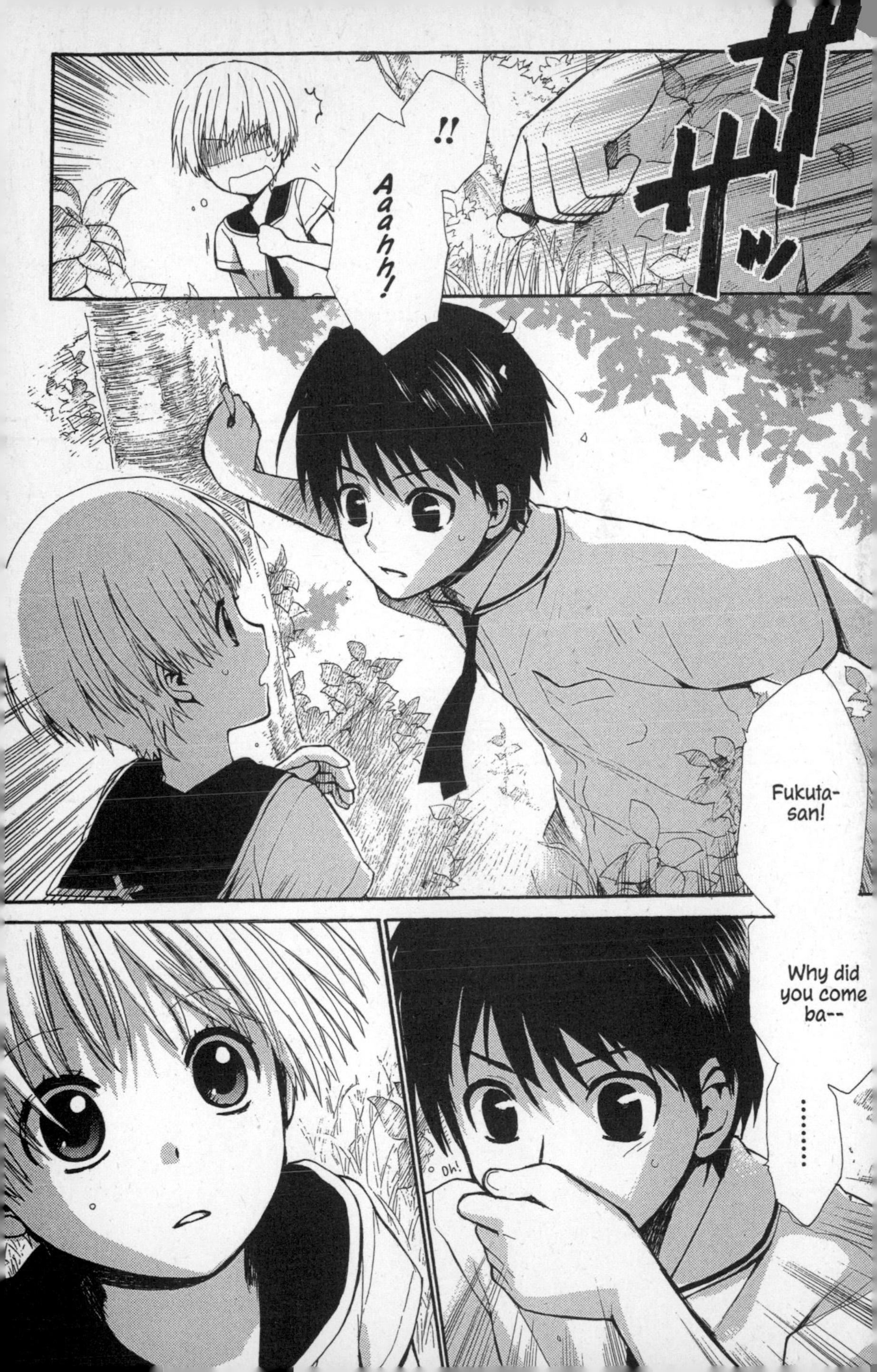
ザザッ
!! Aaaahh!
Fukuta-san!
Why did you come ba--
......
Oh!

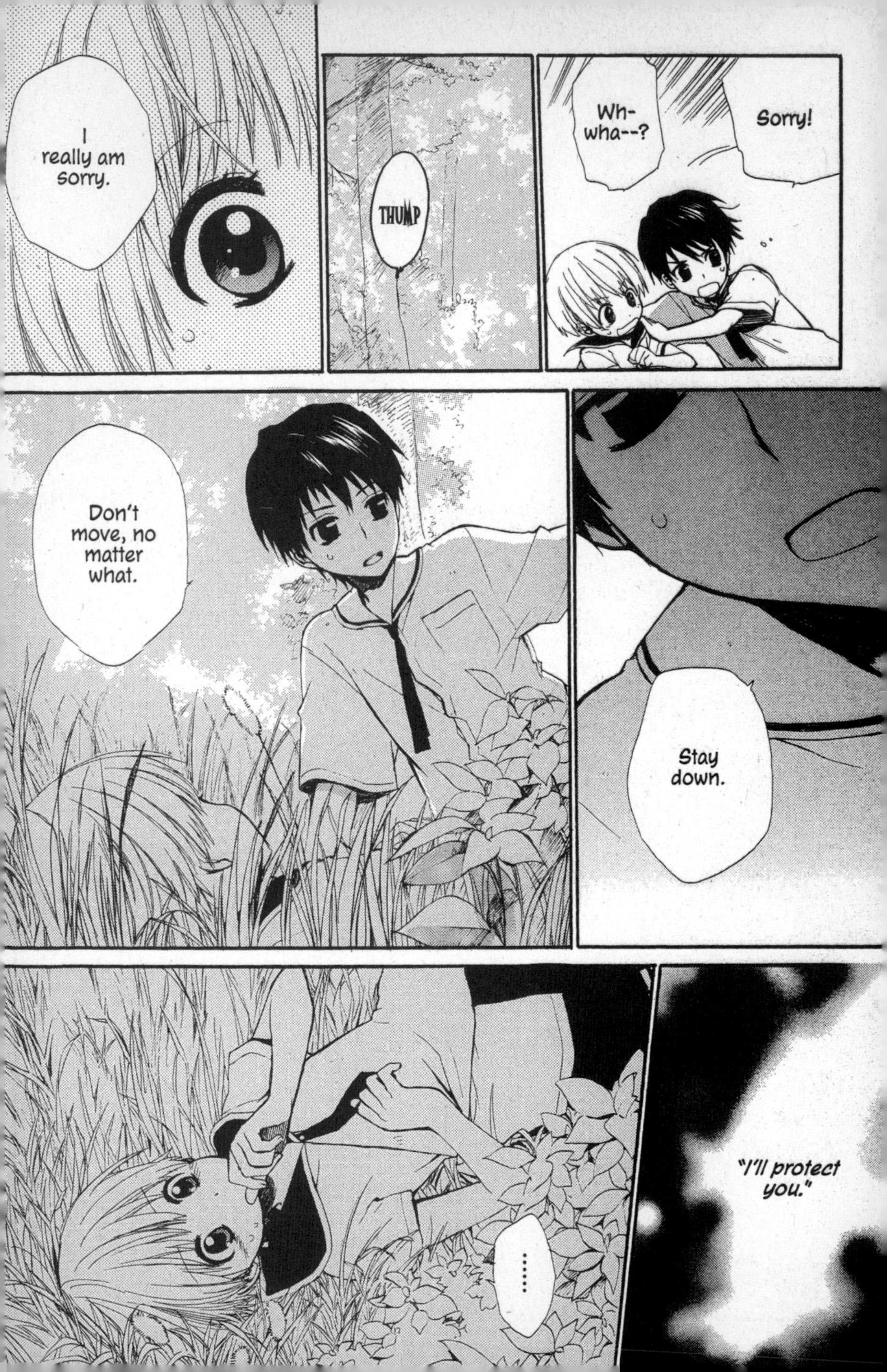
Sorry!
Wh- wha--?
THUMP
I really am sorry.
Stay down.
Don't move, no matter what.
"I'll protect you."
......

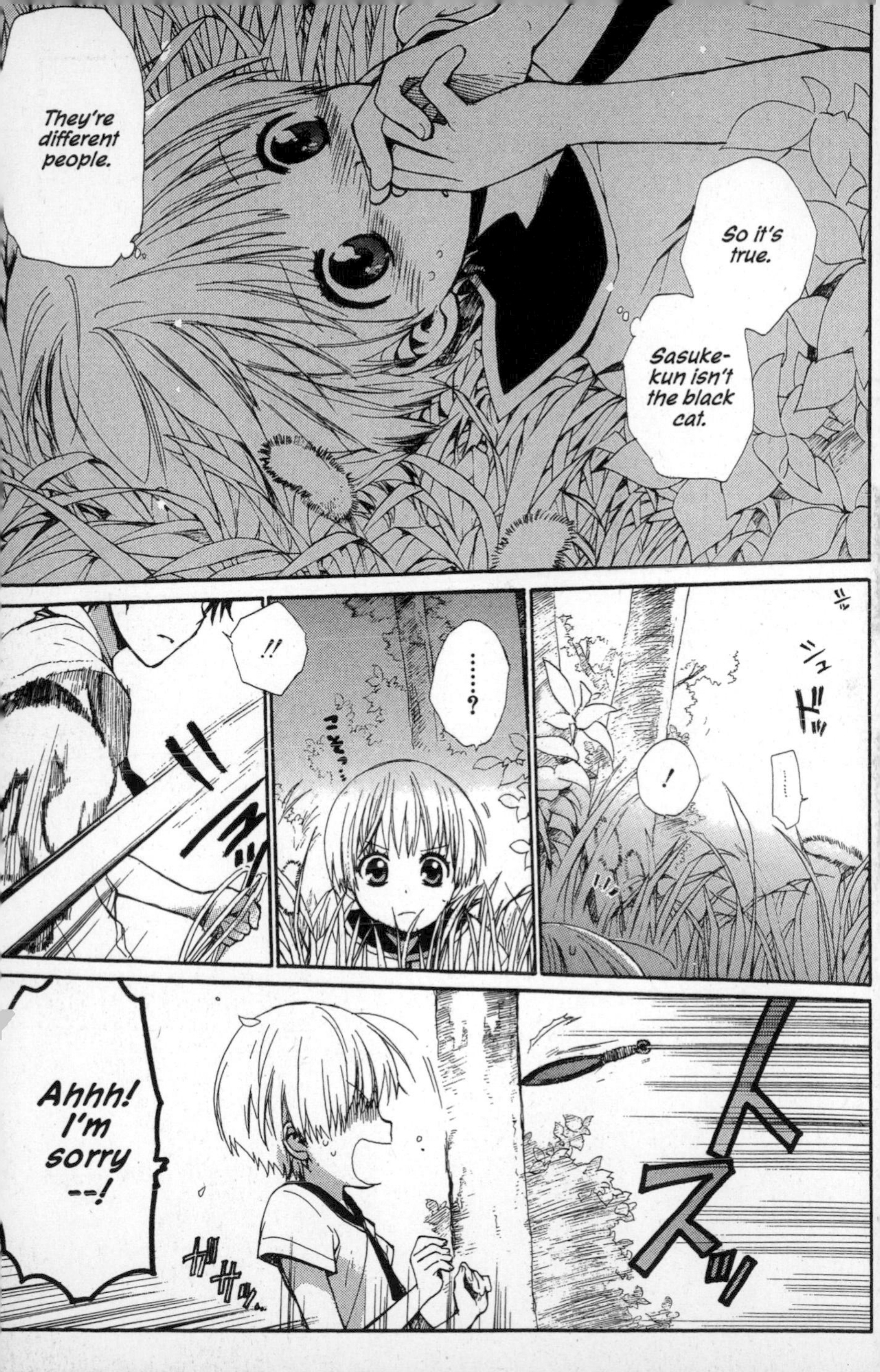
So it's true.
Sasuke-kun isn't the black cat.
They're different people.
!
......
......?
!!
Ahhh! I'm sorry --!

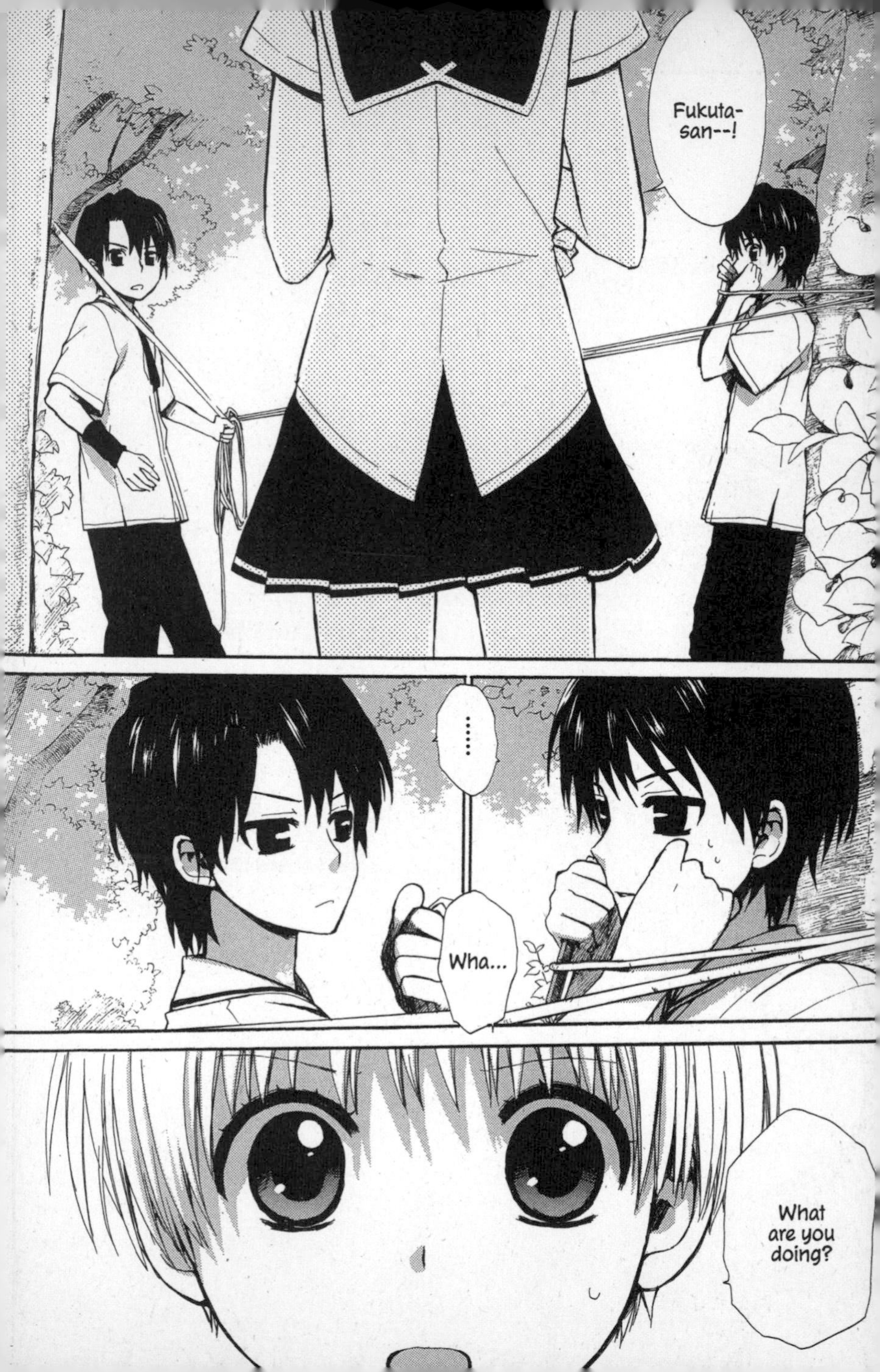

Fukuta-san--!
......
Wha...
What are you doing?

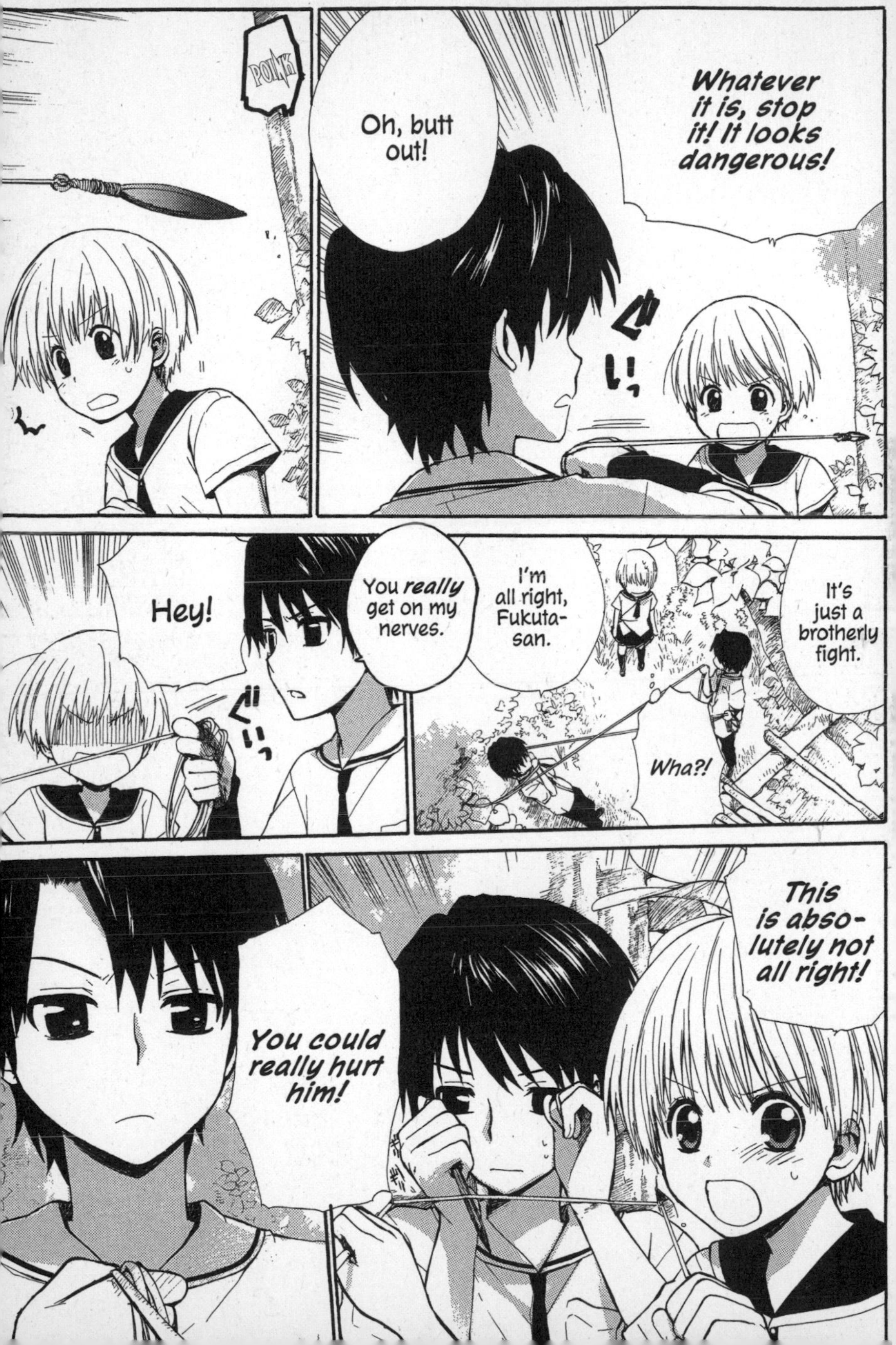
Whatever it is, stop it! It looks dangerous!
Oh, butt out!
POINK
It's just a brotherly fight.
I'm all right, Fukuta-san.
Wha?!
You *really* get on my nerves.
Hey!
This is absolutely not all right!
You could really hurt him!

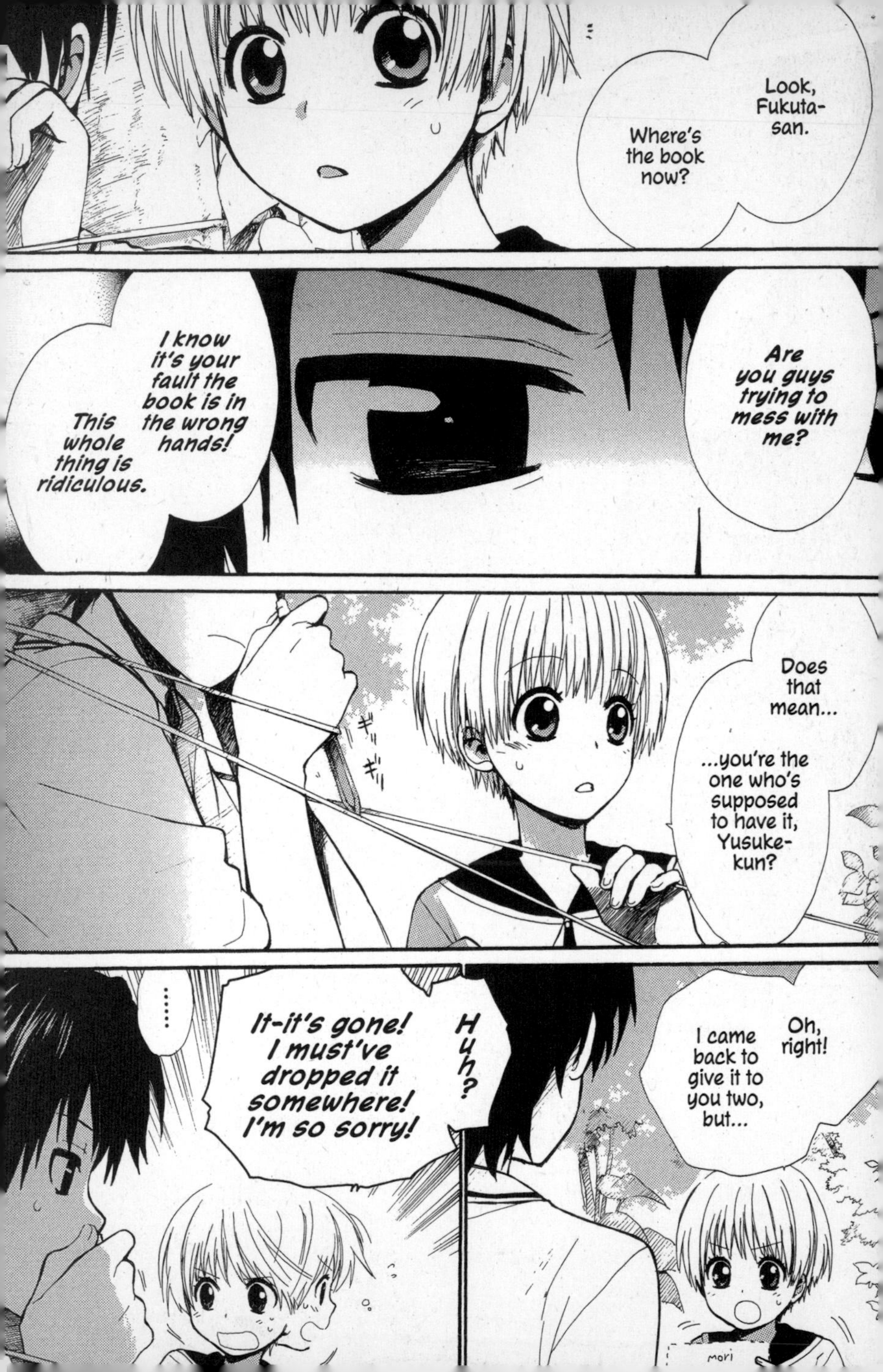
Look, Fukuta-san.
Where's the book now?
Are you guys trying to mess with me?
I know it's your fault the book is in the wrong hands!
This whole thing is ridiculous.
Does that mean...
...you're the one who's supposed to have it, Yusuke-kun?
Oh, right!
I came back to give it to you two, but...
Huh?
It-it's gone! I must've dropped it somewhere! I'm so sorry!
......
mori

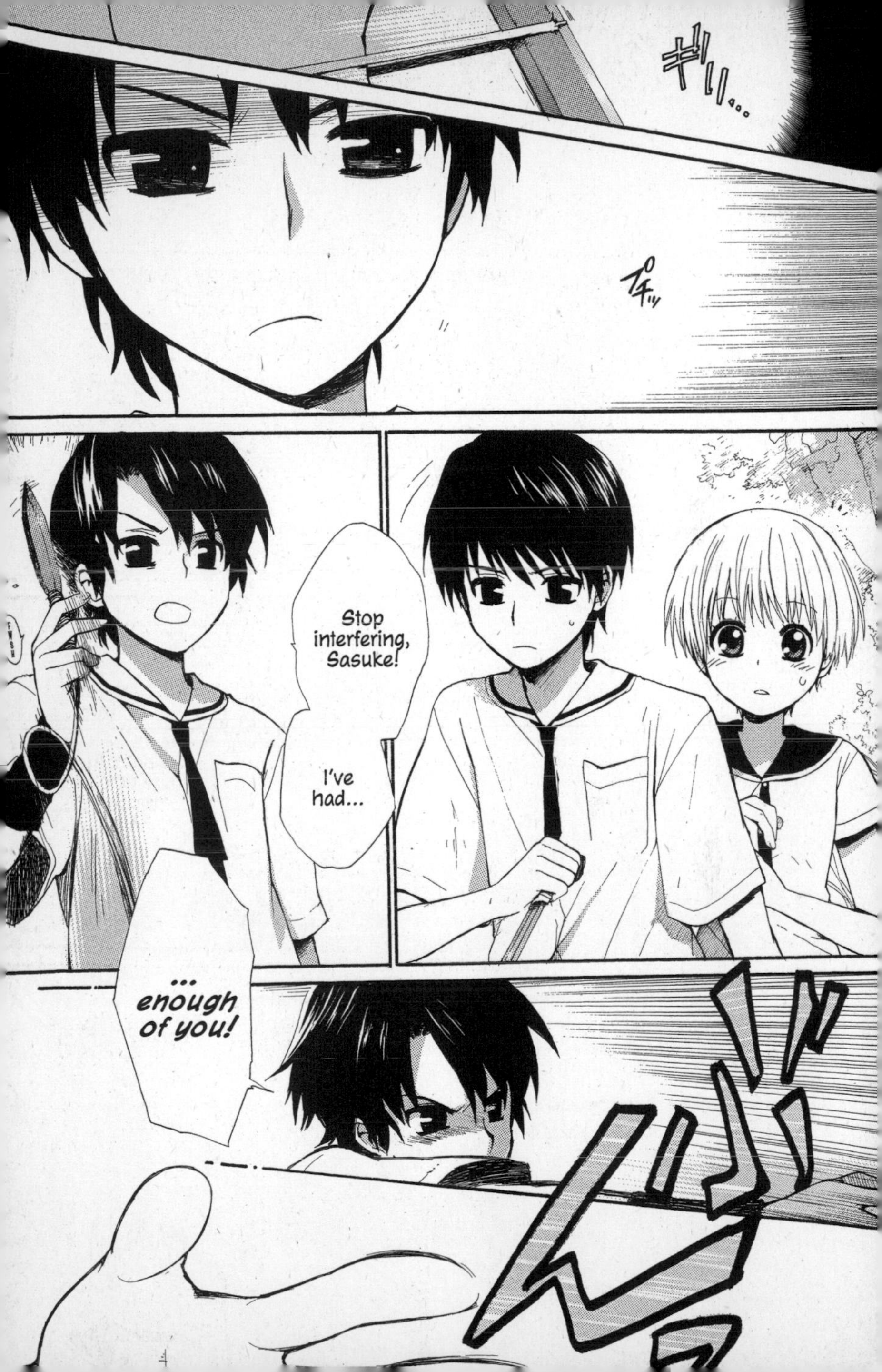
ギリ...
プチッ
FWSH
Stop interfering, Sasuke!
I've had...
...enough of you!

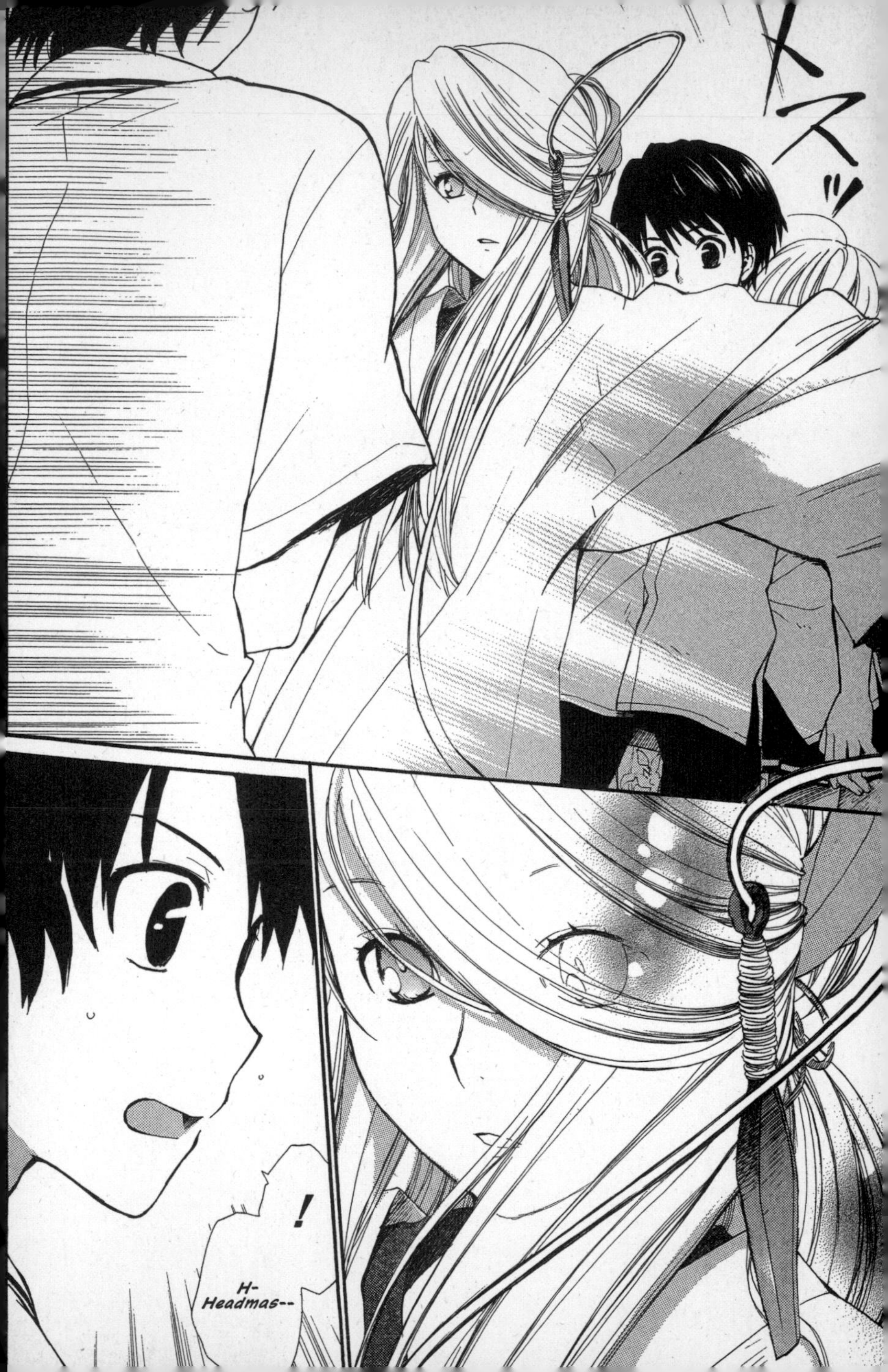
トスッ
!
H-
Headmas--

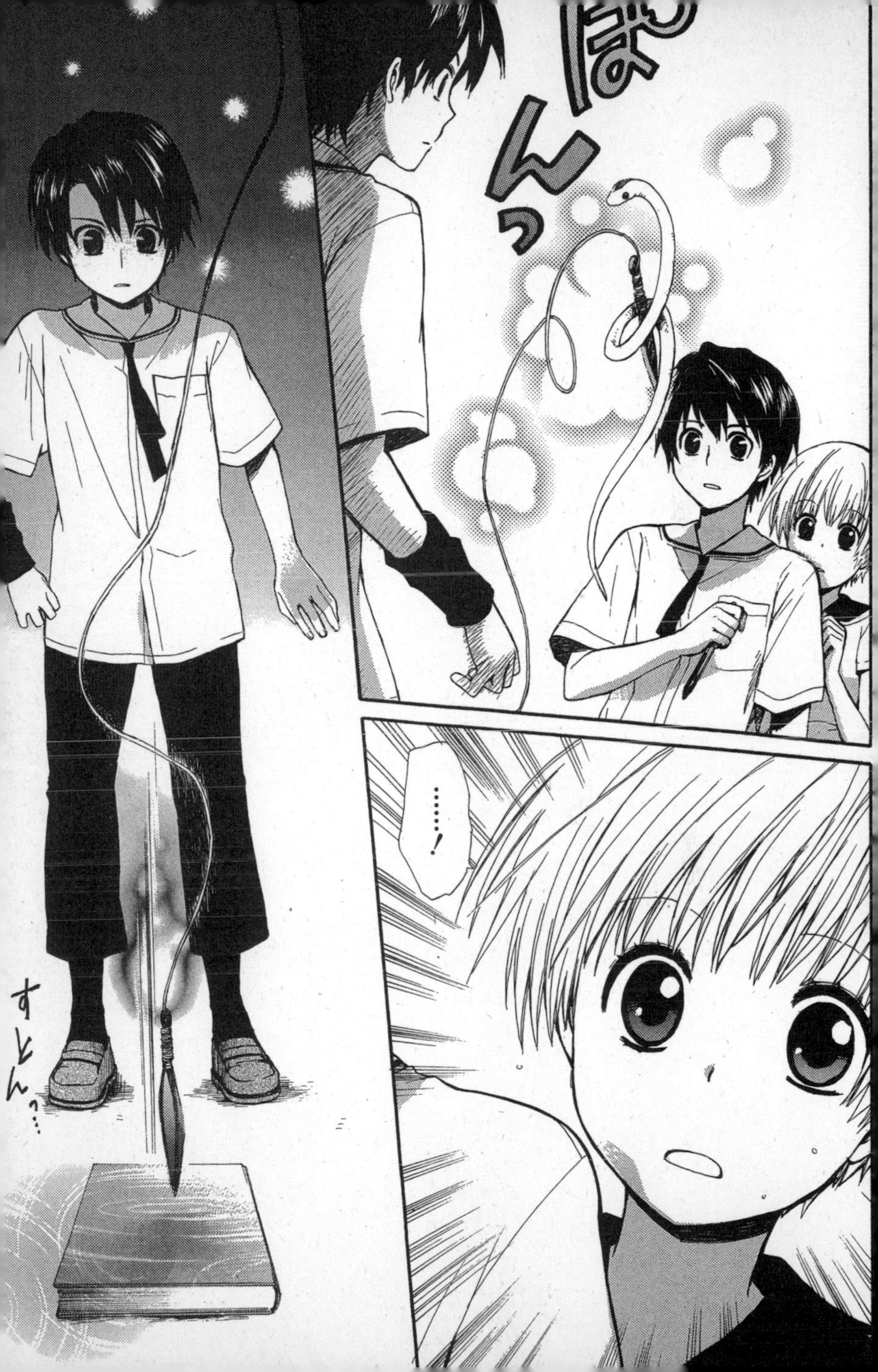
ぽんっ
……！
すとんっ…

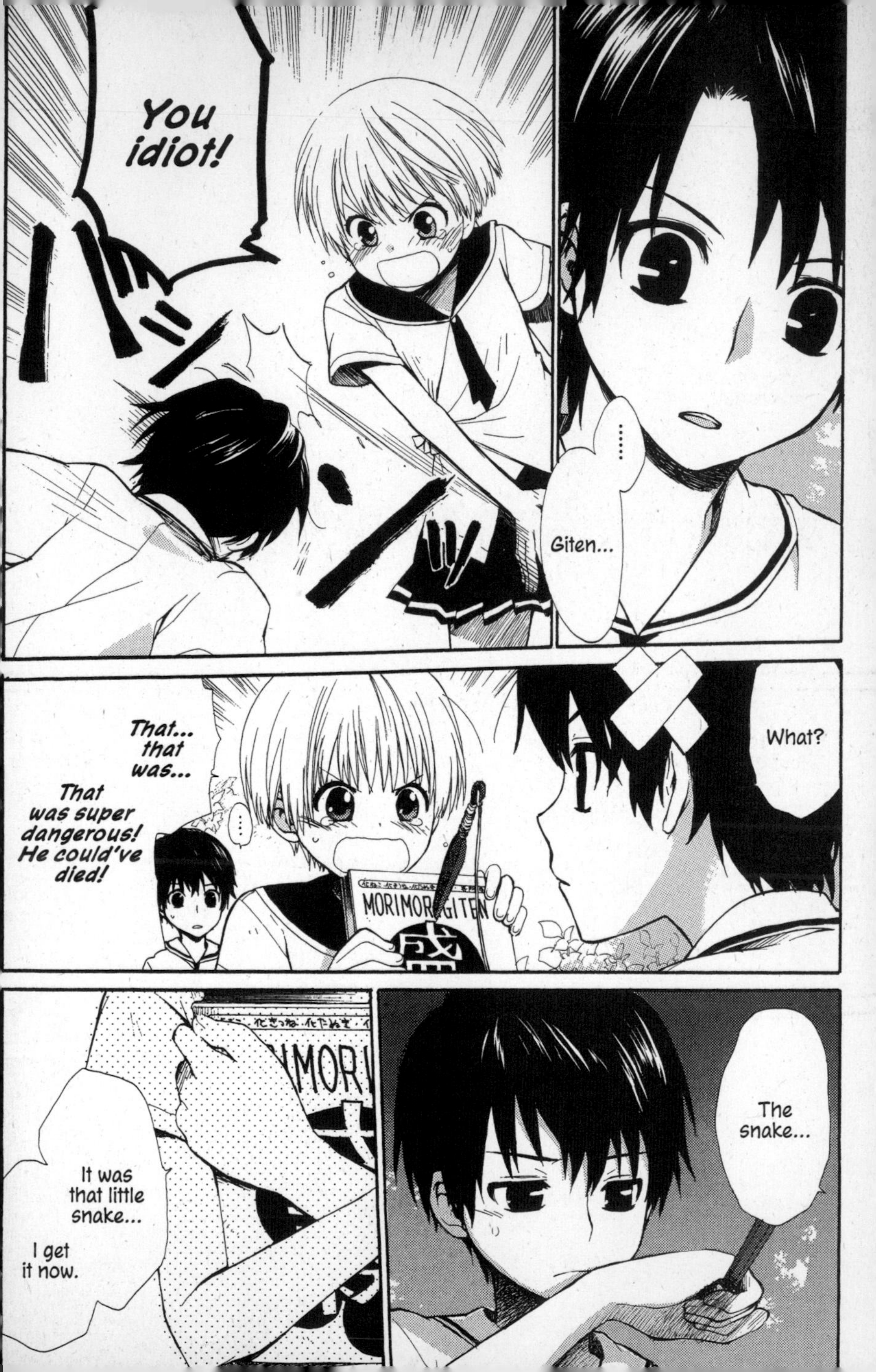
......
Giten...
You idiot!
What?
That... that was...
That was super dangerous! He could've died!
...
The snake...
It was that little snake...
I get it now.

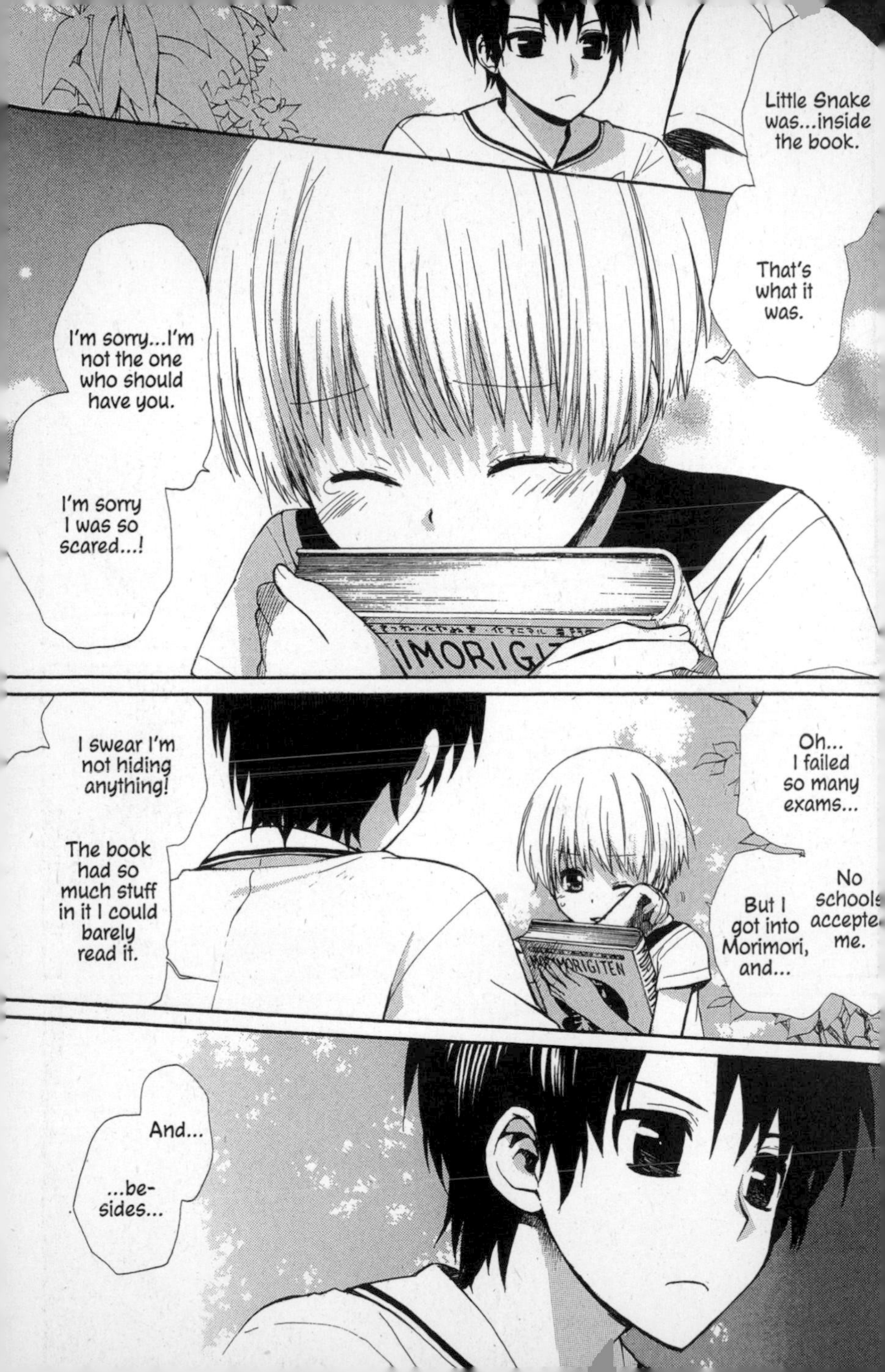

Little Snake was...inside the book.
That's what it was.
I'm sorry...I'm not the one who should have you.
I'm sorry I was so scared...!
Oh... I failed so many exams...
No schools accepte me.
But I got into Morimori, and...
I swear I'm not hiding anything!
The book had so much stuff in it I could barely read it.
And...
...be-sides...

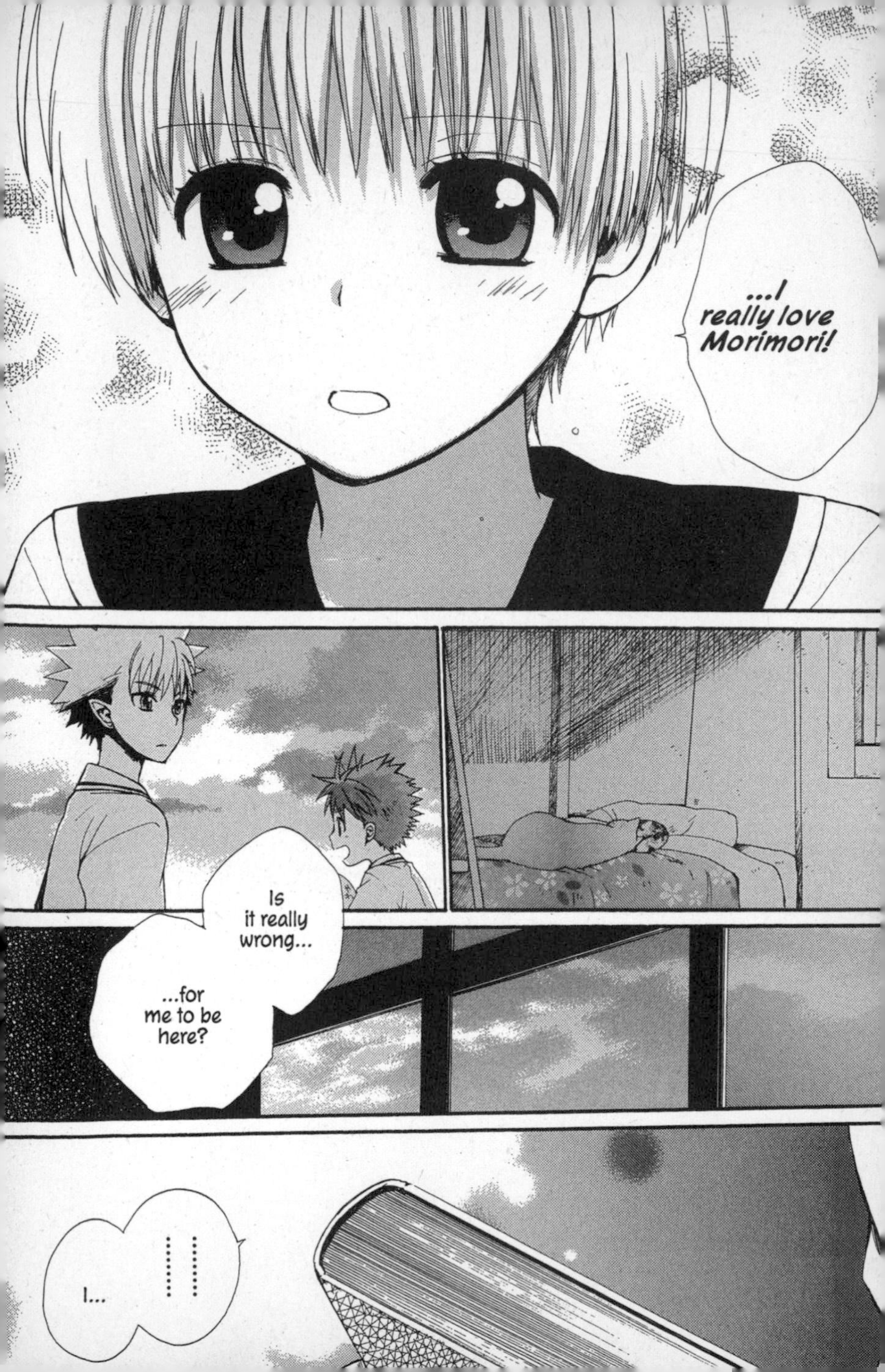
...I really love Morimori!
Is it really wrong...
...for me to be here?
......
I...

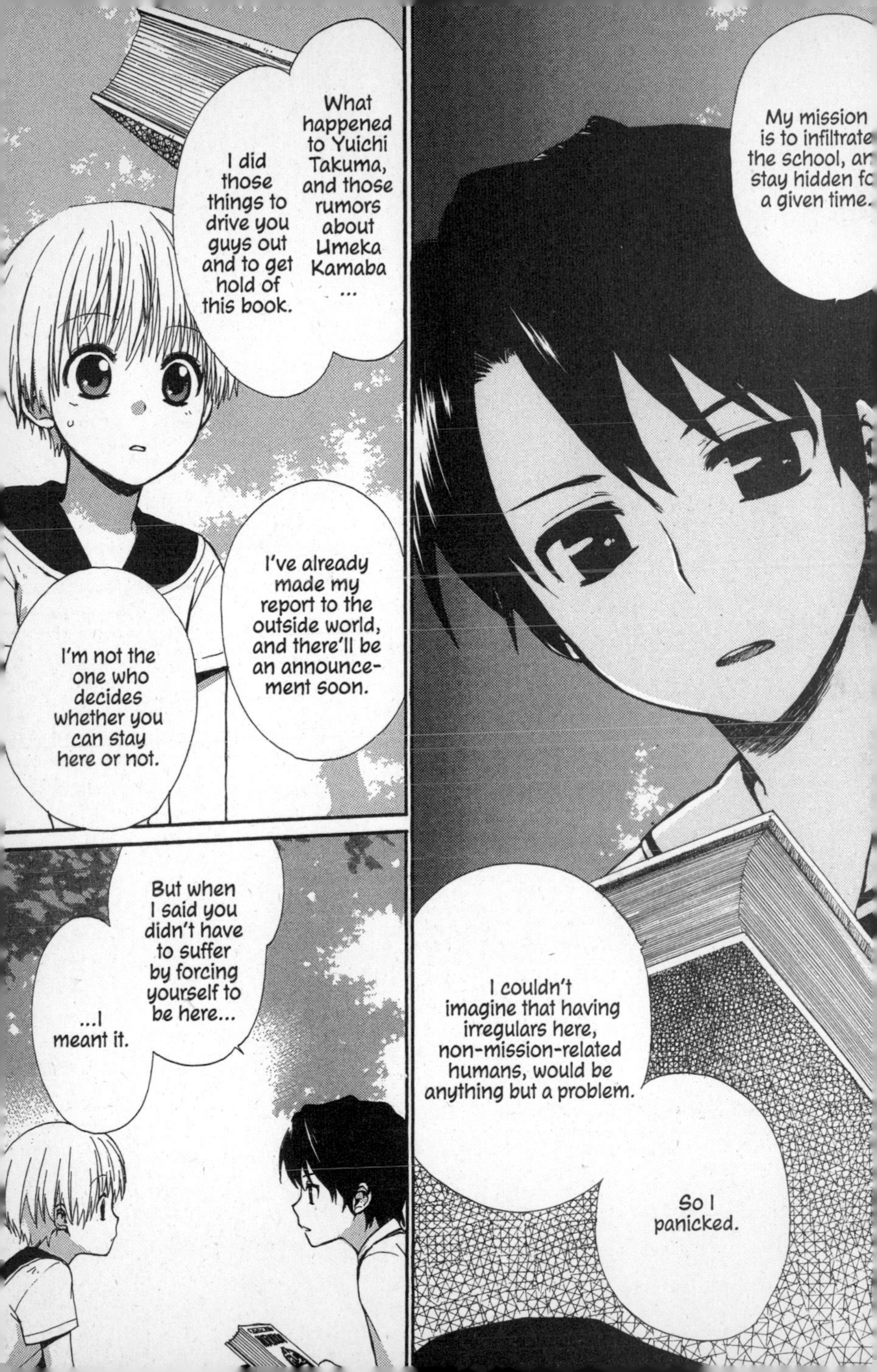
My mission is to infiltrate the school, ar stay hidden fc a given time.
I couldn't imagine that having irregulars here, non-mission-related humans, would be anything but a problem.
So I panicked.
What happened to Yuichi Takuma, and those rumors about Umeka Kamaba ...
I did those things to drive you guys out and to get hold of this book.
I've already made my report to the outside world, and there'll be an announcement soon.
I'm not the one who decides whether you can stay here or not.
But when I said you didn't have to suffer by forcing yourself to be here...
...I meant it.

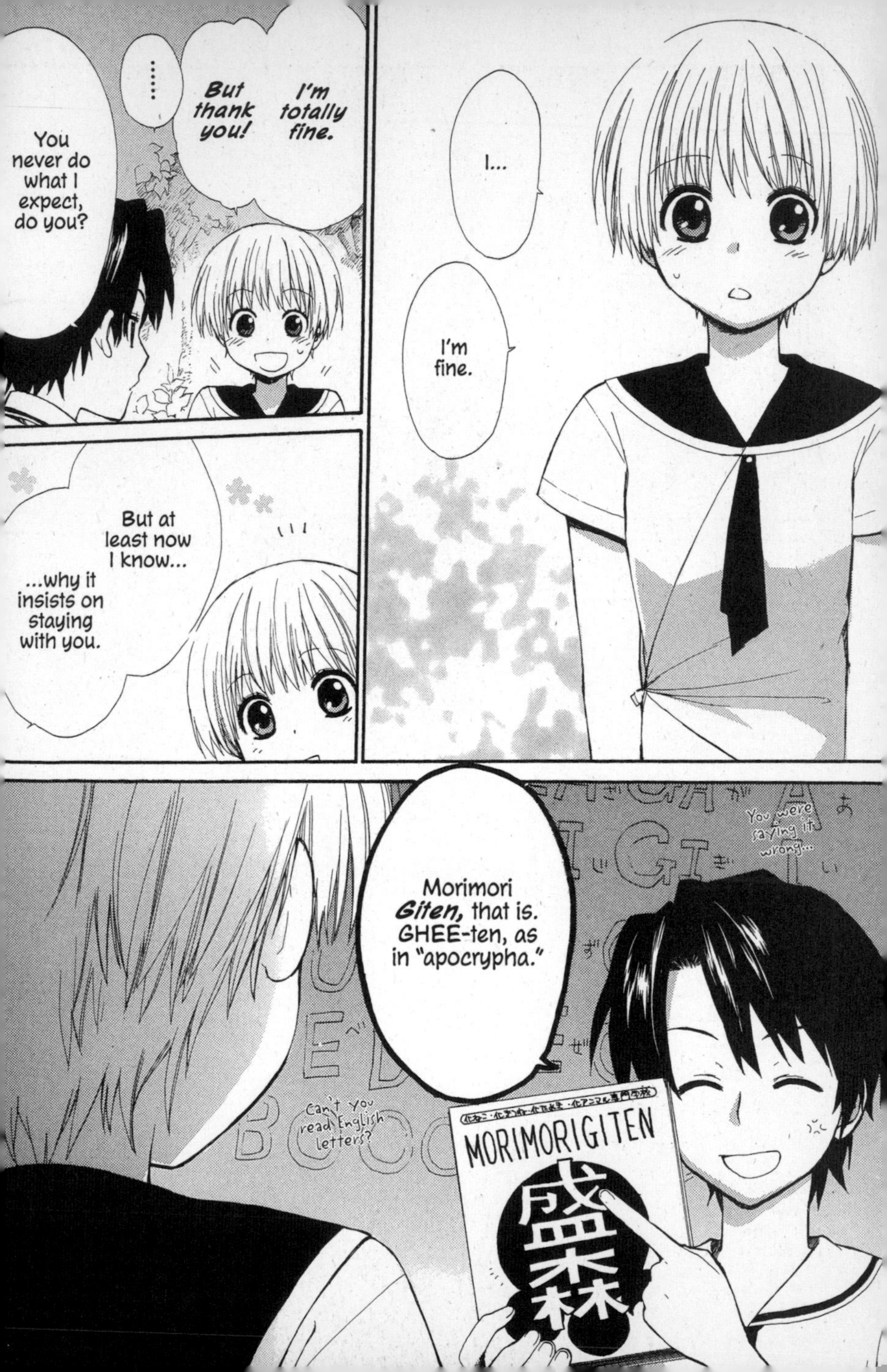
I...
I'm fine.
I'm totally fine.
But thank you!
......
You never do what I expect, do you?
But at least now I know...
...why it insists on staying with you.
You were saying it wrong...
Morimori Giten, that is. GHEE-ten, as in "apocrypha."
MORIMORIGITEN
盛林
Can't you read English letters?

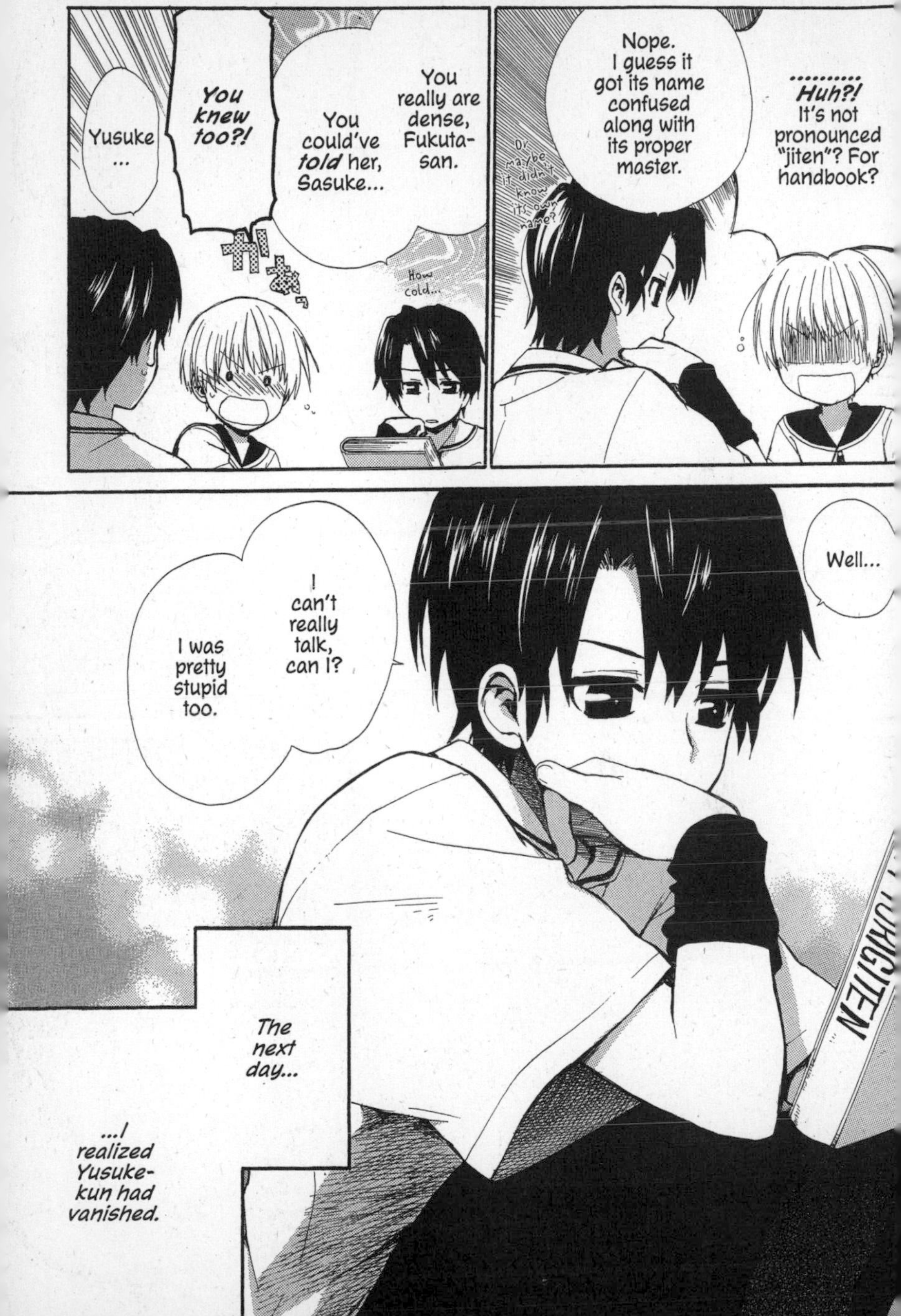
.... Huh?! It's not pronounced "jiten"? For handbook?
Nope. I guess it got its name confused along with its proper master.
Or maybe it didn't know its own name?
You really are dense, Fukuta-san.
You could've told her, Sasuke...
How cold...
You knew too?!
Yusuke ...
Well...
I can't really talk, can I?
I was pretty stupid too.
The next day...
...I realized Yusuke-kun had vanished.

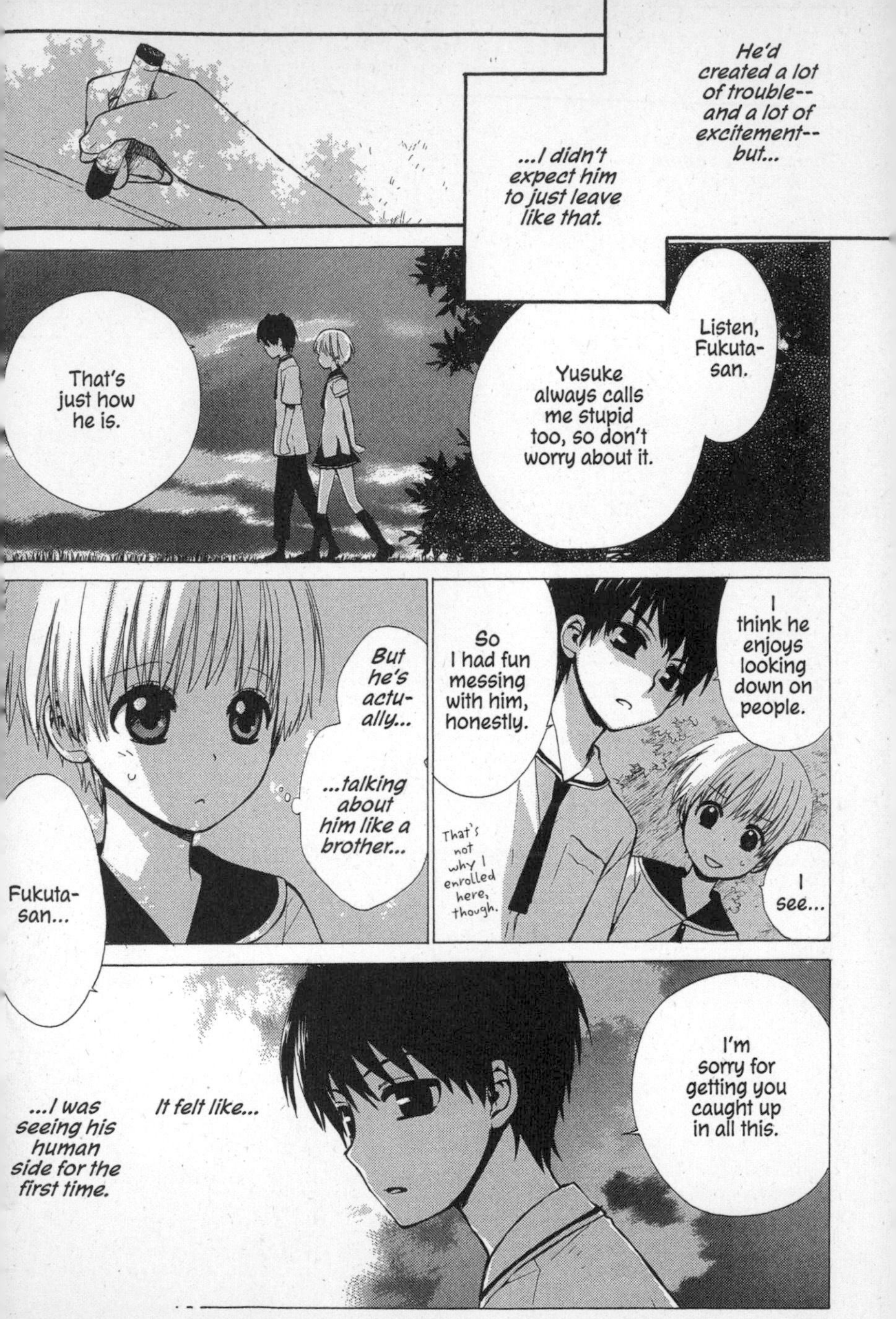
He'd created a lot of trouble-- and a lot of excitement-- but...
...I didn't expect him to just leave like that.
Listen, Fukuta-san.
Yusuke always calls me stupid too, so don't worry about it.
That's just how he is.
I think he enjoys looking down on people.
So I had fun messing with him, honestly.
I see...
That's not why I enrolled here, though.
But he's actu-ally...
...talking about him like a brother...
Fukuta-san...
I'm sorry for getting you caught up in all this.
It felt like...
...I was seeing his human side for the first time.

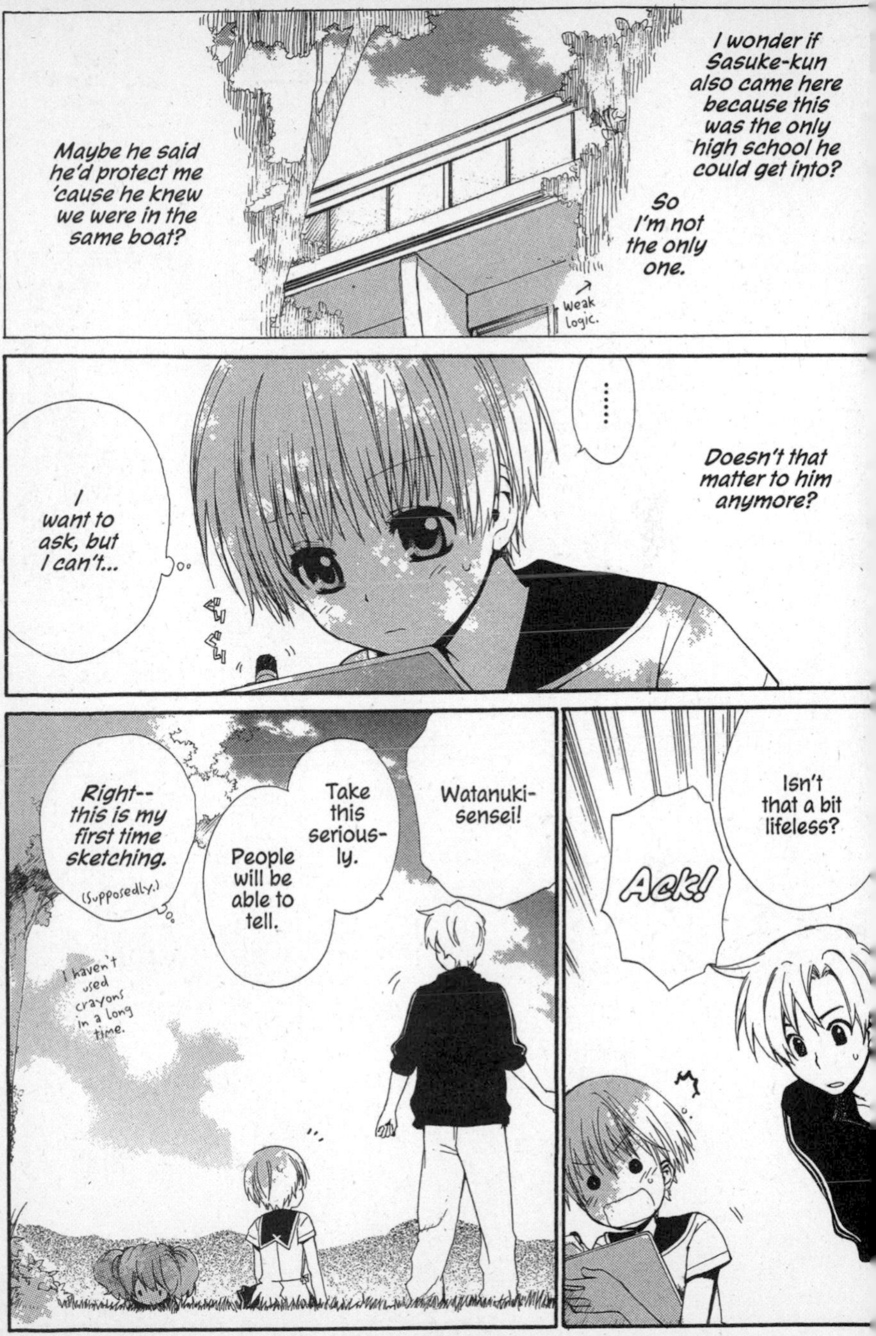
I wonder if Sasuke-kun also came here because this was the only high school he could get into?
So I'm not the only one.
Weak logic.
Maybe he said he'd protect me 'cause he knew we were in the same boat?
Doesn't that matter to him anymore?
......
I want to ask, but I can't...
Isn't that a bit lifeless?
Ack!
Watanuki-sensei!
Take this serious-ly.
People will be able to tell.
Right-- this is my first time sketching.
(Supposedly.)
I haven't used crayons in a long time.

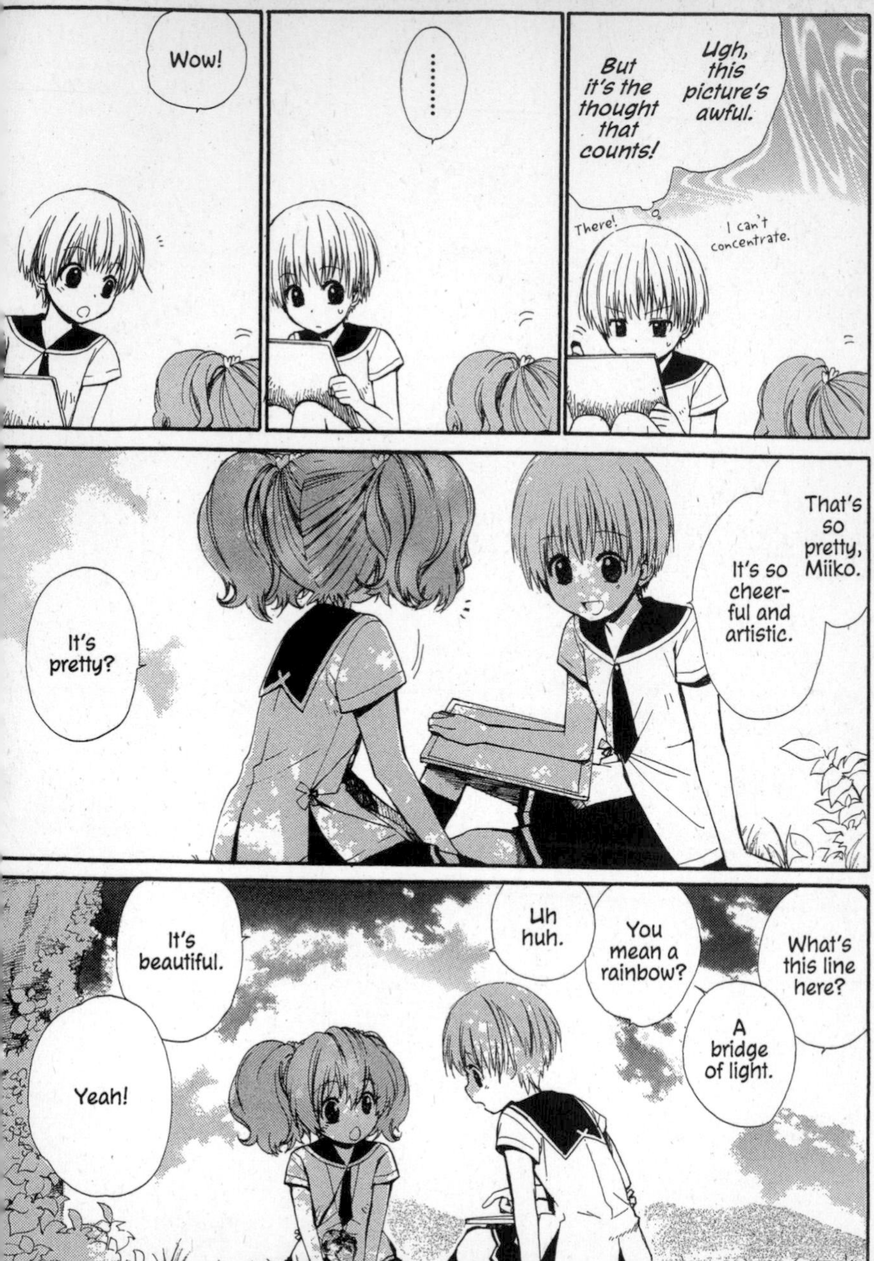
Ugh, this picture's awful.
But it's the thought that counts!
I can't concentrate.
There!
......
Wow!
That's so pretty, Miiko.
It's so cheerful and artistic.
It's pretty?
What's this line here?
A bridge of light.
You mean a rainbow?
Uh huh.
It's beautiful.
Yeah!

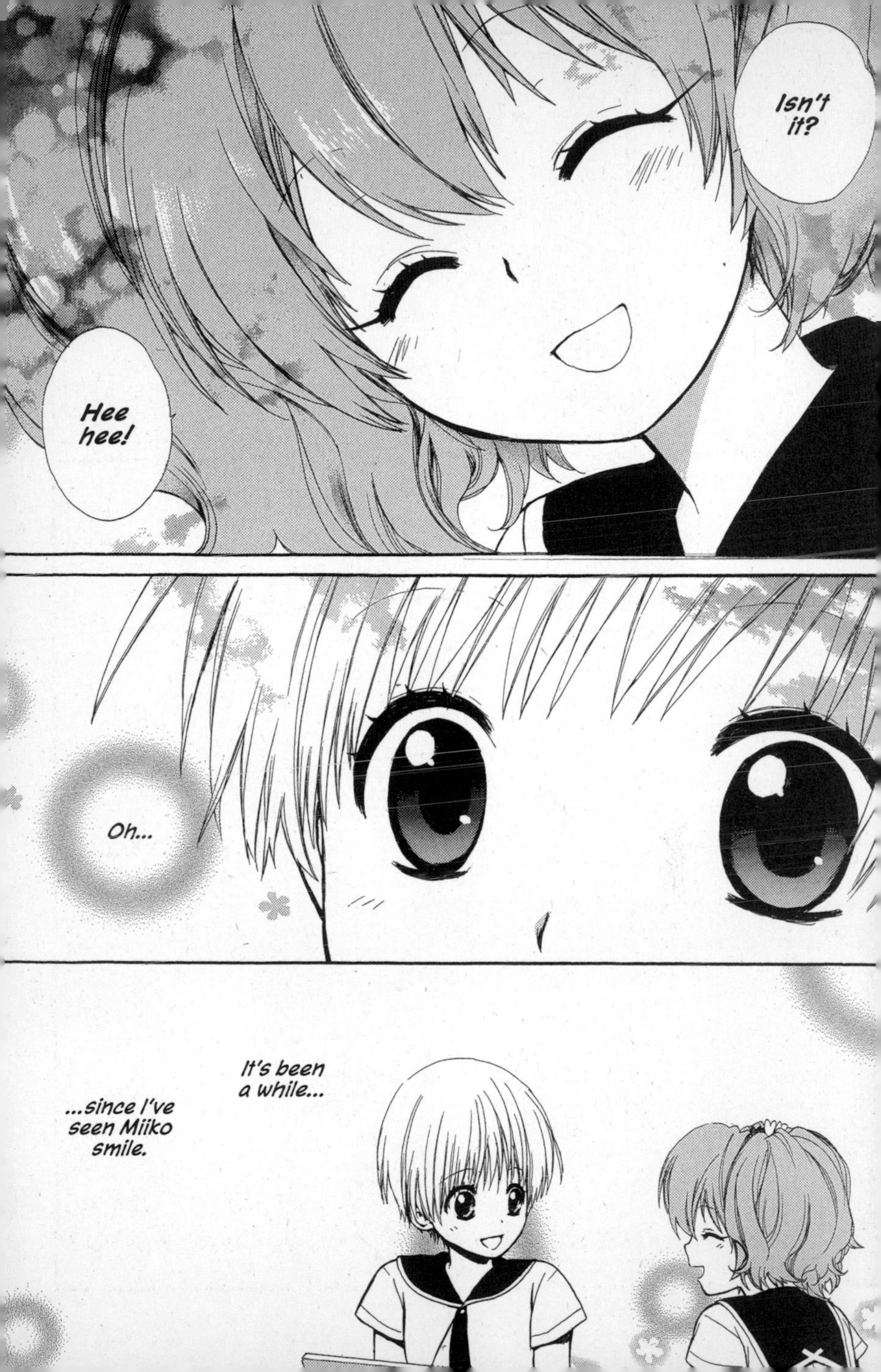
Isn't it?
Hee hee!
Oh...
It's been a while...
...since I've seen Miiko smile.

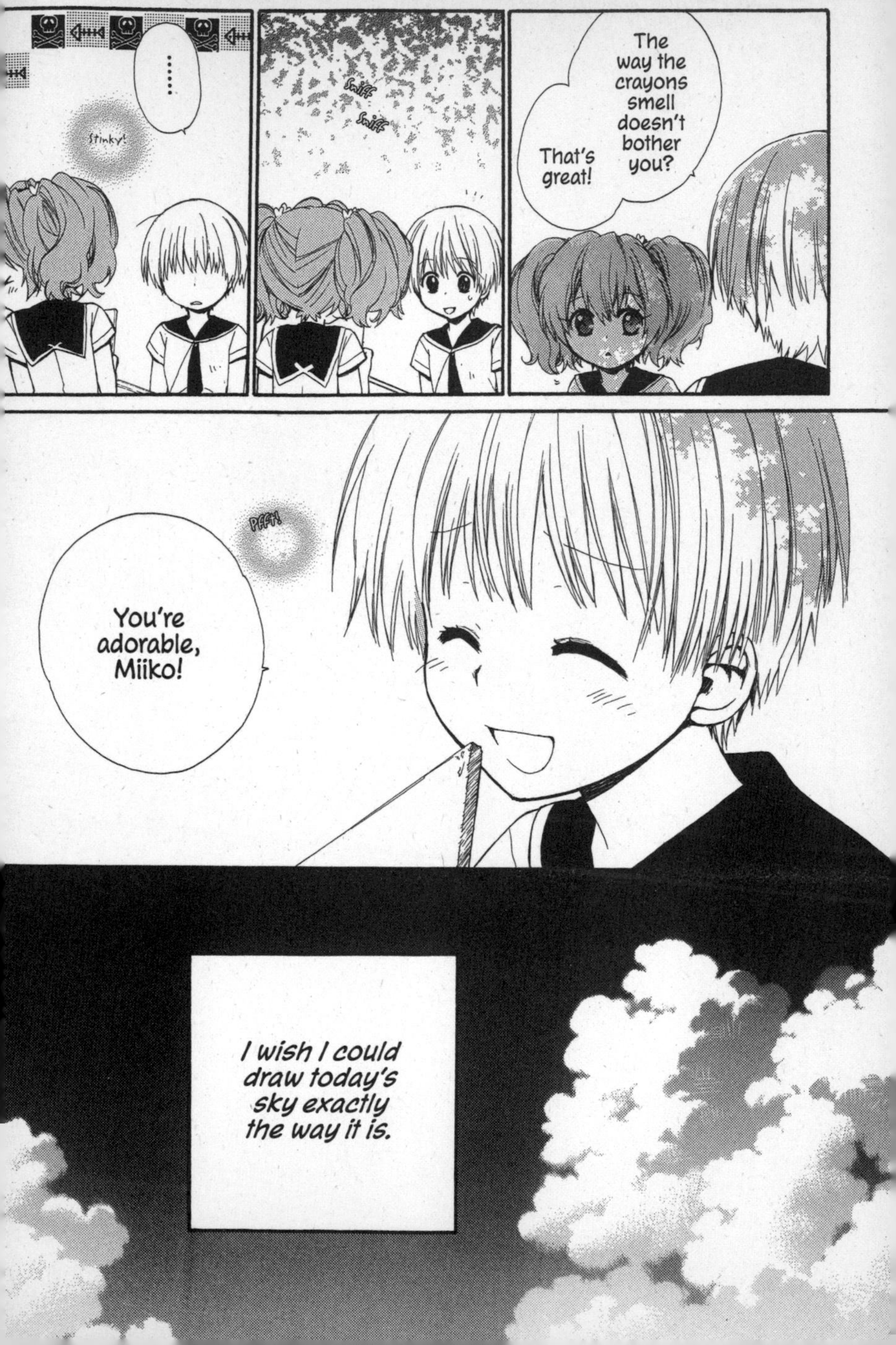
The way the crayons smell doesn't bother you?
That's great!
Sniff
Sniff
......
Stinky!
Pfft!
You're adorable, Miiko!
I wish I could draw today's sky exactly the way it is.

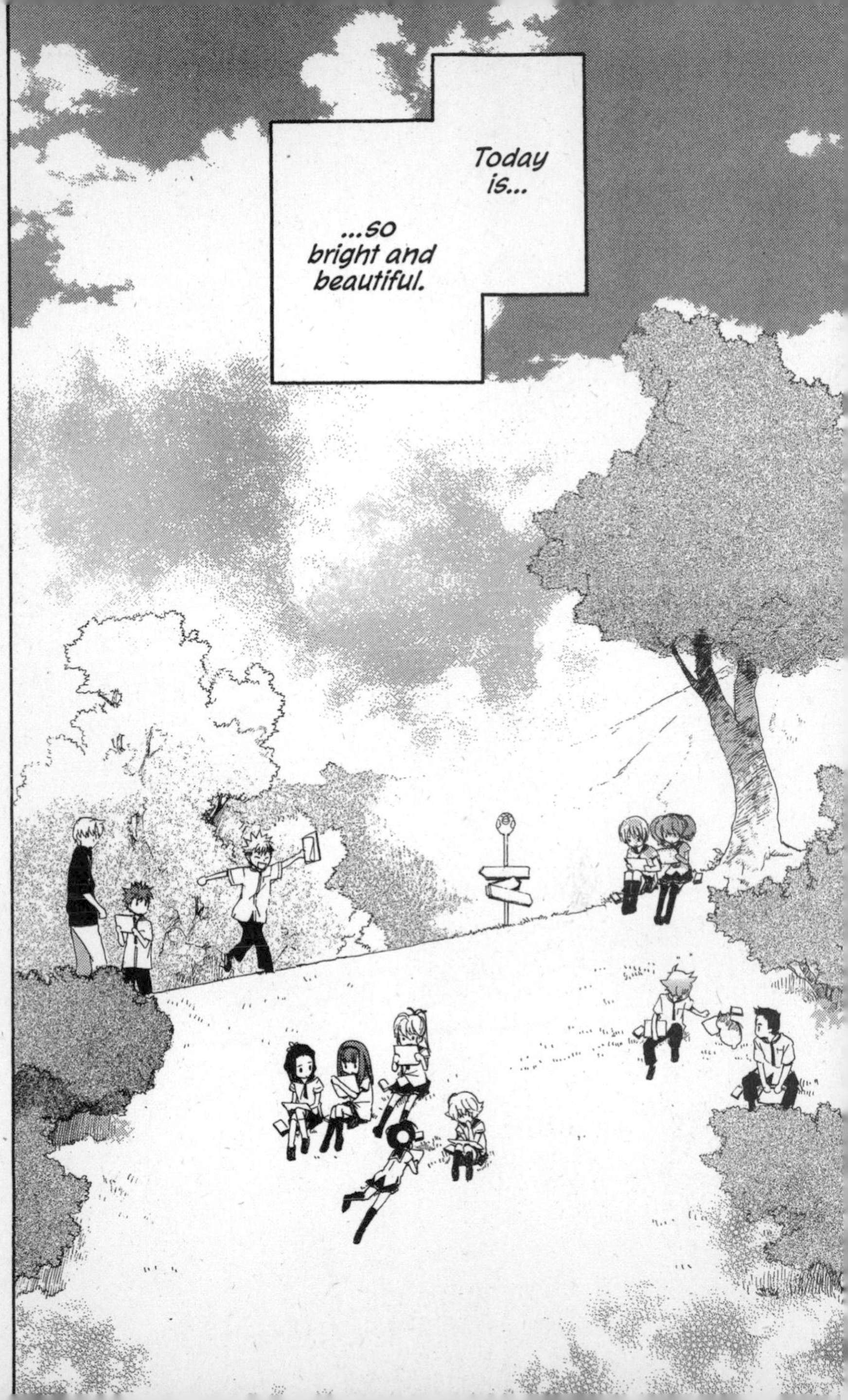
Today is...
...so bright and beautiful.

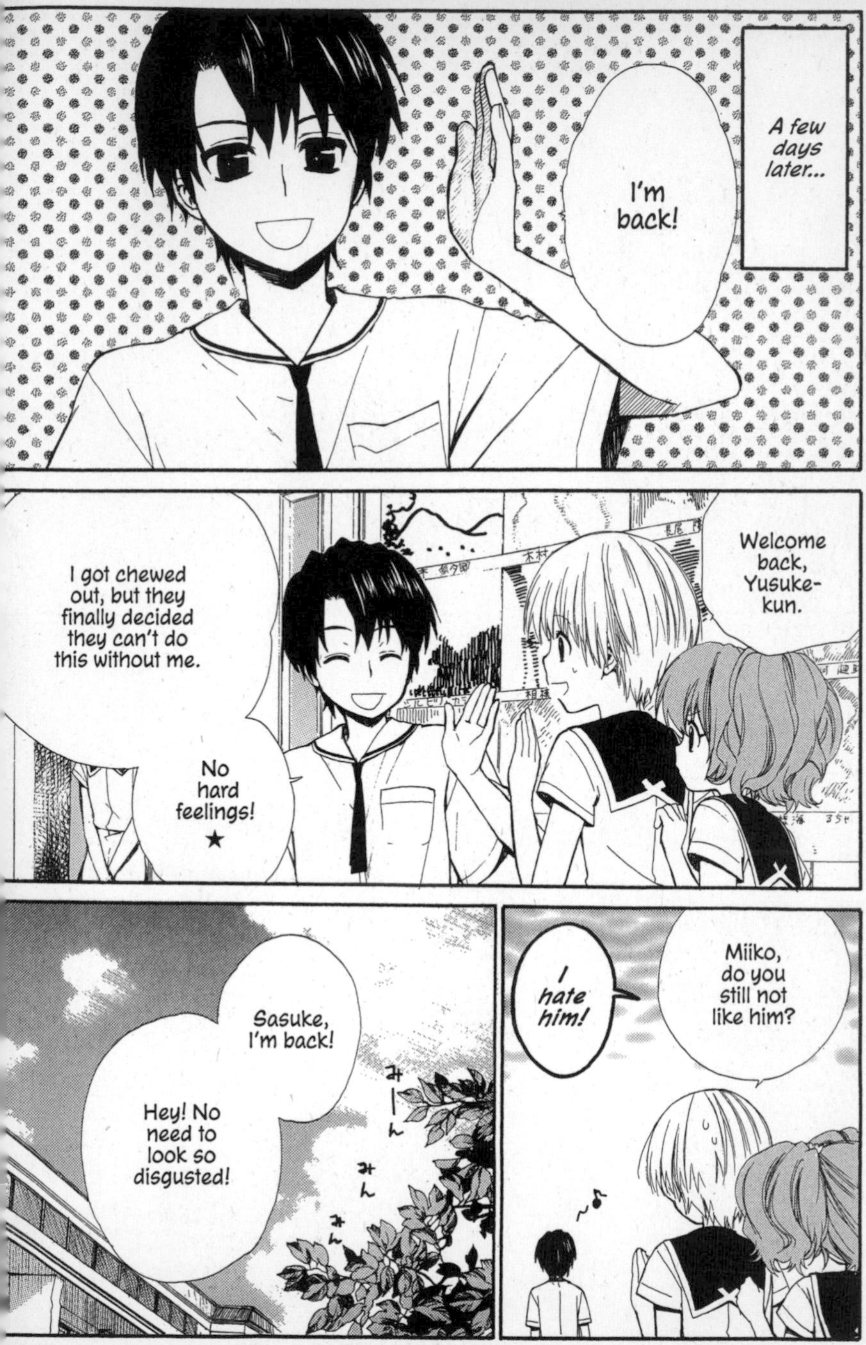
A few days later...
I'm back!
Welcome back, Yusuke-kun.
I got chewed out, but they finally decided they can't do this without me.
No hard feelings! ★
Miiko, do you still not like him?
I hate him!
Sasuke, I'm back!
Hey! No need to look so disgusted!
みーん
みん
みん

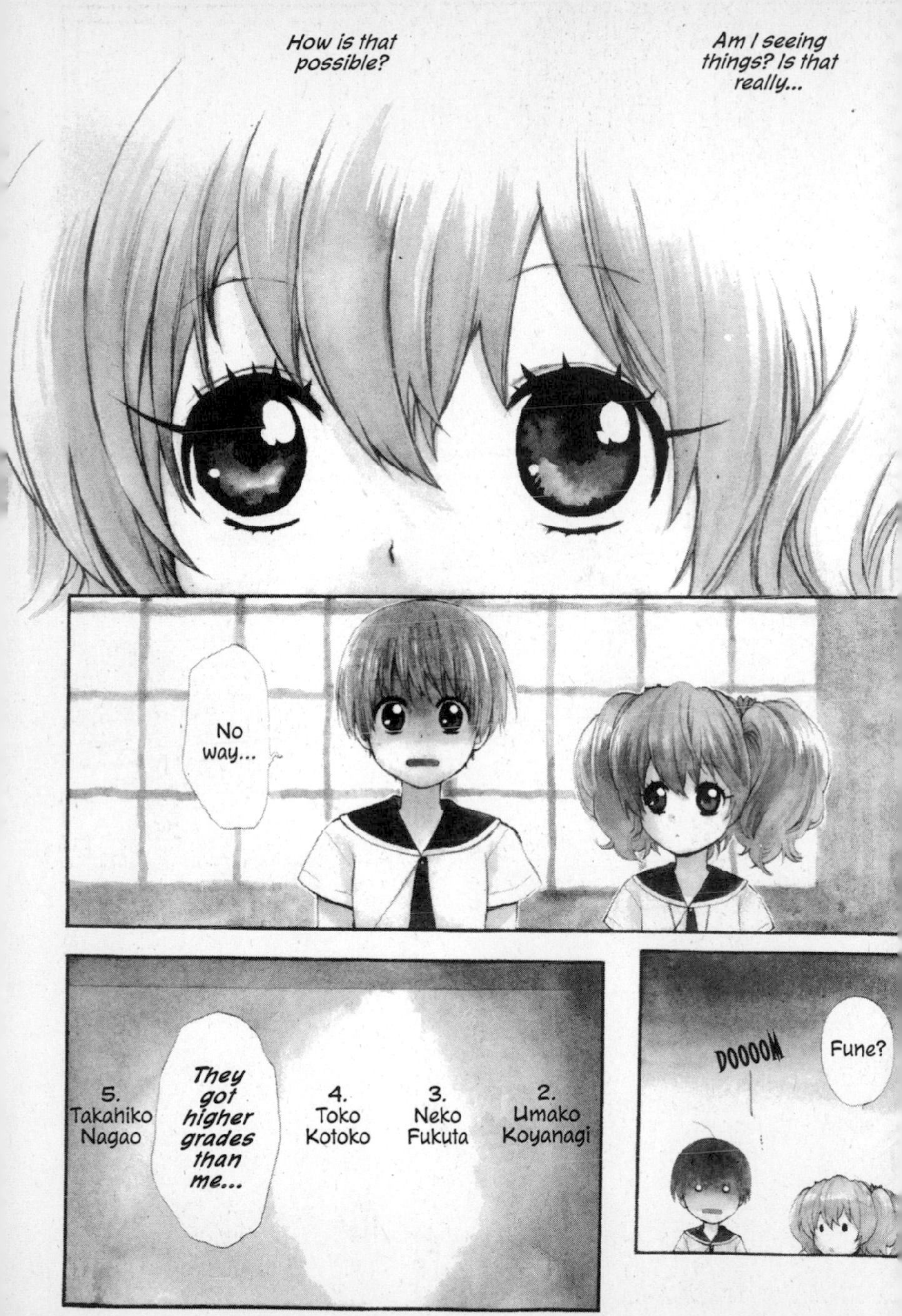
Am I seeing things? Is that really...
How is that possible?
No way...
Fune?
DOOOOM
2. Umako Koyanagi
3. Neko Fukuta
4. Toko Kotoko
They got higher grades than me...
5. Takahiko Nagao

Report.23 The Eternal Name

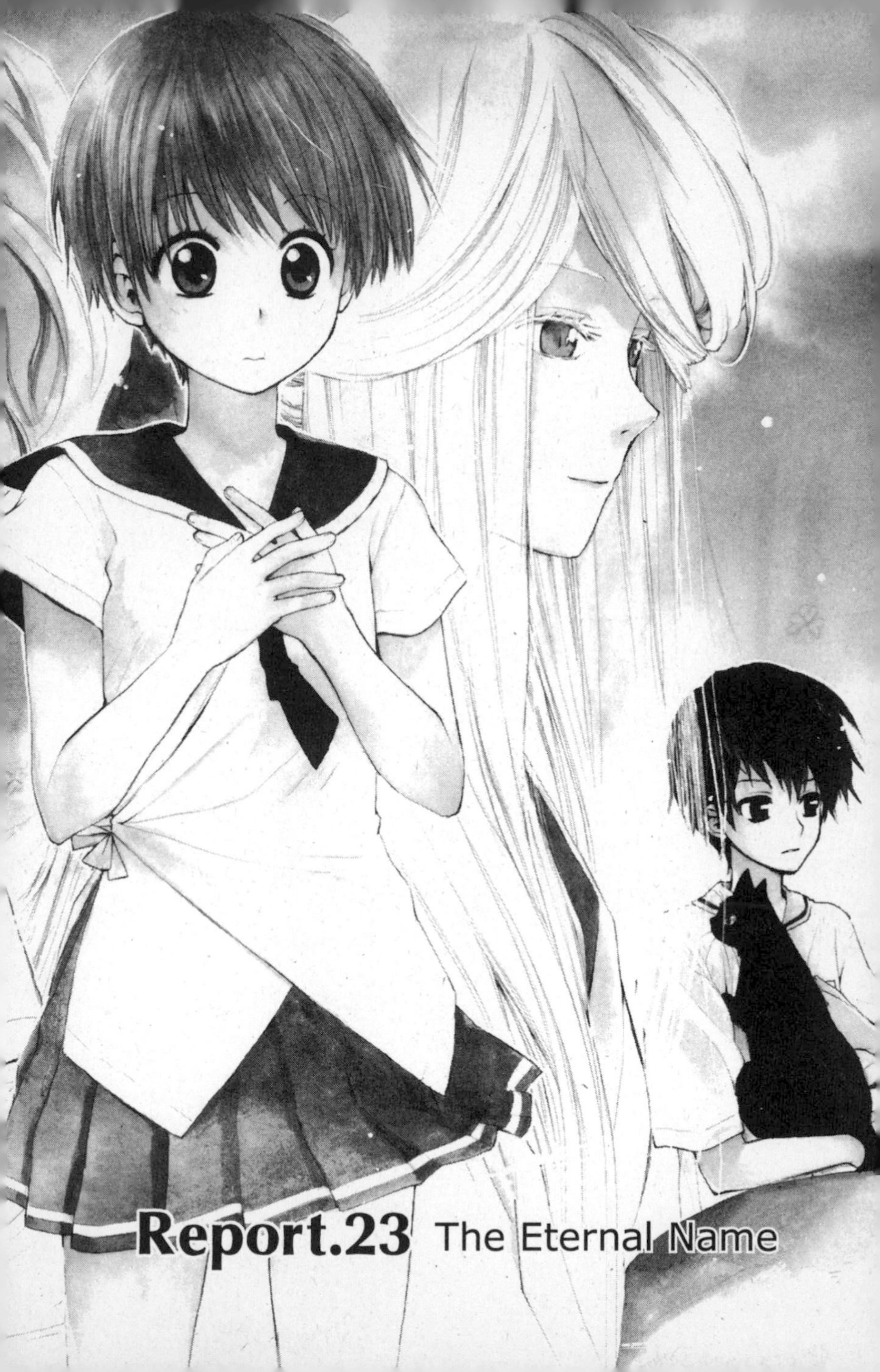

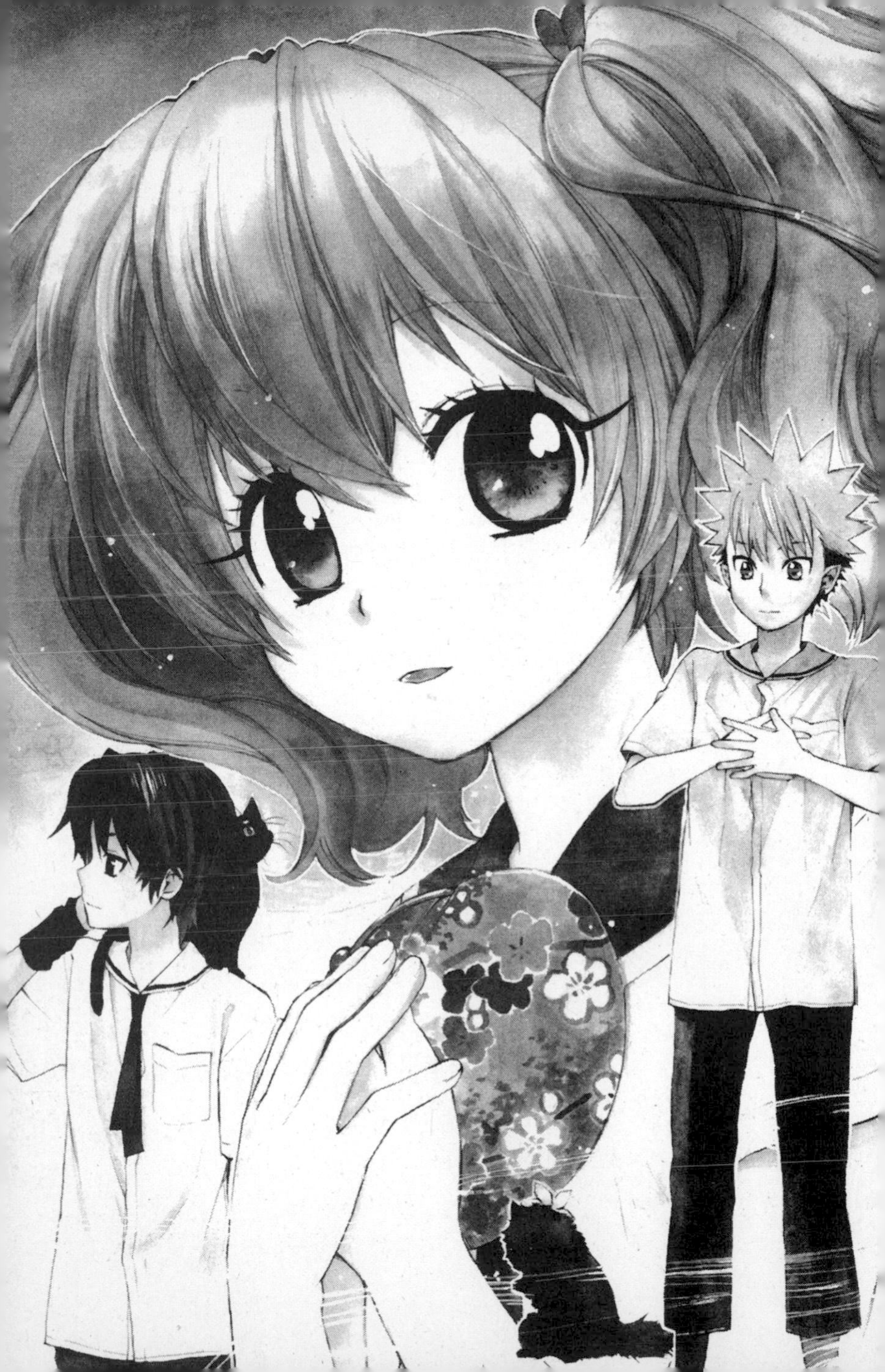

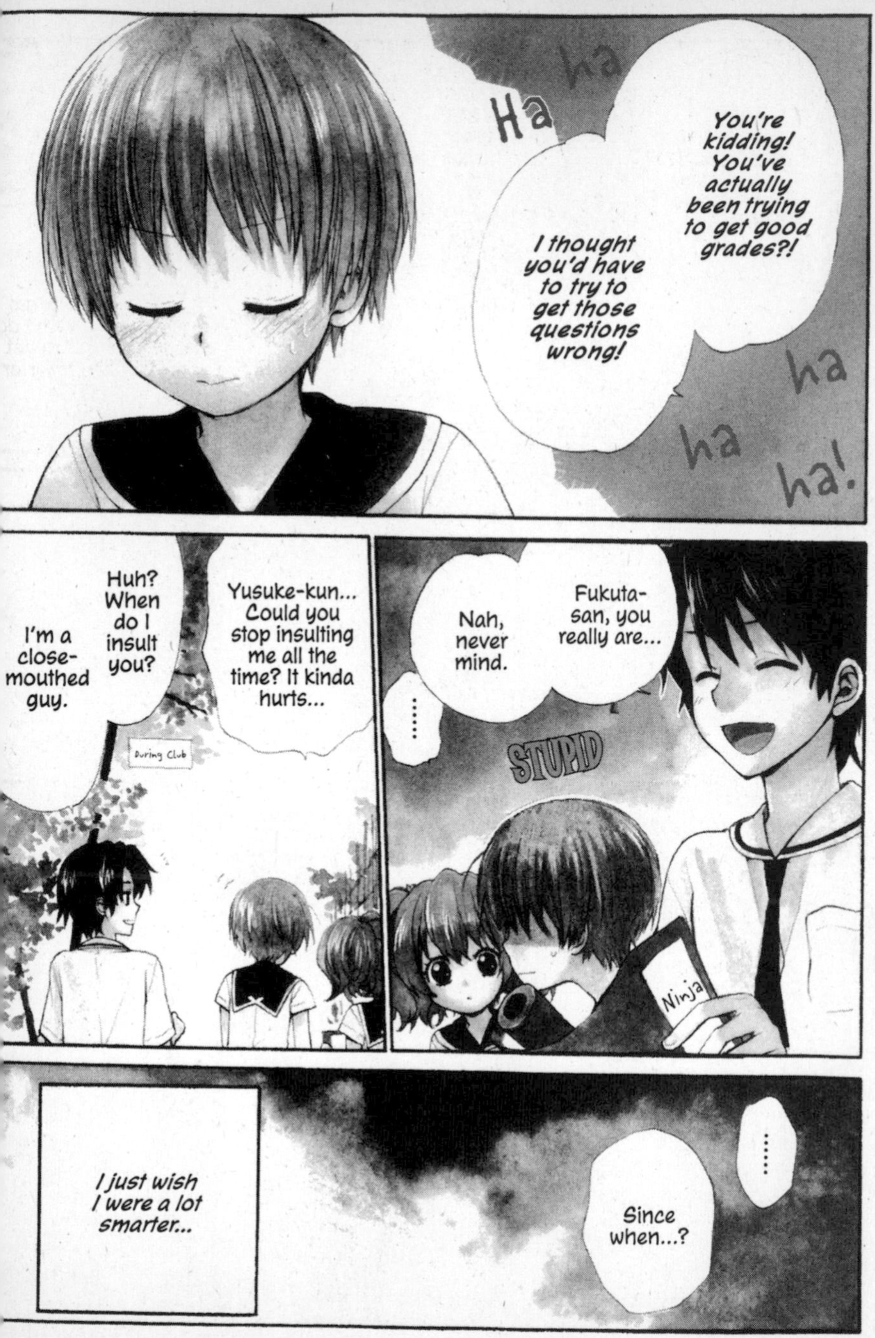
Ha ha
You're kidding! You've actually been trying to get good grades?!
I thought you'd have to try to get those questions wrong!
ha ha ha!
Fukuta-san, you really are...
Nah, never mind.
......
STUPID
Ninja
Yusuke-kun... Could you stop insulting me all the time? It kinda hurts...
Huh? When do I insult you?
I'm a close-mouthed guy.
During Club
......
Since when...?
I just wish I were a lot smarter...

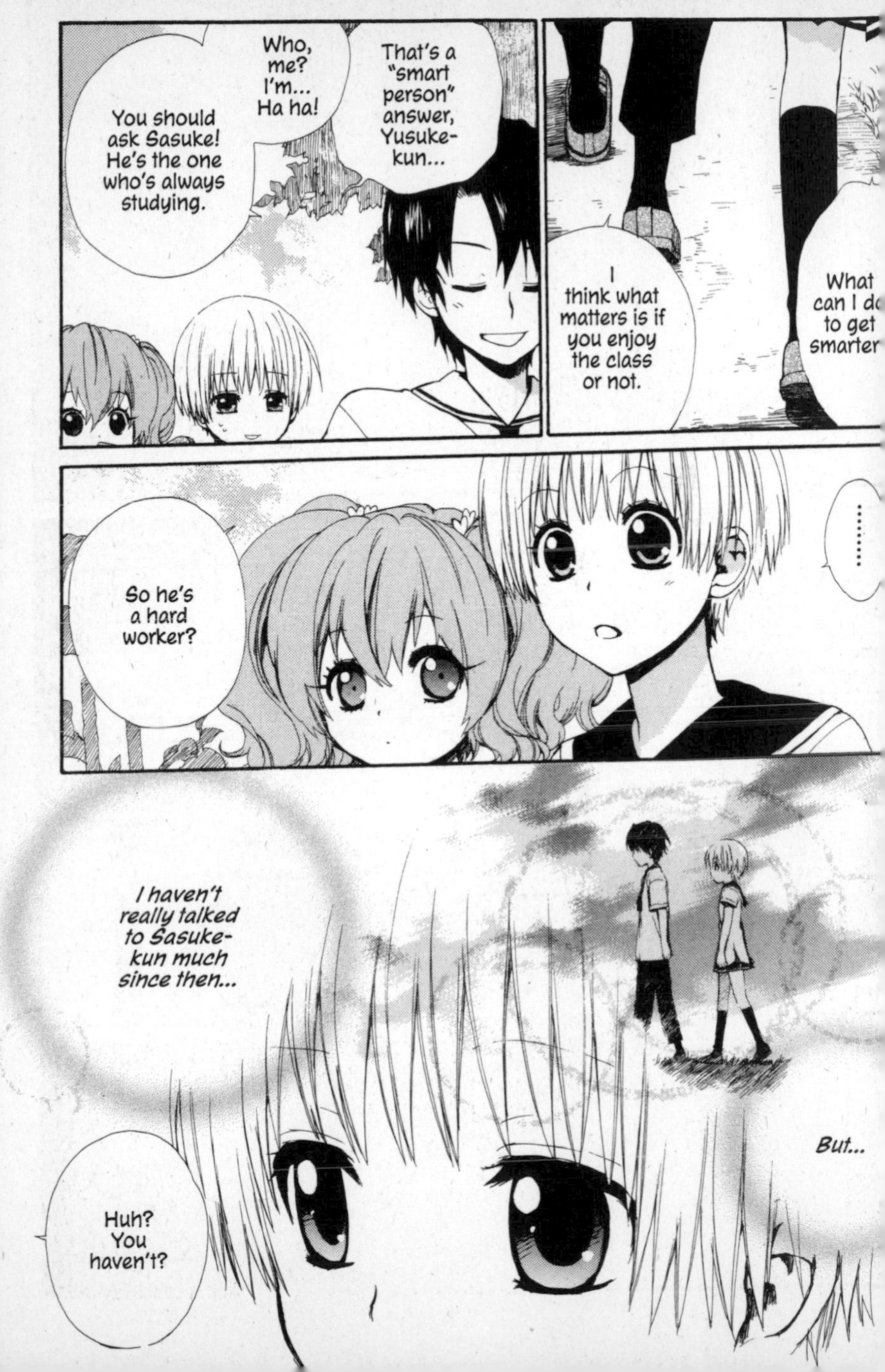
What can I d
to get smarter
I think what matters is if you enjoy the class or not.
That's a "smart person" answer, Yusuke-kun...
Who, me? I'm... Ha ha!
You should ask Sasuke! He's the one who's always studying.
......
So he's a hard worker?
But...
I haven't really talked to Sasuke-kun much since then...
Huh? You haven't?

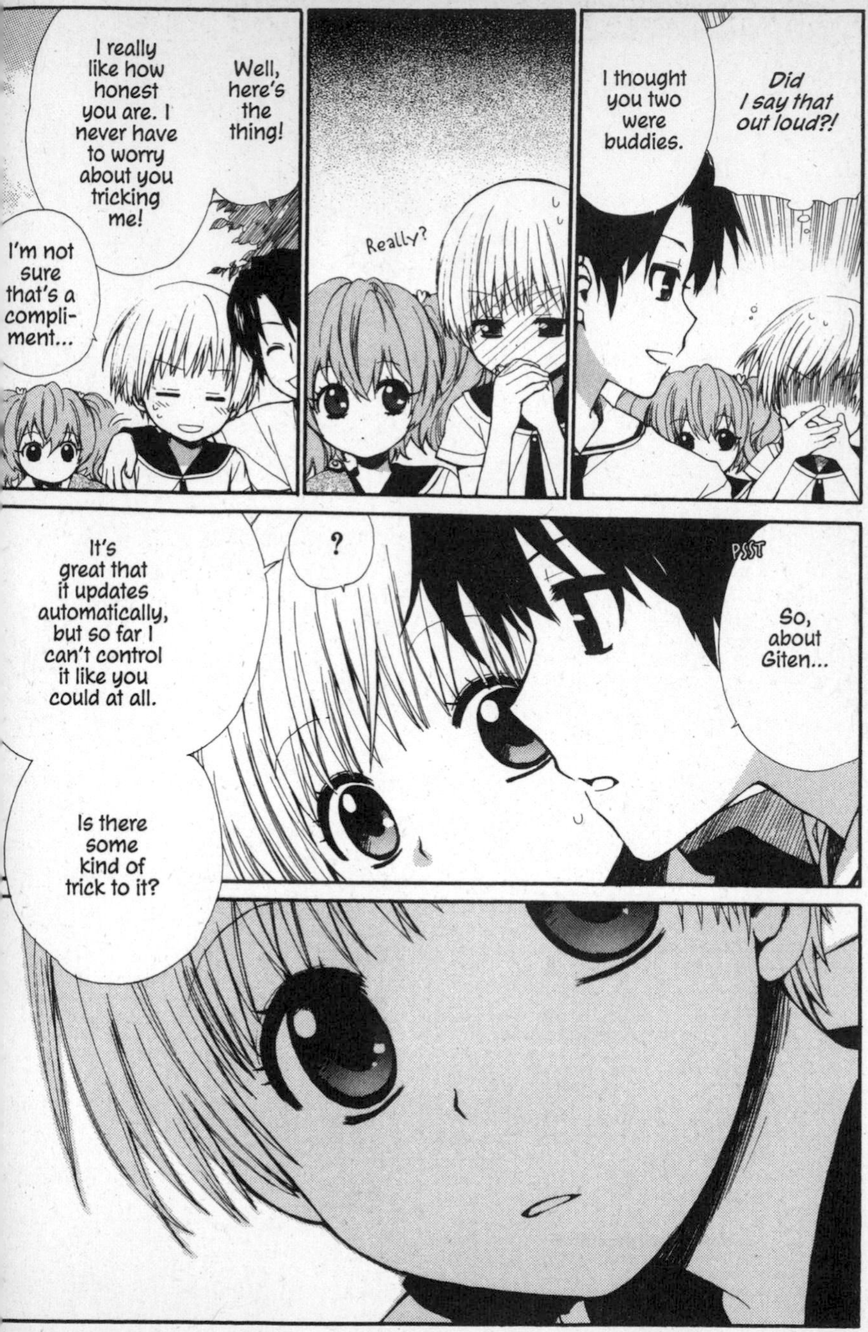
Did I say that out loud?!
I thought you two were buddies.
Really?
Well, here's the thing!
I really like how honest you are. I never have to worry about you tricking me!
I'm not sure that's a compliment...
PSST
So, about Giten...
?
It's great that it updates automatically, but so far I can't control it like you could at all.
Is there some kind of trick to it?

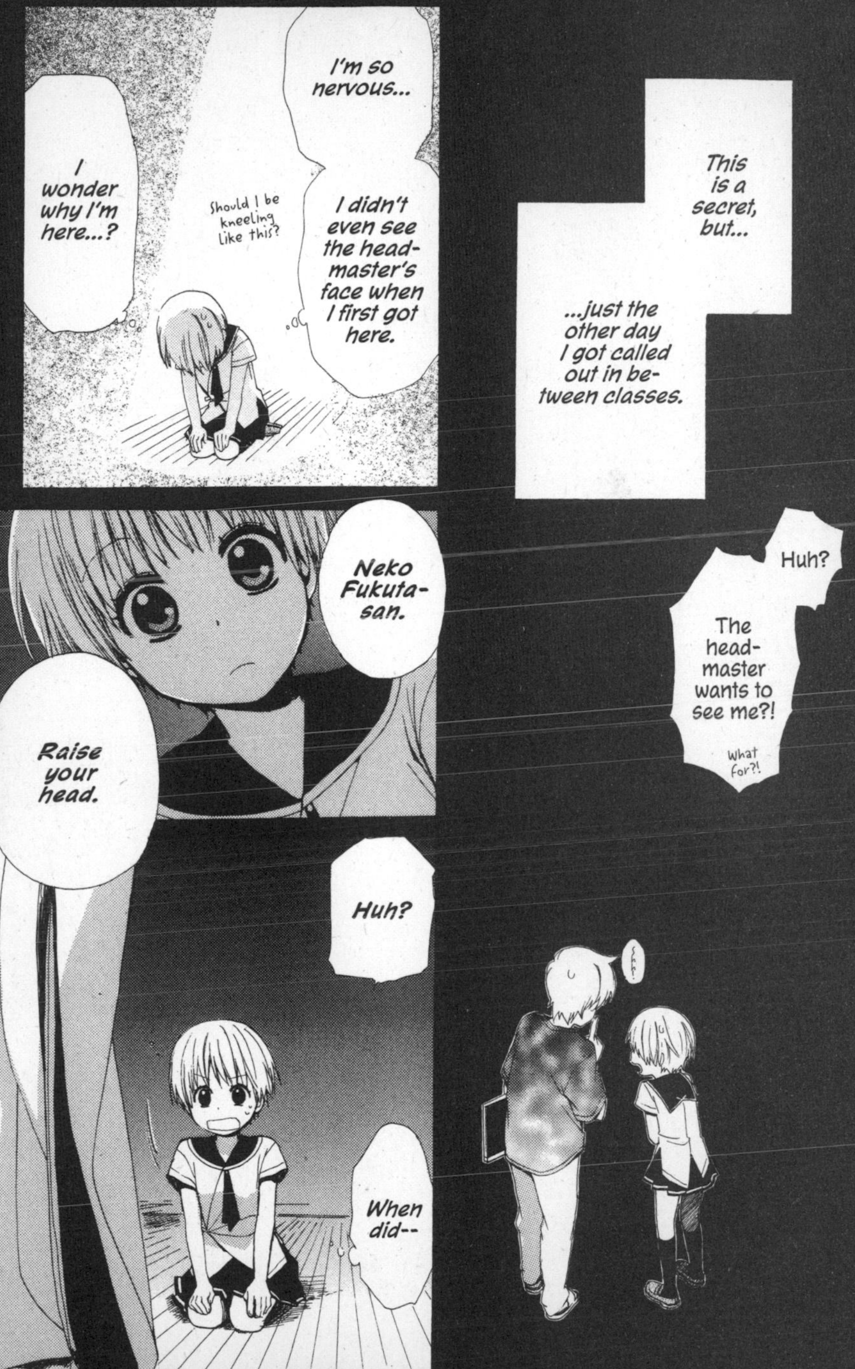

This is a secret, but...
...just the other day I got called out in between classes.
I'm so nervous...
I didn't even see the head-master's face when I first got here.
Should I be kneeling like this?
I wonder why I'm here...?
Huh?
The head-master wants to see me?!
What for?!
Neko Fukuta-san.
Raise your head.
Huh?
When did--

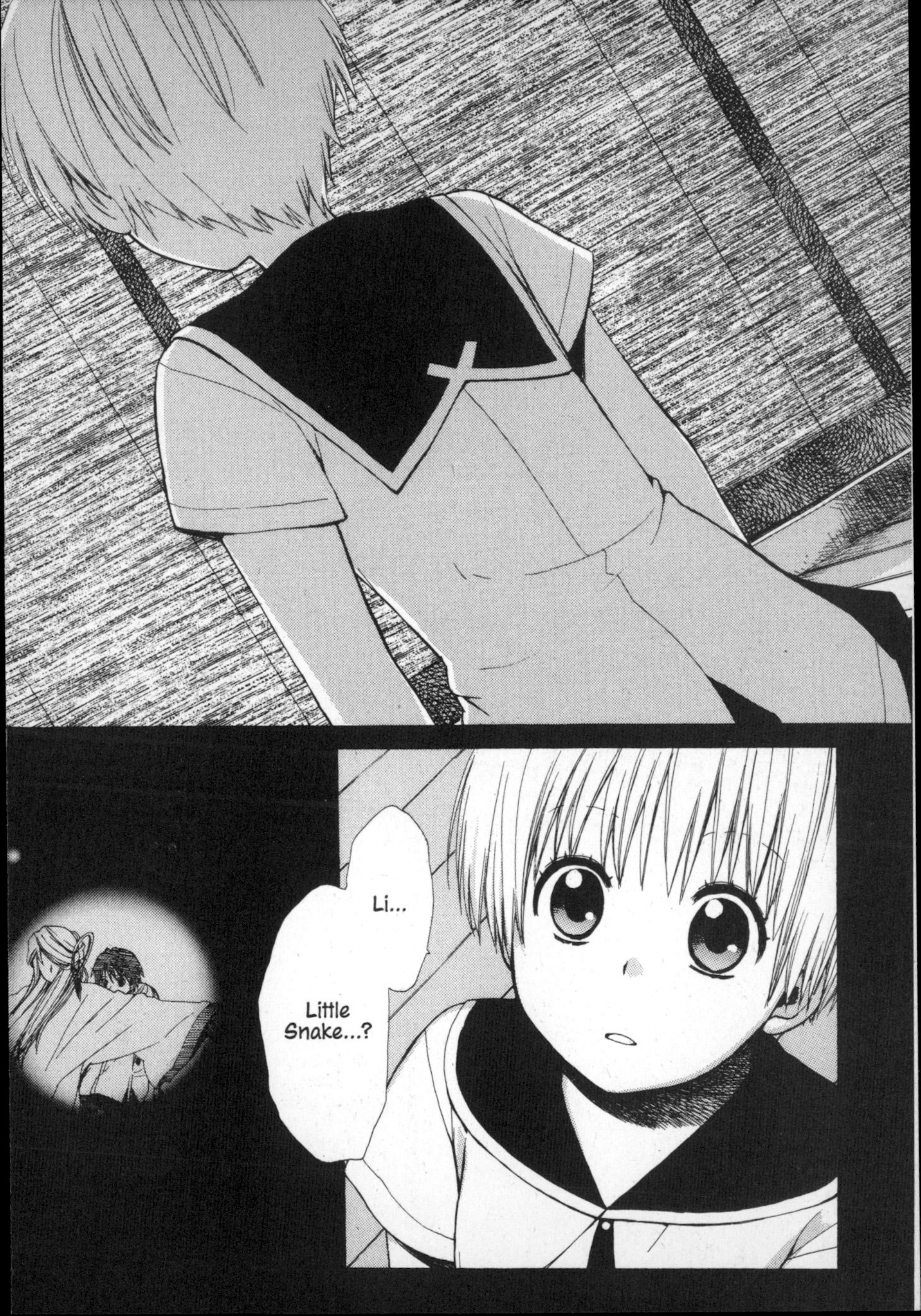
Li...
Little Snake...?

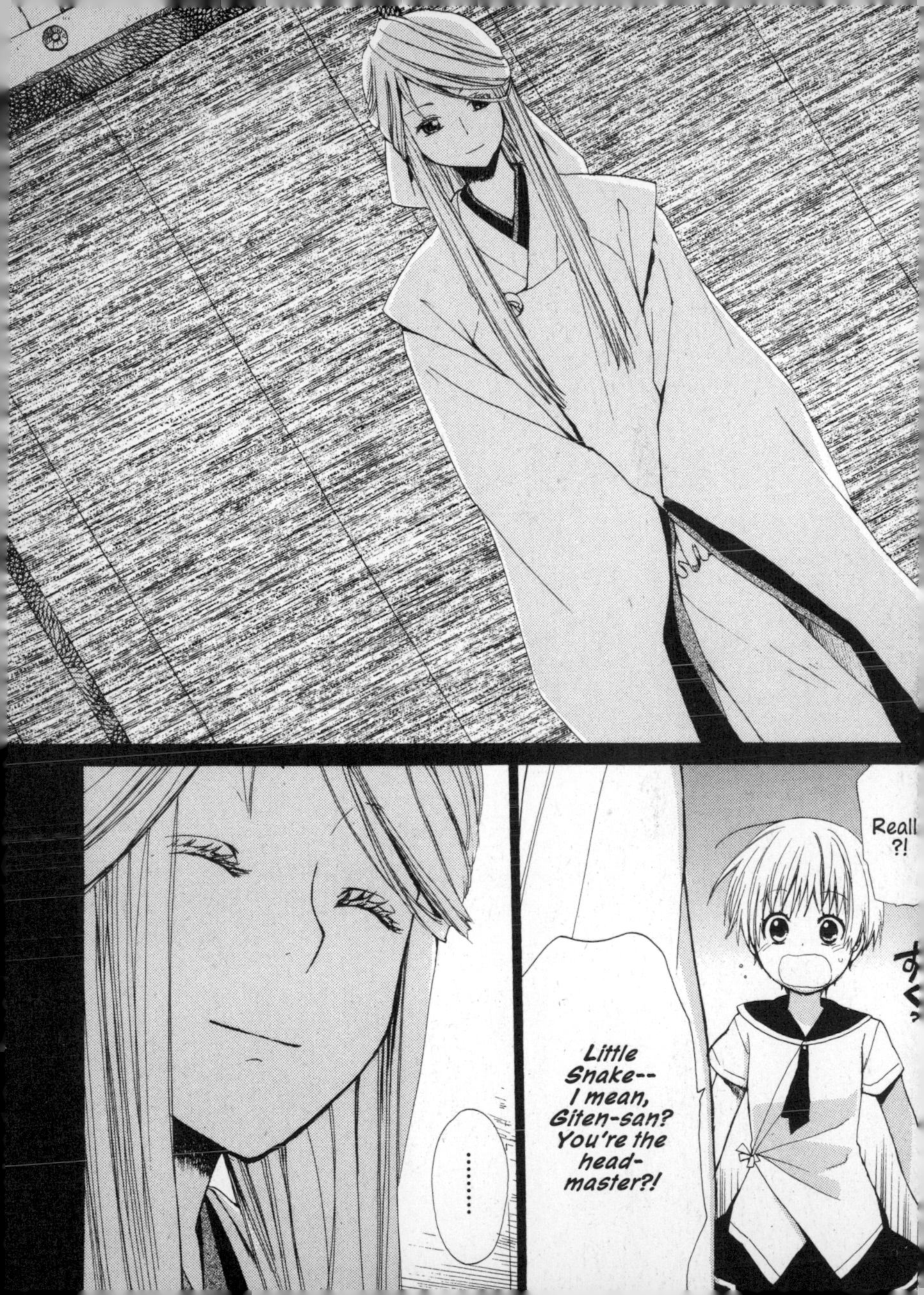
Reall ?!
Little Snake-- I mean, Giten-san? You're the head-master?!
......

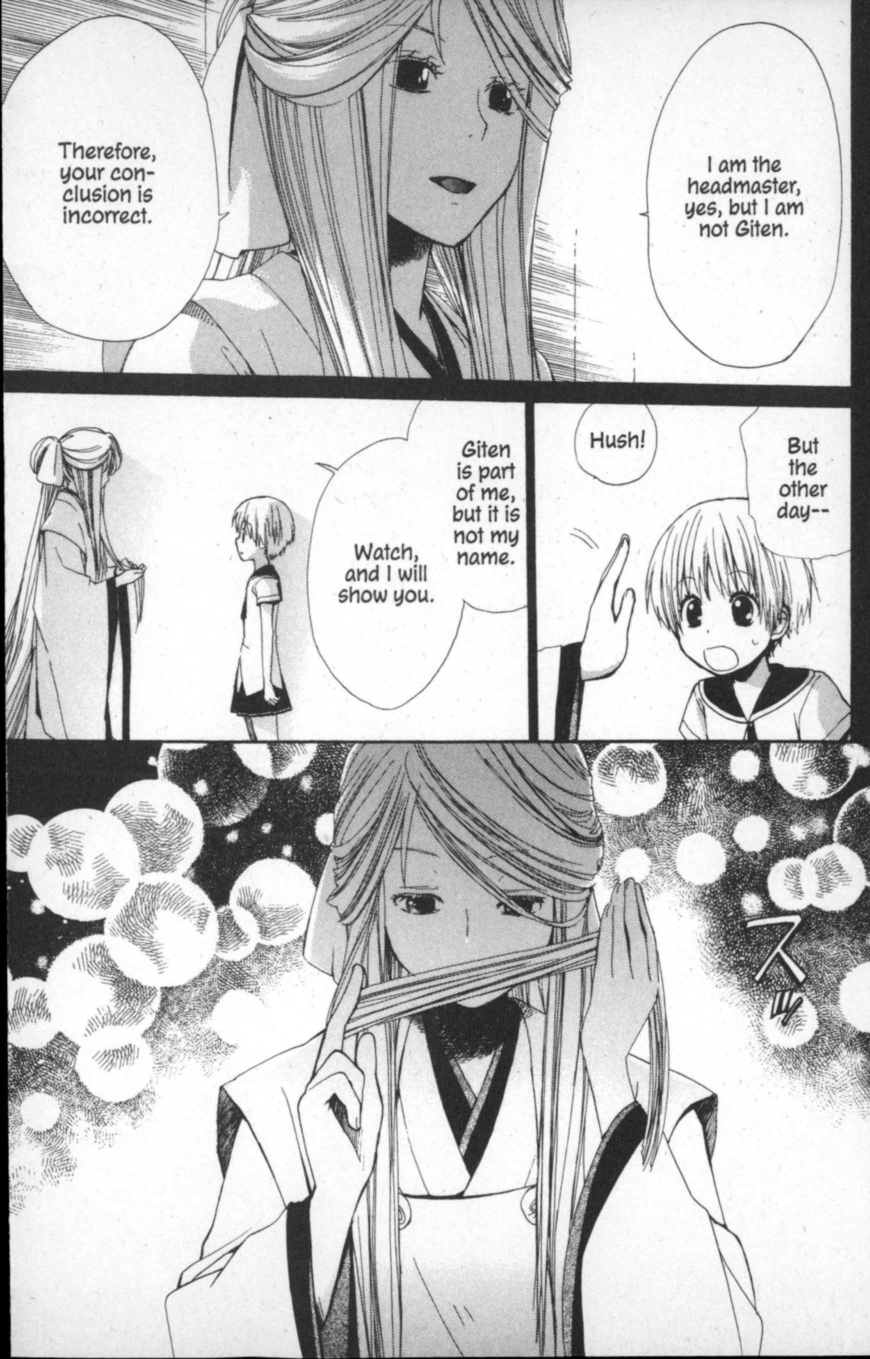
I am the headmaster, yes, but I am not Giten.
Therefore, your conclusion is incorrect.
But the other day--
Hush!
Giten is part of me, but it is not my name.
Watch, and I will show you.
スッ

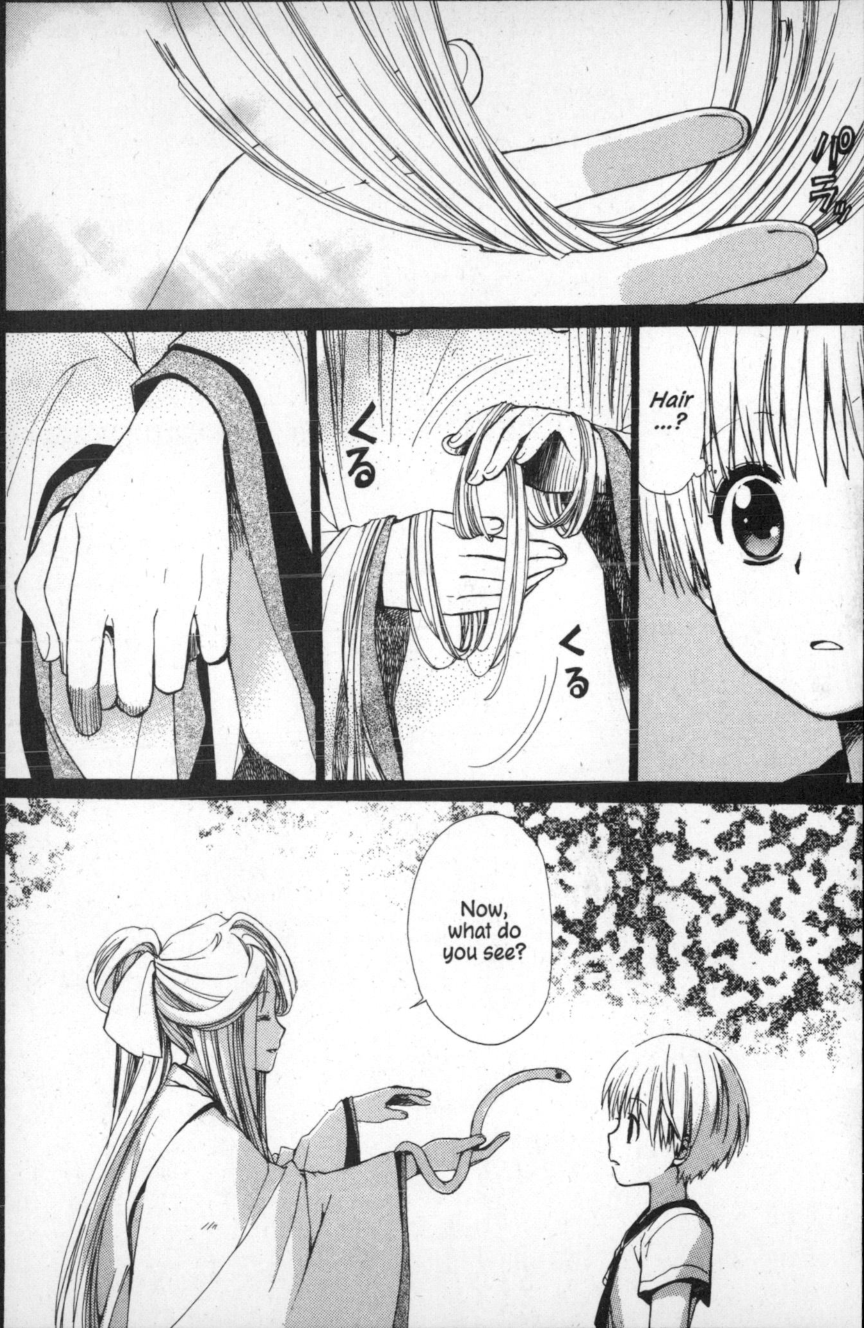
パラッ
Hair ...?
くる
くる
Now, what do you see?

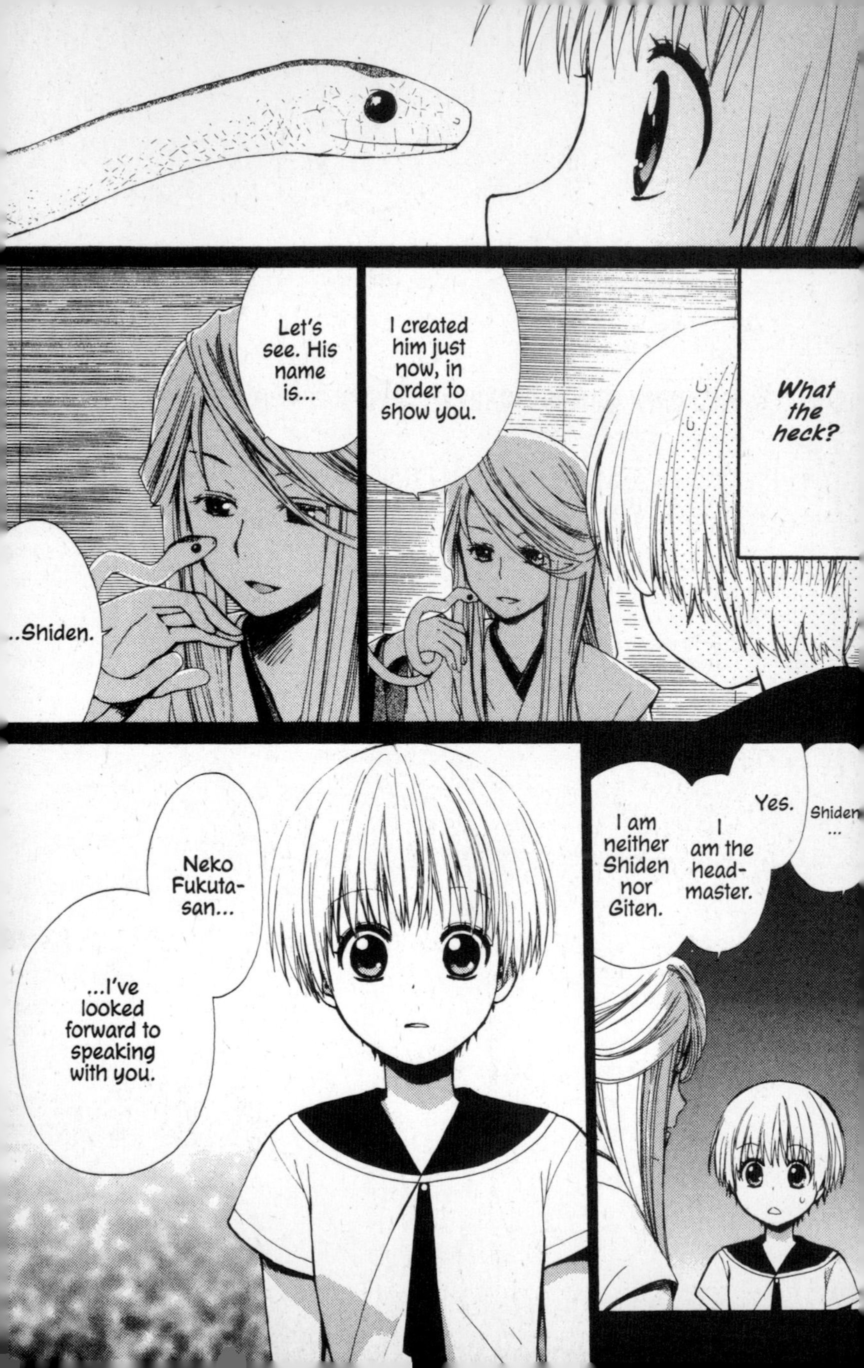
What the heck?
I created him just now, in order to show you.
Let's see. His name is...
..Shiden.
Shiden...
Yes.
I am the headmaster.
I am neither Shiden nor Giten.
Neko Fukuta-san...
...I've looked forward to speaking with you.

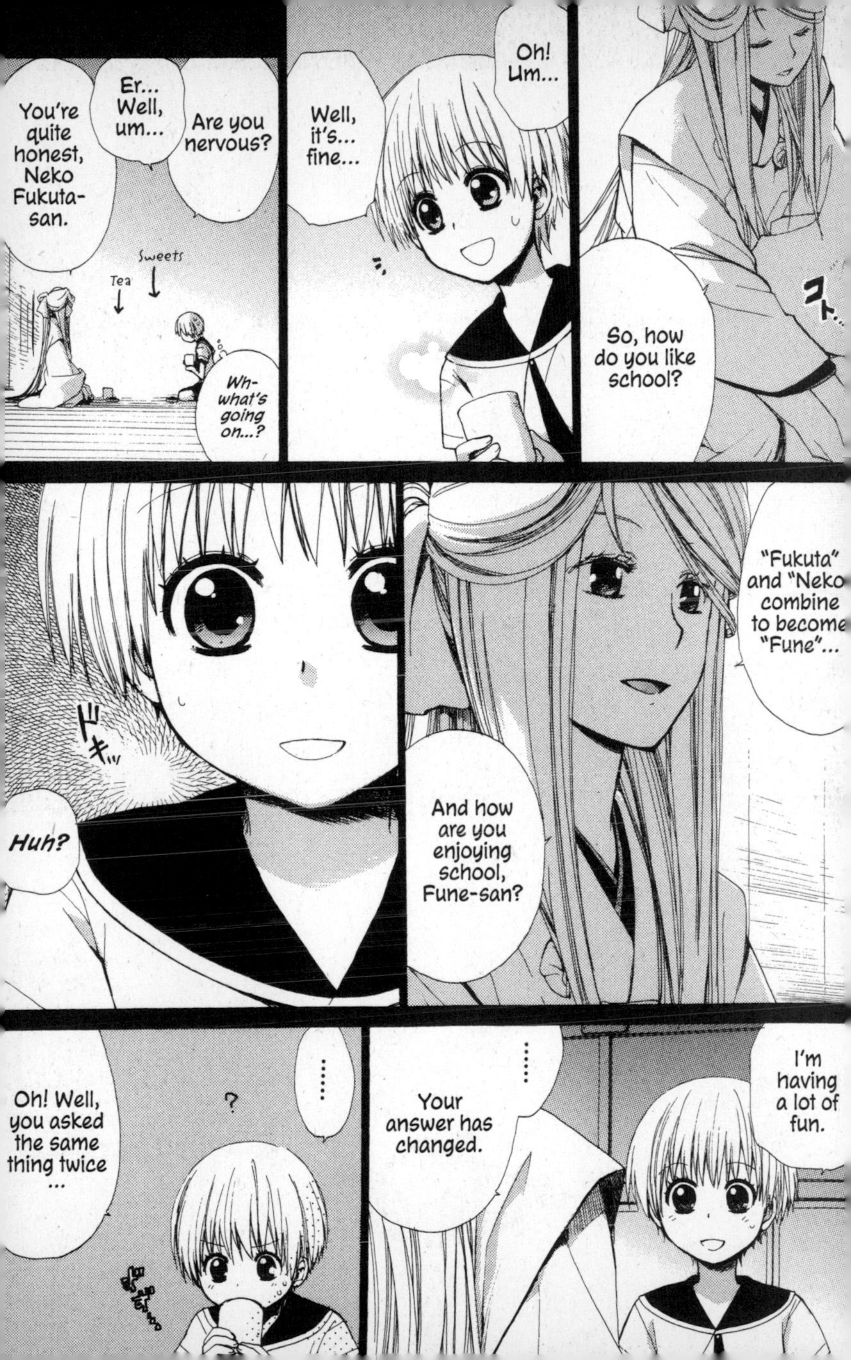
コト...
So, how do you like school?
Oh! Um...
Well, it's... fine...
Are you nervous?
Er... Well, um...
You're quite honest, Neko Fukuta-san.
Sweets
Tea
Wh-what's going on...?
"Fukuta" and "Neko combine to become "Fune"...
And how are you enjoying school, Fune-san?
ドキッ
Huh?
I'm having a lot of fun.
......
Your answer has changed.
......
?
Oh! Well, you asked the same thing twice ...

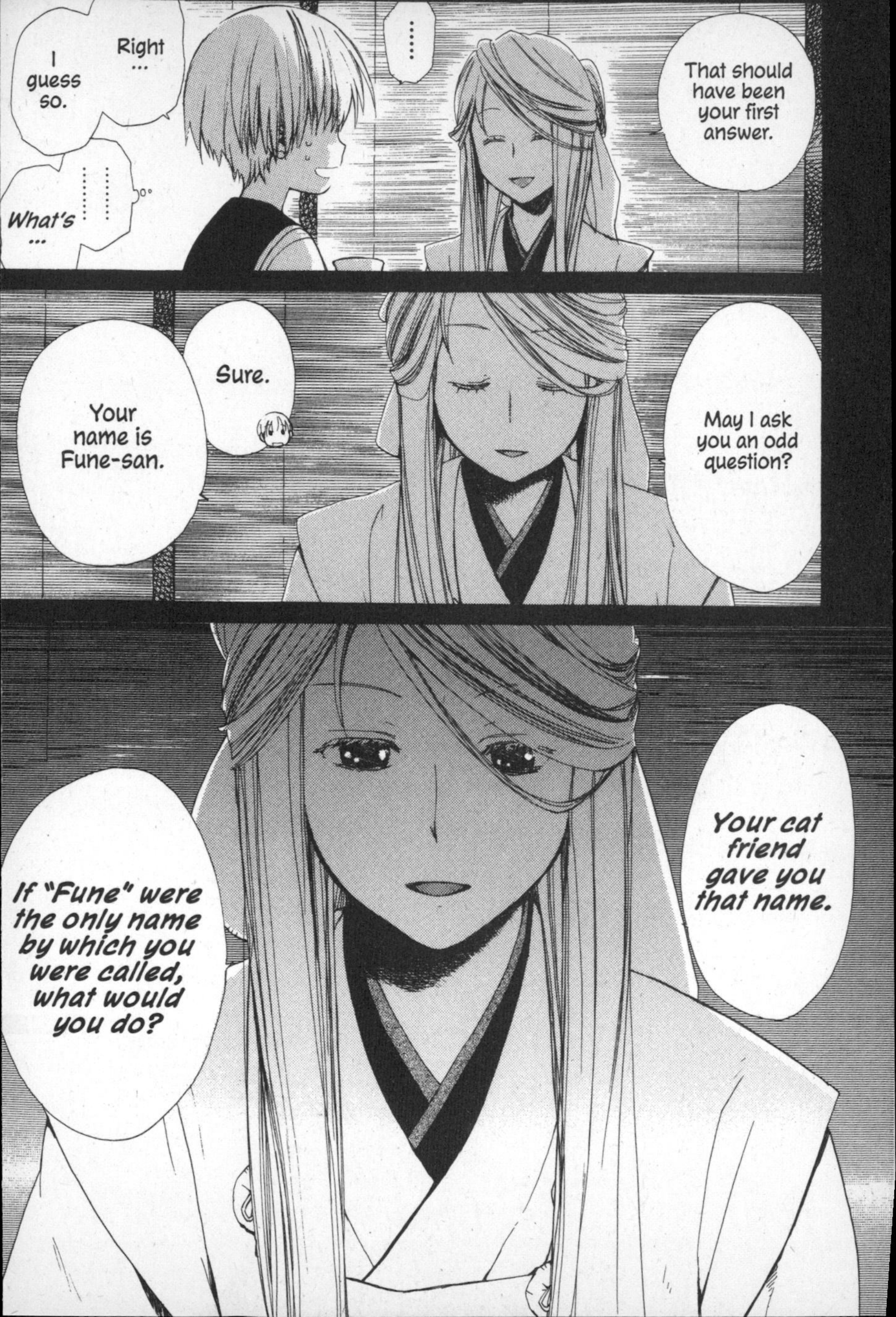
That should have been your first answer.
......
Right ...
I guess so.
......
What's ...
May I ask you an odd question?
Sure.
Your name is Fune-san.
Your cat friend gave you that name.
If "Fune" were the only name by which you were called, what would you do?

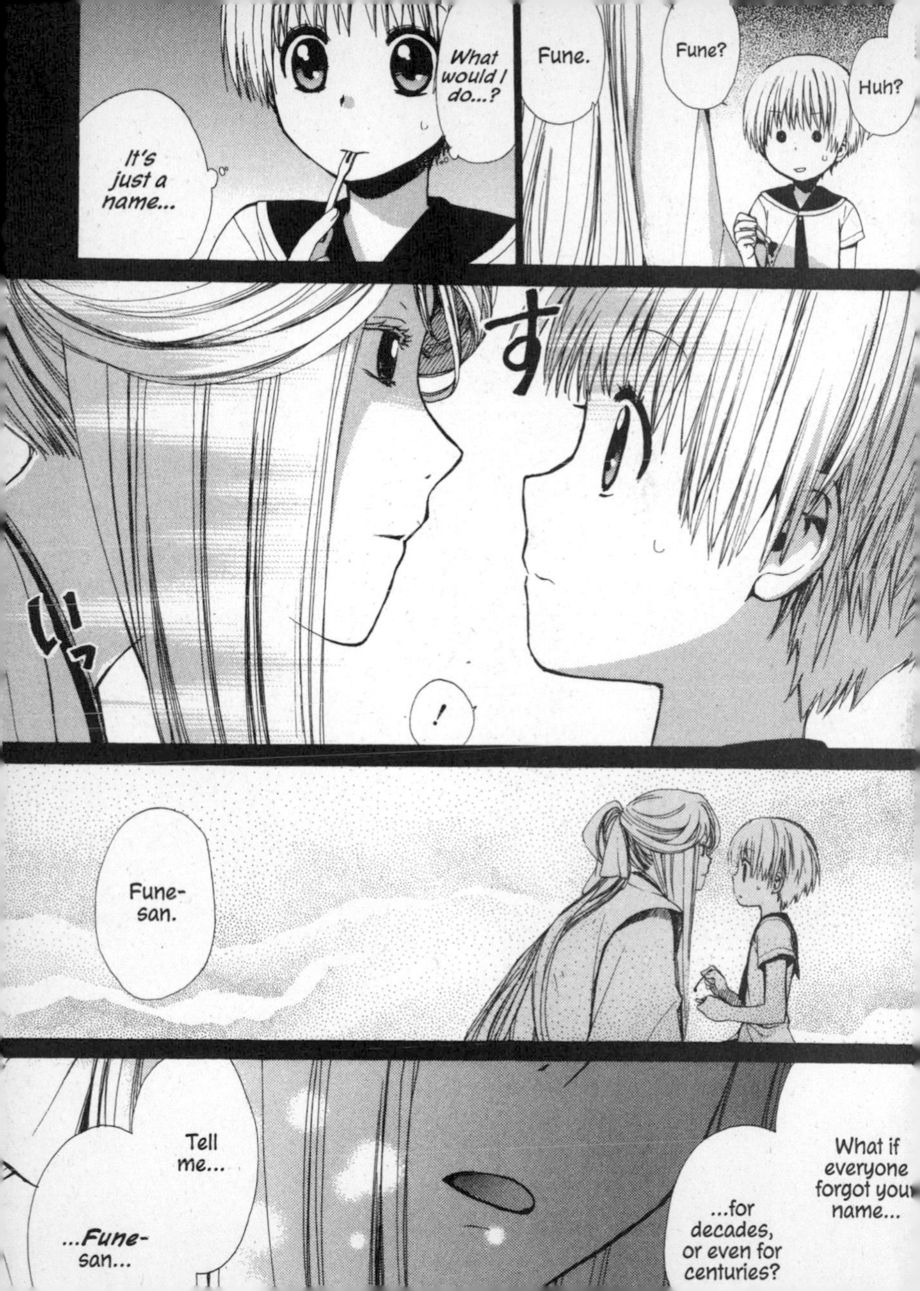
Huh?
Fune?
Fune.
What would I do...?
It's just a name...
す
!
Fune-san.
What if everyone forgot your name...
...for decades, or even for centuries?
Tell me...
...Fune-san...

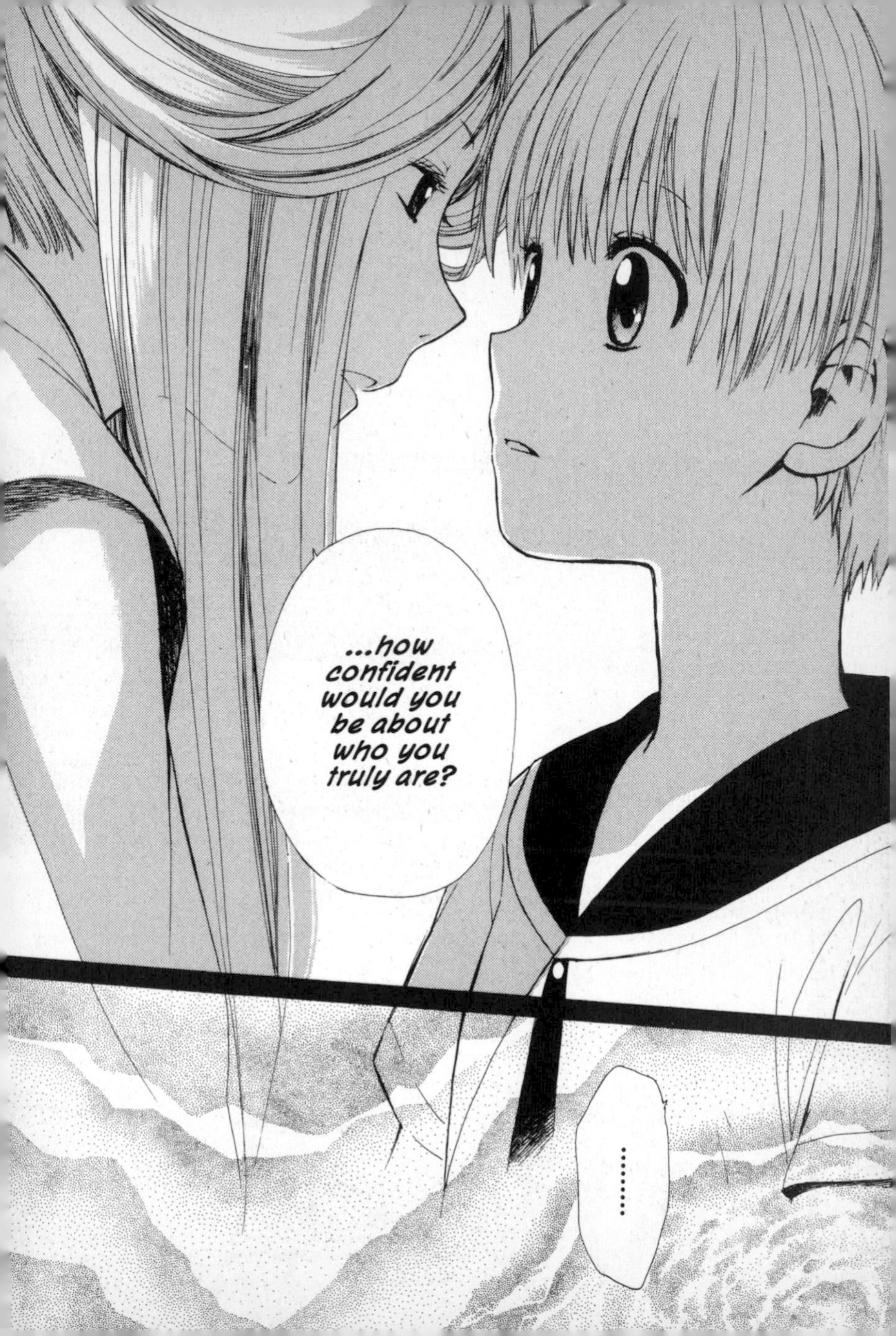
...how confident would you be about who you truly are?
....

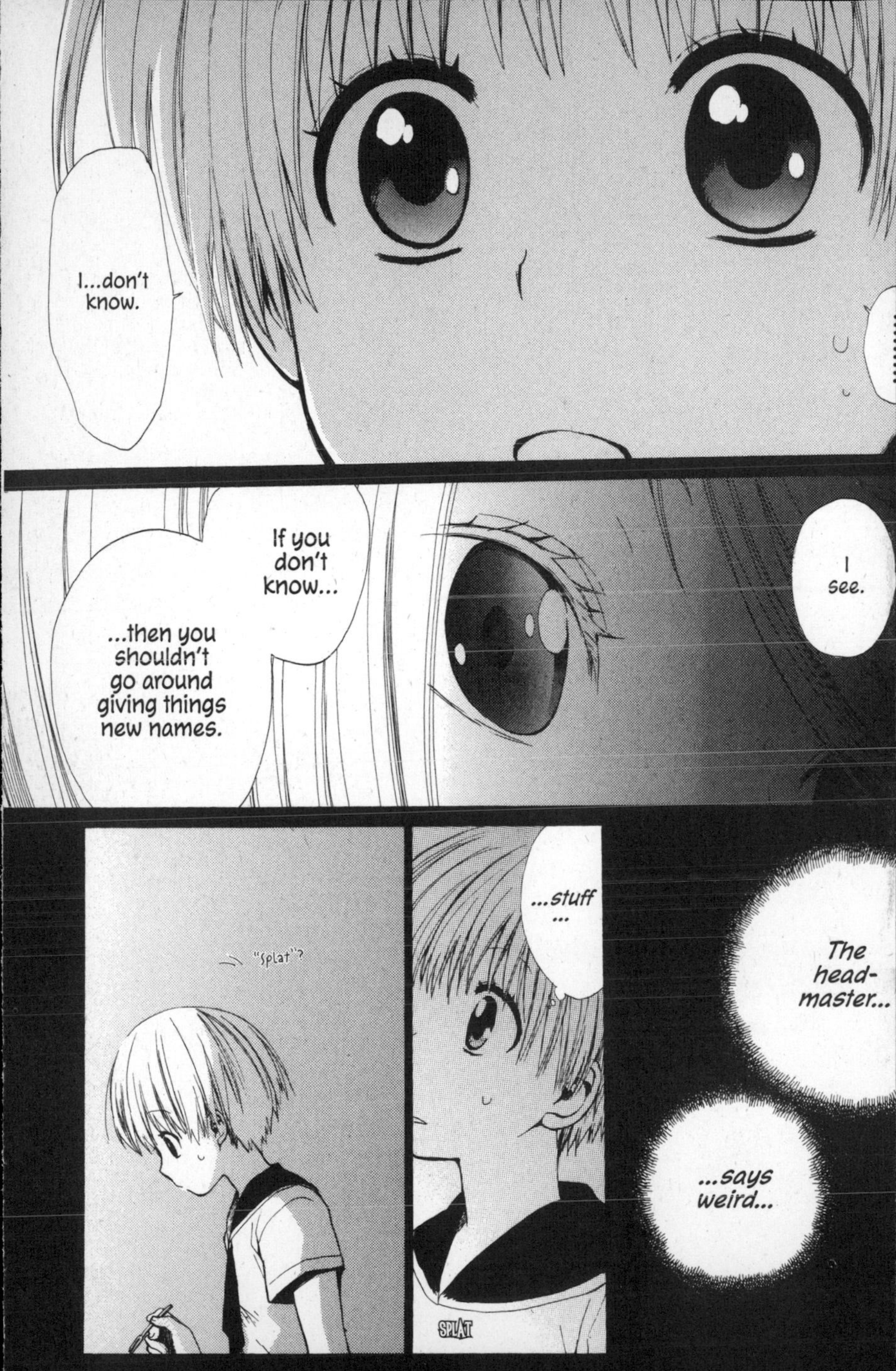
I...don't know.
I see.
If you don't know...
...then you shouldn't go around giving things new names.
The head-master...
...says weird...
...stuff ...
SPLAT
"Splat"?

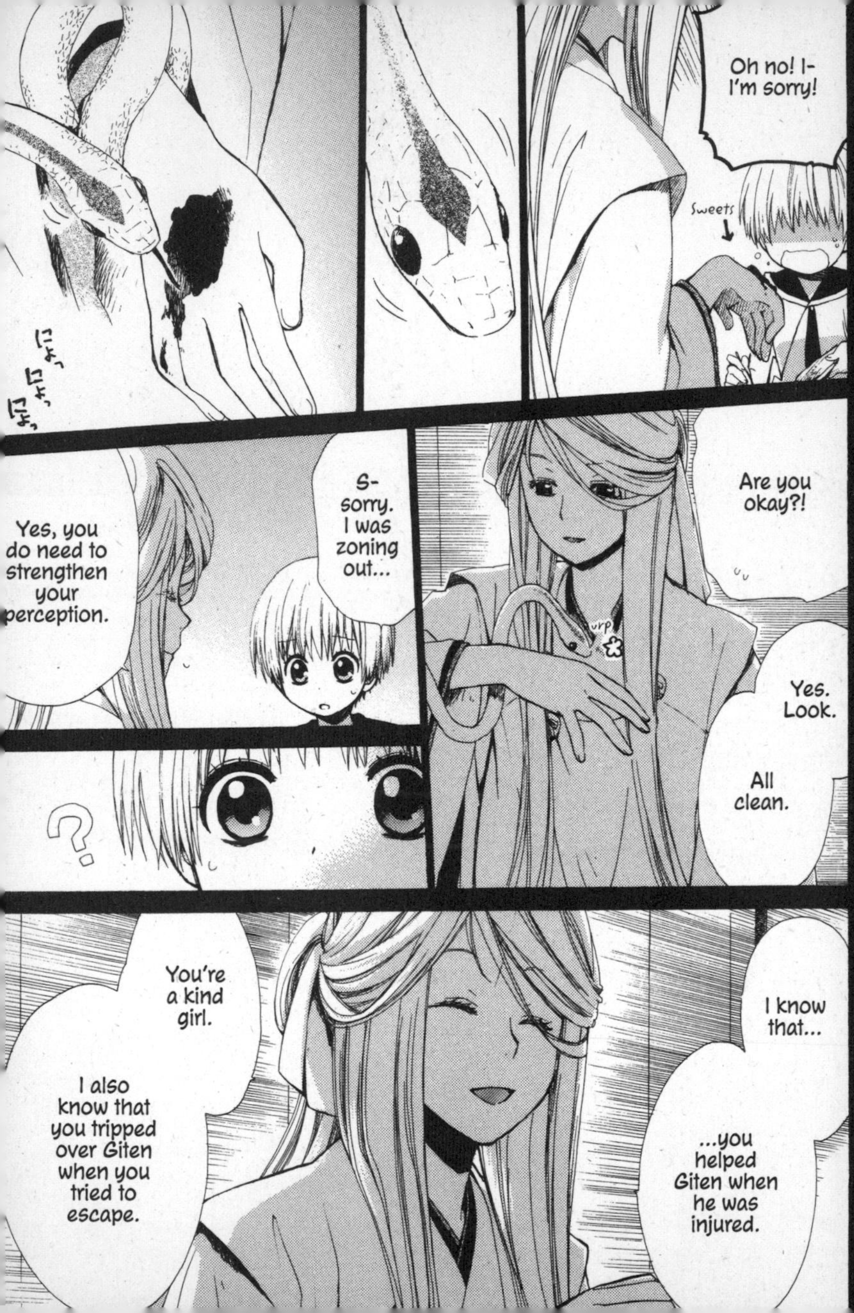
Oh no! I-I'm sorry!
Sweets
にょっ
にょっ
にょっ
Are you okay?!
urp
Yes. Look.
All clean.
S-sorry. I was zoning out...
Yes, you do need to strengthen your perception.
?
I know that...
...you helped Giten when he was injured.
You're a kind girl.
I also know that you tripped over Giten when you tried to escape.

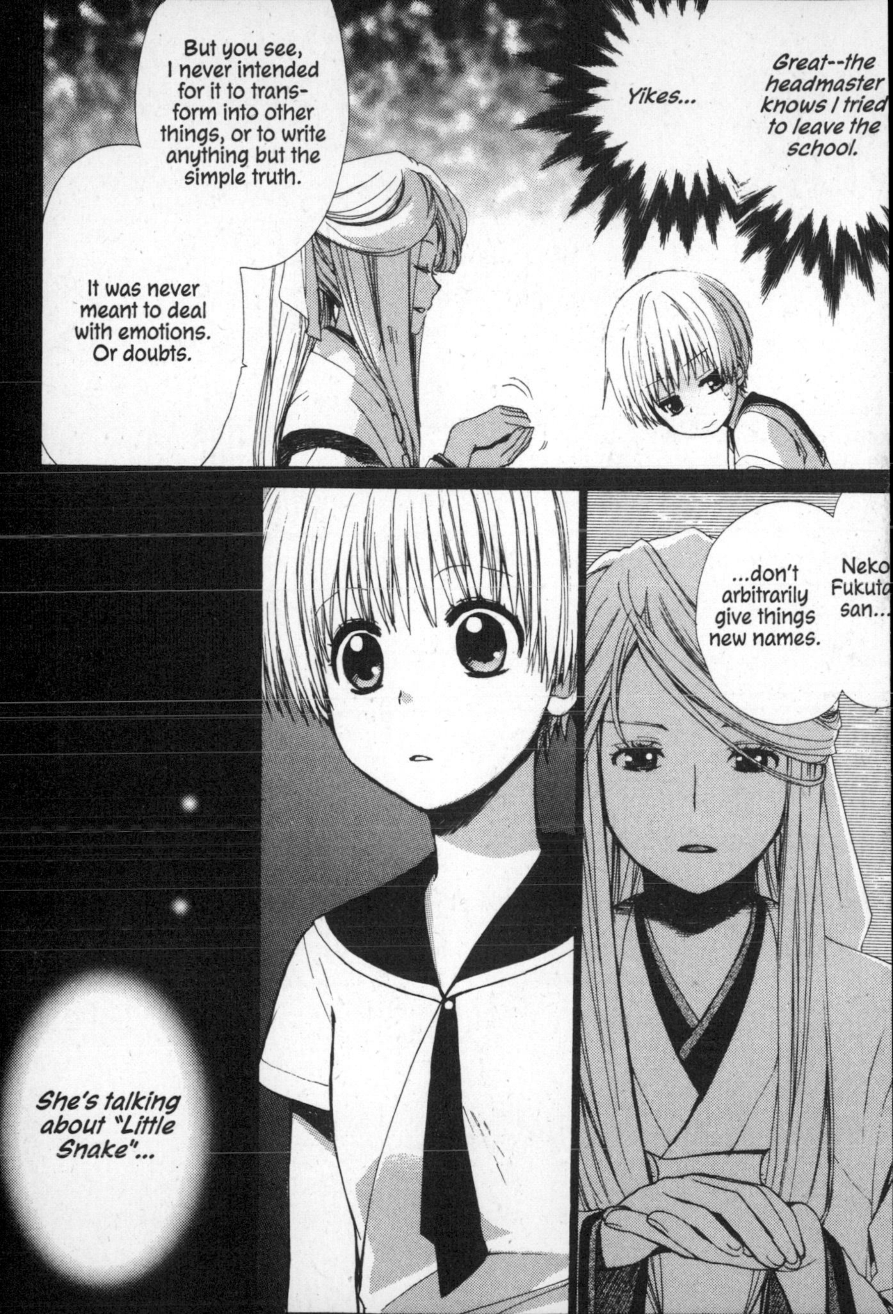
Great--the headmaster knows I tried to leave the school.
Yikes...
But you see, I never intended for it to transform into other things, or to write anything but the simple truth.
It was never meant to deal with emotions. Or doubts.
Neko Fukuta san...
...don't arbitrarily give things new names.
She's talking about "Little Snake"...

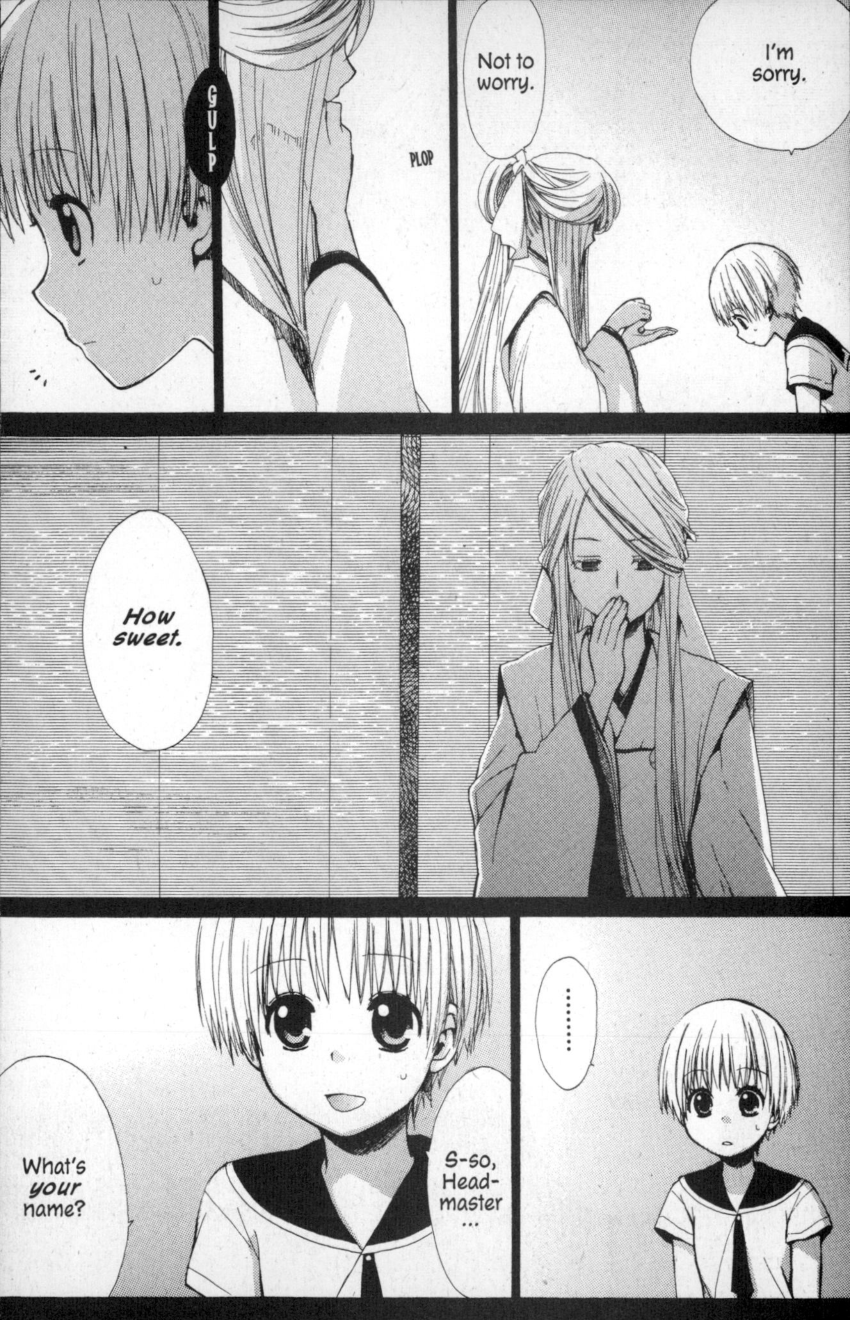
I'm sorry.
Not to worry.
PLOP
GULP
How sweet.
……
S-so, Head-master ...
What's *your* name?

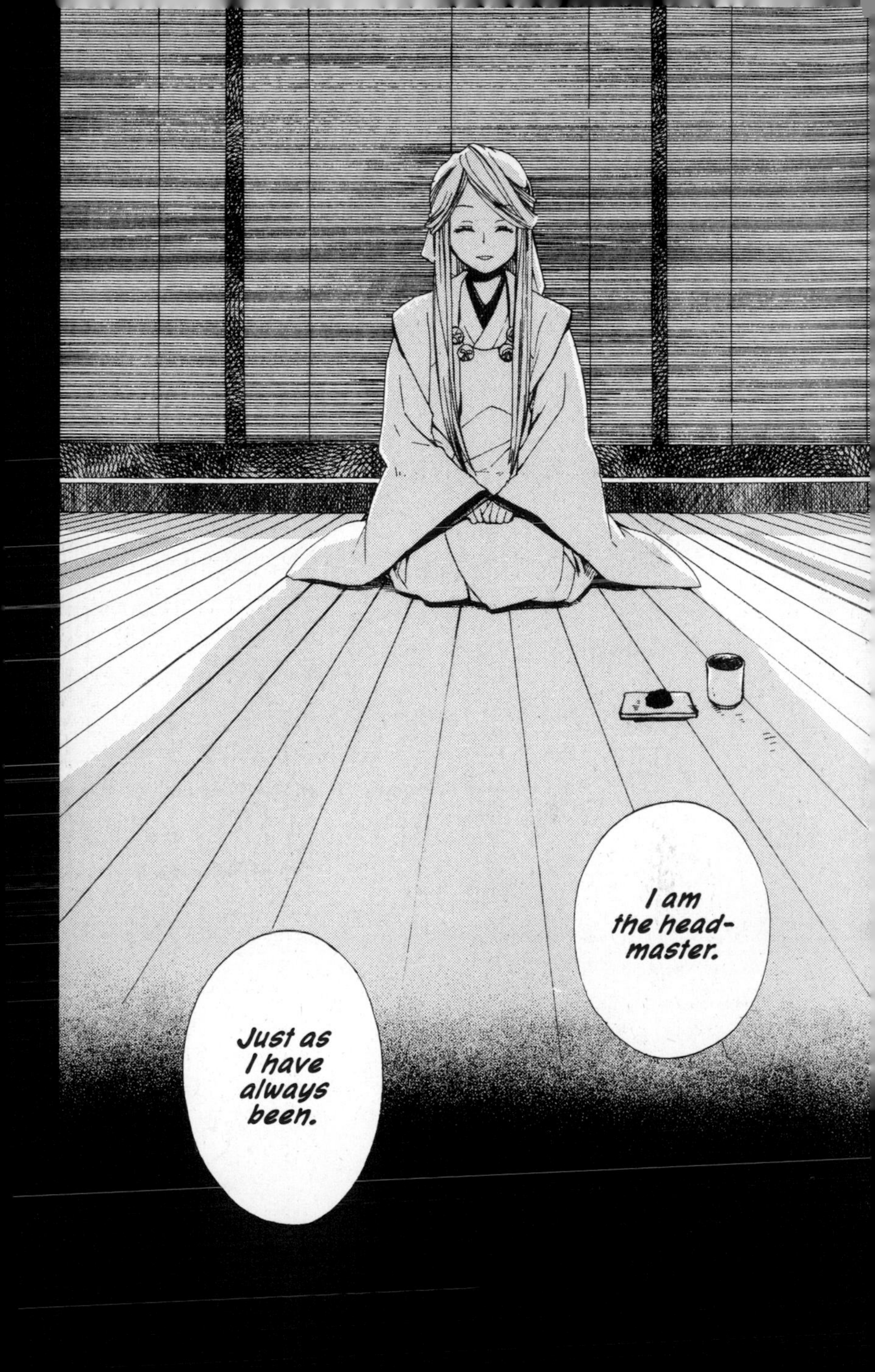
I am the head-master.
Just as I have always been.

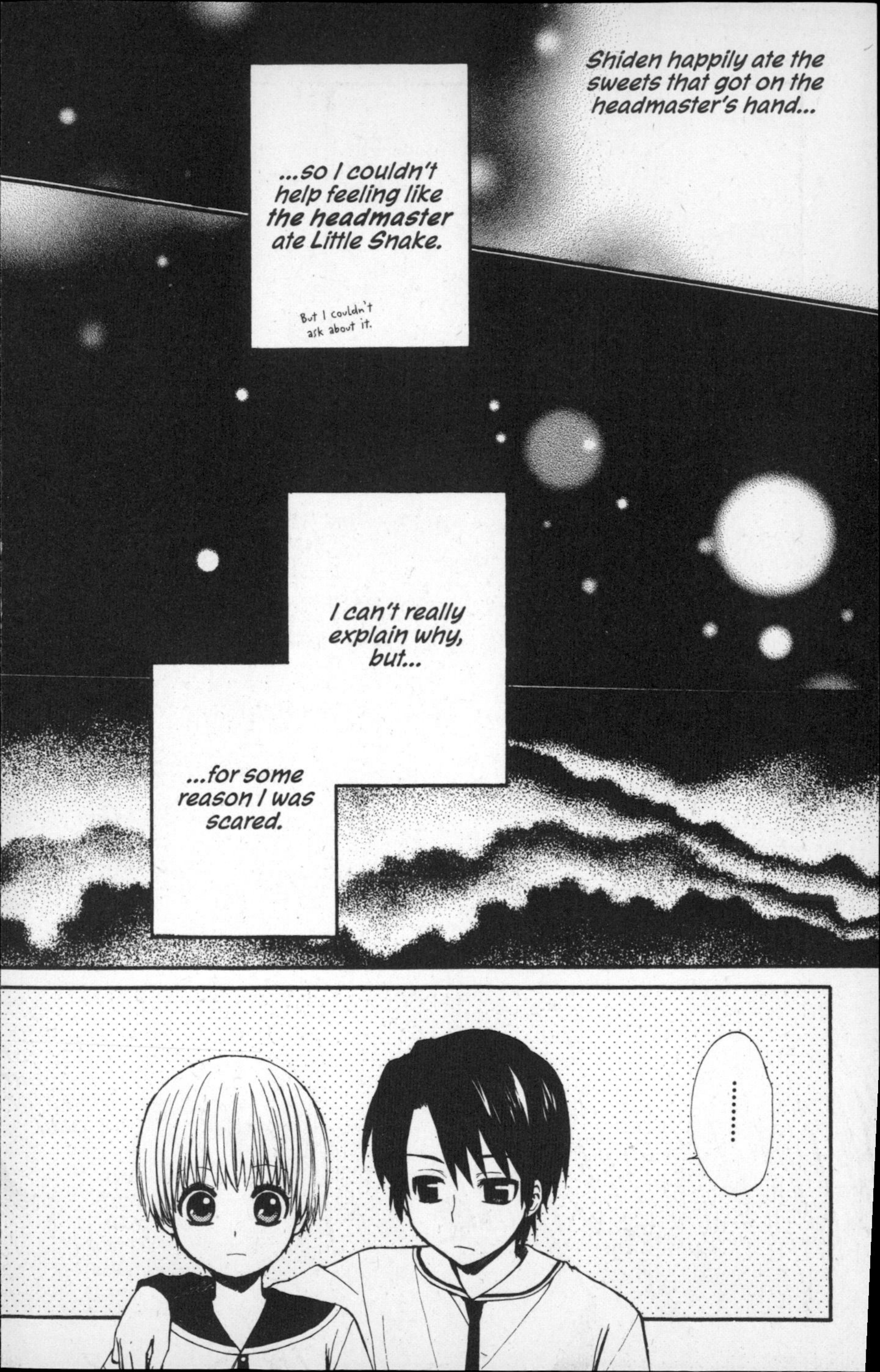

Shiden happily ate the sweets that got on the headmaster's hand...
...so I couldn't help feeling like the headmaster ate Little Snake.
But I couldn't ask about it.
I can't really explain why, but...
...for some reason I was scared.
......

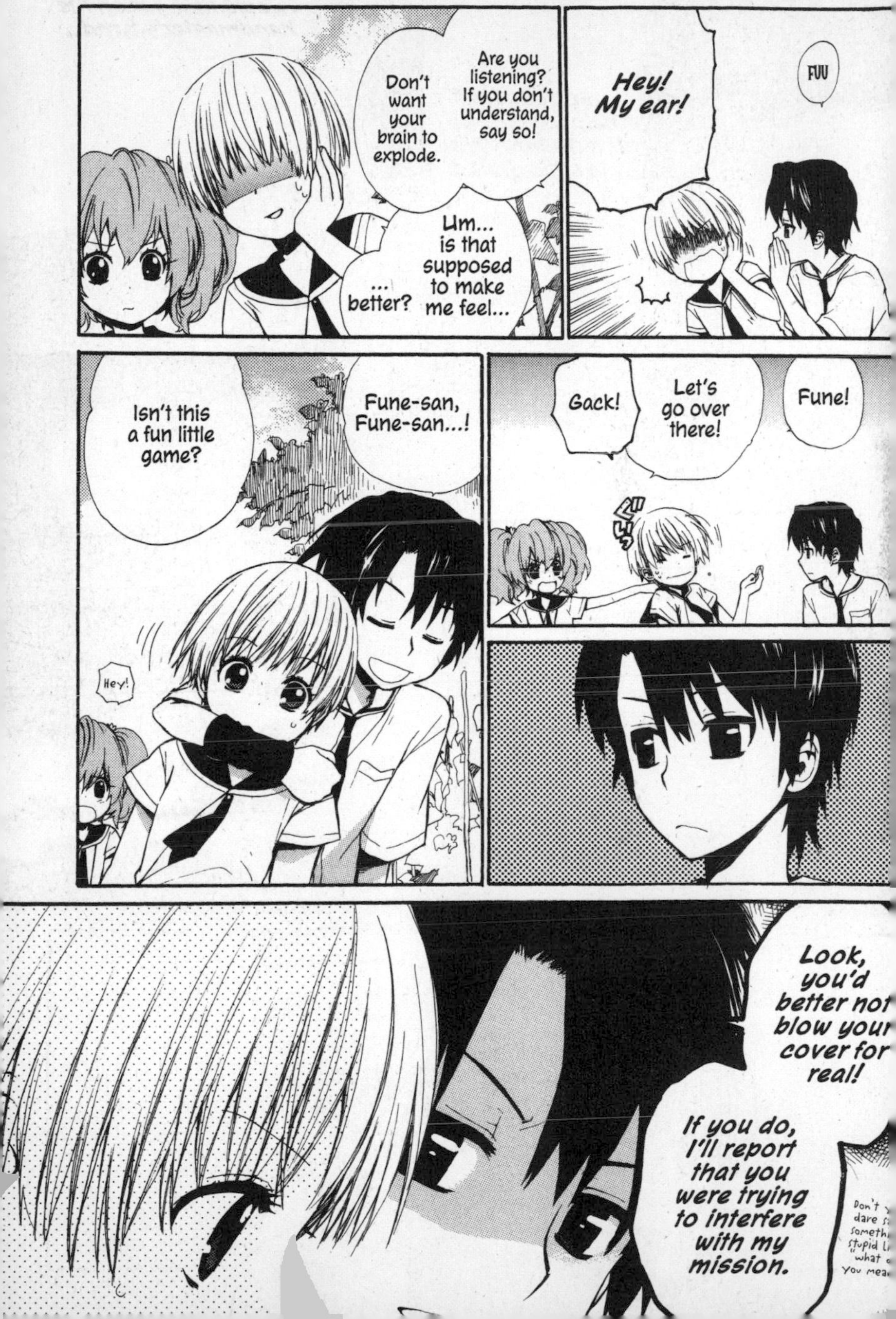
FUU
Hey! My ear!
Are you listening? If you don't understand, say so!
Don't want your brain to explode.
Um... is that supposed to make me feel...
... better?
Fune!
Let's go over there!
Gack!
Fune-san, Fune-san...!
Isn't this a fun little game?
Hey!
Look, you'd better not blow your cover for real!
If you do, I'll report that you were trying to interfere with my mission.

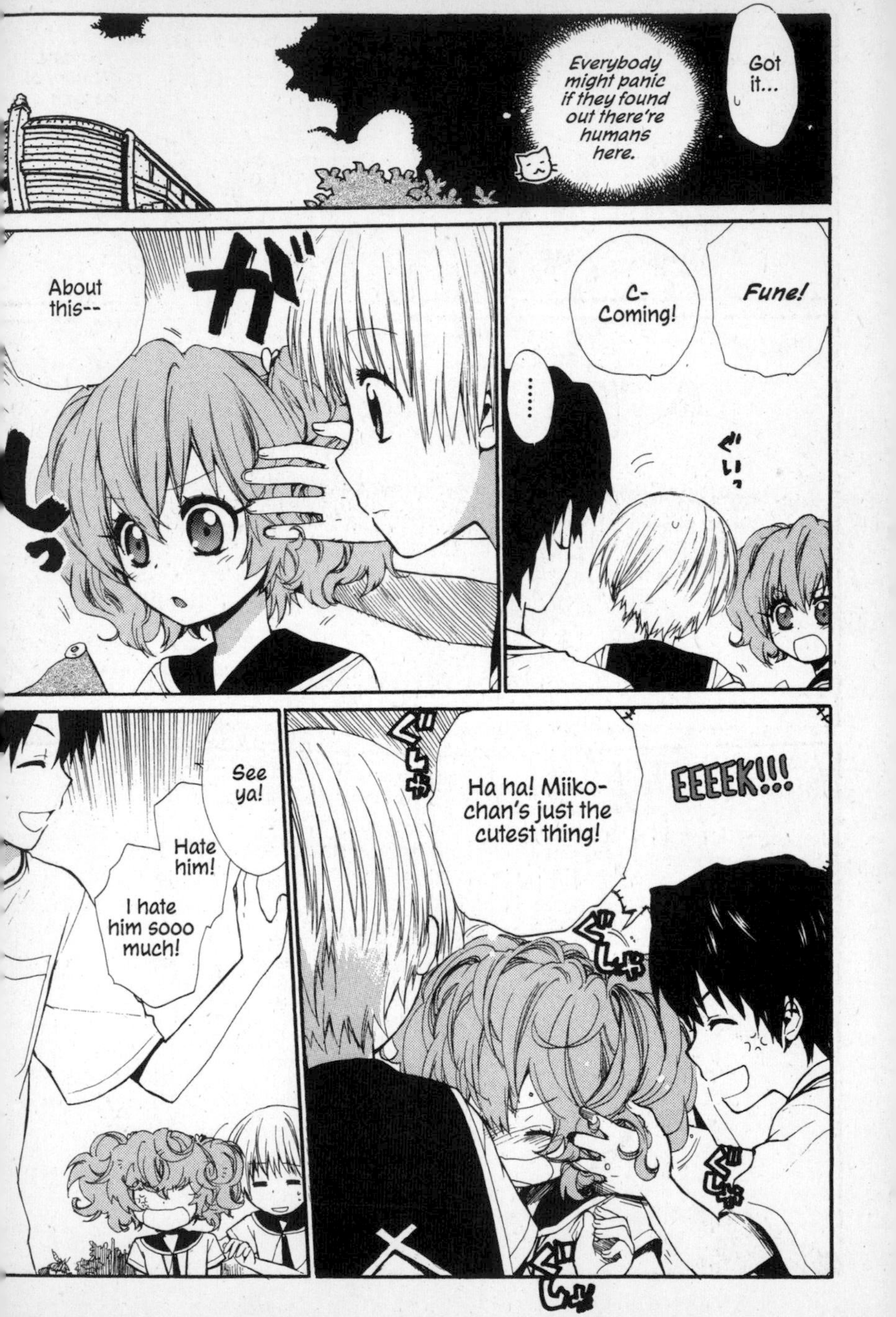
Got it...
Everybody might panic if they found out there're humans here.
Fune!
C- Coming!
......
ぐいっ
About this--
EEEEK!!!
Ha ha! Miiko-chan's just the cutest thing!
See ya!
Hate him!
I hate him sooo much!

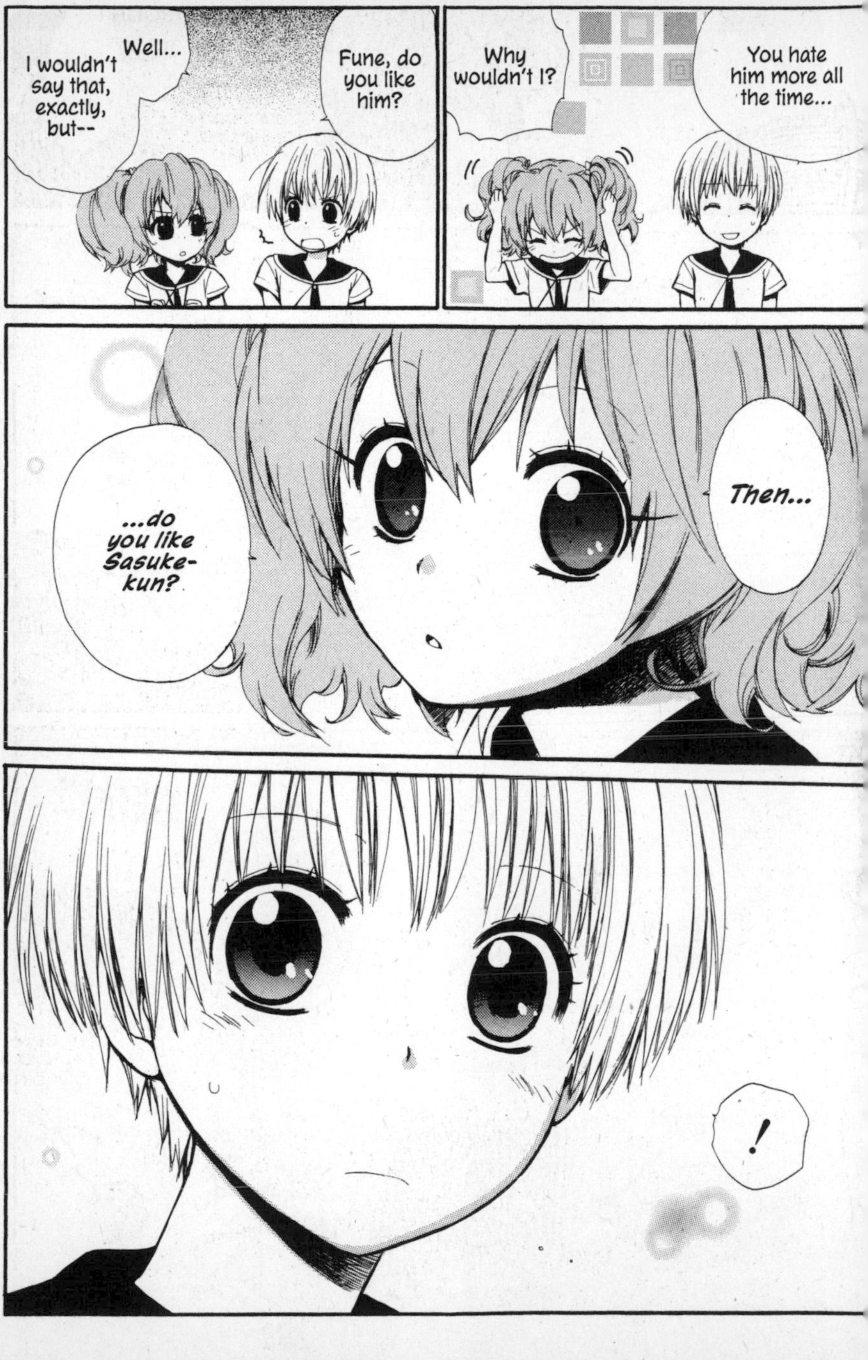
You hate him more all the time...
Why wouldn't I?
Fune, do you like him?
Well...
I wouldn't say that, exactly, but--
Then...
...do you like Sasuke-kun?
!

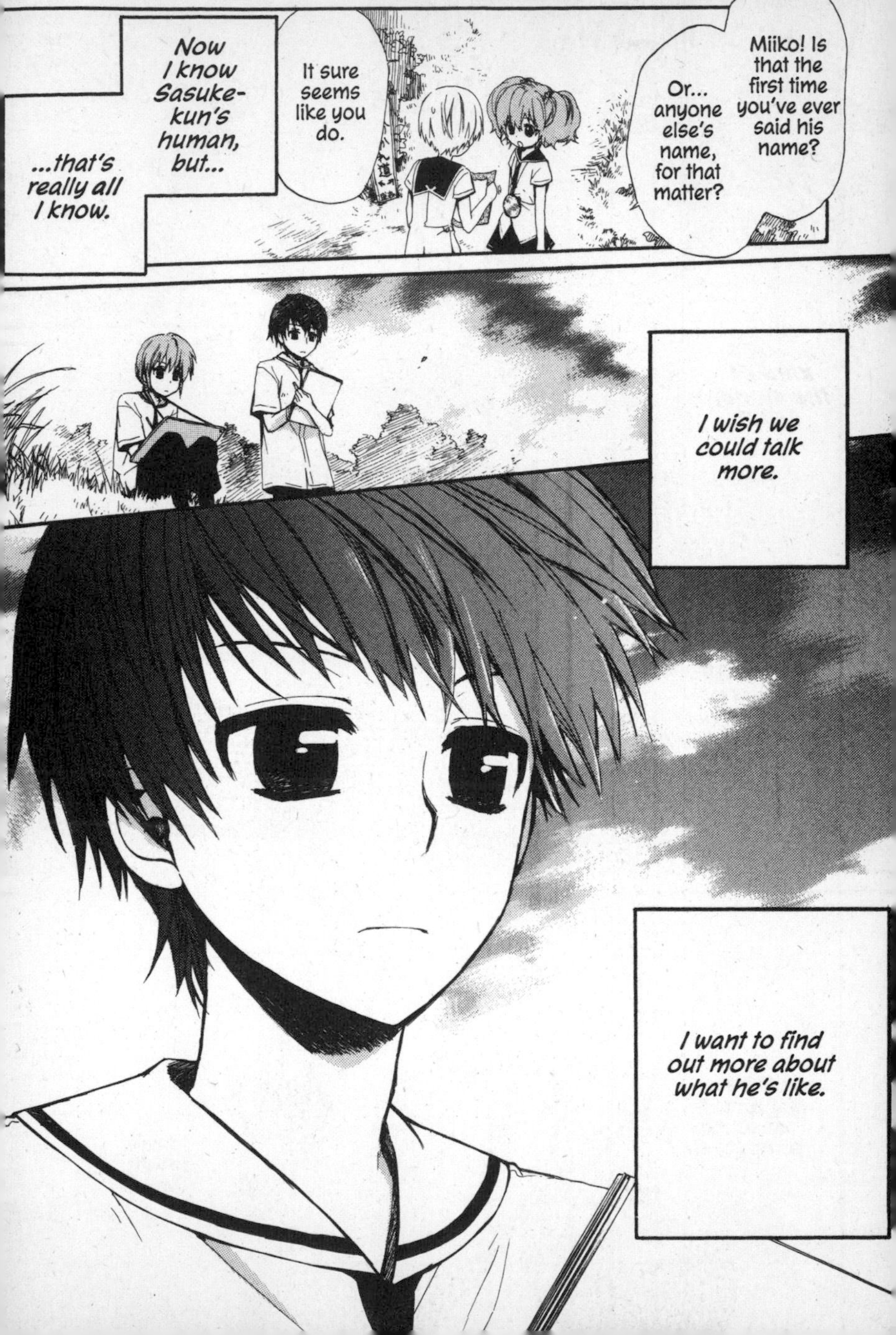
Miiko! Is that the first time you've ever said his name?
Or... anyone else's name, for that matter?
It sure seems like you do.
Now I know Sasuke-kun's human, but...
...that's really all I know.
I wish we could talk more.
I want to find out more about what he's like.

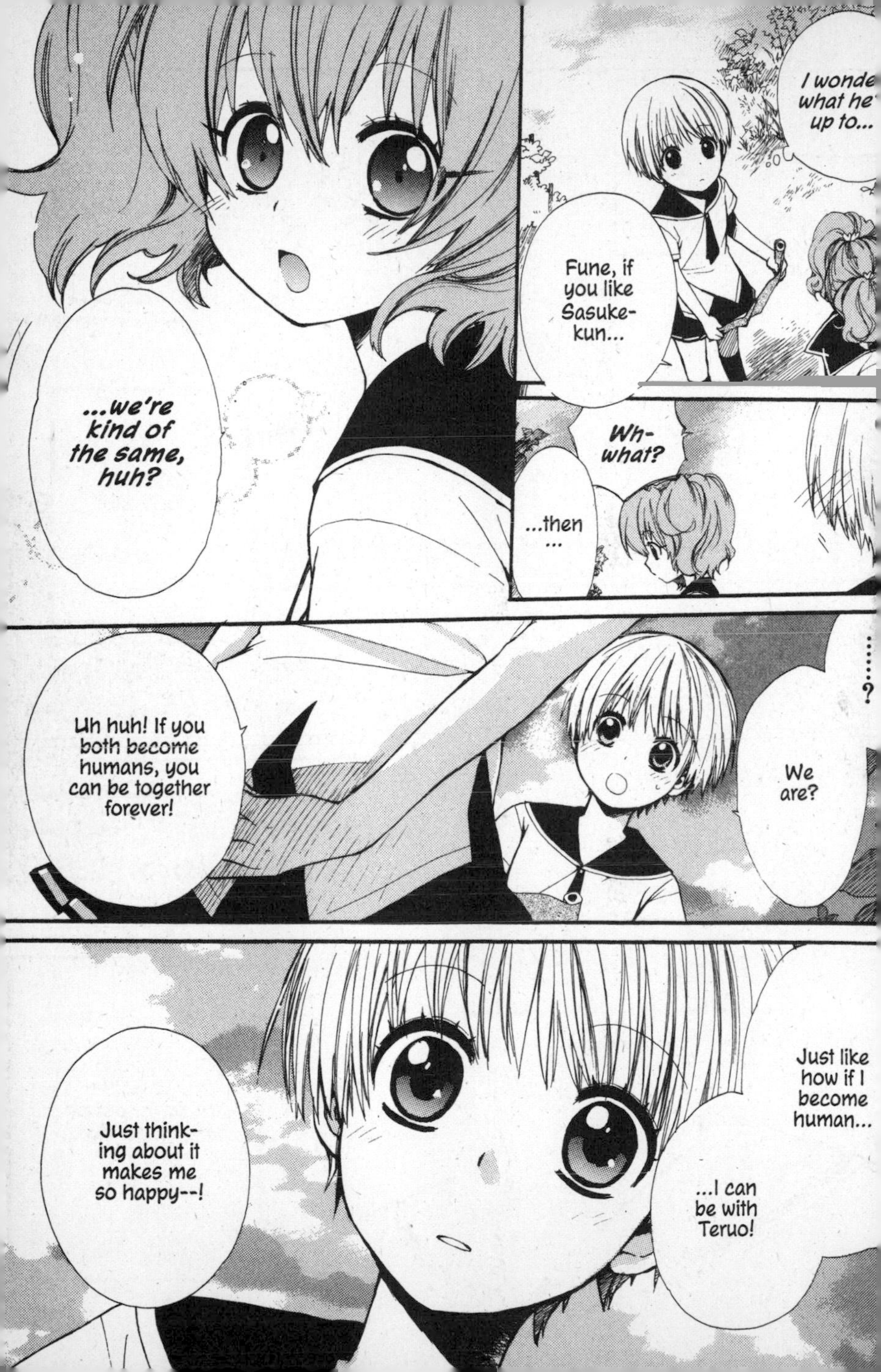
I wonde what he up to...
Fune, if you like Sasuke-kun...
Wh-what?
...then ...
...we're kind of the same, huh?
......?
We are?
Uh huh! If you both become humans, you can be together forever!
Just like how if I become human...
...I can be with Teruo!
Just thinking about it makes me so happy--!

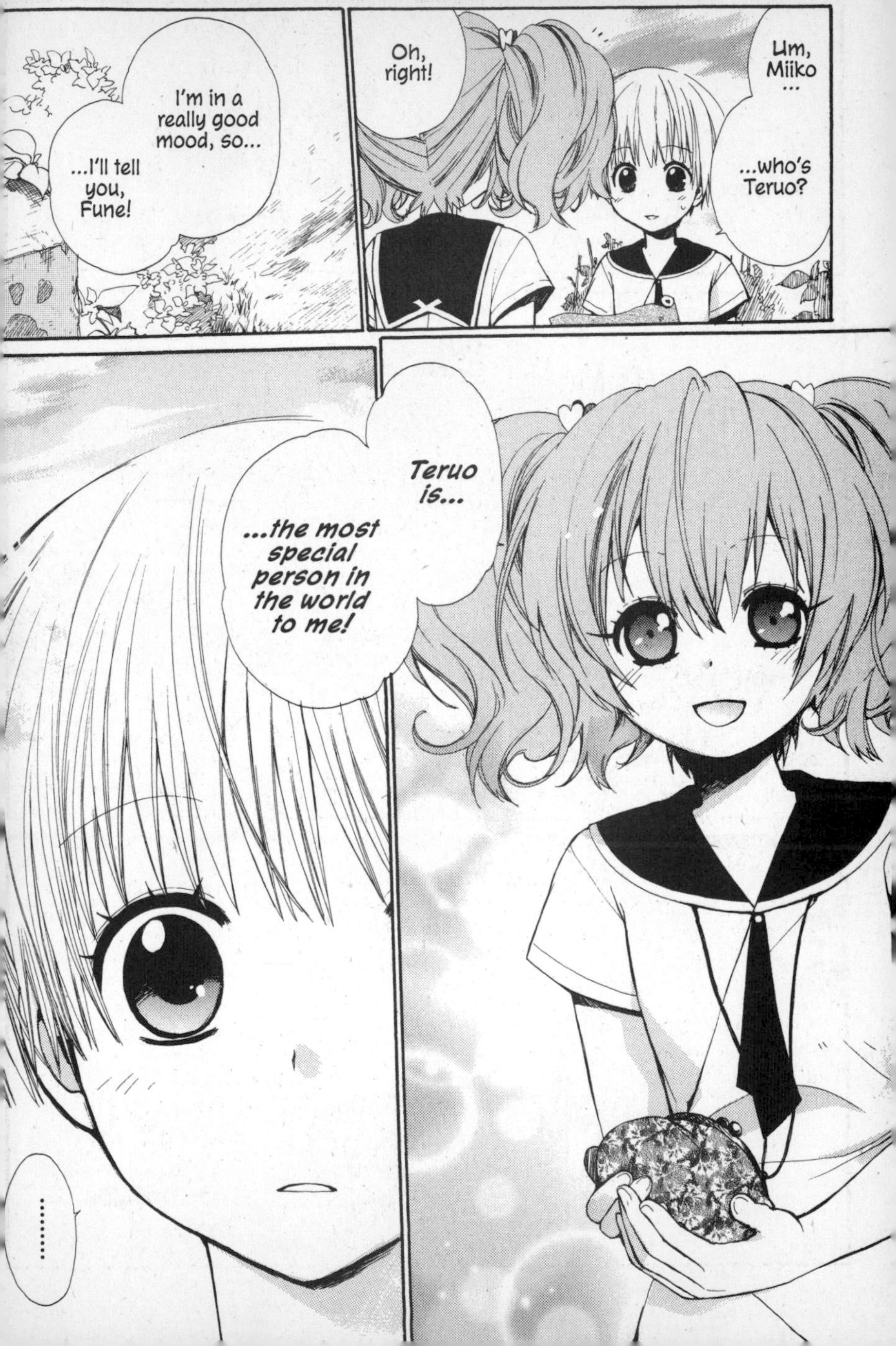
Um, Miiko...
...who's Teruo?
Oh, right!
I'm in a really good mood, so...
...I'll tell you, Fune!
Teruo is...
...the most special person in the world to me!
....

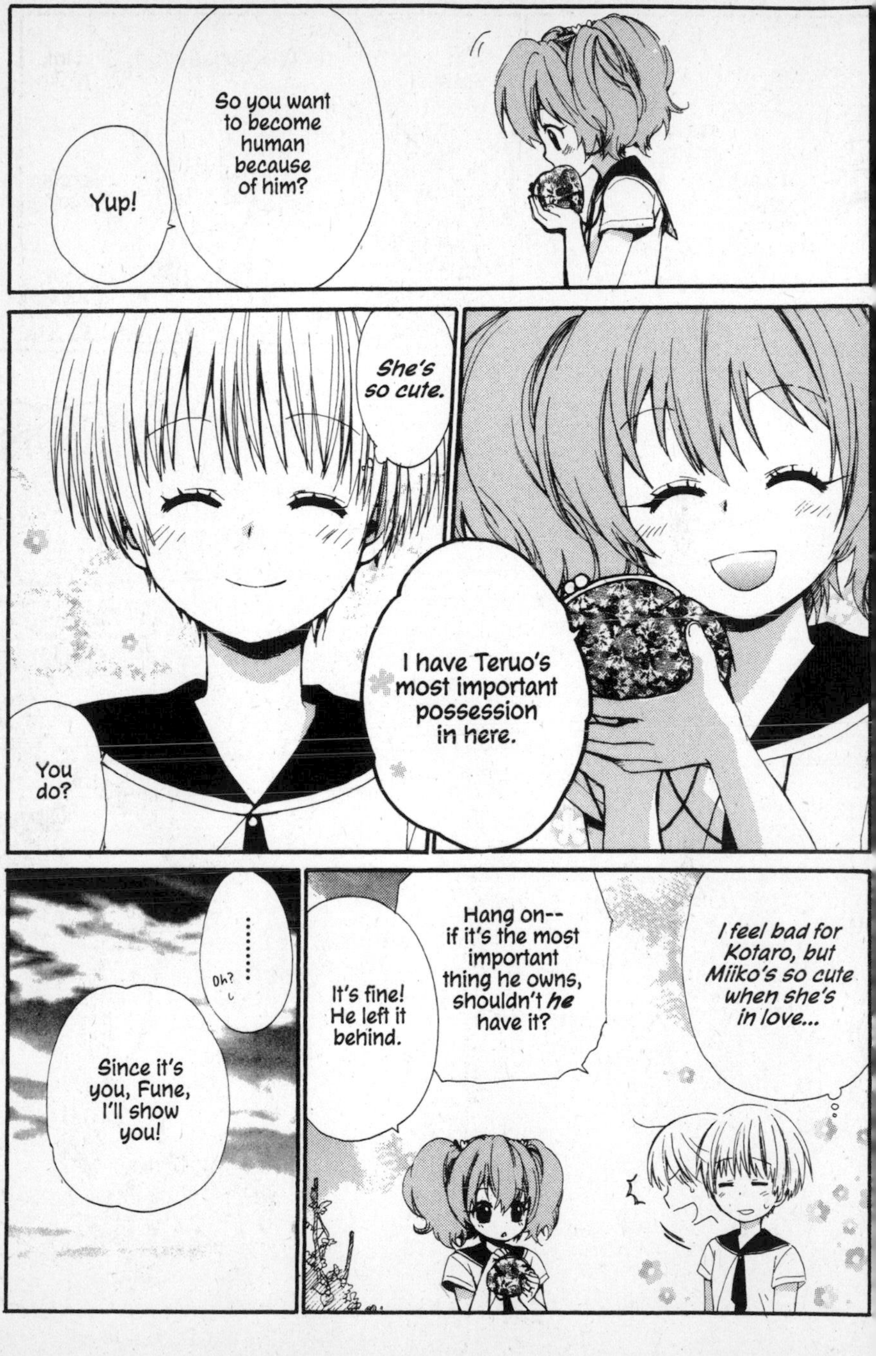
So you want to become human because of him?
Yup!
I have Teruo's most important possession in here.
She's so cute.
You do?
I feel bad for Kotaro, but Miiko's so cute when she's in love...
Hang on-- if it's the most important thing he owns, shouldn't he have it?
It's fine! He left it behind.
......
Oh?
Since it's you, Fune, I'll show you!

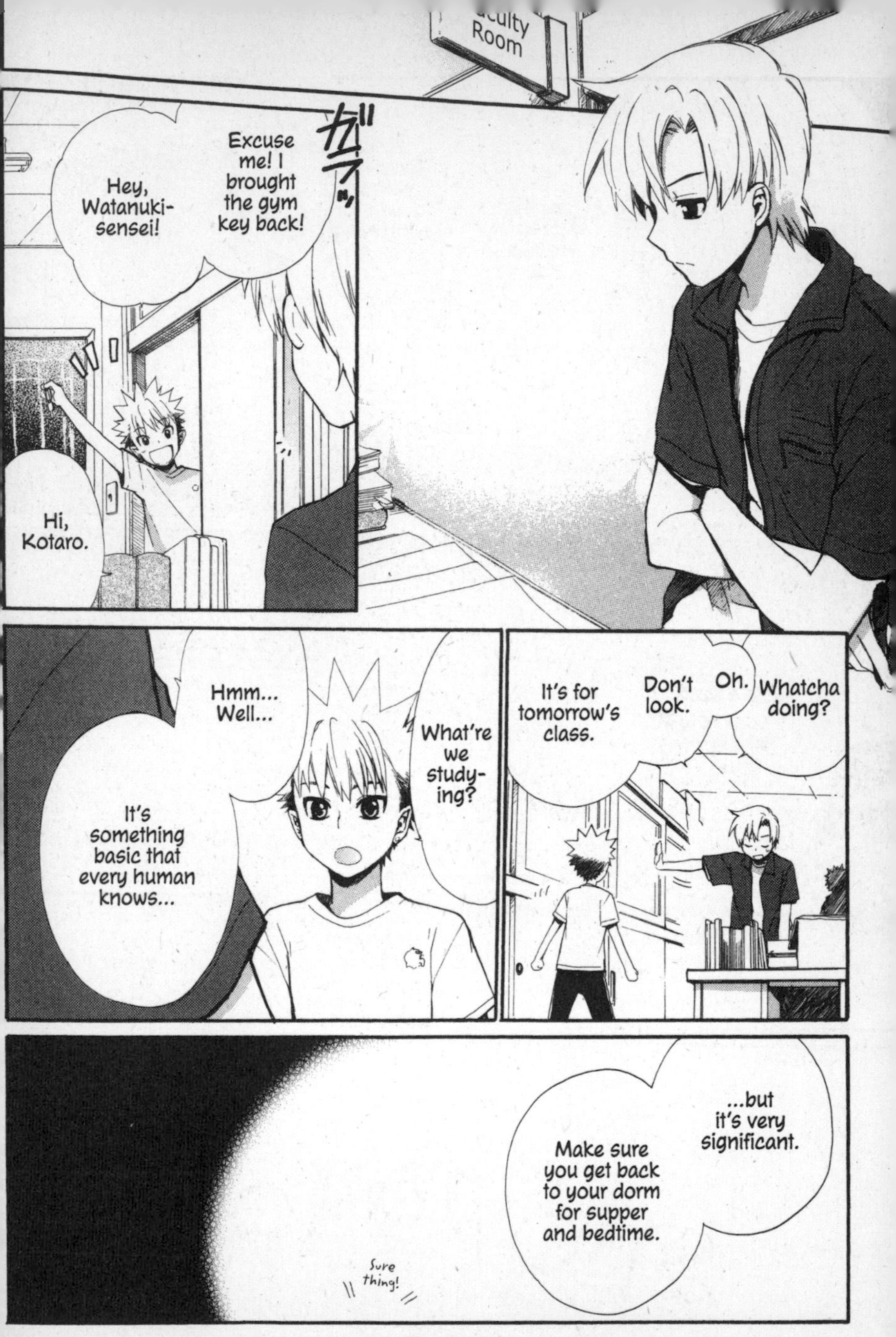
aculty Room
Excuse me! I brought the gym key back!
ガラ
Hey, Watanuki-sensei!
Hi, Kotaro.
Whatcha doing?
Oh.
Don't look.
It's for tomorrow's class.
What're we study-ing?
Hmm... Well...
It's something basic that every human knows...
...but it's very significant.
Make sure you get back to your dorm for supper and bedtime.
Sure thing!

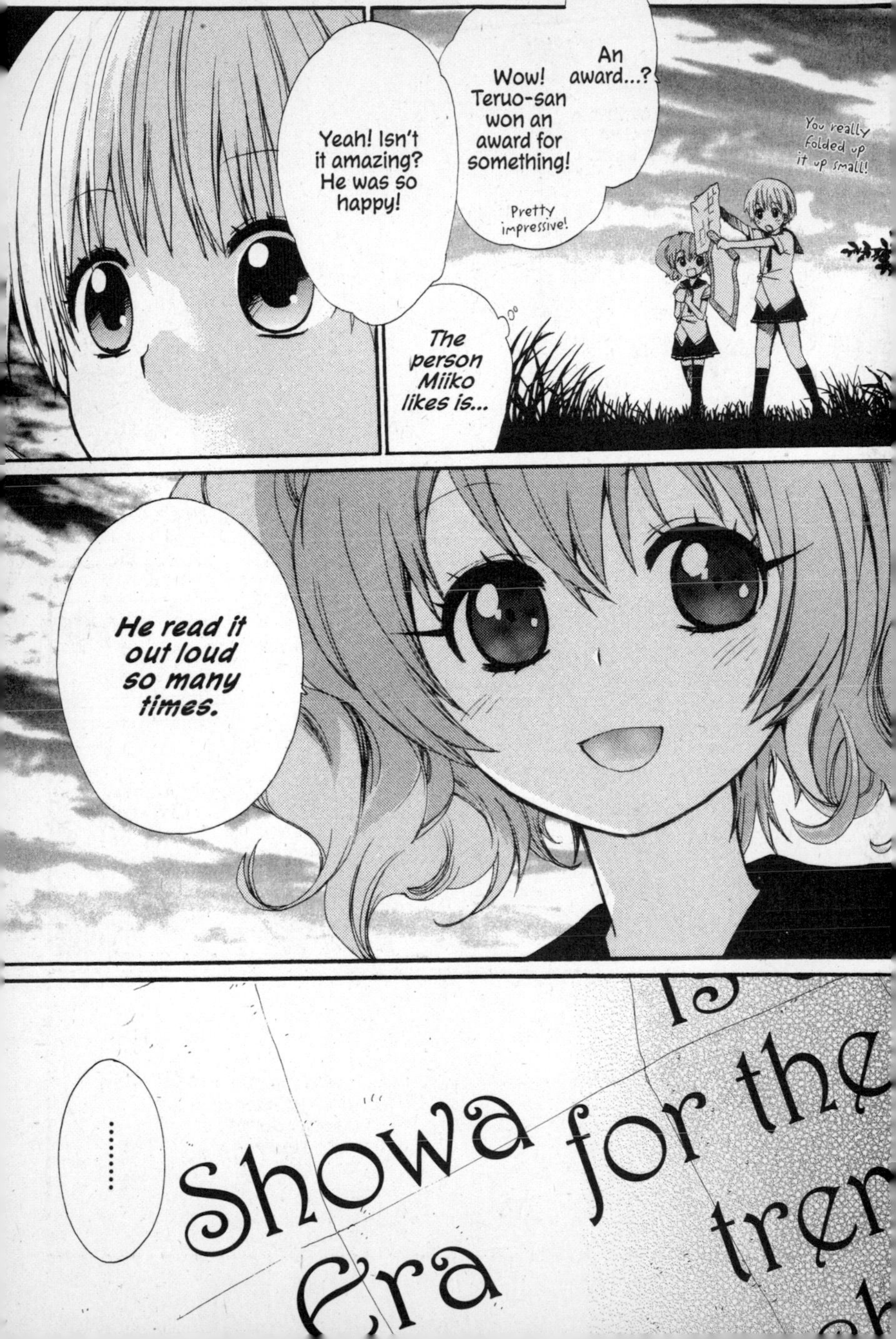
An award...?
You really folded up it up small!
Wow! Teruo-san won an award for something!
Pretty impressive!
Yeah! Isn't it amazing? He was so happy!
The person Miiko likes is...
He read it out loud so many times.
....
Showa Era
for the

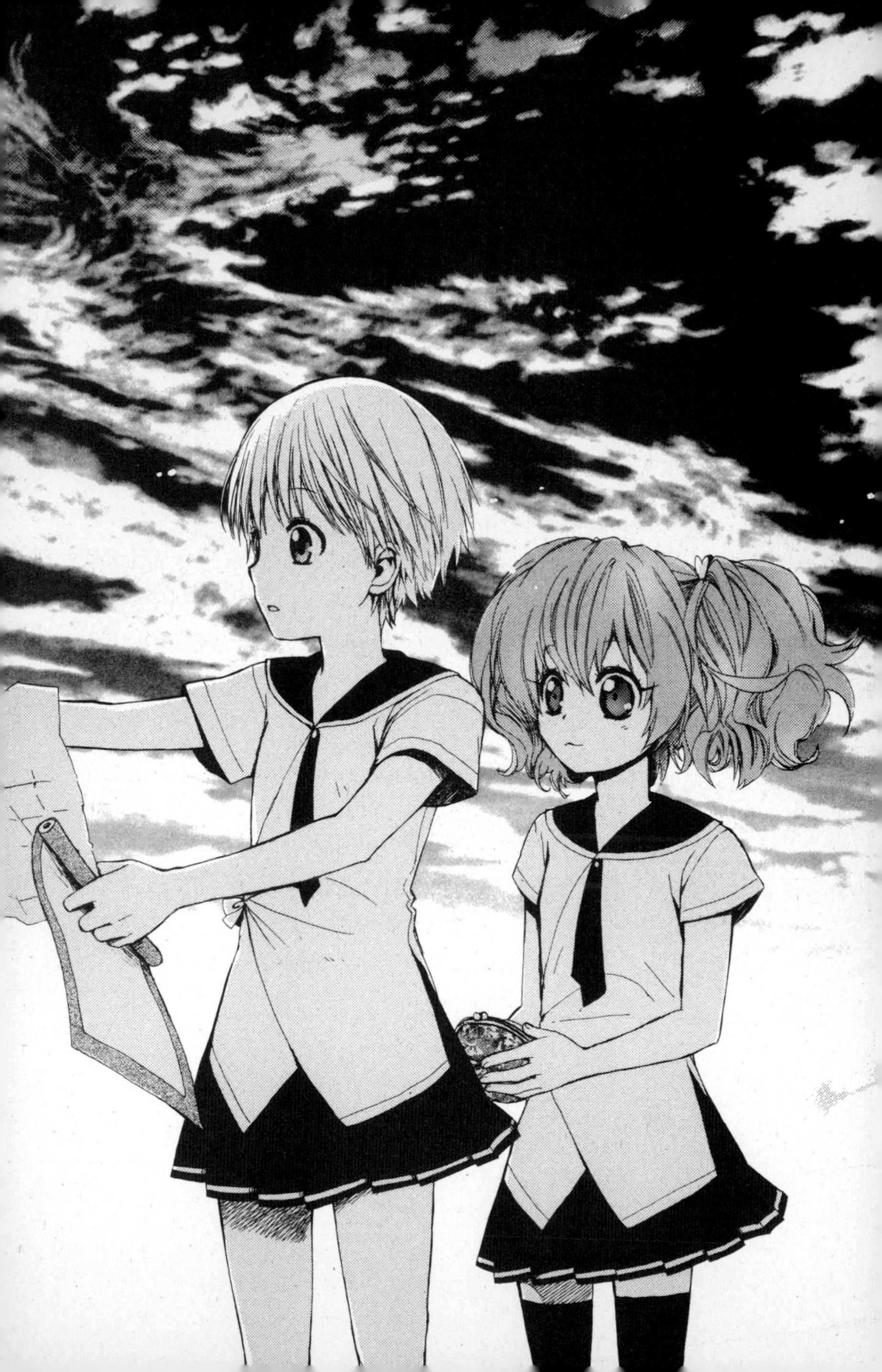

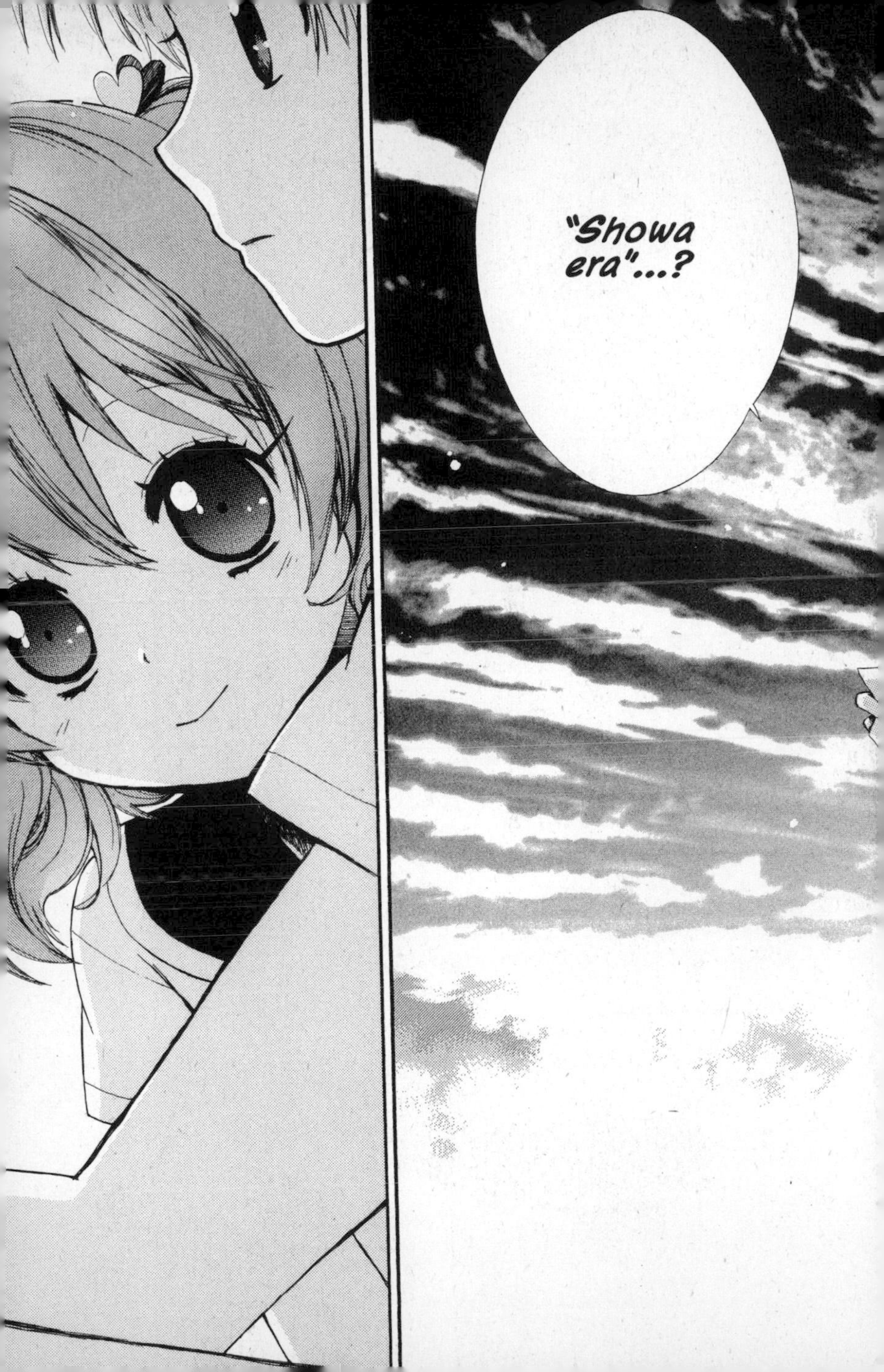
"Showa era"...?

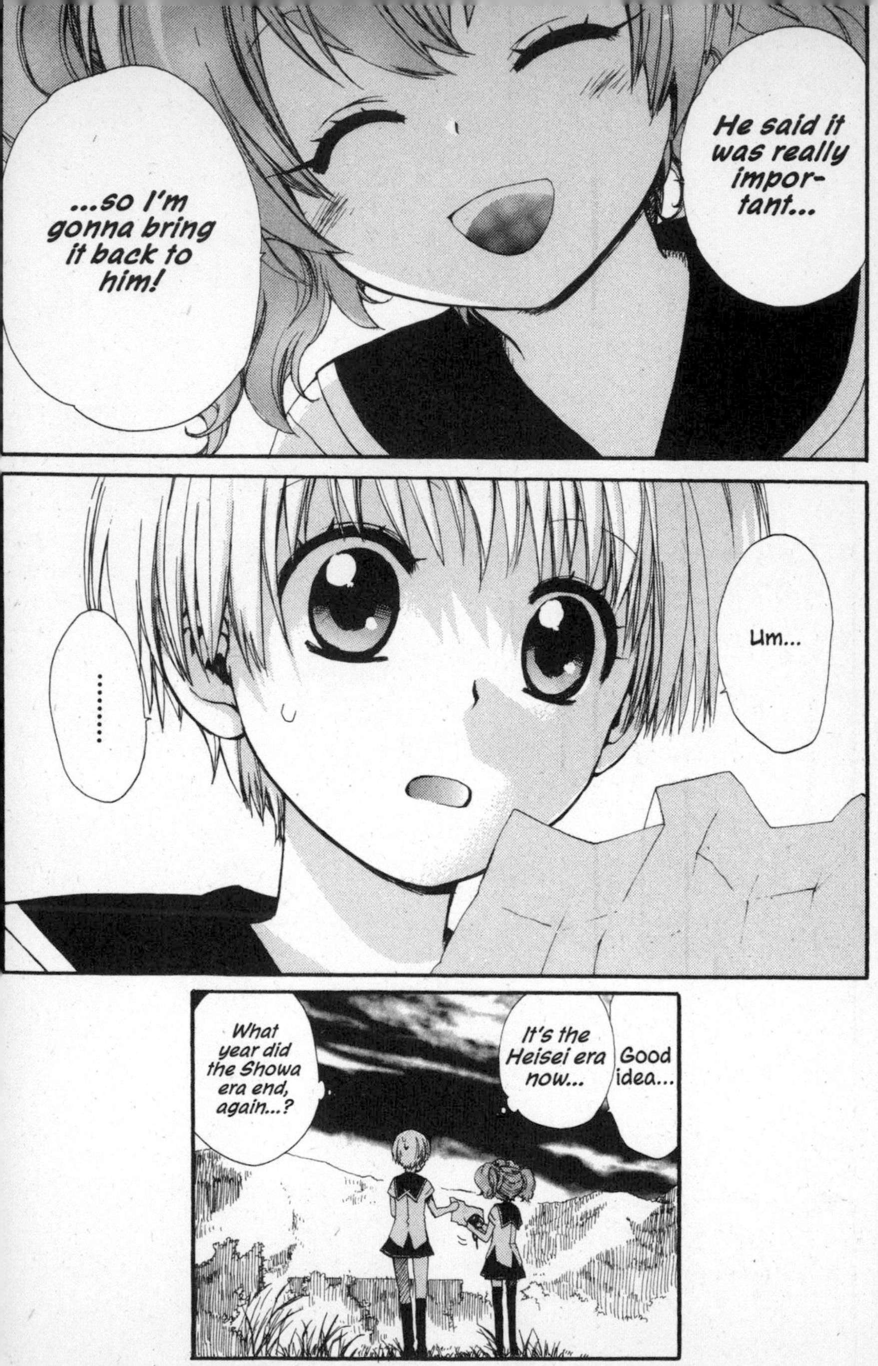
He said it was really important...
...so I'm gonna bring it back to him!
Um...
......
Good idea...
It's the Heisei era now...
What year did the Showa era end, again...?

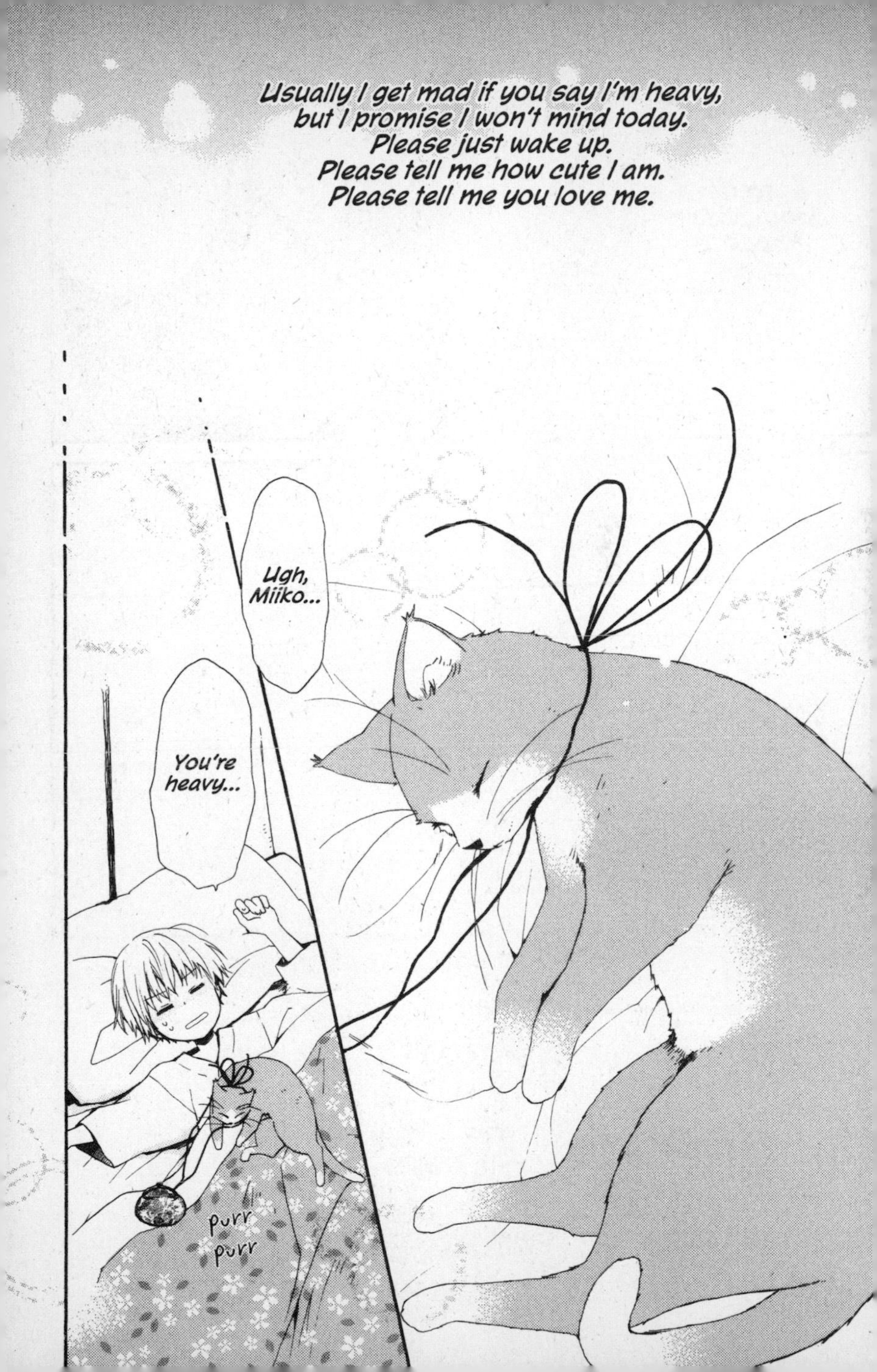
Usually I get mad if you say I'm heavy, but I promise I won't mind today.
Please just wake up.
Please tell me how cute I am.
Please tell me you love me.
Ugh, Miiko...
You're heavy...
purr purr

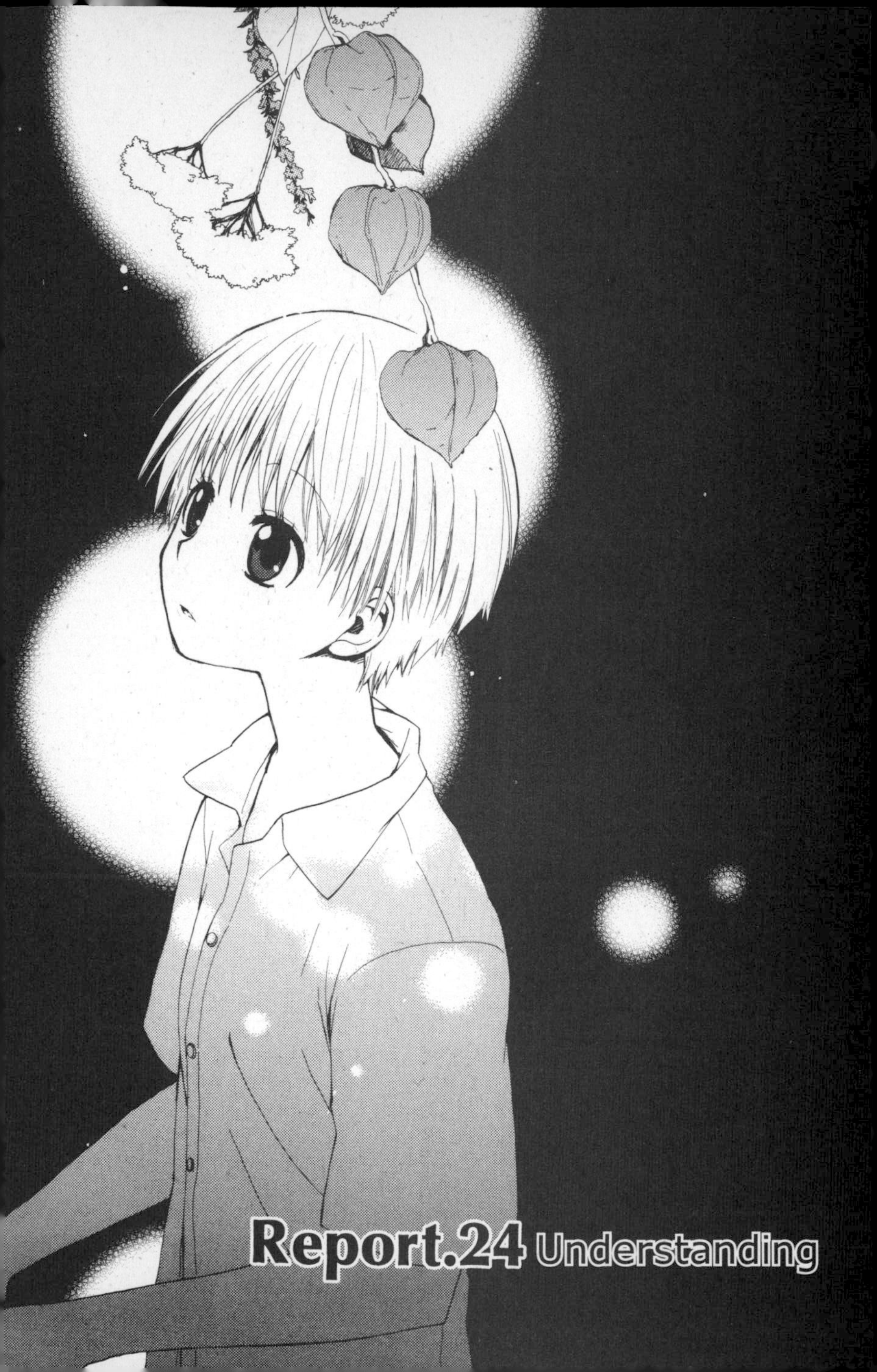
Report.24 Understanding

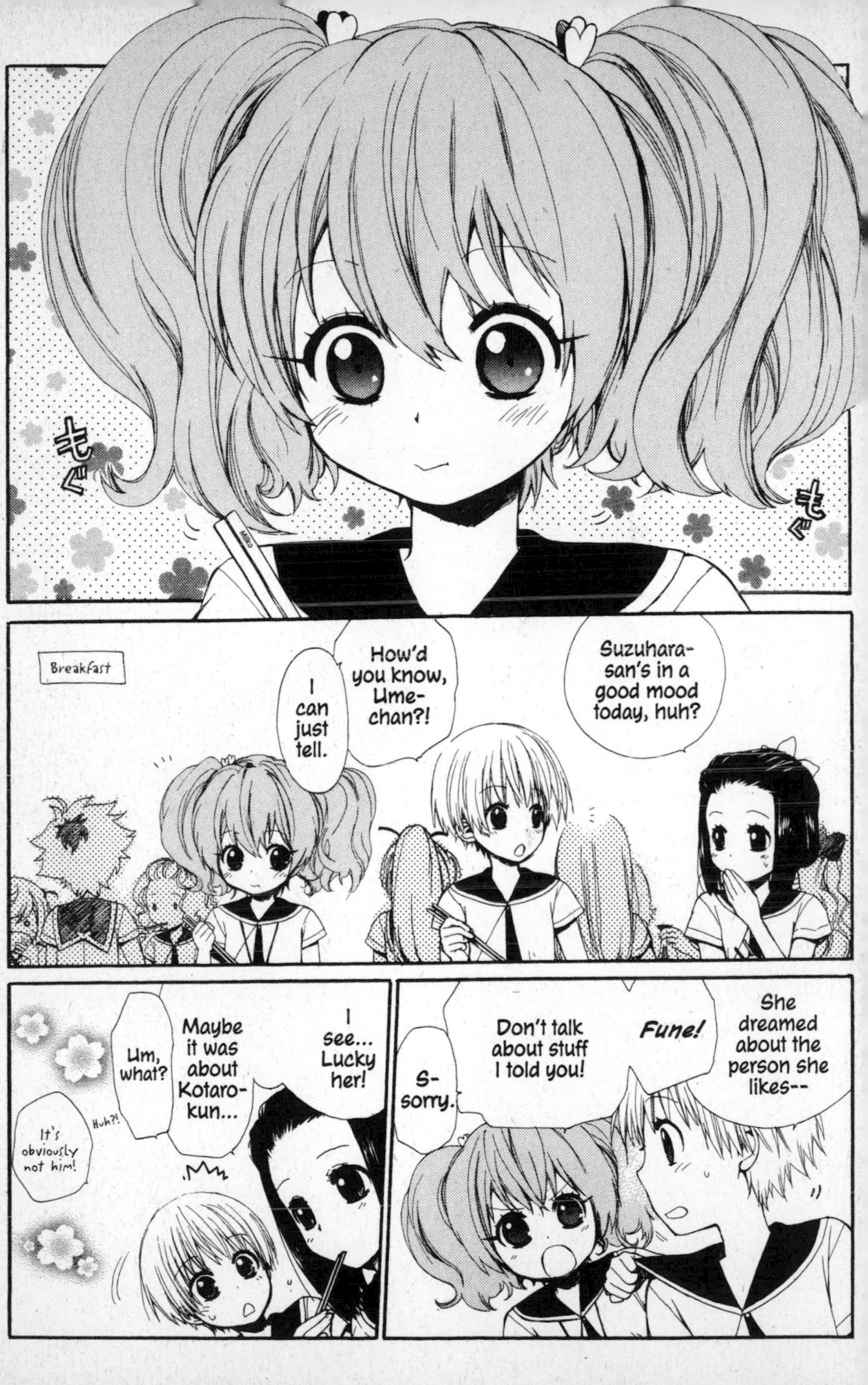
もぐ
もぐ
Suzuhara-san's in a good mood today, huh?
How'd you know, Ume-chan?!
I can just tell.
Breakfast
She dreamed about the person she likes--
Fune!
Don't talk about stuff I told you!
S-sorry.
I see... Lucky her!
Maybe it was about Kotaro-kun...
Um, what?
Huh?!
It's obviously not him!

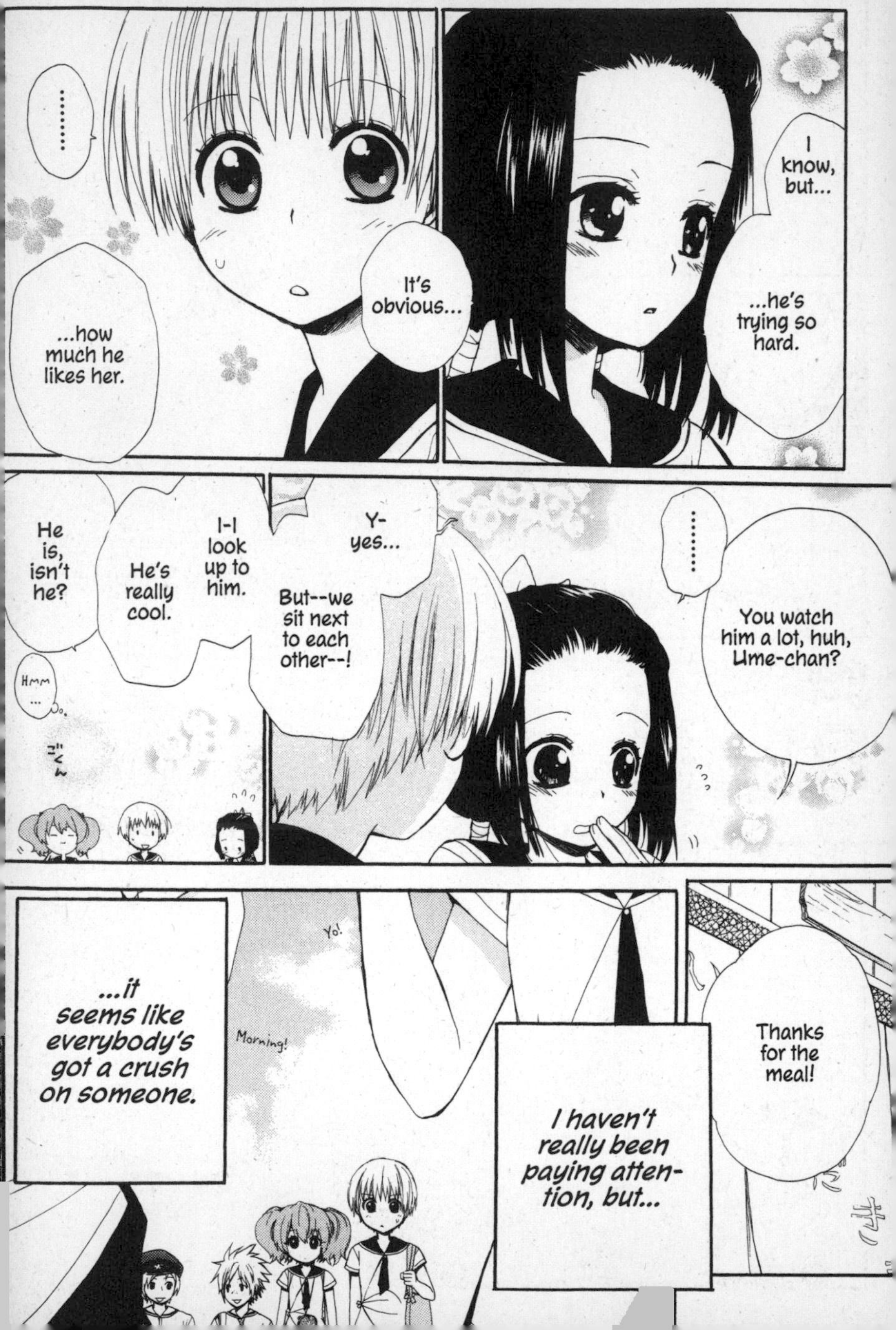
I know, but...
...he's trying so hard.
......
It's obvious...
...how much he likes her.
......
You watch him a lot, huh, Ume-chan?
Y-yes...
But--we sit next to each other--!
I-I look up to him.
He's really cool.
He is, isn't he?
Hmm...
Thanks for the meal!
I haven't really been paying atten-tion, but...
Yo!
Morning!
...it seems like everybody's got a crush on someone.

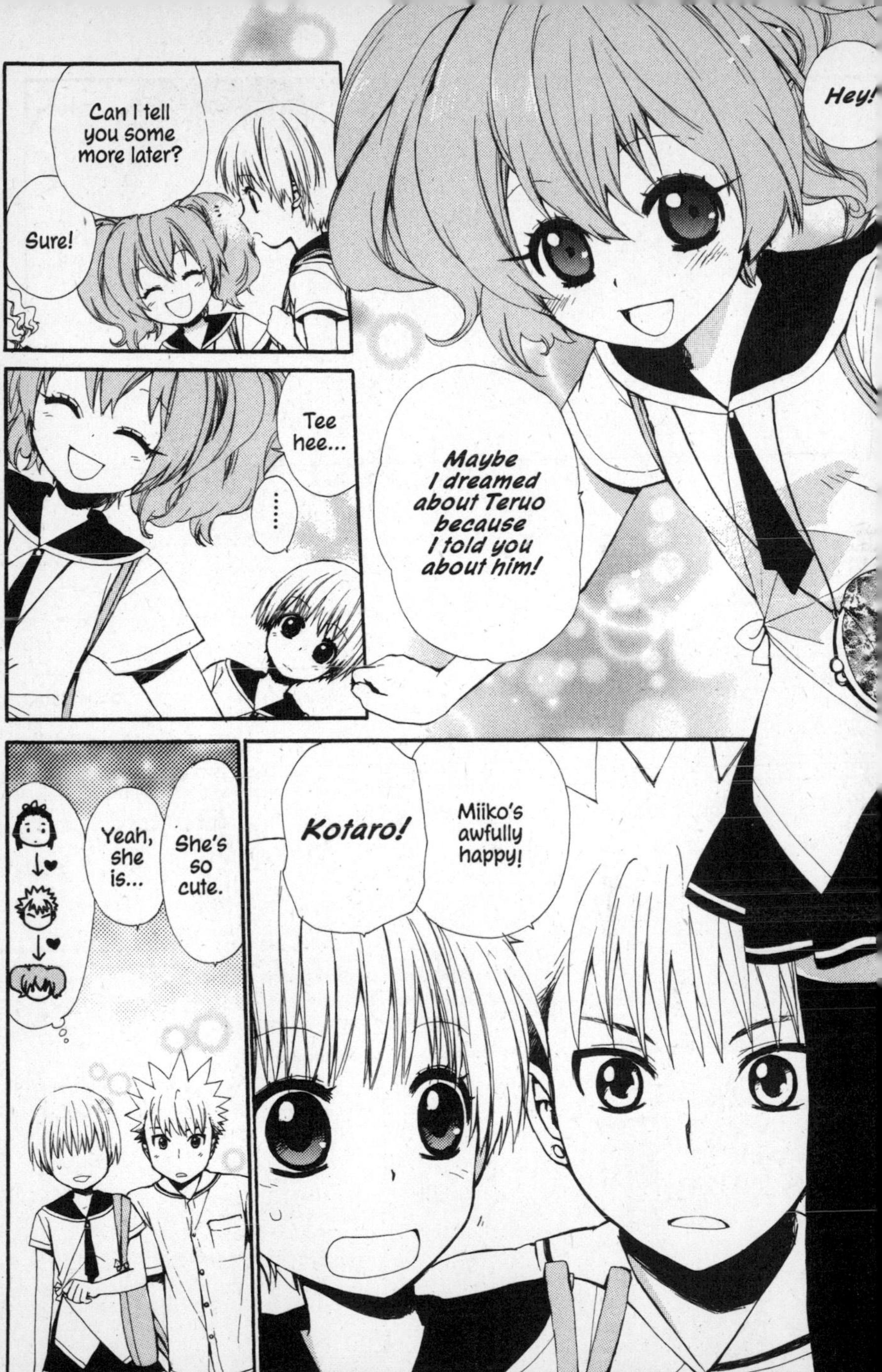
Hey!
Maybe I dreamed about Teruo because I told you about him!
Can I tell you some more later?
Sure!
Tee hee...
......
Miiko's awfully happy!
Kotaro!
She's so cute.
Yeah, she is...

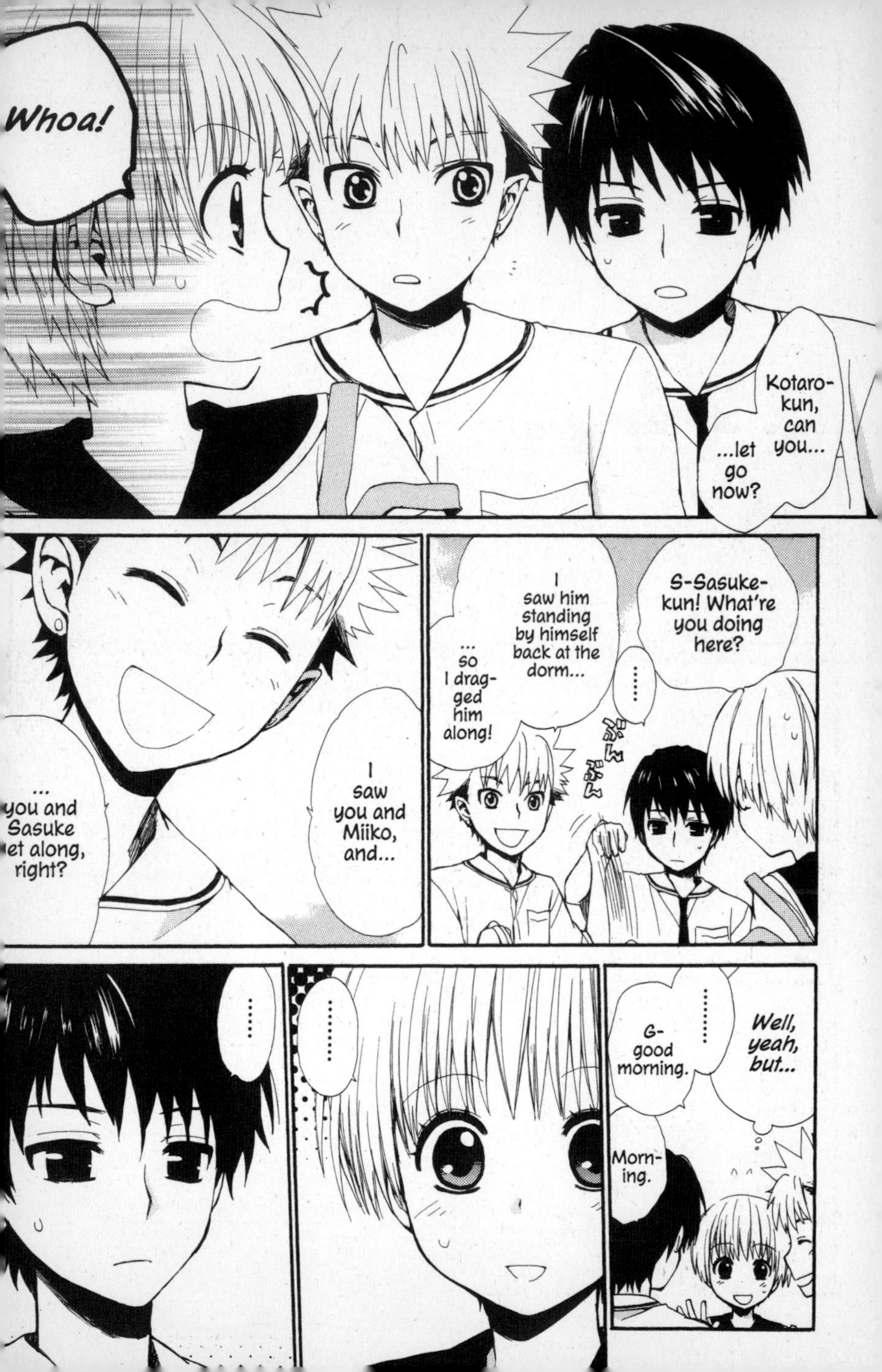
Kotaro-kun, can you...
...let go now?
Whoa!
S-Sasuke-kun! What're you doing here?
......
I saw him standing by himself back at the dorm...
...so I dragged him along!
ぶん ぶん
I saw you and Miiko, and...
...you and Sasuke et along, right?
Well, yeah, but...
......
G-good morning.
Morn-ing.
....
......

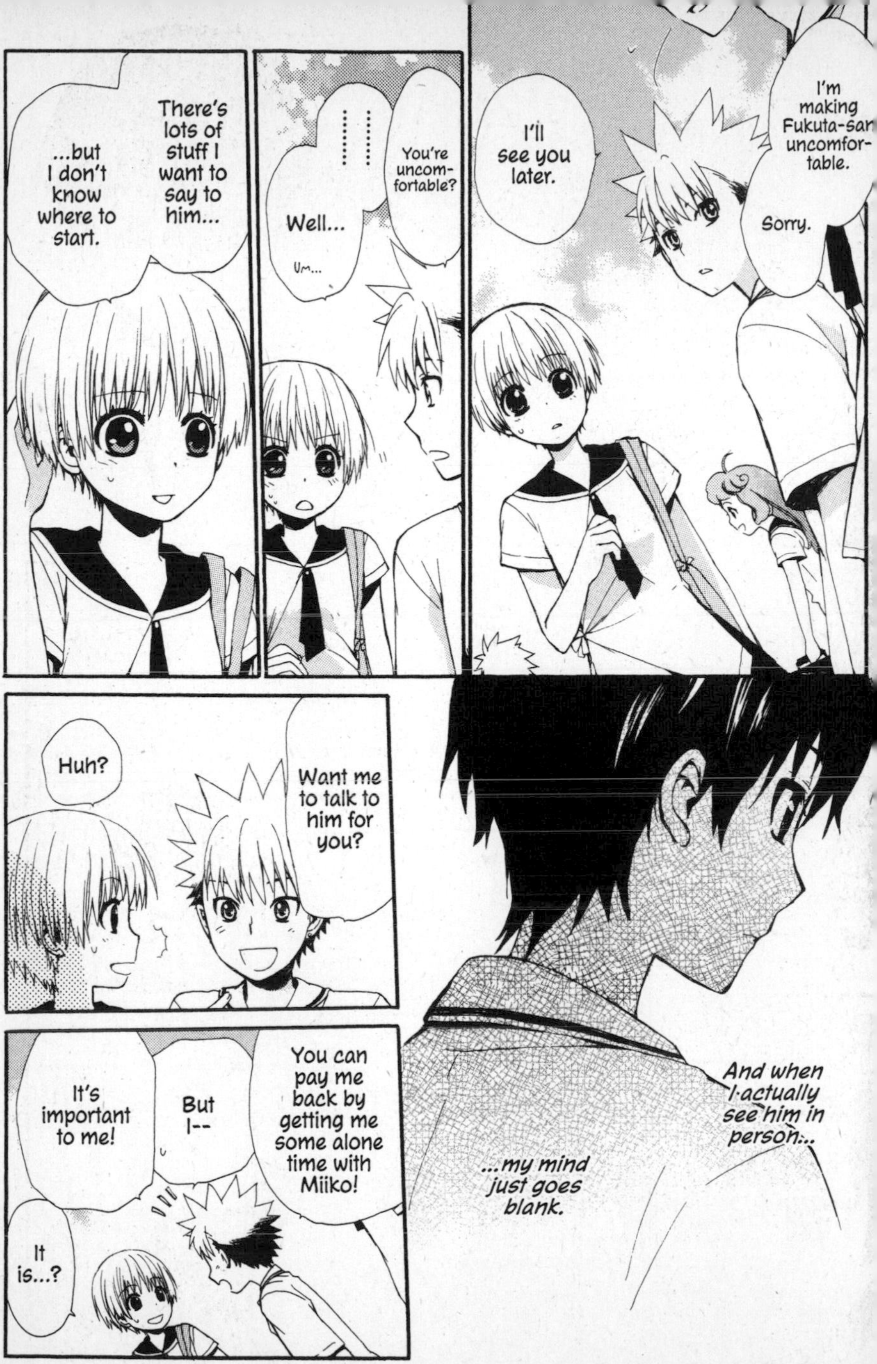
I'm making Fukuta-san uncomfortable.
Sorry.
I'll see you later.
You're uncomfortable?
......
Well...
Um...
There's lots of stuff I want to say to him...
...but I don't know where to start.
And when I actually see him in person...
...my mind just goes blank.
Want me to talk to him for you?
Huh?
You can pay me back by getting me some alone time with Miiko!
But I--
It's important to me!
It is...?

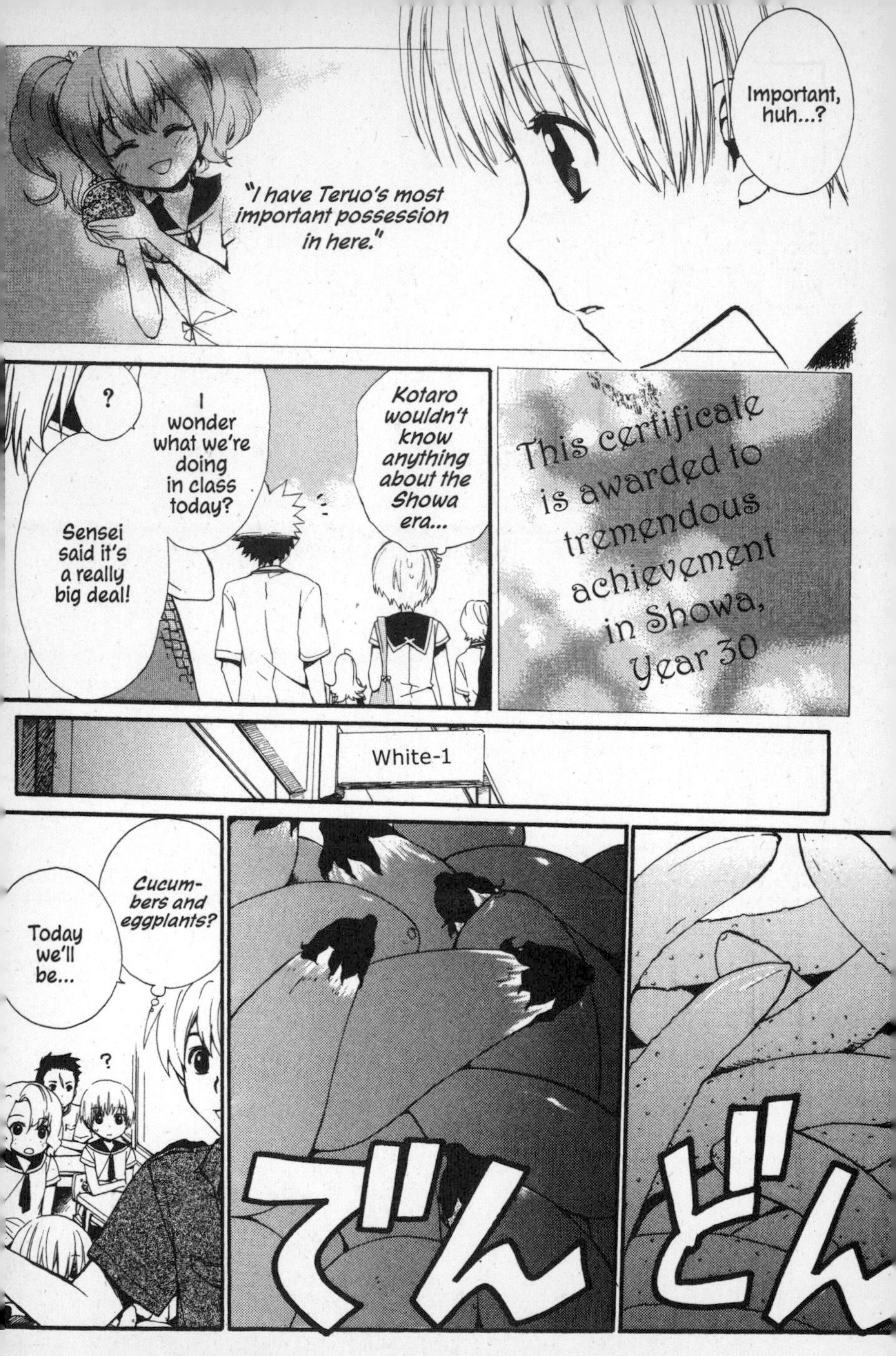
Important, huh...?
"I have Teruo's most important possession in here."
This certificate is awarded to tremendous achievement in Showa, Year 30
Kotaro wouldn't know anything about the Showa era...
I wonder what we're doing in class today?
?
Sensei said it's a really big deal!
White-1
どん
でん
Cucum-bers and eggplants?
Today we'll be...
?

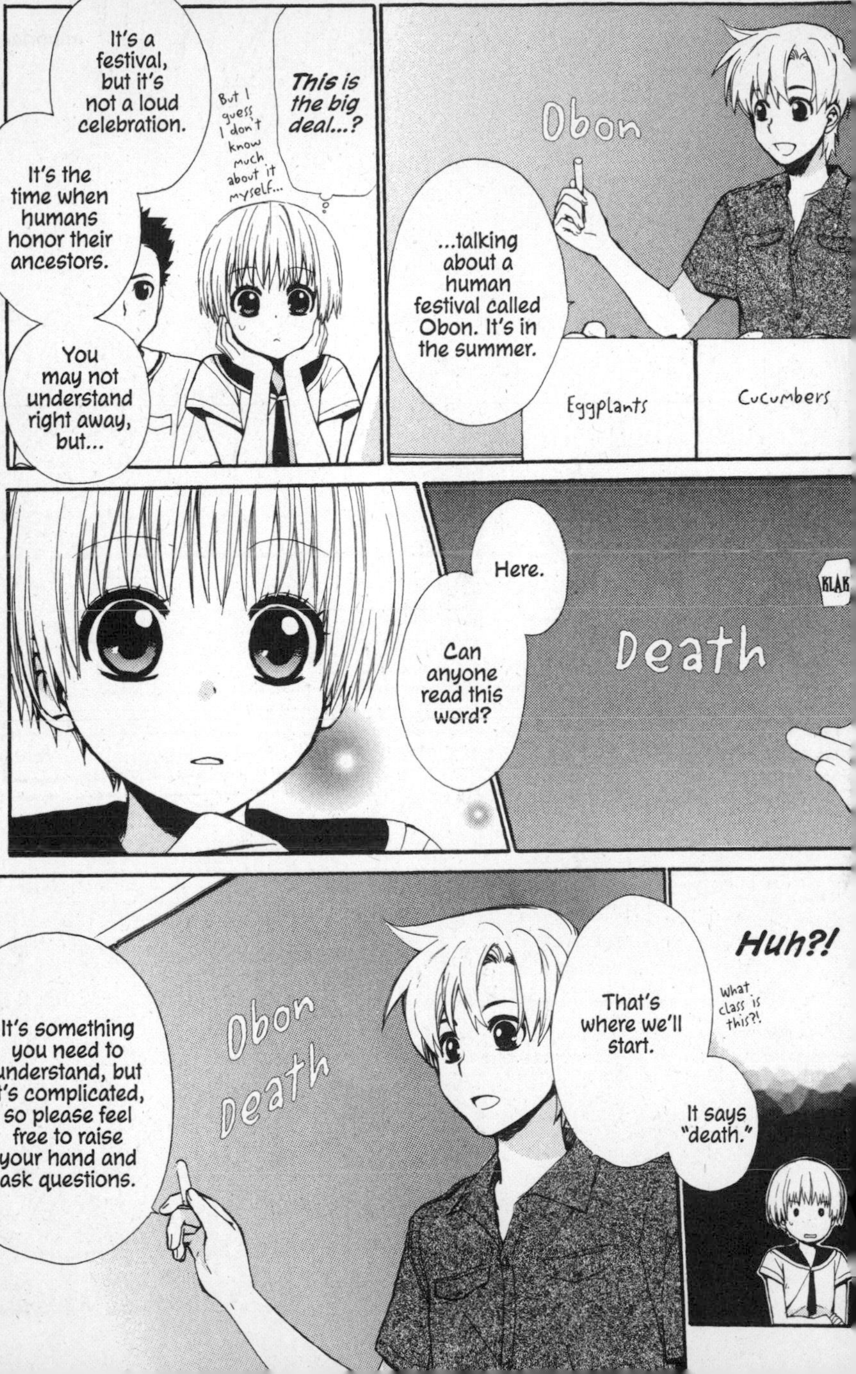
Obon
...talking about a human festival called Obon. It's in the summer.
Cucumbers
Eggplants
This is the big deal...?
But I guess I don't know much about it myself...
It's a festival, but it's not a loud celebration.
It's the time when humans honor their ancestors.
You may not understand right away, but...
KLAK
Here.
Death
Can anyone read this word?
Huh?!
what class is this?!
It says "death."
That's where we'll start.
Obon
Death
It's something you need to understand, but it's complicated, so please feel free to raise your hand and ask questions.

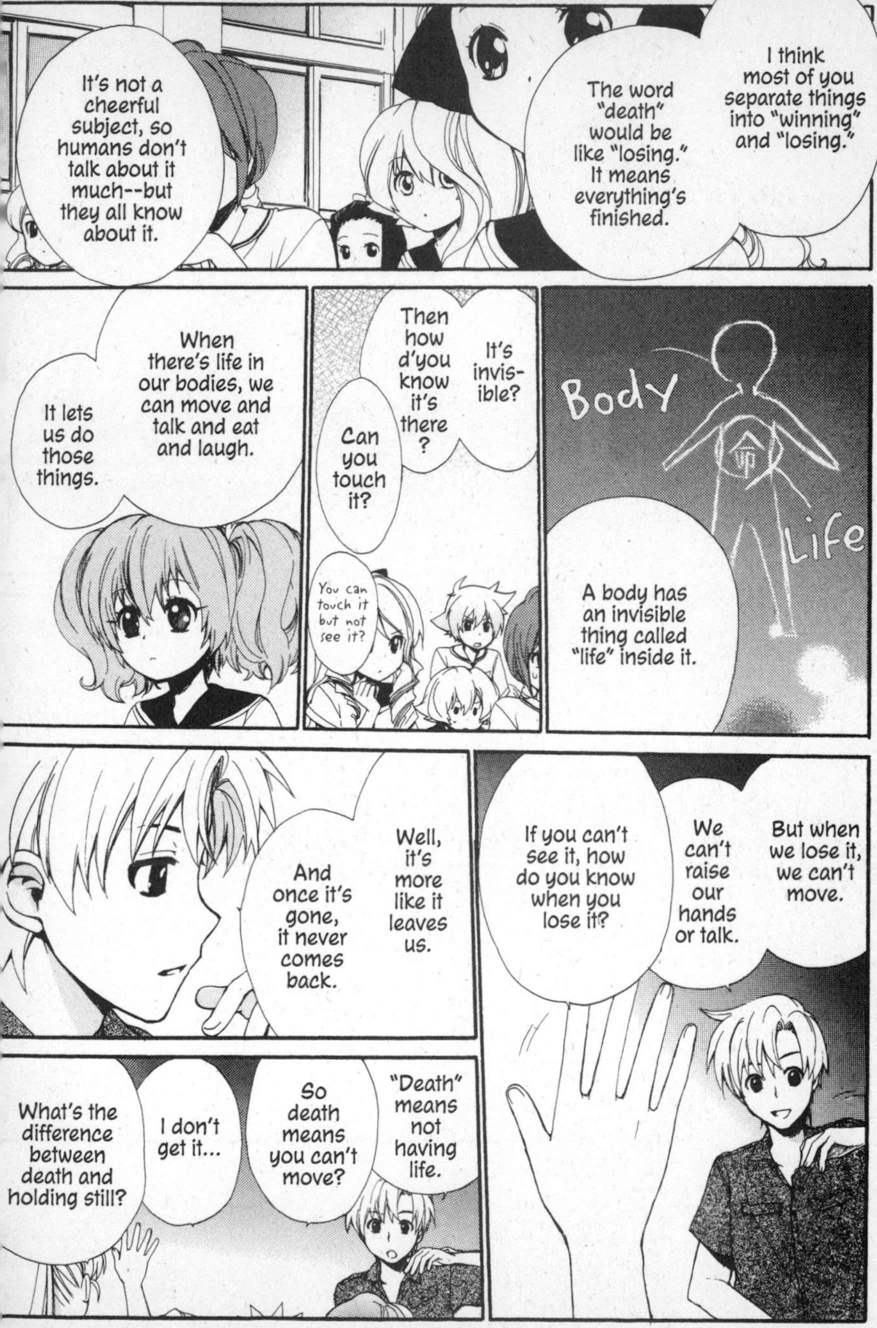
I think most of you separate things into "winning" and "losing."
The word "death" would be like "losing." It means everything's finished.
It's not a cheerful subject, so humans don't talk about it much--but they all know about it.
Body
Life
A body has an invisible thing called "life" inside it.
It's invisible?
Then how d'you know it's there?
Can you touch it?
You can touch it but not see it?
When there's life in our bodies, we can move and talk and eat and laugh.
It lets us do those things.
But when we lose it, we can't move.
We can't raise our hands or talk.
If you can't see it, how do you know when you lose it?
Well, it's more like it leaves us.
And once it's gone, it never comes back.
"Death" means not having life.
So death means you can't move?
I don't get it...
What's the difference between death and holding still?

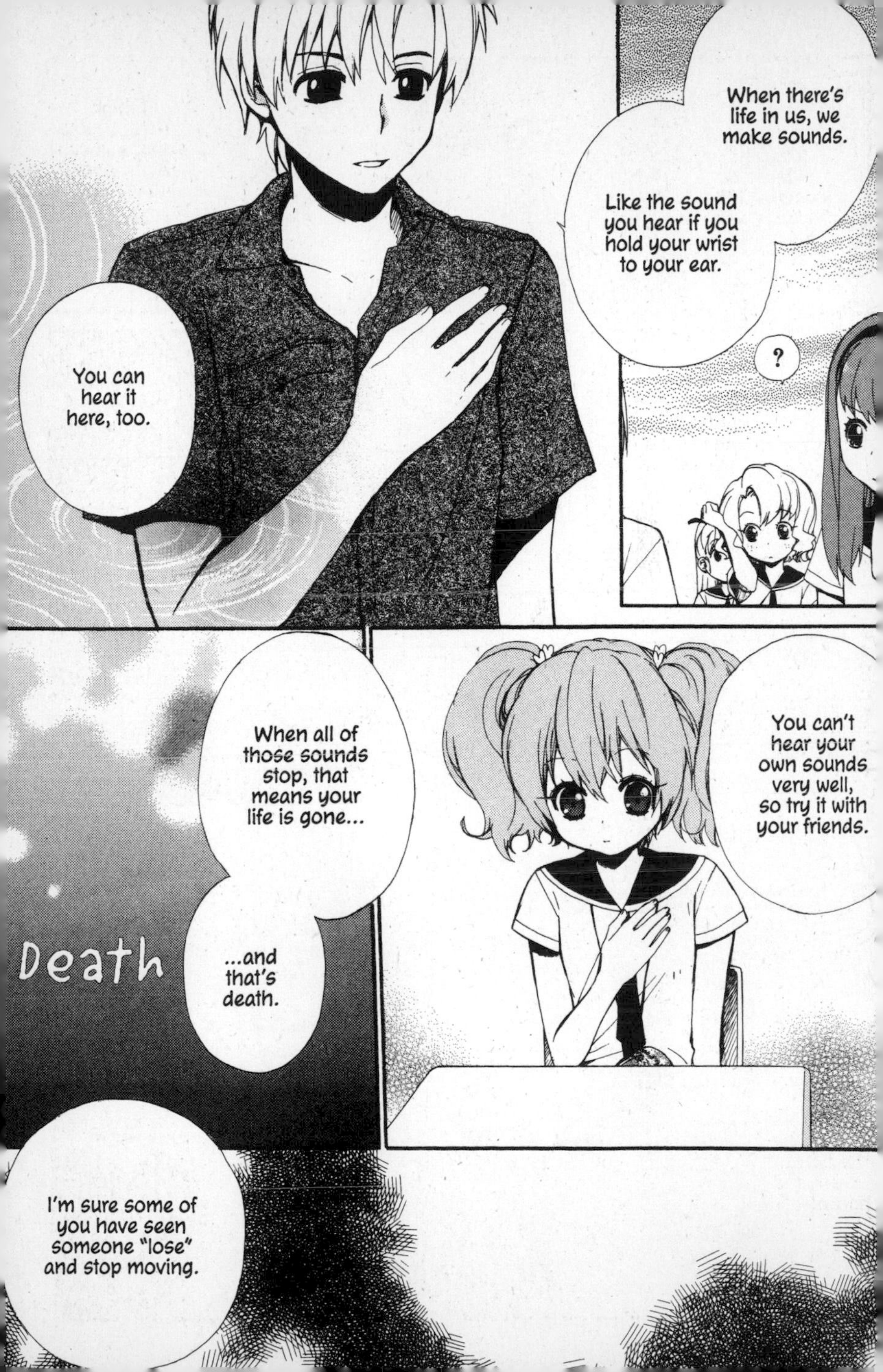
When there's life in us, we make sounds.
Like the sound you hear if you hold your wrist to your ear.
?
You can hear it here, too.
You can't hear your own sounds very well, so try it with your friends.
When all of those sounds stop, that means your life is gone...
...and that's death.
Death
I'm sure some of you have seen someone "lose" and stop moving.

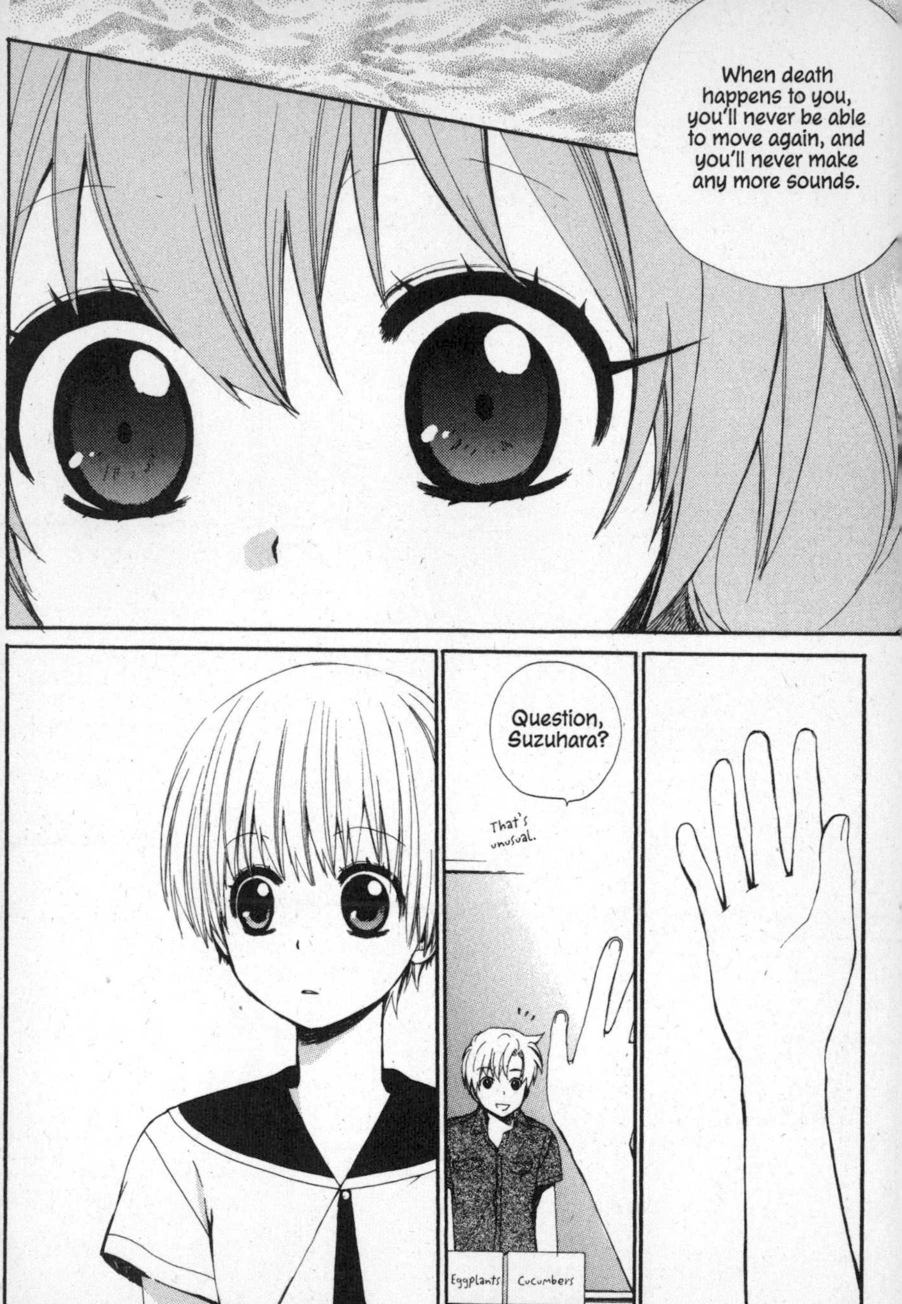
When death happens to you, you'll never be able to move again, and you'll never make any more sounds.
Question, Suzuhara?
That's unusual.
Eggplants
Cucumbers

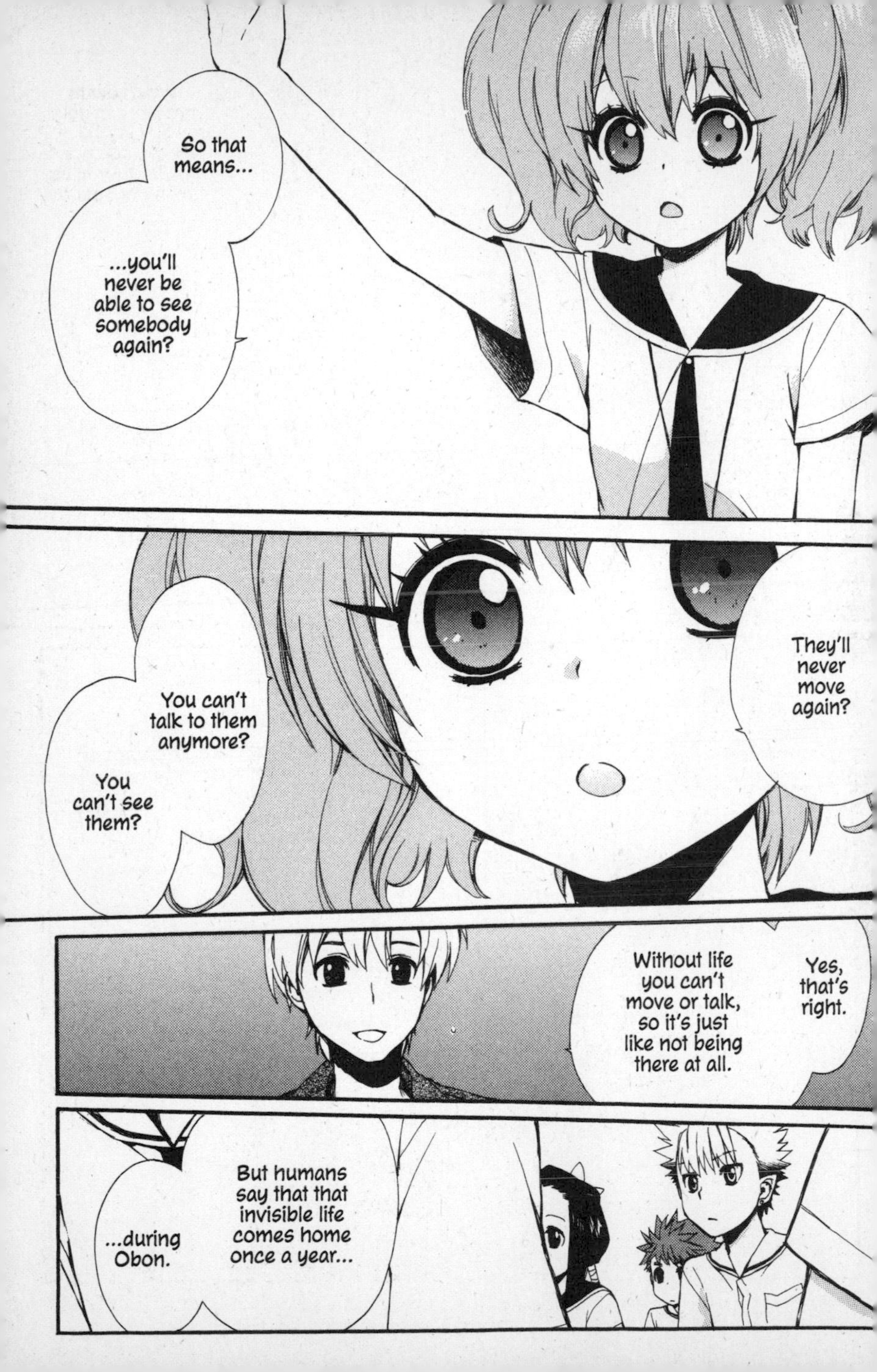
So that means...
...you'll never be able to see somebody again?
They'll never move again?
You can't talk to them anymore?
You can't see them?
Yes, that's right.
Without life you can't move or talk, so it's just like not being there at all.
But humans say that that invisible life comes home once a year...
...during Obon.

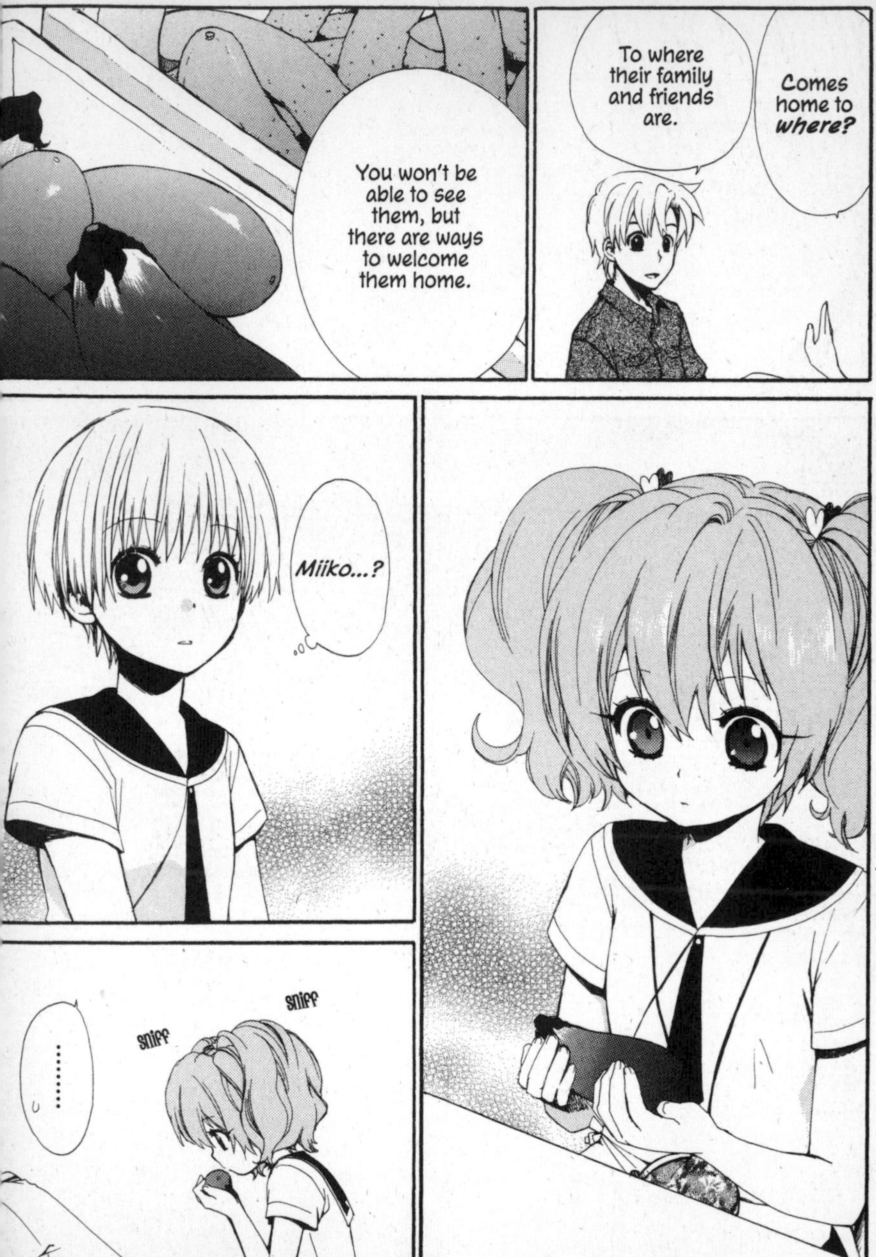
Comes home to *where?*
To where their family and friends are.
You won't be able to see them, but there are ways to welcome them home.
Miiko...?
SNIFF
SNIFF
......

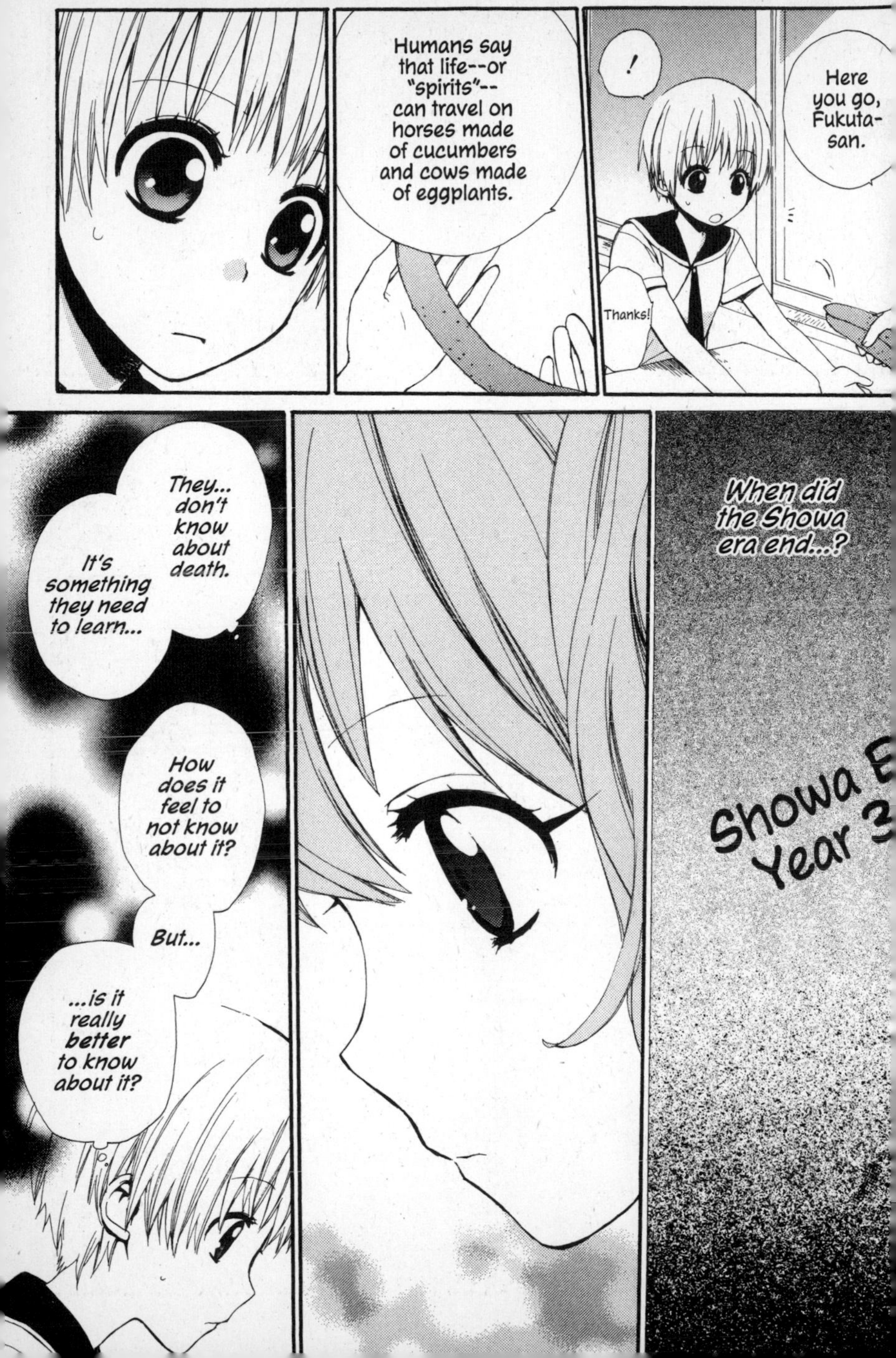
Here you go, Fukuta-san.
!
Thanks!
Humans say that life--or "spirits"--can travel on horses made of cucumbers and cows made of eggplants.
When did the Showa era end...?
Showa E
Year 3
They... don't know about death.
It's something they need to learn...
How does it feel to not know about it?
But...
...is it really better to know about it?

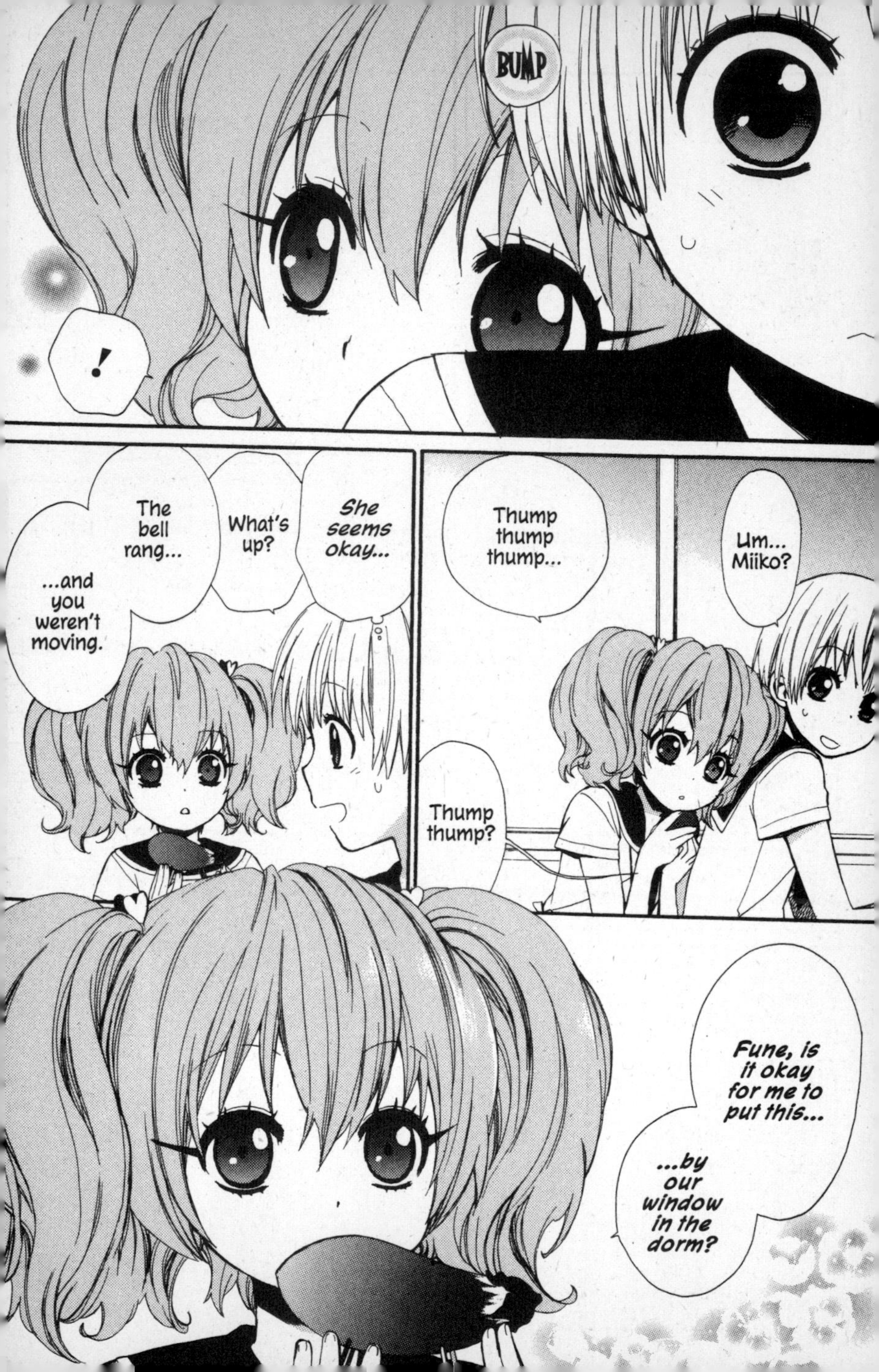
BUMP
!
Um... Miiko?
Thump thump thump...
Thump thump?
She seems okay...
What's up?
The bell rang...
...and you weren't moving.
Fune, is it okay for me to put this...
...by our window in the dorm?

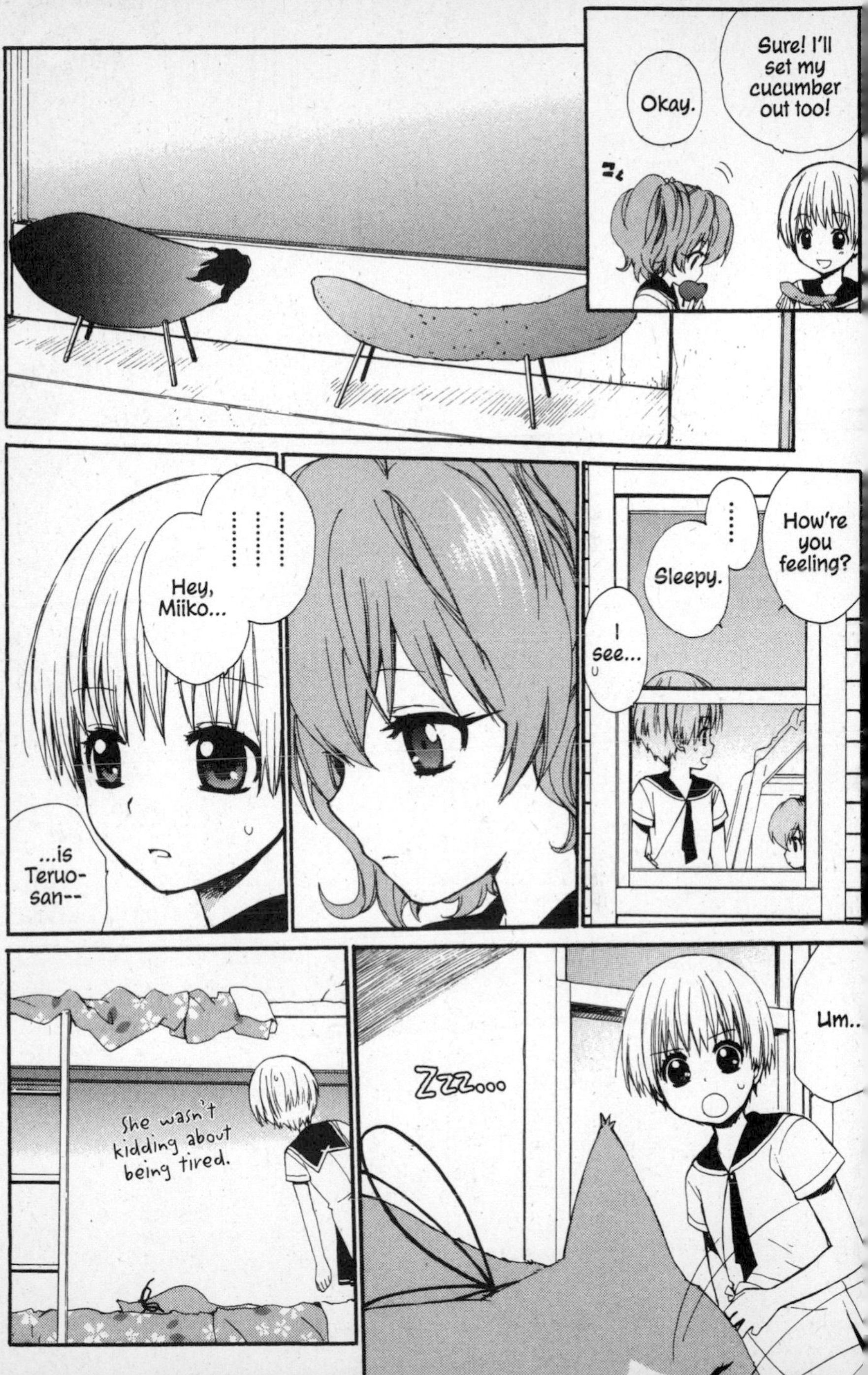
Sure! I'll set my cucumber out too!
Okay.
How're you feeling?
......
Sleepy.
I see...
......
Hey, Miiko...
...is Teruo-san--
Um...
Zzz...
She wasn't kidding about being tired.

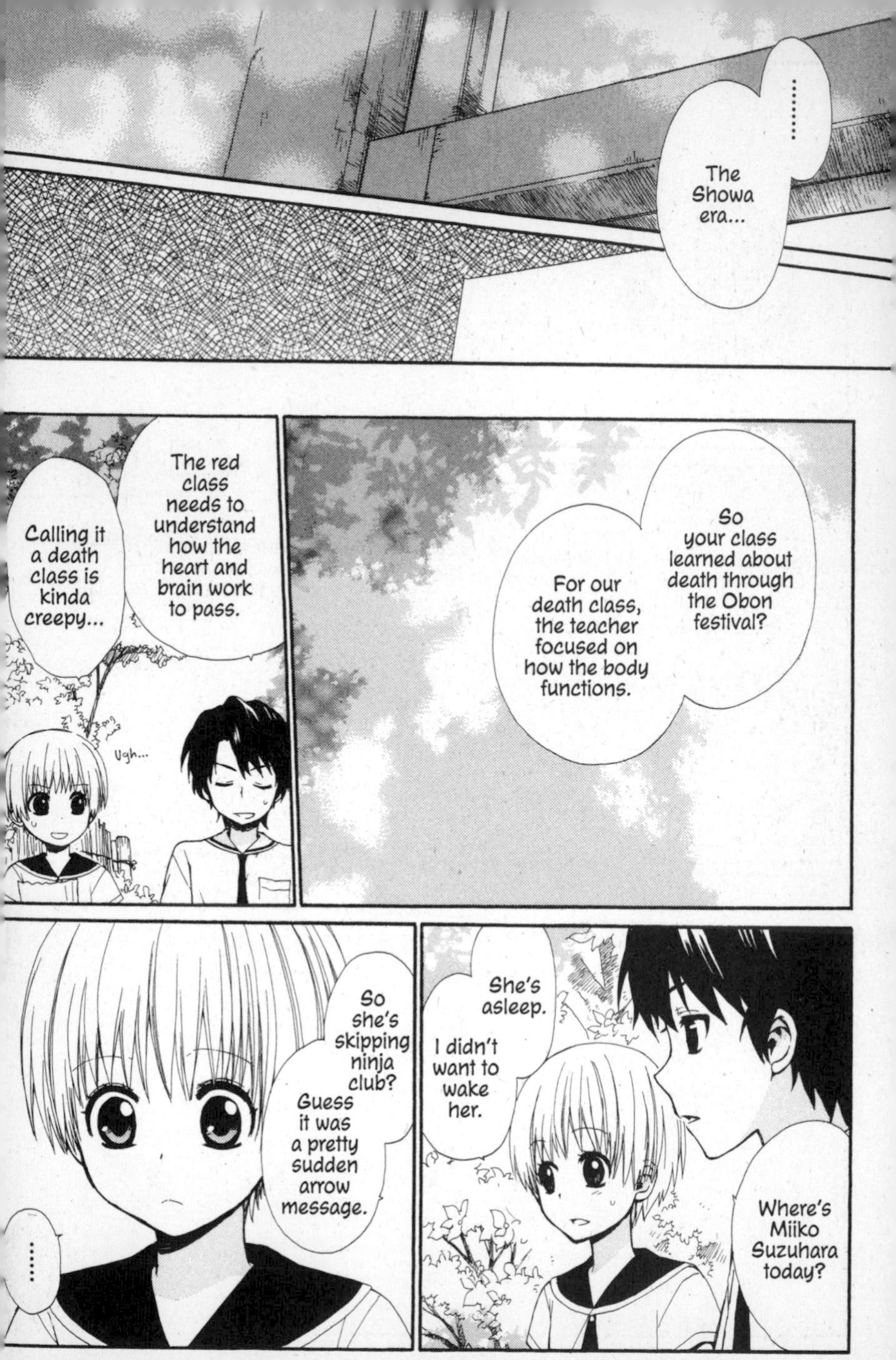
......
The Showa era...
So your class learned about death through the Obon festival?
For our death class, the teacher focused on how the body functions.
The red class needs to understand how the heart and brain work to pass.
Calling it a death class is kinda creepy...
Ugh...
Where's Miiko Suzuhara today?
She's asleep.
I didn't want to wake her.
So she's skipping ninja club?
Guess it was a pretty sudden arrow message.
......

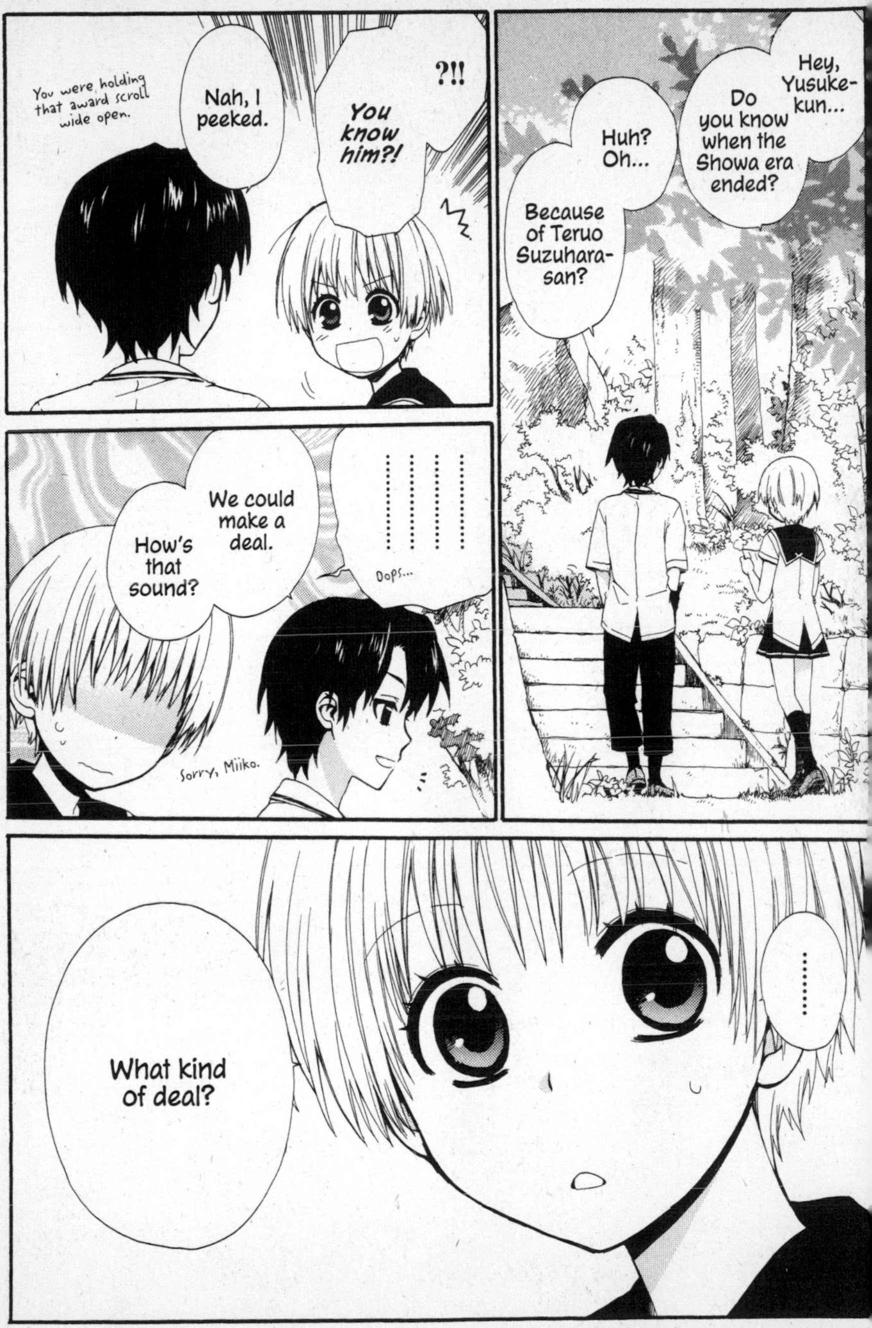
Hey, Yusuke-kun...
Do you know when the Showa era ended?
Huh? Oh...
Because of Teruo Suzuhara-san?
?!!
You know him?!
Nah, I peeked.
You were holding that award scroll wide open.
......
Oops...
We could make a deal.
How's that sound?
Sorry, Miiko.
......
What kind of deal?

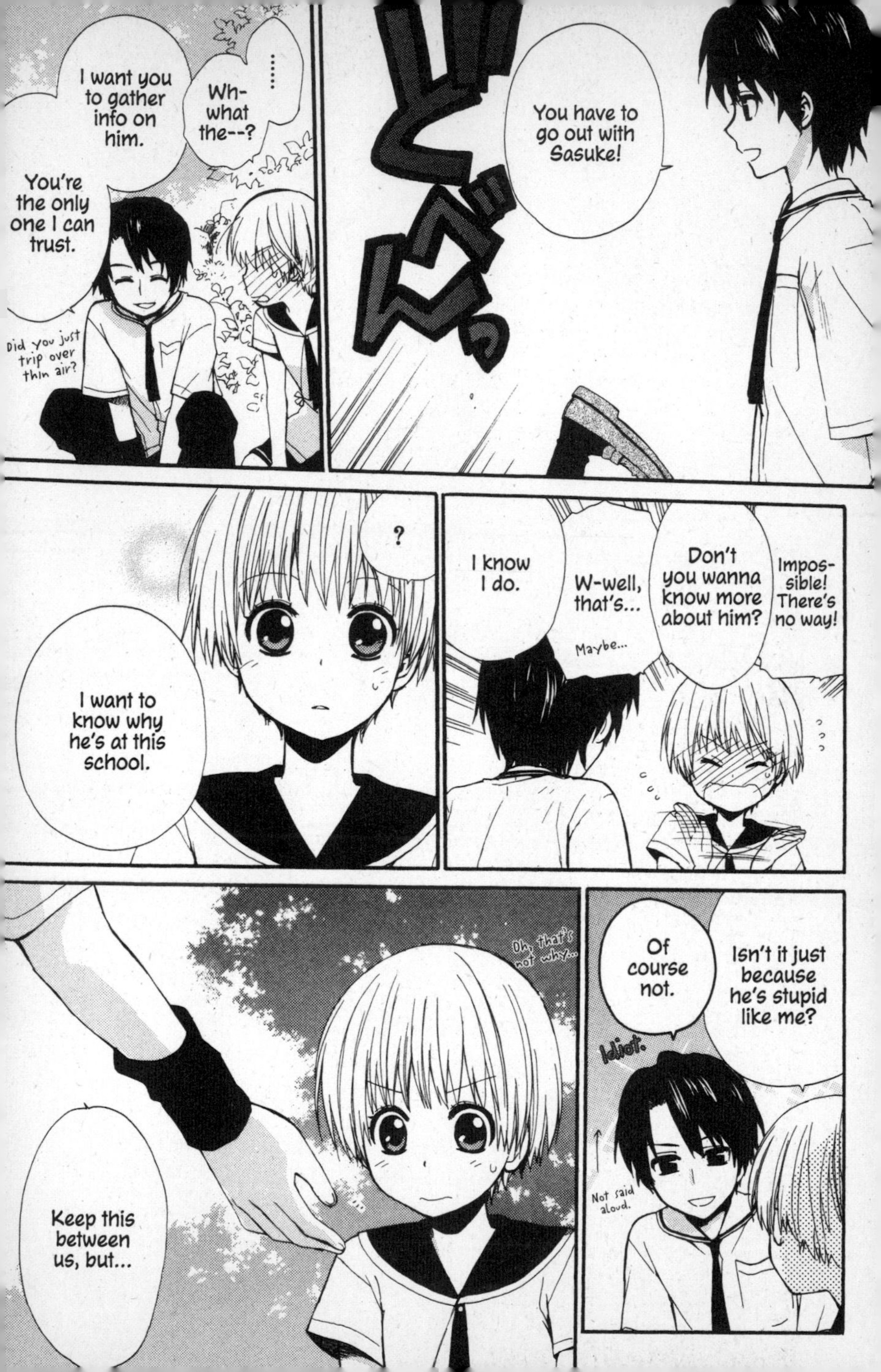
You have to go out with Sasuke!
......
Wh-what the--?
I want you to gather info on him.
You're the only one I can trust.
Did you just trip over thin air?
Impos-sible! There's no way!
Don't you wanna know more about him?
W-well, that's...
I know I do.
Maybe...
?
I want to know why he's at this school.
Isn't it just because he's stupid like me?
Of course not.
Idiot.
Not said aloud.
Oh, that's not why...
Keep this between us, but...

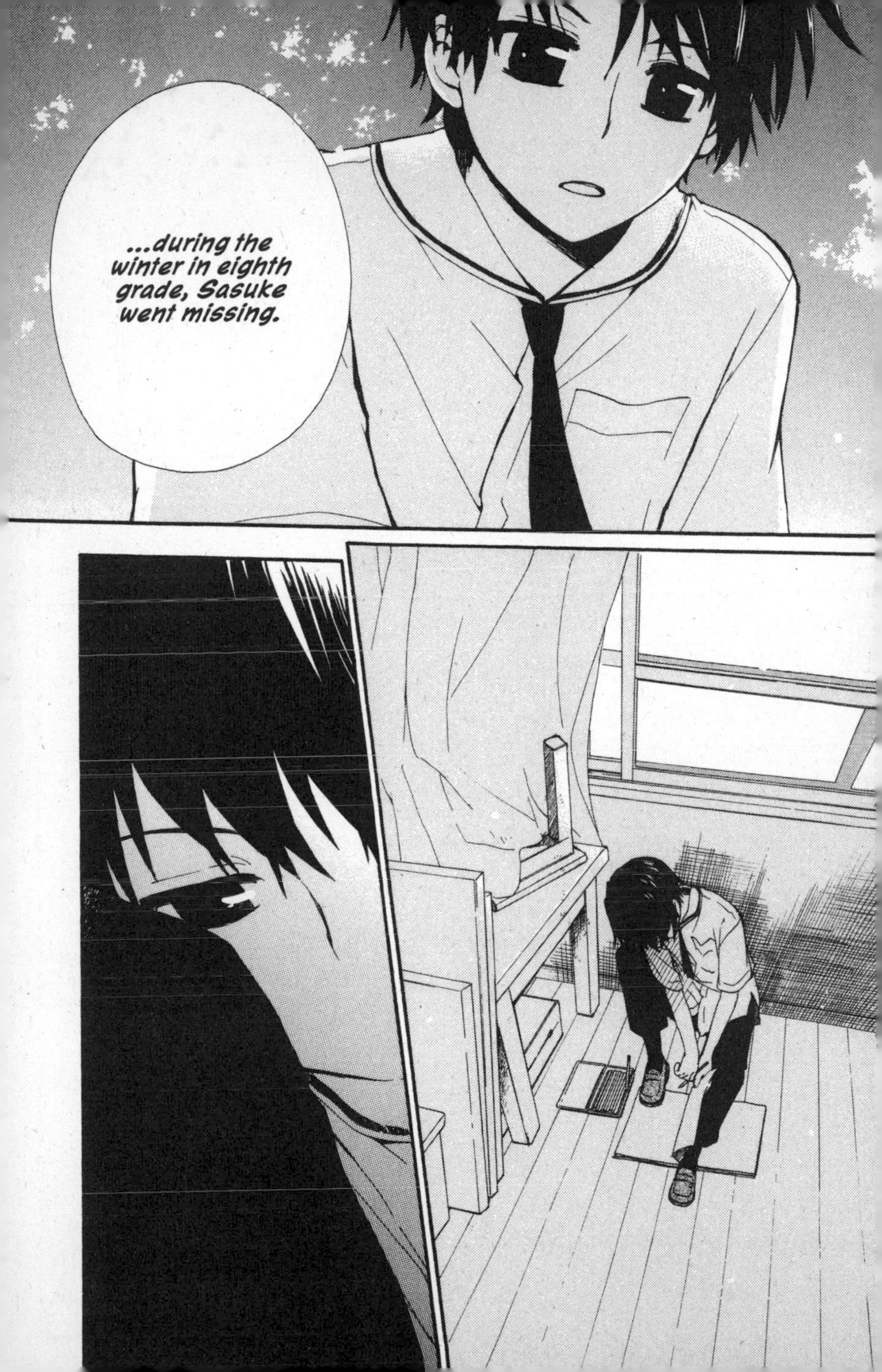
...during the winter in eighth grade, Sasuke went missing.

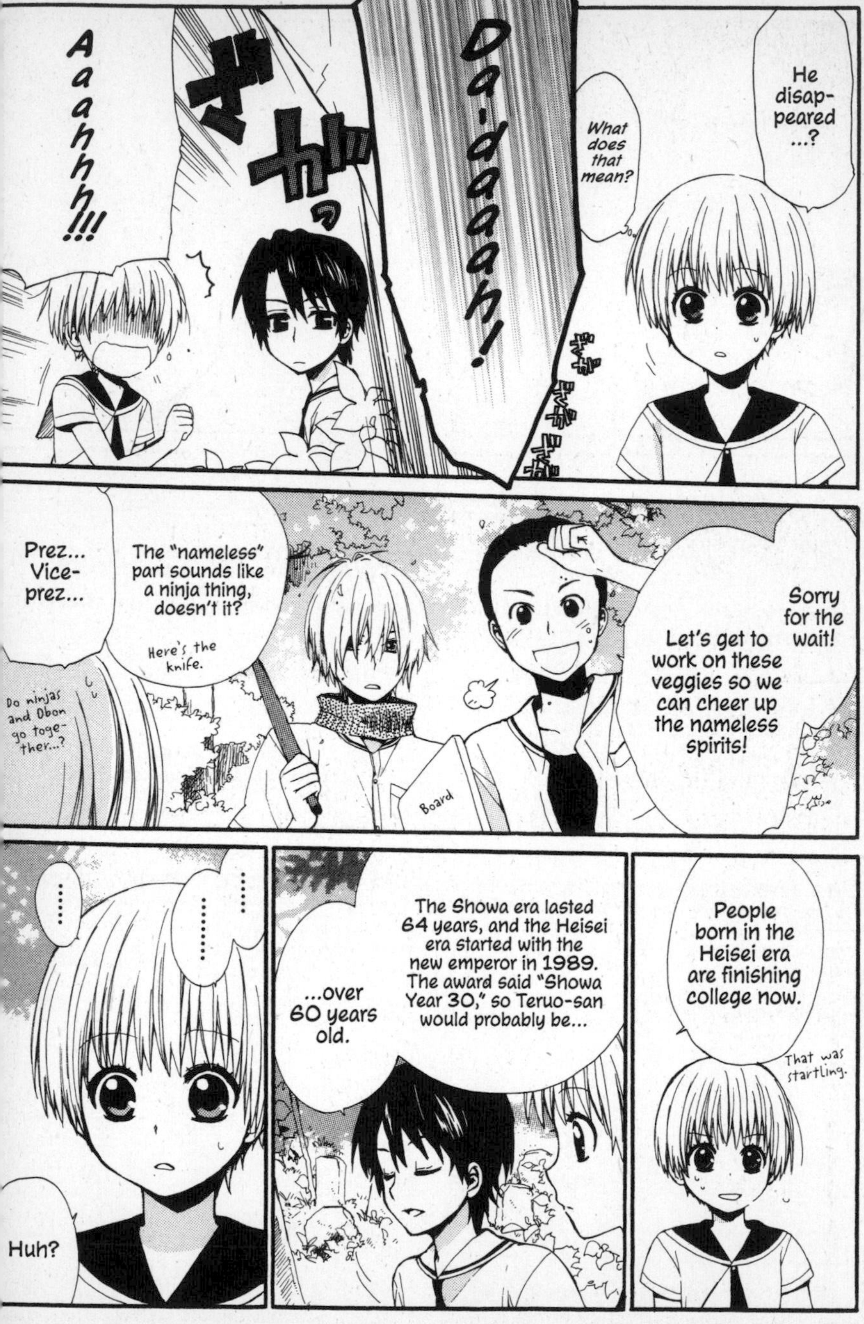
He disap-peared ...?
What does that mean?
Da-daaaaah!
Aaahhh!!!
Sorry for the wait!
Let's get to work on these veggies so we can cheer up the nameless spirits!
Board
The "nameless" part sounds like a ninja thing, doesn't it?
Here's the knife.
Prez... Vice-prez...
Do ninjas and Obon go toge-ther...?
People born in the Heisei era are finishing college now.
That was startling.
The Showa era lasted 64 years, and the Heisei era started with the new emperor in 1989. The award said "Showa Year 30," so Teruo-san would probably be...
...over 60 years old.
......
......
Huh?

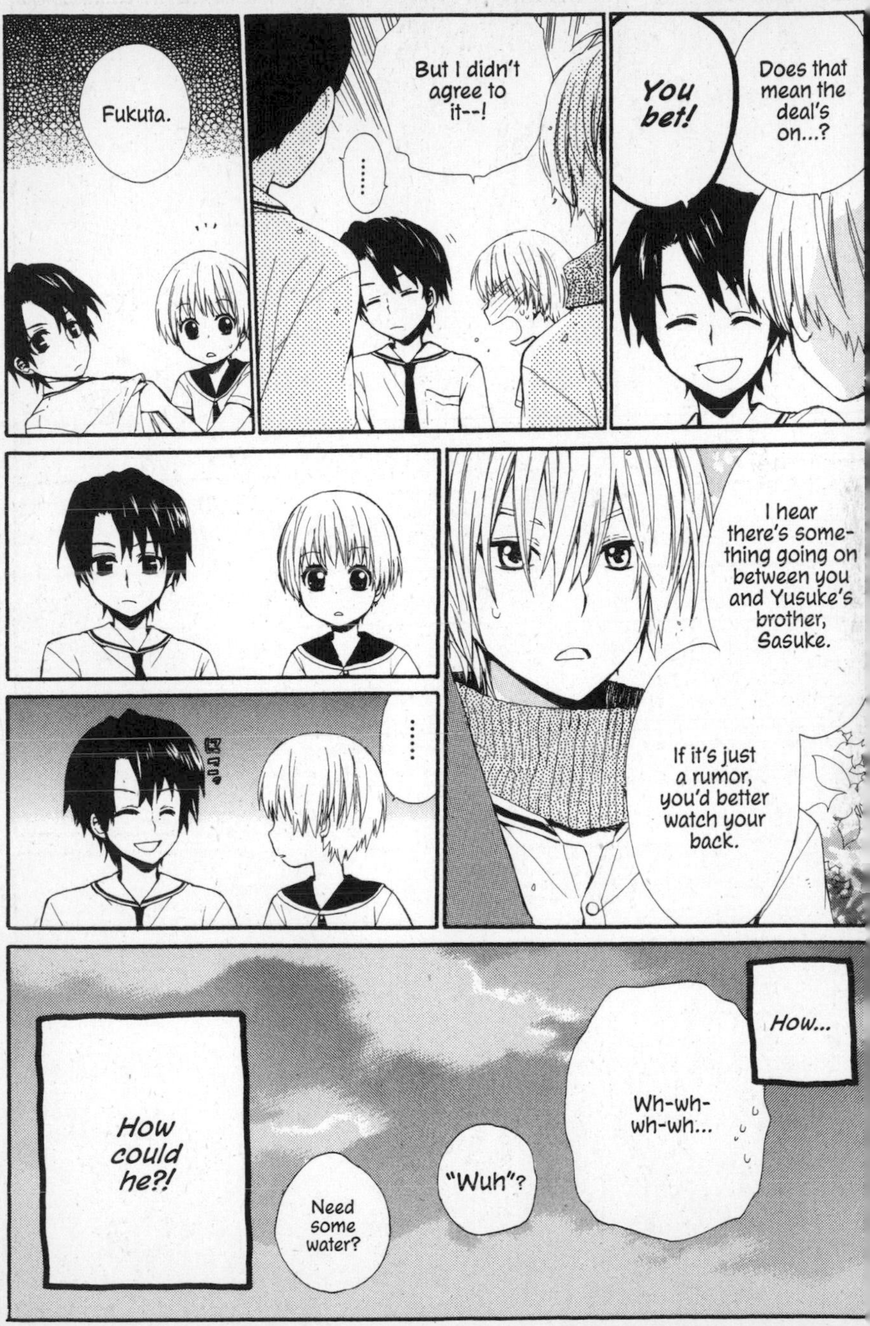
Does that mean the deal's on...?
You bet!
But I didn't agree to it--!
......
Fukuta.
I hear there's some-thing going on between you and Yusuke's brother, Sasuke.
If it's just a rumor, you'd better watch your back.
......
How...
Wh-wh-wh-wh...
"Wuh"?
Need some water?
How could he?!

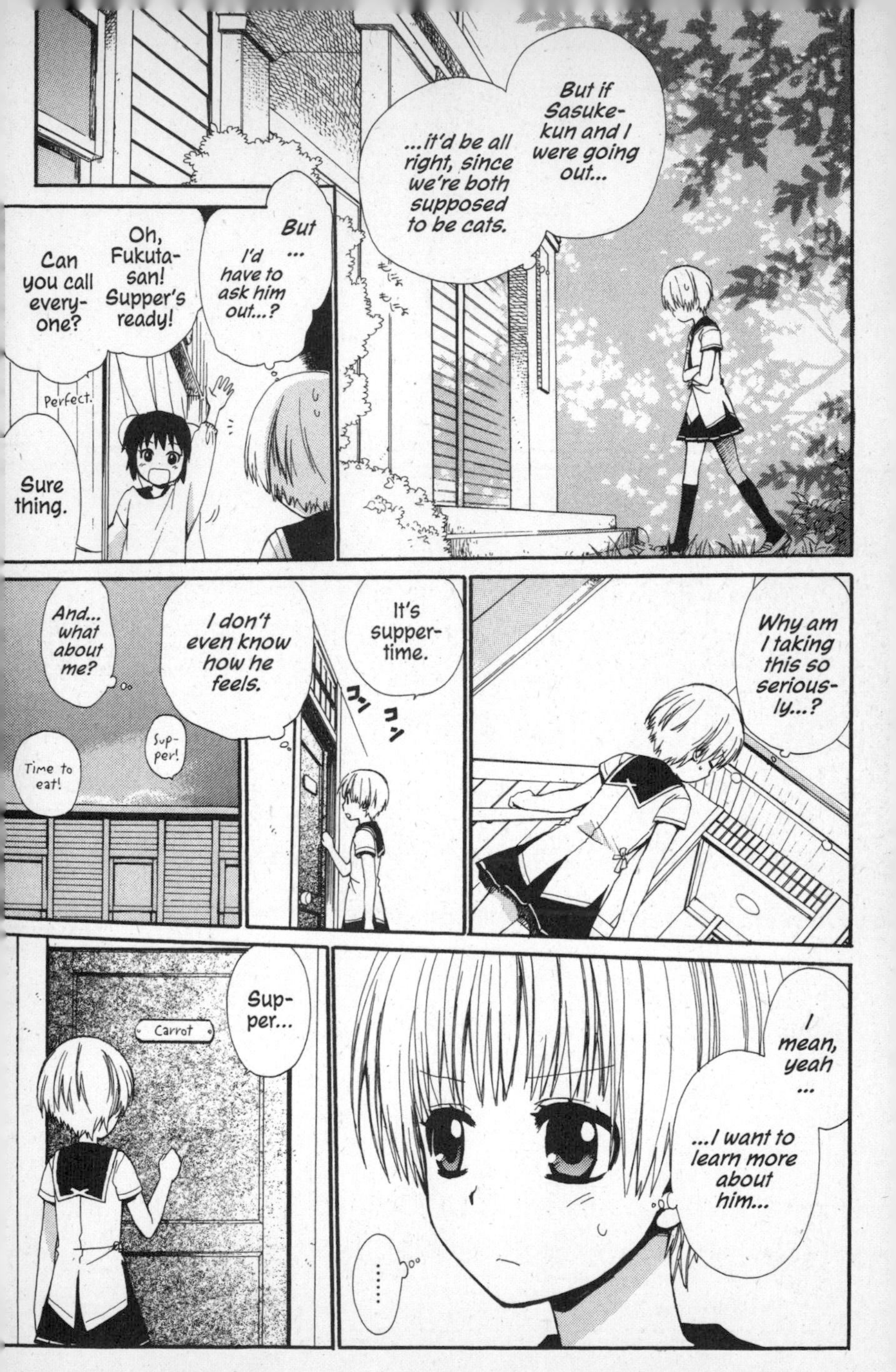
But if Sasuke-kun and I were going out...
...it'd be all right, since we're both supposed to be cats.
But ... I'd have to ask him out...?
Oh, Fukuta-san! Supper's ready!
Can you call every-one?
Perfect.
Sure thing.
Why am I taking this so serious-ly...?
It's supper-time.
コン コン
I don't even know how he feels.
And... what about me?
Sup-per!
Time to eat!
I mean, yeah ...
...I want to learn more about him...
......
Sup-per...
Carrot

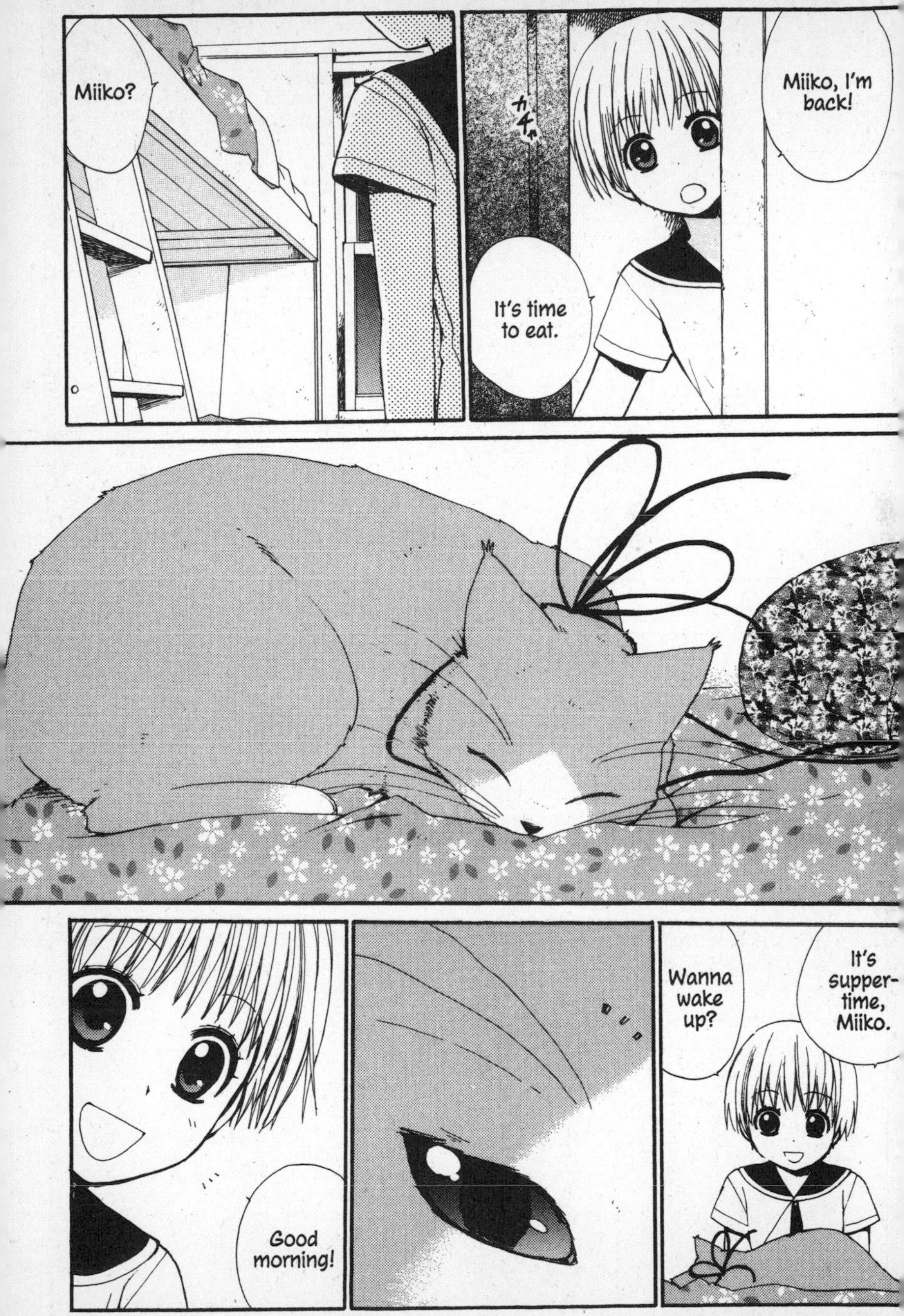
Miiko, I'm back!
カチャ
It's time to eat.
Miiko?
It's supper-time, Miiko.
Wanna wake up?
Good morning!

Hey! Wake up!

Zzz...

Of course, it's actually evening...

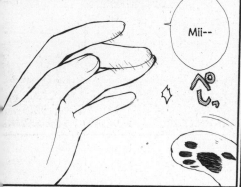

Mii--

Come on, Miiko.

Rrrr...

Don't "rrrr" me!

Don't complain to me if you're hungry later!

......

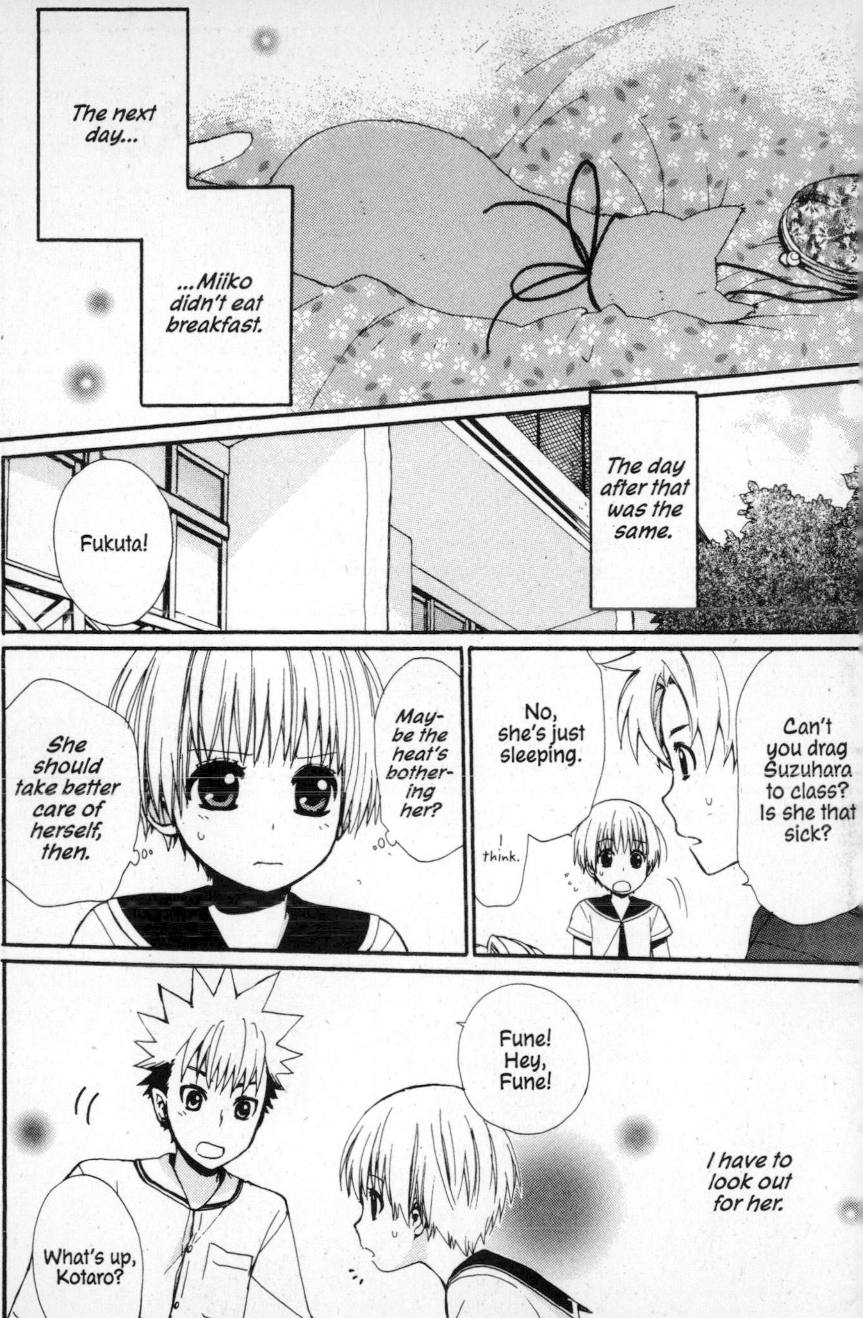
The next day...
...Miiko didn't eat breakfast.
The day after that was the same.
Fukuta!
Can't you drag Suzuhara to class? Is she that sick?
No, she's just sleeping.
I think.
May-be the heat's bother-ing her?
She should take better care of herself, then.
I have to look out for her.
Fune! Hey, Fune!
What's up, Kotaro?

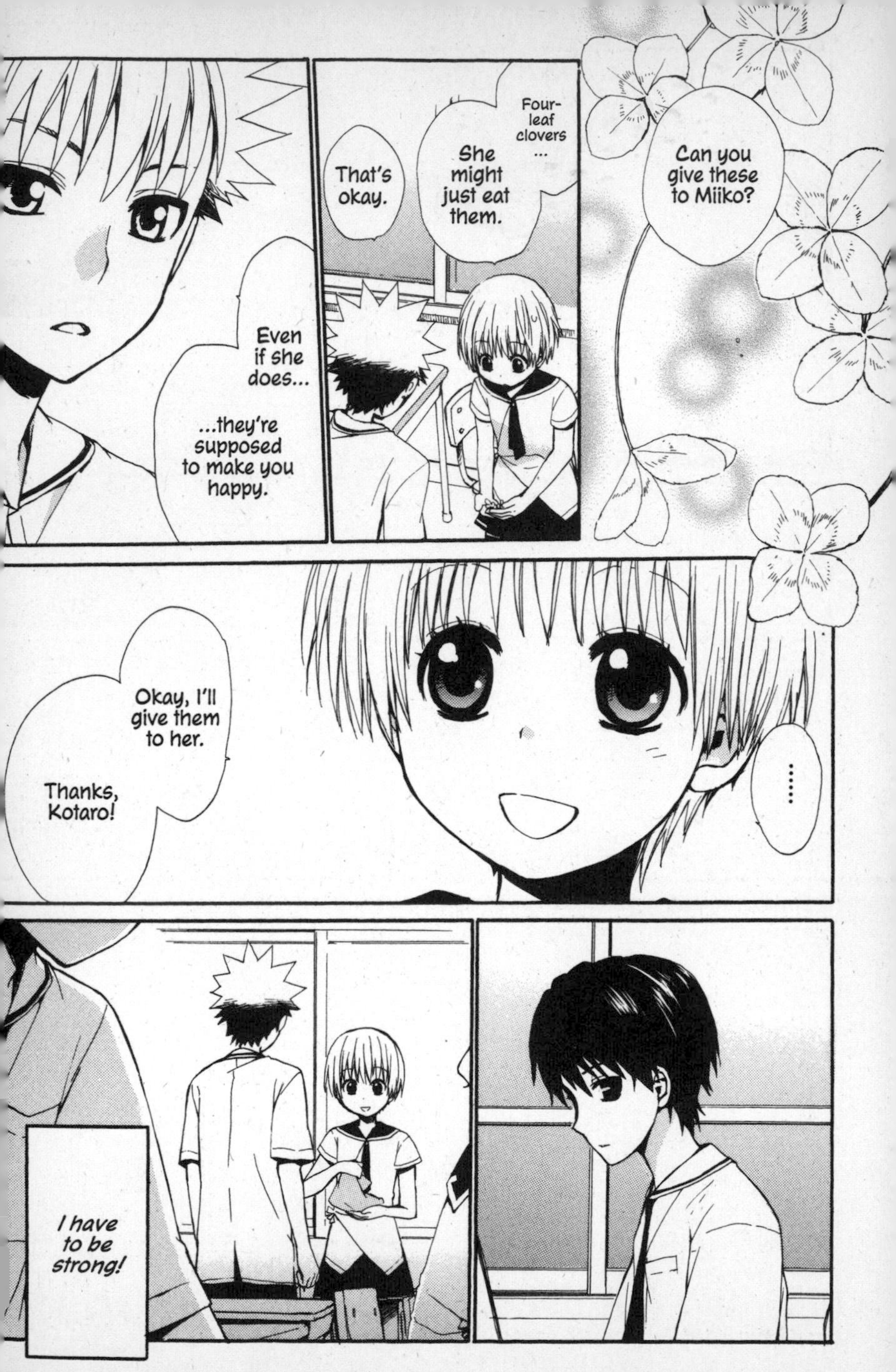
Can you give these to Miiko?
Four-leaf clovers...
She might just eat them.
That's okay.
Even if she does...
...they're supposed to make you happy.
......
Okay, I'll give them to her.
Thanks, Kotaro!
I have to be strong!

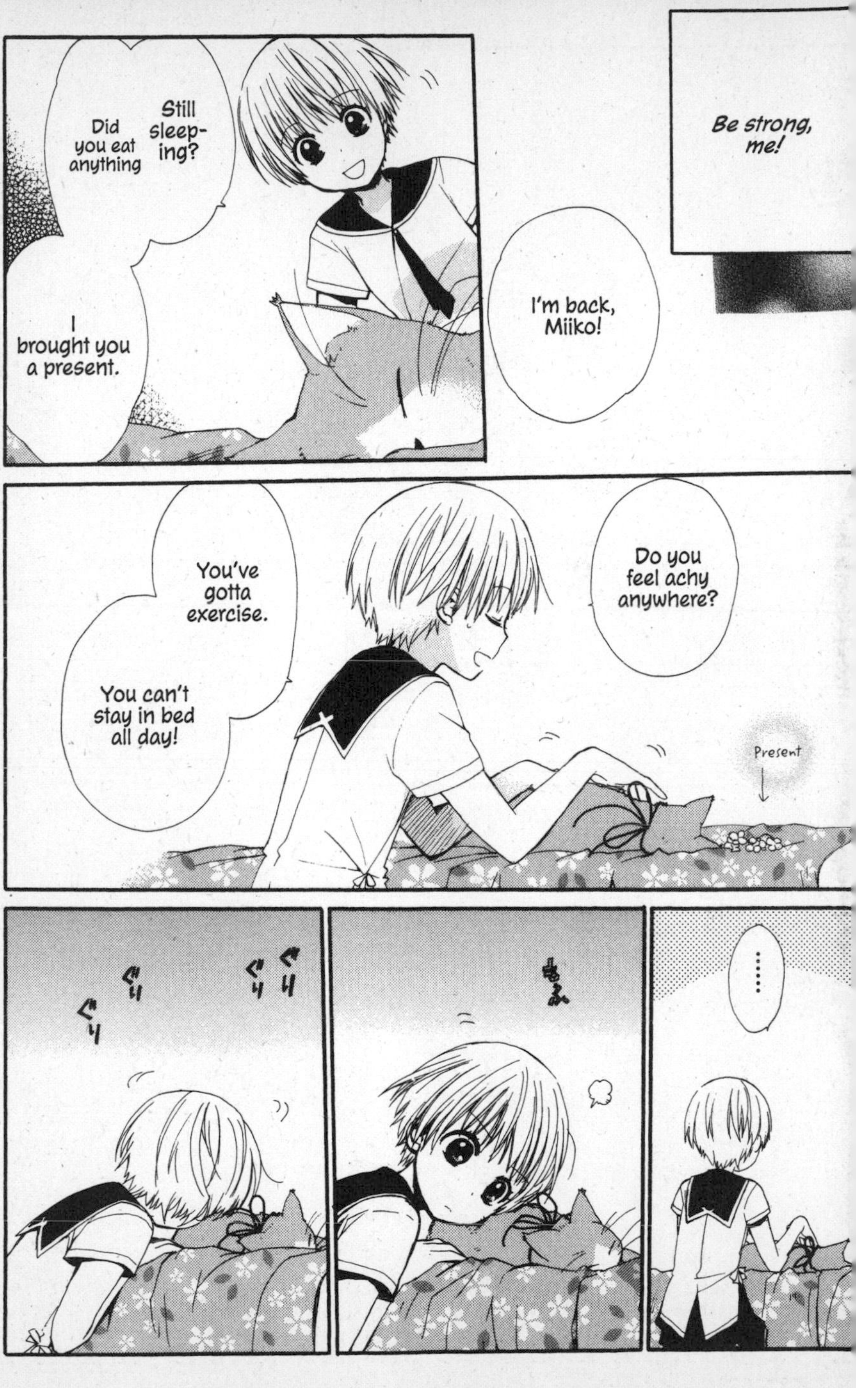
Be strong, me!
I'm back, Miiko!
Still sleeping?
Did you eat anything
I brought you a present.
Do you feel achy anywhere?
Present
You've gotta exercise.
You can't stay in bed all day!
......

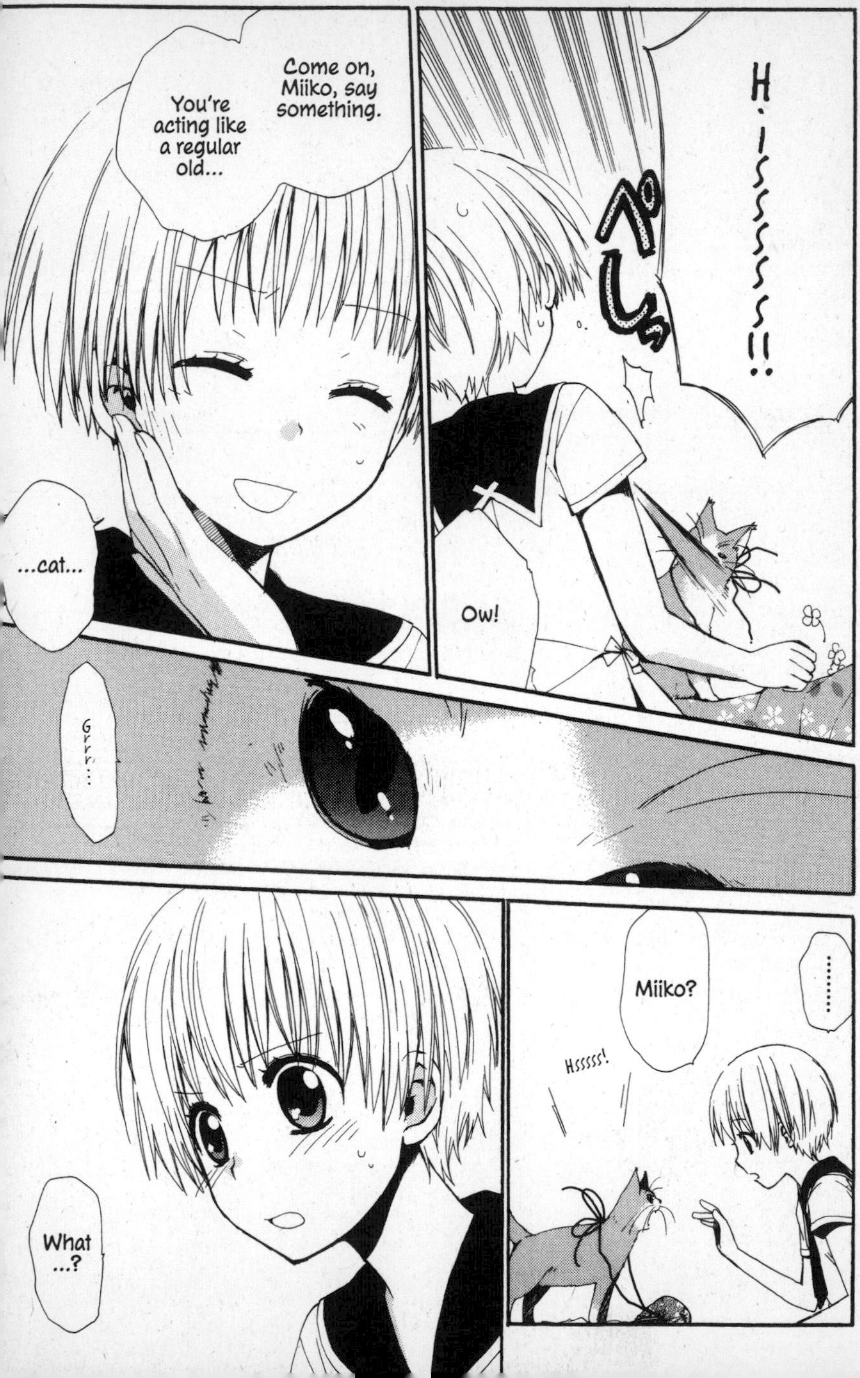
H-issssss!!
ぺしっ
Ow!
Come on, Miiko, say something.
You're acting like a regular old...
...cat...
Grrr...
......
Miiko?
Hsssss!
What ...?

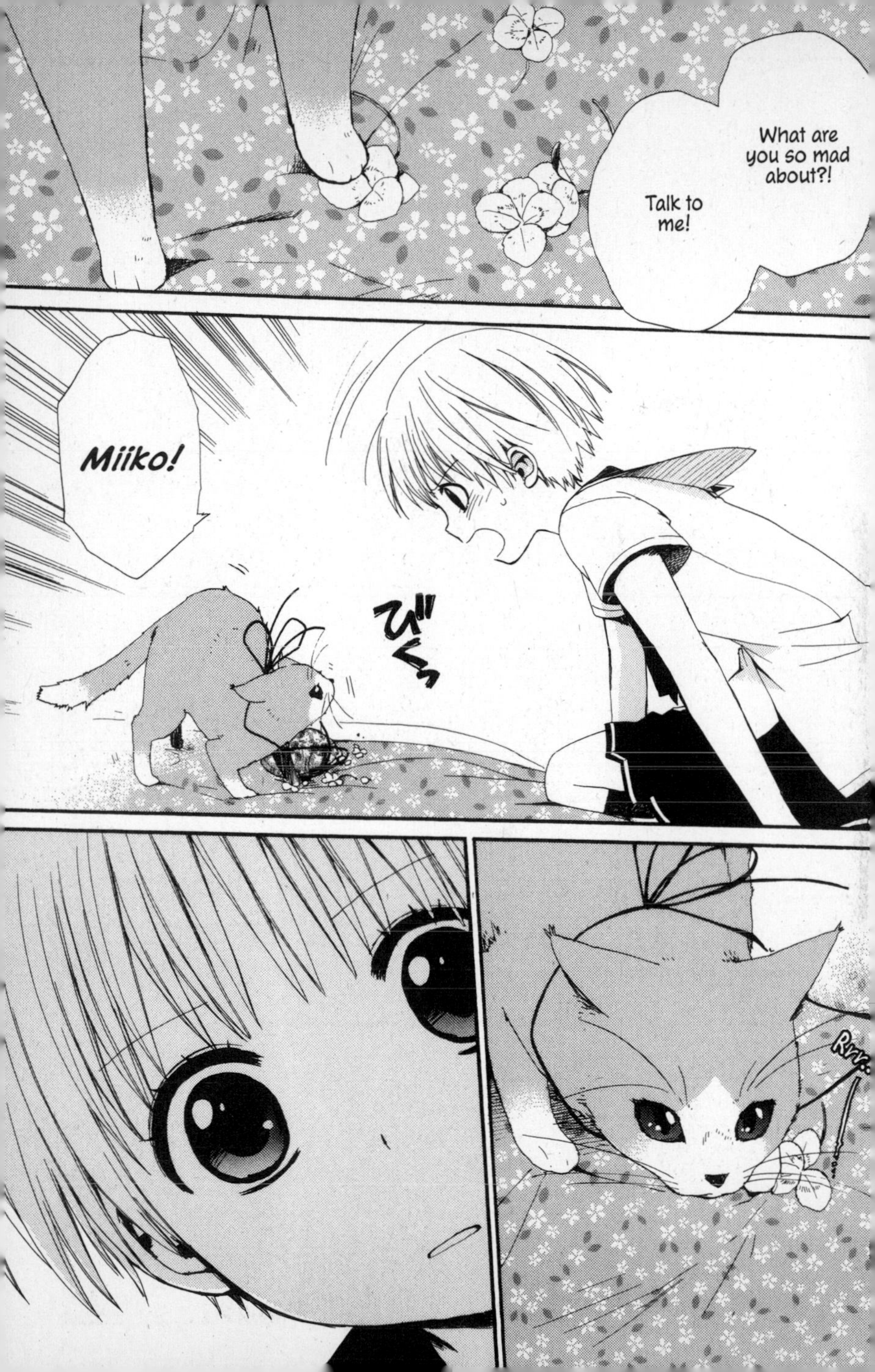
What are you so mad about?!
Talk to me!
Miiko!
びくっ
Rrr..

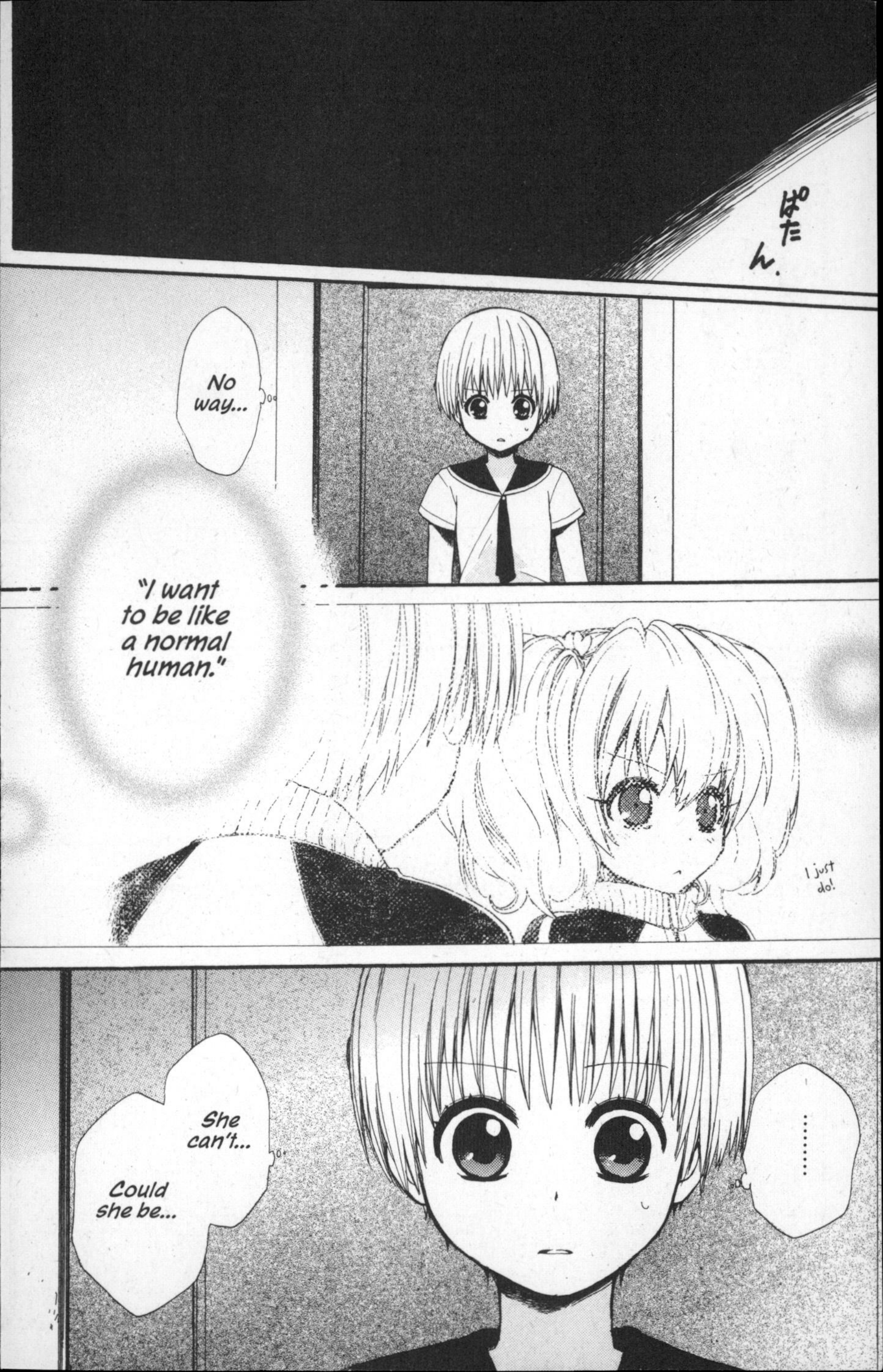
ぱたん.
No way...
"I want to be like a normal human."
I just do!
......
She can't...
Could she be...

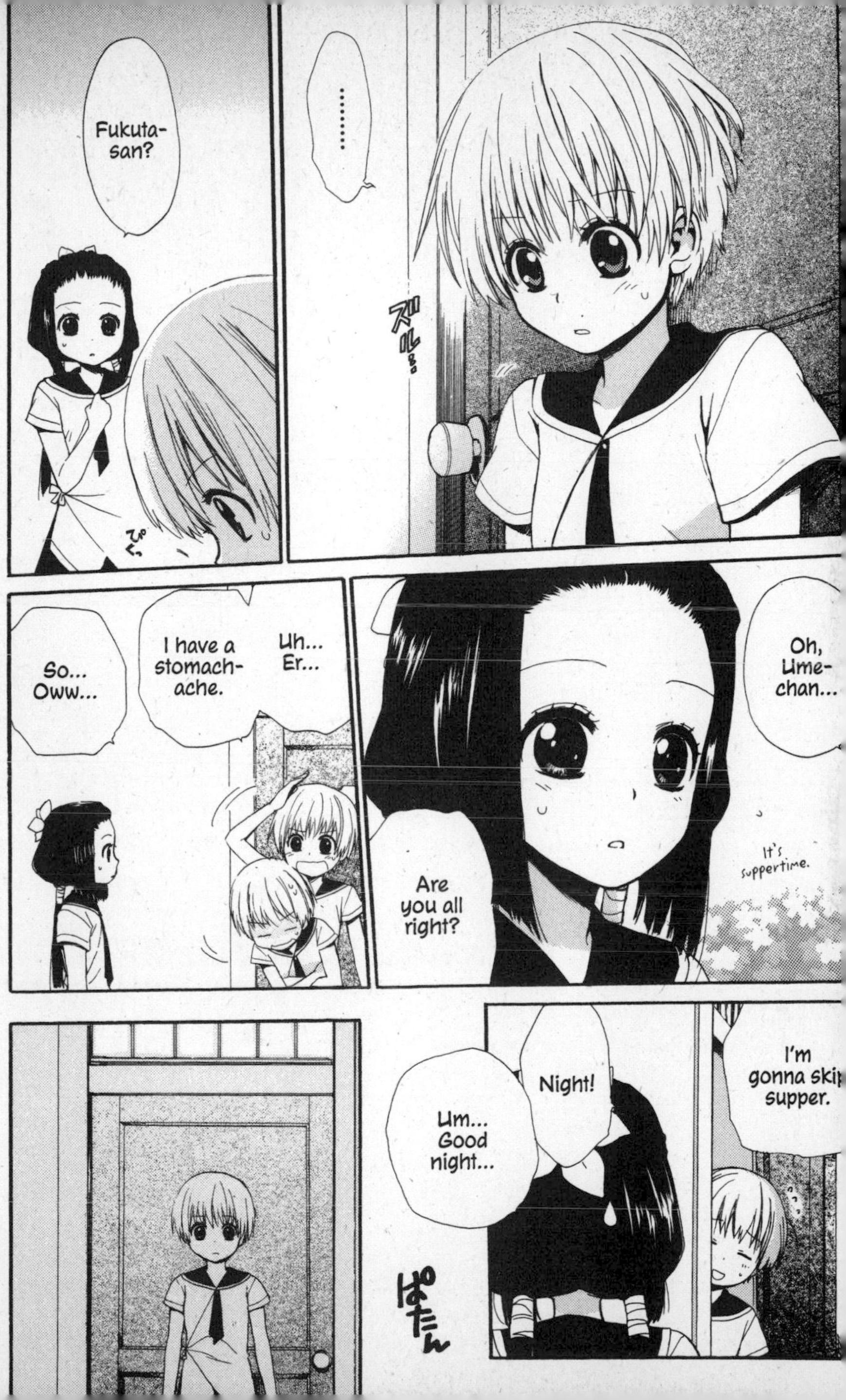
......
ズル…
Fukuta-san?
ぴくっ
Oh, Ume-chan...
It's suppertime.
Are you all right?
Uh... Er...
I have a stomach-ache.
So... Oww...
I'm gonna skip supper.
Night!
Um... Good night...
ぱたん

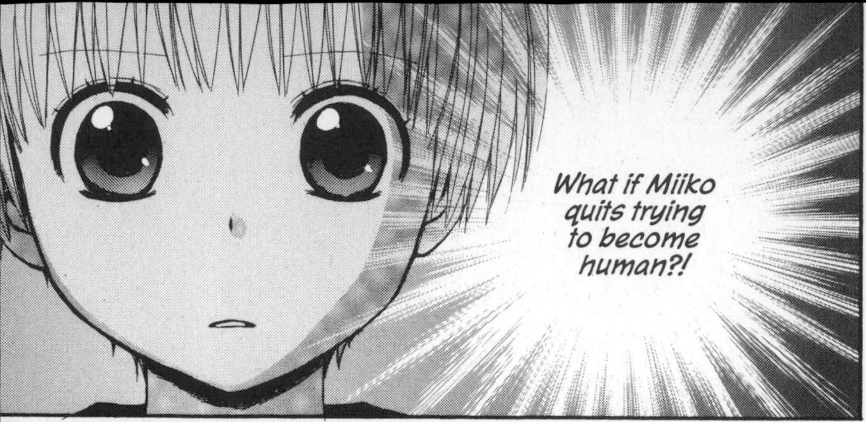
What if Miiko quits trying to become human?!
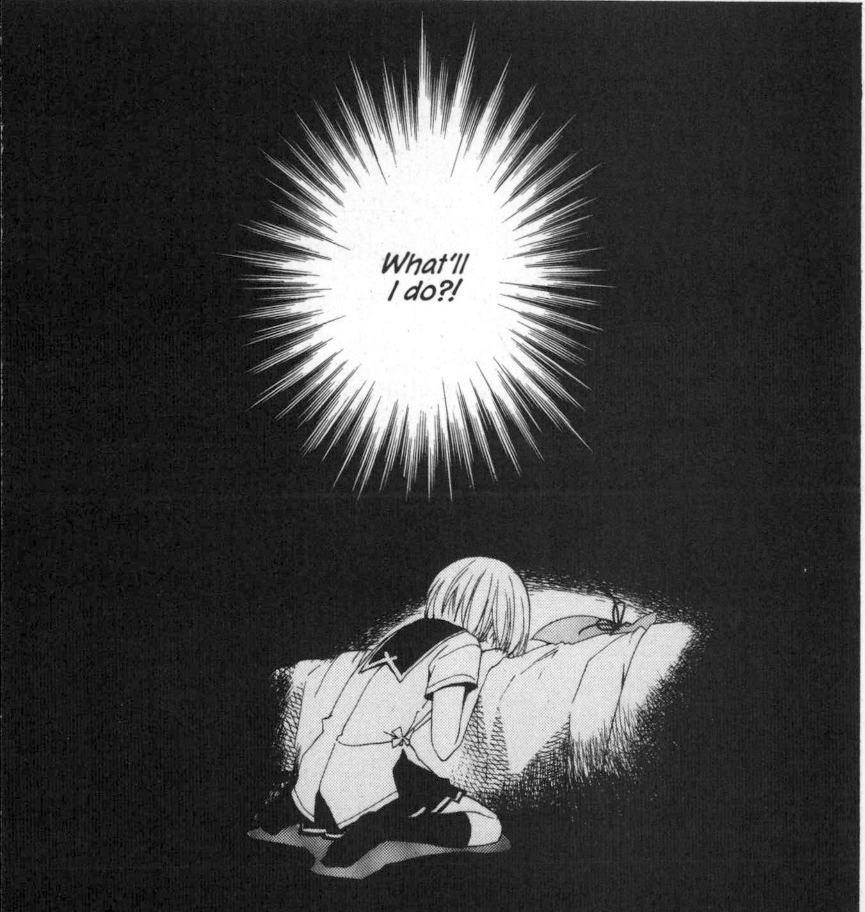
What'll I do?!

Animal Academy 5/END

Postscript

5

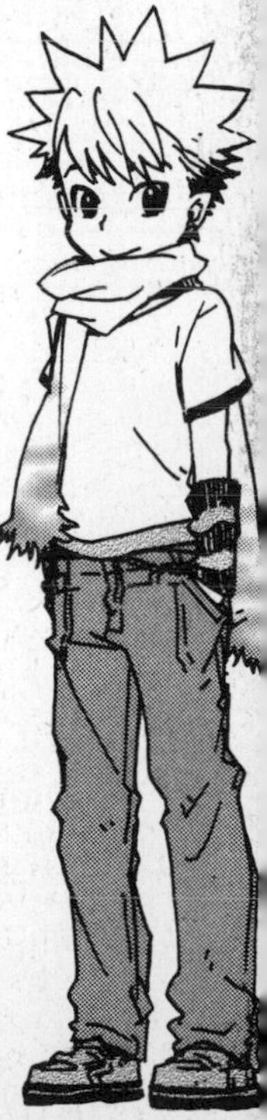

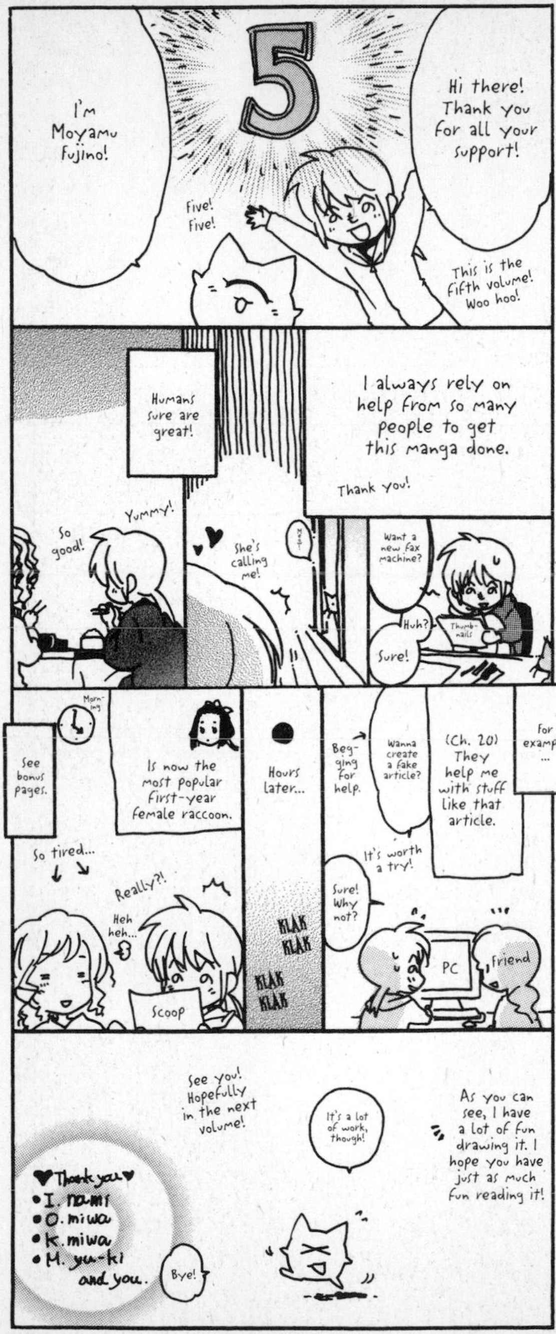
5
Hi there! Thank you for all your support!
I'm Moyamu Fujino!
Five! Five!
This is the fifth volume! Woo hoo!
I always rely on help from so many people to get this manga done.
Thank you!
Humans sure are great!
Want a new fax machine?
Huh?
Thumb-nails
Sure!
She's calling me!
Yummy!
So good!
For example ...
(Ch. 20) They help me with stuff like that article.
Wanna create a fake article?
Beg-ging for help.
It's worth a try!
Sure! Why not?
PC
Friend
Hours later...
KLAK KLAK
KLAK KLAK
Morn-ing
Is now the most popular first-year female raccoon.
See bonus pages.
Really?!
So tired...
Heh heh...
Scoop
As you can see, I have a lot of fun drawing it. I hope you have just as much fun reading it!
It's a lot of work, though!
See you! Hopefully in the next volume!
♥Thank you♥
•I. nami
•O. miwa
•K. miwa
•M. yu-ki
and you.
Bye!

HAKOBUNE HAKUSHO.5

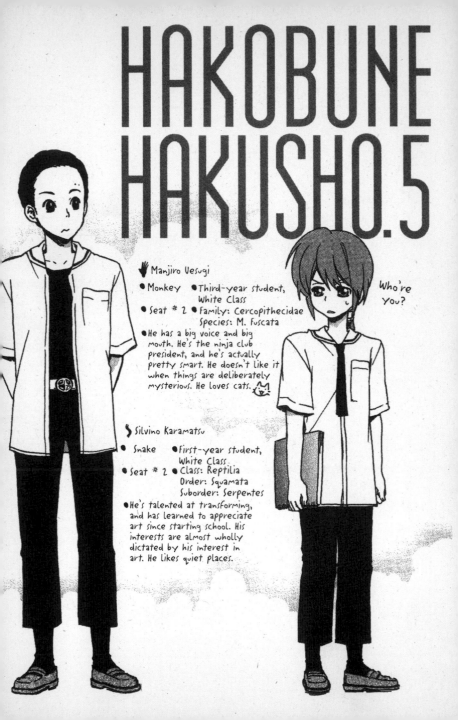

✋ Manjiro Uesugi
- Monkey
- Seat # 2
- Third-year student, White Class
- Family: Cercopithecidae Species: M. fuscata

He has a big voice and big mouth. He's the ninja club president, and he's actually pretty smart. He doesn't like it when things are deliberately mysterious. He loves cats. 🐱

🐍 Silvino Karamatsu
- Snake
- Seat # 2
- First-year student, White Class
- Class: Reptilia Order: Squamata Suborder: Serpentes

He's talented at transforming, and has learned to appreciate art since starting school. His interests are almost wholly dictated by his interest in art. He likes quiet places.

Who're you?

Miiko's Four Seasc

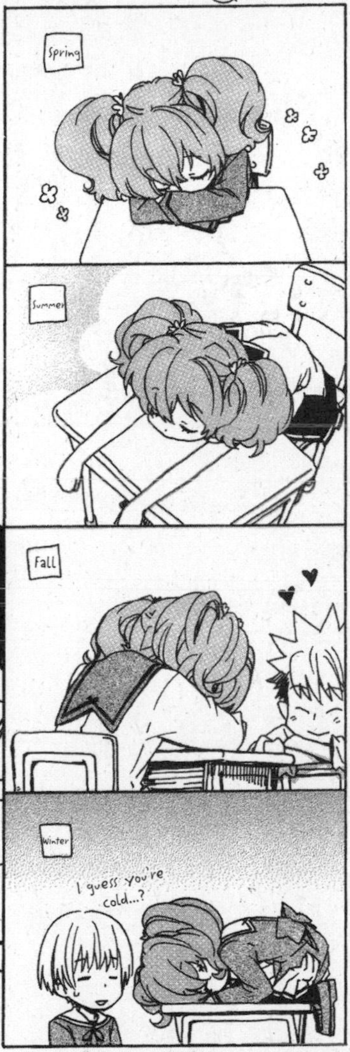
Spring
Summer
Fall
Winter
I guess you're cold...?

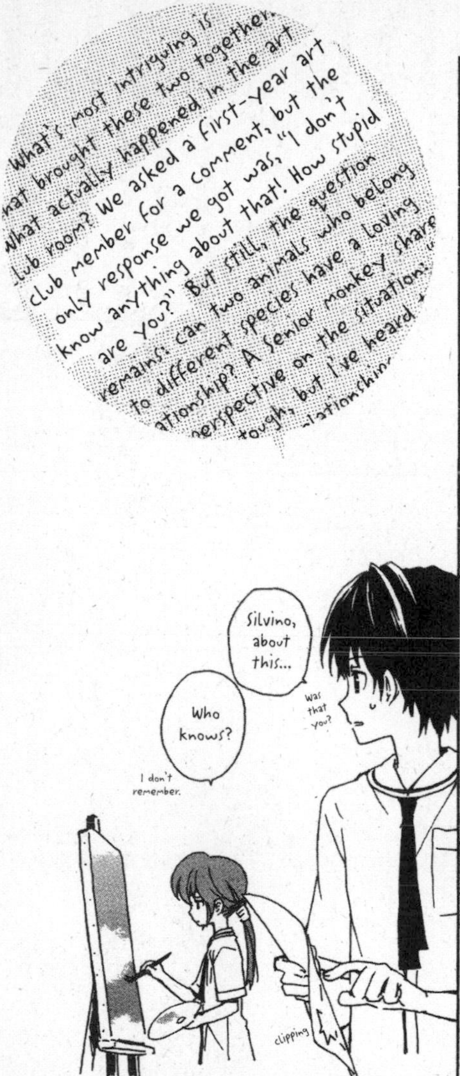
What's most intriguing is
brought these two together.
What actually happened in the art
room? We asked a first-year art
club member for a comment, but the
only response we got was, "I don't
know anything about that! How stupid
are you?" But still, the question
remains: can two animals who belong
to different species have a loving
A senior monkey share
perspective on the situation:
tough, but I've heard
Silvino, about this...
Was that you?
Who knows?
I don't remember.
clipping

In the next volume of...

Animal ACADEMY

HAKOBUNE HAKUSHO

はこぶね白書

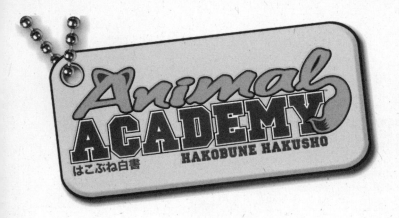

Miiko's sad past with her beloved Teruo is finally revealed, but to what end? And Neko must struggle with her own feelings for Sasuke-- but will Yusuke's advice help or hurt?

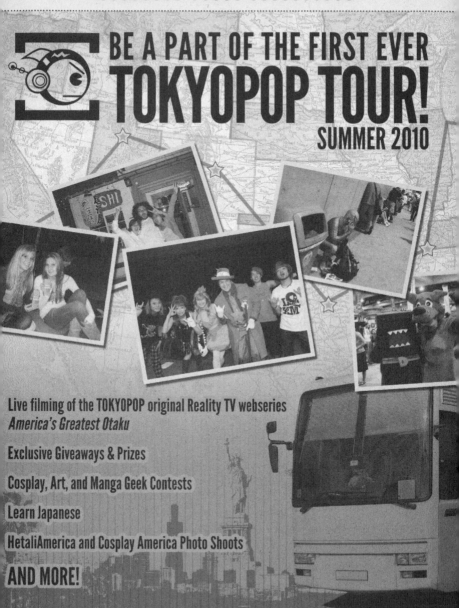

RightStuf.com asks...

"What kind of OTAKU are you?"